The **Problem** of **Perception**

The
Problem
of
Perception

A. D. SMITH

HARVARD UNIVERSITY PRESS

Cambridge, Massachusetts

London, England   2002

Title-page illustration from Robert Hooke, "An Instrument of Use to
take the Draught, or Picture of any Thing," 1726.

Library of Congress Cataloging-in-Publication Data

Smith, A. D.
    The problem of perception / A.D. Smith.
        p. cm.
    Includes bibliographical references (p.) and index.
    ISBN 0-674-00841-3 (alk. paper)
    1. Realism. 2. Perception (Philosophy) I. Title.

B835 .S57 2002
121'. 34—dc21   2002017164

To my father, Ronald Smith
in memoriam

Contents

Preface

This is my first book, so I should like straightaway to record my major philosophical debts. I studied philosophy, both as an undergraduate and a graduate, in Oxford throughout the 1970s. My undergraduate tutors were I. M. Crombie and M. R. Ayers, and my doctoral supervisors were P. F. Strawson, J. A. Foster, and A. J. Ayer. I learnt something from all of them, and am grateful. But perhaps because I received the most extensive exposure to Ayers and Foster, I should like to record an especial debt to them. Although two philosophers of very different styles and outlook, they share a rigorousness and an unconcern for fashion in philosophy that I admire and have hoped to emulate. Although neither, I am sure, will be entirely happy by what they find in these pages, I hope they will detect some positive influence that they have had on me. Whether they like what they find here or not, their influence has been great.

I should also like to record my thanks to Mike Martin for a number of stimulating discussions over the past couple of years, conversations that were genuinely helpful while I prepared this work for publication.

This book has taken me about a decade to write. Throughout this period I have been fortunate to enjoy the unfailing support and encouragement of Rosemary Sherratt, to whom I should like to express an equal though different kind of gratitude.

L'examen de l'opération de l'esprit qui consiste à passer de nos sensations aux objets extérieurs, est évidemment le premier pas que doit faire la Métaphysique.

—d'Alembert

τῶν αἰσϘήσεων μέντοι μὴ καταλαμβανουσῶν τὰ ἐκτόϜ, οὐδὲ ἡ διάνοια ταῦτα δύναται καταλαμβάνειν

—Sextus Empiricus

The eye's plain version is a thing apart,
The vulgate of experience

—Wallace Stevens

. . . τὰ πάϘη μόνα φησὶ καταλαμβάνεσϘαι

—Cyrenaic doctrine

Introduction

I THINK I may have solved the Problem of Perception. "Which problem of perception?" and "What problem of perception?" are two responses that this claim, indeed the very title of this work, may well elicit. The first is a perfectly sensible question, since perception is a multifaceted phenomenon, posing many questions to philosophers, psychologists, physiologists, and, these days, information theorists and cognitive scientists. This, however, is a work of philosophy; and when philosophers speak of "the" problem of perception, what they generally have in mind is the question whether we can ever directly perceive the physical world. This issue is a *problem* because of certain arguments that have been put forward to the effect that such direct perception is impossible. Although there are other questions, even of a distinctively philosophical stamp, that are raised by perception, at least almost all of these need to be addressed at some stage in a thoroughgoing treatment of this central issue—which, from now on, I shall frequently refer to simply as the "Problem."

More precisely, the topic of this work is the philosophical position known as "Direct Realism"—a position that combines this issue of directness with a Realism about the physical world. Such Realism holds that the physical world has an existence that is not in any way dependent upon its being "cognized"—that is, perceived or thought about. The physical world is not, as it is usually put, dependent on "consciousness," at least not finite consciousness.[1] Such Realism is opposed to

1

Idealism: the view that whatever seems to be physical is either reducible to, or at least supervenient upon, cognitive states of consciousness.[2] For the Realist, the purely physical elements of this physical world of ours would, or at least could, be just as they are even if no perceiving or thinking subjects had ever come into existence.[3] Of course there could not, in the absence of such subjects, be a world that contained, say, houses, or knives and forks. All such artefacts are, however, fashioned out of naturally occurring material, the existence of which is, according to the Realist, independent of the existence of conscious subjects without qualification. If you are a Realist, not only could *a* physical world exist devoid of consciousness; this world of ours, in respect of its purely material stratum, could so exist, and doubtless actually did in its early history before the emergence of conscious life. Moreover, such existence is not to be analysed in terms of some merely hypothetical truths about what conscious subjects would have perceived if they had come into existence earlier than they did.

As a matter of fact, a number of writers, especially in the "continental tradition" of philosophy, who would not regard themselves as Idealists, would range far beyond artefacts, and such other obviously subject-related items as language and social institutions, in identifying things that cannot be credited with existence in the absence of conscious subjects. Jean-Paul Sartre, for example, claimed that no event of destruction could take place in a world devoid of consciousness; nor would there be any distances.[4] Such things, according to him, involve an element of negativity, which necessarily has its source in conscious beings. Indeed, the very notion of a *world* wholly independent of consciousness makes no sense for him, nor for the Phenomenological tradition generally. Although there is, for Sartre, a realm of self-subsistent being wholly independent of consciousness, which contains, though not destructions and distances, at least distributions of masses possessing various lengths—things that are purely positive, and which he liked to characterize in terms of density, and a compaction of being—a "world" is a meaningful environment that is articulated out of such brute being by the projects of conscious, active subjects. There is a story, not apocryphal I hope, of a disagreement between A. J. Ayer and Georges Bataille over whether dinosaurs existed before human beings came on the scene. Bataille demurred. This was not, I take it, an assertion of Idealism. Bataille was not claiming that nothing can exist without conscious subjects being present, but rather that nothing in such a situation could properly be termed a "dinosaur"—something that makes sense only with respect to human taxonomic interests. For Sartre, at least, a domain without consciousness can at least properly be said to contain such things as redistributions of masses, and lengths; though if the line of thought attributed to Bataille is pursued, there is at least a question of how *any* specification of a domain could be supposed to be wholly independent of human concerns. Be this as it may, if such a position really is not a form of Idealism, it must at least be agreed that there is a purely physical aspect or stratum to a world. Direct Realism is the claim that we can be directly aware of objects that themselves possess such a stratum.

Idealists about the physical world can easily, and usually do, credit us with direct awareness of it. Berkeley is a clear example of this. Direct *Realism*, however, is much more difficult to make out as a coherent position. The worry over such coherence is at the heart of the Problem to be addressed in this work. Now, one way of "solving" the Problem would be to show that Direct Realism is indeed incoherent, and to embrace the only two alternatives: Idealism or Indirect Realism—the latter being the view that although Realism is true of the physical world, we are not directly aware of that world through perception. What I am attempting here, however, is a more straightforward solution to the Problem: showing how Direct Realism may be defended against the various arguments that have been brought against it.

"What problem of perception?" is typically the response of those who recognize that Direct Realism is indeed the issue in question, but who suppose either that the problem has been solved, or that there never really was any such problem, but a mere pseudo-problem and philosophical confusion—philosophy itself being regarded in certain quarters as itself a form of confusion. Indeed, it is sometimes suggested that the belief that there is a genuine philosophical problem here is a symptom of "Modernism"—an intellectual illness into which we have fallen, perhaps as a result of the "New Way of Ideas" that emerged in the seventeenth century. This, at least, is certainly not true. As the last of the epigraphs to this work indicates, the Problem dates back at least to the time of the ancient philosophical sect of Cyrenaics: "Only sense-impressions are apprehensible."[5] Be this as it may, to those who think that my Problem is but a pseudo-problem, I can only suggest that they read on. For although my ultimate purpose is to defend Direct Realism from one sort of attack, a subsidiary purpose is to show that certain arguments do indeed raise serious worries for this view—far more serious than is generally recognized today. If, on the other hand, it is accepted that there is a genuine problem here, but one that has been solved, then I should like to know who is supposed to have solved it. None of the accounts of perception that have been offered in the "analytical tradition" of philosophy (together with what is regarded as this tradition's prehistory) achieves this in my view—for reasons that we shall investigate. Although the account of perception proposed in these pages in some respects has more in common with the "continental" tradition in philosophy, especially with the Phenomenological school, one cannot find an adequate response to the Problem there either. The two writers in this tradition who have given the most attention to perception are Maurice Merleau-Ponty and Edmund Husserl, and they are both Idealists.[6] Sartre was certainly no Idealist. He sees our relation to the world as a coming into contact with a realm of "being in itself" that is wholly independent of, indeed prior to, consciousness;[7] but he espouses a view that I shall call "Naive Realism," and as we shall see in Chapter 1, it has nothing to be said for it. Heidegger was, perhaps, not an Idealist either.[8] The problem with Heidegger's account of perception is somewhat complex, and it will be dealt with more fully in the body of this work. One aspect of it may, however, be mentioned here: he explicitly eschews all reference to conscious, sensory experience. In doing so, he ignores, or by-passes, the Problem of Perception rather than solves it. This is not necessarily meant as a criticism of Heidegger; he is after other, and bigger, game.[9] Nevertheless, it does mean that we shall find no help with our Problem from this quarter. Indeed, it means that Heidegger is to be classed with those who think that there never was any real problem to be solved. The first chapters of the two parts of the present work are designed to show that there *is* a problem.

I do not, however, wish to give the impression that I have come up with a radically new solution to the Problem of Perception. I do not believe in radical novelties in philosophy; not, at least, at this stage of the enterprise. There are, as we shall see, many writers who have made significant and positive contributions to the solution of the Problem as I see it. There is even a sense in which the solution is already to be found in the annals of philosophy. The difficulty is that addressing the Problem takes in a lot of philosophical territory; many positions have to be taken on local issues, and they have to be coördinated in an overall perspective. Although congruence with the thought of several philosophers is to be found in what follows—most notably, perhaps, with that of the later Husserl—I know of no one who has knitted things together in precisely the way here proposed. I think that unless just those positions that are defended here are knitted together in just the way that I propose, any overall account of perception that is meant to sustain Direct Realism will, on inspection, unravel.

Finally, I should make it clear that I am not here attempting to defend Direct Realism against all arguments that can be marshaled against it. I do not claim to show that Direct Realism is true, or even possibly true. What I do claim is that Direct Realism cannot be shown to be false within that area of philosophy known as the Philosophy of Perception. There is nothing specifically *about perception* that requires its denial. Many Idealist and Indirect Realists have believed that, given only various generally accepted facts about the physical world, reflection on the nature of perception itself leads to a recognition of the falsity of Direct Realism. More particularly, what they have thought is that if Realism with respect to the physical world is assumed for the sake of argument, the Direct Realist's claim to *directness* in our perceptual awareness of such a world can be controverted. *This* is what I hope to show not to be possible. Perhaps, however, Direct Realism can be shown to be false for other reasons. In particular, perhaps Realism as such, with respect to the empirical world, can be shown to be false. Kant's argument about the ideality of space, and of the entire empirical realm that it somehow "contains," has little directly to do with perception—other than the general observation that it is phenomenally spatial in character—and yet it would constitute, if sound, a refutation of Direct Realism. Husserl gives an analysis of *reality* according to which the kind of Realism that is here in question is, as he liked to put it, a *"nonsens."* And more recently John Foster and Howard Robinson have put forward related arguments, based on the necessity of identity, against any form of physical Realism.[10] So perhaps Direct Realism really is false. What this work is intended to show is that if this is indeed the case, it cannot be shown to be so by reflecting on the nature of perception. As a distinctive position within the Philosophy of Perception, Direct Realism can, I think, be sustained.

LET US THEREFORE ASSUME, for the sake of argument, that Realism about the physical world is true. What we are to concern ourselves with is the claim that we can be directly aware of that world. Should this idea have to be given up, a natural inference would be that we are only ever, at best, *indirectly* aware of the physical world. Let us try and get some purchase on what such indirectness would involve by considering an everyday illustration of a distinction that we are all happy to make between direct and indirect perception. If you go into a camera obscura, you can see the surrounding terrain by directing your gaze on to the tabletop in the middle of the room.[11] Even though you are here in some sense viewing the surrounding terrain, you see it only in virtue of your seeing something that is not that terrain: an image on the table, or perhaps the tabletop itself carrying the image. Here we have an example of one thing being perceived in virtue of something else being perceived. When one thing is thus perceived *in virtue of* some distinct item being perceived, we can say that perception of the latter mediates perception of the former, and that this former object is not the *immediate*, but only the *indirect, object* of perception.[12] Items are immediate objects of perception when they are not perceived *by proxy*.[13] Assuming a Realist perspective on physical objects, our question is whether such objects are only ever perceived, and could conceivably only ever be perceived, in virtue of our perceiving something distinct from them. Answering this question affirmatively is definitive of Indirect Realism.[14]

This characterization of Indirect Realism requires two small qualifications. First, given that Indirect Realism holds that we never directly perceive physical objects, it is natural to infer that it holds that we do so in virtue of perceiving something else. Now, as we shall soon see, according to most Indirect Realist accounts, the thing that "goes proxy" for a physical object in perception has a nature at least analogous to a sensation; it has, indeed, often been termed a "perceptual sensation." And it is at least unusual to speak of ourselves as "perceiving" such typical examples of sensation as headaches and pins and needles. We say, rather, that we "feel" them, or are "aware of" them. Since we also speak of ourselves as being aware of physical objects, the issue of directness is best couched in term of the notion of an "awareness" of objects. The issue is whether we can be perceptually aware of any physical object only in virtue of being aware of some "proxy" thing distinct from that object.

This brings us to the second qualification. For to say that we are never directly aware of physical objects entails, given that we are sometimes directly aware of something or other, that the immediate objects of perception are non-physical. Now, although most Indirect Realists have indeed held this view, this is no part of Indirect Realism as such. Bertrand Russell, for example, was, for part of his career, an Indirect Realist who held that our immediate perceptual objects are physical because they are parts of our brains. Hence his notorious statement that "what the physiologist sees when he looks at a brain is part of his own brain, not part of the brain he is examining."[15] So perceptual proxies, mere internal images though they may be, were, for Russell, themselves physical in nature. The crucial issue for Indirect Realism, then, is not whether the immediate objects of perceptual awareness are physical or not, but whether they are the physical objects that we take them to be. I shall commonly refer to these as "normal" objects.[16]

Illustrating the thesis of Indirect Realism with such an everyday distinction between direct and indirect perception as applies to a camera obscura is, of course, hardly adequate. Indeed, J. L. Austin wrote that "it is quite plain that the philosophers' use of 'directly perceive,' whatever it may be, is not the ordinary, or any familiar, use; for in that use it is not only false but simply absurd to say that such objects as pens or cigarettes are never directly perceived. But we are given no explanation or definition of this new use—on the contrary, it is glibly trotted out as if we were all quite familiar with it already."[17] Everyday illustration can take us only a short way to appreciating the Indirect Realist's notion of a perceptual proxy because, according to the "ordinary use," when one object is perceived in virtue of our being aware of something else, the latter is itself a "normal" physical object, whereas Indirect Realism banishes *all* such items from the class of immediate objects of awareness. All that the everyday illustration achieves is the introduction of the notion of a person being aware of one entity in virtue of being aware of some distinct entity: that is, the introduction of the general notion of a perceptual proxy. What we now need to see is why such mediation has been thought to be present even in cases of perceptual awareness of normal objects that common sense would regard as direct.

The general idea that is in play here is, at a first approximation, that our perceptual experiences, rather than giving us an immediate awareness of our physical environment, are *themselves* our immediate objects of awareness, so that we are cognitively trapped behind a "veil of perception," as it is commonly put.[18] A classic statement of the idea can be found in Sextus Empiricus: "For perception does not present external objects to the mind, but reports its own state of being affected [*pathos*] ... Since, then, it is agreed by all that what is grasped in virtue of something else is hidden, and all things are perceived [*lambanetai*] in virtue of our own states of being affected, which are different from the former, all external objects are hidden."[19] Why, however, should we believe any such thing? Austin himself goes on to refer us to A. J. Ayer: "The answer, he says, is provided 'by what is known as the argument from illusion.'"[20] In fact, even when the phrase "argument from illusion" is used so widely as to cover arguments concerned with hallucination and the perspectival nature of perception, it is not the case that the argument from "illusion" is the only basis on which philosophers have rejected the idea of direct perceptual contact with the physical world. Nor, therefore, is it the only argument by which they have tried to introduce a notion of direct awareness other than the everyday one. What all such arguments do have in common is a reliance on Leibniz's Law.[21]

Leibniz's Law is pertinent to the philosophy of perception because Direct Realism must be understood as making an identity claim: that the immediate object of awareness in standard perceptual situations is a normal physical object—in other words, that it is *identical* to some such object. Arguments against Direct Realism therefore all attempt to refute this suggestion by finding some fact concerning the immediate object of awareness that does not hold of the normal object, or conversely. There are a limited number of possible discrepancies here, possible violations of Leibniz's Law, that fix the number of possible arguments against Direct Realism. The possibilities are the following. Concerning the immediate object of awareness and the normal object: (a) one possesses a genuine attribute that the other lacks;[22] (b) one bears a genuine relation to another item that the other does not; (c) one exists at a place where the other does not; (d) one exists at a time when the other does not; (e) one exists and the other does not. Each of these discrepancies has been alleged by some opponent of Direct Realism. Thus, those who accept the distinction between primary and secondary qualities, and who also hold that this is incompatible with Direct Realism, adopt a form of argument (a): they hold that the immediate objects of visual perception are, for example, sensuously coloured, but that no physical object is.[23] Hume's principal argument for his claim that we are immediately aware only of our own "perceptions" focuses on (b): what we are immediately aware of is dependent, both as to its character and its very existence, on the functioning of our brains and sensory systems in a way that no normal object is.[24] Such a thought may then motivate an additional argument concerned with (c): the immediate objects of perception exist in our brains, whereas normal objects typically do not. Russell, as we have seen, and also, arguably, Hume himself, argued this.[25] An argument that has been surprisingly popular from the seventeenth century on, to the effect that we can be immediately aware only of what is "locally present to the seat of consciousness," together with the observation that normal objects typically are not so present (since they are at a distance from us, in particular from our brains), also concerns (c).[26] The so-called Time-Lag Argument concerns (d).[27] Finally, arguments against Direct Realism that focus on hallucination, afterimages, or double vision concern (e).

In this work we shall be concerned with just two such arguments: what I shall call the "Argument from Illusion" and the "Argument from Hallucination"—forms of arguments (a) and (e), respectively. It is these two arguments that are here required to introduce the supposedly arcane notion of "direct awareness" according to which it is a genuine question whether we are directly aware of normal objects or not. I focus on these two because they are the ones that I believe pose the most serious challenge to Direct Realism from within the Philosophy of Perception, and consequently raise the widest range of issues involved in a proper philosophical understanding of perception. Other arguments based on the facts of perception can, I believe, either be deflected *ambulando* or be independently answered without too much difficulty.

Although we need to wait upon the presentation of our two arguments to understand the precise way in which we are supposed to be but indirectly aware of normal objects, and therefore directly aware of some kind of non-normal object, the notion of awareness that is in play is, in fact, neither arcane nor technical. We begin with a perfectly ordinary, intuitive understanding of being aware of something. All we are required initially to accept is that at a certain time we are aware, say, of something coloured, or even just that at a certain time we are aware of something or other. This is vouchsafed to us by reflexion, by the apperceptive awareness that we have of our conscious states.[28] The notions of directness and indirectness are introduced as a result of the recognition that the normal object that we should ordinarily be thought to be perceiving on such occasions either lacks the feature in question (such as colour) or does not exist at all. In the latter case, we are clearly not aware of a normal object at all; and in the former, if we can be said to aware of one, we can be so only indirectly. If this can be shown to be our predicament whenever we take ourselves to be perceiving a normal physical object, we are condemned to at best merely indirect awareness of such physical objects universally. We should indeed be trapped behind a "veil of perception."

The present work therefore falls into two parts, the first of which deals with the Argument from Illusion, the second with the Argument from Hallucination. The first part is considerably longer than the second—not because the former argument is more challenging (indeed, I believe the opposite to be the case), but because a large number of philosophical issues are relevant to both of these arguments. Part II therefore relies to a considerable extent on the findings of the earlier part. Part I begins with a chapter devoted to a longer-than-usual presentation of the Argument from Illusion. Such length is, I believe, demanded by the fact that most contemporary philosophers need to be convinced that the argument in question really does present a serious challenge to Direct Realism. In the course of the first chapter, various quick "refutations" of the argument are themselves refuted, and it is claimed that nothing less than a full-blown philosophical theory of perception is needed if we are to withstand the force of the argument. After this first chapter, the course of the argument takes a negative turn. In Chapters 2 and 3 it is argued than none of the standardly recognized accounts of perception is acceptable. In Chapter 4 I take stock of the negative findings that have previously emerged, and with them in mind outline the general form that any acceptable account of perception must take. In the final two chapters of Part I my own positive response to the argument is concretely developed. Part II begins with an exposition of the Argument from Hallucination, where it is argued that this poses an even more serious problem for Direct Realism than the earlier argument concerning illusion, and that despite the findings of Part I, it may not be clear how the Argument from Hallucination is to be answered. The second chapter of this part argues against the adoption of a currently popular way of dismissing the argument. And the final chapter presents my own positive response to it.

BY WAY OF A FINAL WORD of introduction, let me briefly explain why the fact that Direct Realism may face serious problems is a matter of philosophical importance. In my experience, little justification of the importance of this topic is required for those who come to our two arguments afresh. In general, such persons readily feel the force of the Problem, and regard its solution as a matter of considerable importance. On the other hand, the Philosophy of Perception is hardly a central focus of philosophical concern at the present time, in the way that it was but a generation or two ago. There can be little doubt that the Philosophy of Language, together with "Philosophical Logic" and more recently, "Cognitive Science," have come to overshadow all other areas of theoretical philosophy within the analytical tradition, and that discussions in this area are typically conducted in a manner that avoids any sustained confrontation with the Problem of Perception.[29] Nor do we find a sustained confrontation with the Problem in the tradition of recent continental philosophy; it, too, has been principally concerned with issues concerning meaning.[30] And yet, when you think about it, the idea that anything definitive can be said about language, or thought, in abstraction from a proper understanding of perception is bizarre. After all, one of the most important aspects of language and thought, and arguably the most important, is reference or directedness to the world; and is it not perception that constitutes our most fundamental mode of access to, or contact with, the world? As Sextus Empiricus puts it in one of my epigraphs, "If external things are not apprehended by the senses, neither will thought be able to apprehend them."[31] Not, of course, that we can speak of nothing other than what is perceptible; we can speak intelligibly about photons, for example. Perception is primary, rather, in that if we did not first perceive the world, we could not speak about it at all. Language manages to be something other than unanchored, freewheeling expostulation only because it receives its world-directed focus from perception. Moreover, there are certain sorts of entities, such as photons, to which we can re-

fer *only because* we can make reference to certain other sorts of entities—namely, macroscopic, perceptible objects. Reference to the former is, as Husserl put it, "founded" on reference to the latter. And it is
surely beyond serious dispute that it is perception that furnishes us
with our basic referents. And yet the idea, deriving from Quine, has
gained ground that we can conduct our semantic inquiries in a wholly
third-personal manner, being warranted in implementing any "interpretation" of speakers that leads to predictive success concerning verbal utterances. To take the classic example, we may, on such an approach, be justified in interpreting a subject as referring not to rabbits,
but to time-slices of rabbits, or undetached rabbit parts, or Lord knows
what other kind of gerrymandered entity.[32] Indeed, if no such interpretative scheme is better on behavioural grounds than some rival candidate, it is supposed to be actually indeterminate what this subject is
referring to. Now, there have been notable attempts, abiding by the
constraints of such an "interpretative" approach, to show that such indeterminacy can be at least cut down, if not eliminated. Need for such
ingenuity might have been altogether avoided, however, if more attention had been paid to the question of what such subjects are aware of
in perception. Could any conceivable creature perceive time-slices as
such? And if not, could time-slices possibly be basic entities in a creature's "ontology"? Surely the Stoics were nearer to the mark when they
claimed, according to Diogenes Laertius, that "the theory of assent, or
of understanding and thought . . . cannot be constructed without [that
is, as I take it, without reference to] sense-perception. For sense-perception comes first; and then thought, which is expressible, puts forth
in speech what it receives from sense-perception."[33] At least it is extraordinary that such questions were not even raised. More recently, as
a result of the growing appreciation of the fundamental and indispensable role played by indexical expressions in language, more attention is
being accorded to perception in semantic inquiries. Yet even here the
Problem of Perception is seldom directly addressed.

   A second reason for decline in philosophical interest in perception,
one that it is perhaps even more important for us to consider, is the idea
that the issue over Direct Realism is not even of any great moment
within the domain of the Philosophy of Perception itself. For if Direct
Realism is false, only two positions remain between which we must
choose: Idealism and Indirect Realism. Idealism is almost totally out of

favour today, so it is Indirect Realism that is most commonly thought to be the real rival to Direct Realism. Now, far and away the most common criticism that has been levelled against Indirect Realism is that it brings epistemological disaster in its wake. The thought is that, if we are constitutionally incapable of directly perceiving the physical world, but are cognitively confined within the circle of our own perceptions, then there is just no good reason to suppose that there is a physical world at all outside this domain, behind this veil. It is, therefore, standard practice for Indirect Realists, in turn, to defend their position by arguing that it has no such dire epistemological consequences.[34] Such a defence usually takes the form of pointing out that good non-deductive inference at least often has the form of an "inference to the best explanation," and that the overwhelmingly best explanation of the harmonious course of perceptual experience, which none but the extreme sceptic would deny, is that it is the upshot of our causal dealings with a physical world. Many in the philosophical community have come to feel that this is not an implausible move to make. It is for this reason that it may well be felt that the issue of Direct Realism is not of the first importance, since the whole issue now seems to reduce to a perhaps stymied debate over epistemological credentials. I believe that the issue of Direct Realism is far more important than this. The point about Indirect Realism is not that it is epistemologically suspect, but that it is incoherent. If Direct Realism is false, we must embrace some form of Idealism. And this I take to be a matter of the first philosophical importance.[35]

Although this is not the place for a full discussion of such an issue, I should perhaps briefly indicate my reasons for saying that Indirect Realism is incoherent. We need, first, to be clear precisely what it is that this position invites us to be Realists about. The domain in question is that of the physical components of the *empirical world*. An empirical world is an environment of which we are cognizant through perception—one that contains entities we can and do perceive. Such a world may well contain things that we could not, even in principle, perceive; but any such imperceptibles would be part of the empirical world only in virtue of being contained in the spatio-temporal, causal system that also contains perceptible entities. Any hypothesized realm of concrete, non-conscious elements—elements that should, therefore, perhaps be deemed "physical"—with which we could have no perceptual dealings whatever, which contained *no* entity that we could possibly perceive, would not be *our* physical world. In case it is not immediately clear that Indirect Realism, equally with Direct Realism, is concerned with the empirical world in this sense, consider that these two positions differ from one another over just one issue: directness. Hence, they agree in being forms of Realism with respect to the same domain of entities. Since it is certainly our empirical world about which the Direct Realist is a Realist, so must it be for the Indirect Realist. This is the world that contains ordinarily perceived everyday objects such as tables and chairs, animals and plants, rainbows and odours, as well as ourselves. Both positions are, therefore, to be contrasted with any form of Idealism with respect to just such an empirical world.

What, however, is the empirical world according to an Indirect Realist? It is, of course, not that which we can directly perceive, for that is precisely how it differentiates itself from Direct Realism. A realm is empirical, is our world, only in virtue of elements in it being perceptible; but for the Indirect Realist this can be a matter only of indirect perception. So this realm is supposed to be *both* empirical *and yet* irremediably behind a "veil of perception." It is precisely here that the ultimate incoherence in Indirect Realism lies: such a "concealed" world cannot conceivably be our empirical world.

Faced with a Direct Realist, an Indirect Realist will be happy to discourse with him about, say, this page that you are now reading. This page, for him, is a real entity, not a construction out of experiences or whatever. The Indirect Realist does not take himself to be discussing anything other than what the Direct Realist can recognize and refer to. This is essential. A domain that does not contain objects to which we can make common reference on the basis of their being open to being perceived equally by several subjects—*public* objects, as they are commonly termed—is not an empirical world. In particular, an empirical world is one that contains entities to which we can make demonstrative reference: *this* page, *that* tree, and so on. The Indirect Realist's *only* disagreement with the Direct Realist is that the former believes such public objects of common reference are not directly perceived; at best they give rise to sensations, or sense-data, that somehow represent these objects. According to the Indirect Realist, to say there is indeed a real empirical object that I am perceiving, one that you too could in principle perceive, one to which you too could make reference, is always to go *beyond* what is *given* to us in experience. But in what sense is it, there-fore, *this page* of which the Indirect Realist speaks when he speaks of what is physically real in this situation? How can two people be in a po-sition to make demonstrative reference to the same object, when each of them is aware of it only indirectly?

Now, there is nothing in general impossible about two people mak-ing reference to one and the same thing even though neither of them can perceive it directly, even in principle. Two scientists, for example, could talk to one another about a certain electron—one that has, say, just left a path in their cloud chamber. Electrons are too small to be perceived individually by any, perhaps any possible, sense, and our two scientists of course know this. They are able, nevertheless, to speak of *that* individual electron in virtue of thinking of it as the one responsible for making this track in the cloud chamber. Such a possibility lends no credence whatever to Indirect Realism, however, since such a labora-tory situation presents two striking disanalogies to our perception of the physical world in general. In the first place, both scientists directly saw the same track in the cloud chamber—for if they did not, they would be talking at cross purposes; whereas, according to the Indirect Realist, no two people can ever be directly aware of the same object, on the basis of which common reference they could build a reference to an individual that is but indirectly perceivable. In the second place, our two scientists think of their electron as standing in a commonly under-stood relation to that of which they have a joint perception, whereas we most certainly do not think of empirical objects merely as things stand-ing in some sort of relation to what we are perceptually aware of. The Indirect Realist may think of physical objects in this way, or at least aver that he does, but we do not. This is critical, since the Indirect Re-alist must make the case that he is dealing with the empirical objects to which he and we make common reference. It is doubtless for this reason that many Indirect Realists have suggested that representing something as the cause of our experience is ingredient in even everyday perceptual consciousness. We shall consider this idea later, but it has nothing to be said for it.

When, therefore, we return from the analogy to a typical perceptual situation in which all but the Indirect Realist would say that we are di-rectly aware of a physical object, the situation is as follows. When you look at this page, what you are directly aware of is, according to the Indirect Realist, not a page of a book. When you speak and think about *this* thing, your mind is, therefore, directed to some mere proxy for a physical object. When you say "This is a page," you are mis-categorizing a private, proxy item as a page of a book, as a kind of public object. The only stance that the Indirect Realist can plausibly take on the nature of ordinary perceptual consciousness is an Error Theory: he must endorse Hume's notorious claim that "the vulgar confound perceptions and objects, and attribute a distinct continu'd existence to the very things they feel or see."[36] Now, when I look at the "same" page as you, I am immediately aware of a different proxy. My *this* is different from yours. This means that we do not agree when we both say "This is a page." Indeed we *cannot* agree, since we are speaking of what we are thinking of, and we are thinking of what we are aware of—indeed, given that in everyday life we are not Indirect Realists, we are thinking of what we are *directly* aware of. And necessarily we are, according to the Indirect Realist, directly aware of different things, different proxies. This infringes the requirement that an empirical world contain public objects susceptible to common reference. On such a view, a domain is empirical even though not a single element in it ever enters our ken. This cannot be right.

Whatever it is that such an Indirect Realist is being a Realist about, therefore, it is not our empirical world. If we are not sceptics and there is such a world, then given that it cannot be *identified* with our actual perceptions, the only possibility left is that it is ideal. If we are not Direct Realists, we must be Idealists. Because of this, Indirect Realism will not surface again in this work as a real option. I shall, however, often refer to this position in expounding the two arguments we shall be considering against Direct Realism. This is because such arguments initially push us in the direction of Indirect Realism. We all start out being Direct Realists. If an argument shakes our faith in this position, our initial reaction is to cling fast to the Realism, but to conclude that we are not directly aware of physical objects in the way we initially thought. It is sometimes helpful to present arguments against Direct Realism in this light. It should, however, not be forgotten that such an initial move can find no secure resting place. Idealism is, no doubt, an extreme view, one that is standardly adopted only after two moves have been made: recognizing that Direct Realism is false, and then recognizing that the next natural port of call, Indirect Realism, is also false. I have already argued that the second move is mandatory. In the rest of this work we shall be concerned with the first. The importance of this issue should now be clear. It involves nothing less than a choice between Realism and Idealism about the physical world. If this is so, d'Alembert cannot be far off the mark when he says, in the first of my epigraphs, that "the examination of the operation of the spirit that consists in passing from our sensations to exterior objects is clearly the first step that metaphysics must take."[37]

The **Argument** from **Illusion**

I

The Argument

1

THE ARGUMENT FROM ILLUSION—for short, "the Argument"—is held in low respect by most philosophers today. This is not merely because the majority of contemporary philosophers endorse some form of Direct Realism, and hence regard all arguments against this position as unsound. Even many who reject Direct Realism spurn this particular reason for rejection as being hopelessly weak. Frank Jackson, for example, is a leading contemporary proponent of Indirect Realism who can yet write of "the notorious arguments from illusion, variation, perceptual relativity, and so forth" that "I think these arguments prove nothing."[1] As will emerge, I myself do believe that the Argument can be resisted. It will, however, take over half of the present book to demonstrate how this may be done. (Jackson devotes about four pages to the task.) In my view, the Argument genuinely presents a serious challenge to Direct Realist theories of perception, and we can learn much about the nature of perception by forcing ourselves to address this challenge seriously. In fact, the only way to block the Argument is subtle and non-obvious. The accounts of perception that are generally purveyed today simply do not face up to the Argument's puzzling power.

The Argument claims that the physical world can appear to us in perception other than it really is, *and that this very fact is incompatible with Direct Realism*. Stated thus baldly the claim appears not just far from seriously worrying, but wildly implausible. Many opponents of the Argument have pounced at this early point. The following passage from G. Dawes Hicks is typical: "Suppose that the petals of a rose are veritably characterised by a specific shade of red. Is there, in that case, any occasion for surprise in the fact that their actual colour will seem different to two observers who view the rose from different distances, or when one of them observes it in daylight and the other in twilight, or when one sees it through a pair of dark spectacles and the other with the naked eye? Surely the surprising thing would be if the fact were otherwise."[2] J. L. Austin makes a similar point in his characteristically forthright manner: "What is wrong, what is even faintly surprising, in the idea of a stick's being straight but looking bent sometimes? Does anyone suppose that if something is straight, then it jolly well has to look straight at all times and in all circumstances?"[3] The term "Naive Realism" has been used by some as a label for the view that in perception we always perceive the world exactly as it is. Dawes Hicks and Austin are surely right in insisting that Naive Realism, so understood, is no part of a common-sensical, pre-theoretical, Direct Realist view of our perceptual relation to the world. The view in question is not just naive, but downright silly.

Proponents of the Argument, however, do not suppose otherwise. After all, the very basis of the Argument is that reality and appearance can indeed diverge: its fundamental premise is that *illusions can occur.* What the Argument does, rather, is to challenge common sense, and, indeed, any Direct Realist view, to give an adequate account of such a possibility. Its claim is not that ordinary people have overlooked certain recherché facts of experience, but that they are incapable of giving an adequate account of phenomena that they fully recognize. The charge against common sense is not that it is incomplete, but that it is incoherent. For common sense embraces two theses: that we are directly aware of the physical world (realistically construed), and that illusion is possible. The Argument attempts to demonstrate that the second thesis, when thought through, issues in a recognition that the first is false. Furthermore, it argues that since the latter thesis is indisputable, it is the former, Direct Realist claim that must be abandoned. It is, therefore, simply irrelevant to point out that common sense recognizes a distinction between appearance and reality. Of course it does—but illegitimately, given its commitment to Direct Realism. So the Argument attempts to show. I intend to consider the Argument in its most ambitious, and hence interesting, form: as claiming to demonstrate that the kind of direct awareness of the physical world that is embodied in Direct Realism is *impossible*. No possible physical object could ever be directly perceived by any possible subject. Even in this strongest of forms, I suggest, the Argument is difficult to resist.

Our Argument begins, as I have said, with the premise that perceptual illusion can occur. The term "illusion" is to be understood here as applying to any perceptual situation in which a physical object is actually perceived, but in which that object perceptually appears other than it really is, for whatever reason.[4] It is therefore irrelevant whether the subject of an illusion is fooled by appearances or not. More importantly, the term "illusion" is to be understood as ranging much more widely than its common use would allow. For example, the world appears differently to those who are colour-blind and to those who are not. This involves an illusion, in the possibly unnatural sense here employed. For if I, being colour-blind, cannot tell red and green things apart, but you can, at least one of these colours must look different to the two of us. So, for at least one of us, that colour cannot look the way it really is. That there "really" is a way the object is "objectively" is a presupposition of the Direct Realism that is under investigation here, and so will not itself come up for discussion. One can, of course, take a differential attitude towards the various "qualities" that normal physical objects are commonly held to possess, and embrace some form of the primary / secondary quality distinction. One could, for example, hold that there is no "objective fact" about what colour a thing is; or hold that colour does not really inhere in normal physical objects at all, but is merely "subjective." So long as *some* qualities that are objectively possessed by normal objects are directly perceived, it may be thought, we can be credited with direct perception of those objects. Such views are, to be sure, themselves often arrived at as a result of feeling the Argument's force; but be that as it may, the Argument will attempt to convince you that there is no secure resting place beyond a wholly naive view of physical objects and their qualities that stops short of a complete rejection of Direct Realism in any form.

Given that the Argument is attempting to prove that we have no direct access to the world through perception at all—indeed, that the very idea of such direct perception is incoherent—it may perhaps be thought that the premise that illusions can occur must be taken as applying to every sense we possess and to every perceptible feature of every physical object (or even as applying to every possible sense and every possibly perceivable physical quality). As we shall see, the Argument, even in its strongest form, can get by with a weaker premise than this. Still, such a universal claim is true. Every sense we actually possess is certainly subject to illusion. I cannot be the only person to have been genuinely surprised, after having chosen some article of clothing under the artificial illumination of a shop, to discover its "true" colour in broad daylight. Tastes and smells are affected both by various ailments and by prior exposure to strongly contrasting stimuli. The famous example of the lukewarm water—that feels warmer to one hand than to another when they have just been immersed separately in cold water and hot—shows that tactile perception is also subject to illusion. A "popping" of the ears resulting in unchanging sounds seeming louder than before, and a heavy cold making them seem fainter, demonstrate the presence of "illusion" in hearing; and certain audio recordings are available that demonstrate a wide range of little known, but sometimes striking, auditory illusions.[5] It is, moreover, not just the "proper sensibles" that are subject to illusion, as Berkeley famously pointed out.[6] There is, for example, the somewhat hackneyed, though still undeniable, case of the straight stick that looks bent in water;[7] and distorting lenses can lead us to misperceive the shape, size and position of objects. Nor are illusions of the "primary qualities" restricted to sight. As a result of the common dominance of sight over touch, a straight stick felt with the hands can feel curved when it is observed while wearing lenses that make the stick look curved; and objects feel lighter than they otherwise would after a particularly heavy object has been held. It is also common experience to misperceive both the direction and the distance of sounds.[8]

So much for the classical five senses to which alone the Argument is usually directed. We should also, however, consider our quasi-perceptual awareness of our own bodies—especially as it is tempting to think that because our bodies are, as it were, so close to us, the scope for illusion here is minimal.[9] In fact, however, recent research in this area has presented some of the most striking illusions in all the literature. If, for example, you hold your nose between thumb and index finger, suitably vibrating the muscles in your arm can make it feel to you as if your arm is straightening and your nose is being pulled out to be about two feet long; and if you place your fingertips on the top of your head, a contrary vibration can make it feel as if you are pushing your fingers into your skull.[10]

What, however, of other possible senses by which we, or some other possible creature, could perceive the physical world? Well, surely, when we reflect on the matter, we realize that any possible sense that any possible creature might possess will be in principle subject to illusion because any sense involves the functioning of sense receptors that can, in principle, malfunction. It is not for nothing that traditional theology denied sensory perception to God, as being incompatible with unconditioned, infallible knowledge.

So much for the first premise: there is no type of physical feature that may not appear differently from the way it really is to any sense that could possibly perceive it. The next step of the Argument is an inference from this: that whenever something perceptually appears to have a feature when it actually does not, we are aware of something that does actually possess that feature. So, if you are looking at a white wall, which because of the illumination looks yellow to you, you are aware of something yellow. This inference is commonly known as the "sense-datum inference," with the immediate object of awareness that the inference introduces termed a "sense-datum." This is the heart of the Argument. Indeed, all of Part I of this work is effectively devoted to consideration of this claim and to attempting to see a way around it. This is because, as I shall now argue, if this inference is accepted, the Argument is effectively home and dry.

The third step in the Argument consists in pointing out that since the appearing physical object does not possess that feature which, according the previous step, we are immediately aware of in the illusory situation, it is not the physical object of which we are aware in such a situation; or, at least, we are not aware of it in the direct, unmediated way in which we are aware of whatever it is that possesses the appearing feature—that direct way in which we formerly took ourselves to be generally aware of normal physical objects. In the previous example, since the wall is white, not yellow, but what we are immediately aware of is yellow, not white, what we are immediately aware of cannot be the wall. This third step is but an application of Leibniz's Law to illusory situations. If the so-called sense-datum inference is accepted, this further step may seem unavoidable, since Leibniz's Law is not to be contested.

We are now in a position to see why the scope of the illusions that are required by the Argument's first premise need not be as wide as one might think. The universal pretension of the Argument notwithstanding, we can now see that all that is required is the claim that *some* perceptible feature of any physical object be subject to illusion for every possible sense by which we might perceive that object. For suppose that we see a red tomato that looks black as a result of unusual lighting. We conclude, by the second and third steps of the Argument, that we are aware of a black sense-datum distinct from any physical tomato. Now although in this situation the shape of the tomato is not, we may suppose, subject to illusion, we cannot maintain that we are directly aware visually of the tomato's shape, because, simply in virtue of one of the visible features of the tomato being subject to illusion, a sense-datum has replaced the tomato as the object of visual awareness as such. For the shape you see is the shape *of something black*, and the tomato is not black. I shall refer to this as "sense-datum infection."

The conclusion of the Argument thus far is that in no illusory situation are we directly aware of the physical object that, as we should initially have put it, "appears" to us other than it is. The final step in the Argument is what we may call the "generalizing step": we are immediately aware of sense-data, and only at best indirectly aware of normal physical objects, in all perceptual situations, veridical as well as illusory. If this final step is taken, all, of course, is lost for the Direct Realist. The usual reason given for taking it is the subjective indiscernibility of veridical and possible illusory situations. To put it crudely, being aware of a sense-datum is *exactly like* perceiving a normal object. But a sense-datum, whatever it may turn out precisely to be, is clearly a radically different type of thing from a normal physical object—at least as the latter are usually (that is, realistically) conceived. So how could awareness of two such radically different types of object be experientially identical? How could we *mistake* one for the other? As H. H. Price asks, "Is it not incredible that two entities so similar in all these qualities should really be so utterly different: that the one should be a real constituent of a material object, wholly independent of the observer's mind and organism, while the other is merely the fleeting product of his cerebral processes?"[11] If this is indeed a problem, it seems to grow worse when we reflect that these two radically different sorts of perceptual object may form, subjectively, a smoothly connected series: that there could, as Price put it, be a "sensibly continuous transition" from a state of veridical perception to an illusory state, and conversely. Indeed, it is presumably possible that a transition from a veridical to an illusory perception should involve no apparent change in the object whatsoever, if the physical object itself undergoes some change that precisely compensates for the onset of the illusion. Can it really be thought that at a certain subjectively undetectable point in such a situation the subject becomes aware of a radically new type of object? Such an appeal to intuition is resistible, however, as the following response from Austin indicates: "Even if we were to make the prior admission . . . that in the 'abnormal' cases we perceive sense-data, we should not be obliged to extend this admission to the 'normal' cases too. For why earth should it not be the case that, in some few instances, perceiving one sort of thing is exactly like perceiving another?"[12] I shall now argue that if the earlier moves of the Argument are accepted, the final generalizing step is indeed mandatory.

Let us just reflect on how radically Austin's response (or, to be fair, one that he was willing to make for the sake of argument) contradicts our ordinary picture of our perceptual relation with the physical world —the very picture that opponents of the Argument are keen to preserve. Consider, for example, the common phenomenon of looking at an article of clothing under the artificial lighting of a shop and discovering its "real" colour in daylight. To deny the generalizing step is to suppose that as you walk out of the shop while looking at your purchase, you only become directly aware of that physical item as you emerge into daylight (assuming that this is when an object shows its true colours). Only then does that physical object suddenly leap into your perception *in propria persona*. Before then you were dealing with a train of mere perceptual proxies, or sense-data. Or consider the way in which our awareness of the colours of objects changes as dawn gives way to the full light of morning, or as dusk descends. There is not even anything artificial about dawn or dusk. Anyone who followed the Austinian suggestion—accepting the earlier stages of the Argument and attempting to block it only by denying the last, generalizing step— would be forced to conclude that at some point between dawn and, say, noon, we are suddenly vouchsafed a direct glimpse of physical objects themselves, and that as dusk descends there comes a point at which we begin radically to lose touch with reality. And what about moderately short-sighted people who remove their spectacles? And colour-blind people all the time? It is clear that the notion of direct contact with reality that is being defended here is not one that a Direct Realist should welcome, since it finds no place in the common-sense view of the world that the Direct Realist is trying to defend. Such a manoeuvre in response to the Argument is committed to an absurdly static view of what constitutes awareness of the world. Genuine, direct awareness of the physical world consists, on such a view, of a number of shots of the world taken from ideal positions (in some sense), with any departure from these ideal poses constituting a perceptual loss of the world itself. The picture of our daily commerce with the world through perception that therefore emerges is one of a usually indirect awareness of physical objects occasionally interrupted by direct visions of them glimpsed in favoured positions. If one is unhappy with the Argument from Illusion because of its clash with basic everyday convictions about our perceptual commerce with the physical world, denying it only at the last step is not the way to respond to it.

What has gone wrong here is that Austin's suggestion simply contradicts the very nature of illusion. It does this because the whole point about the concept of illusion, from which the Argument starts, is that in an illusion we really are perceiving a certain physical object, but misperceiving it. This, after all, is how illusion differs from hallucination. To deny the generalizing step, while accepting the rest of the Argument, is to regard us as being as radically out of touch with our environment when subject to mere illusion as we are generally agreed to be when wholly hallucinating. This is simply not the Direct Realist's conception of an illusion. Even though a red tomato may look black to you, it is the tomato itself that you are seeing. In other words, it is crucial to our understanding of illusion, as opposed to hallucination, that *we are aware of the same object in an illusion that we could perceive veridically.* Thus the very nature of illusion demands acceptance of the generalizing step of the Argument. For if, in illusion, we are aware of the same object as we should be aware of were we perceiving veridically, and it has been shown that in illusion we are not aware of a normal physical object, but of a mere sense-datum, it follows that we are not aware of such physical objects even in veridical perception, but only of sense-data. To deny this is to treat illusions as hallucinations— the topic of Part II of this work.

Incidentally, Austin, and many like-minded "ordinary language philosophers," were keen on pointing out that illusions are somewhat rare
phenomena. This supposed fact was supposed to have some bearing on
the force of the Argument. As we have seen, given the sense in which
the term "illusion" is employed here, illusions are far from uncommon.
But even if they were, this would have no bearing on the soundness of
the Argument, because, as we are now in a position to see, the Argument does not even require that illusions ever happen.[13] All that is required is that, for any object perceptible in any sense-modality, illusion
be barely possible. From such a mere possibility the Argument then
proceeds as follows: It is of the very nature of illusion, as opposed to
hallucination, that *were* we to perceive something illusorily, we should
be aware of the same kind of object as we could be aware of veridically;
by the sense-datum inference, we should be aware of a sense-datum in
the possible illusory situation; so such a sense-datum, not a normal
physical object, is the kind of object we are aware of even when perceiving veridically.[14]

If, therefore, we are to block the Argument at all, it must be at either
Stage Two or Stage Three. A number of philosophers—those, for example, associated with the so-called New Realism that flourished at
the beginning of the twentieth century—have attempted to block it
at Stage Three. The New Realists accept the sense-datum inference:
when the tomato looks black to me, I am aware of something black.
They deny, however, that I am therefore not aware of a normal physical
object. Indeed, they deny that I am therefore not aware of the very tomato in question. For why should not the blackness that I see be a genuine feature of the tomato? The suggestion is not that the tomato in
question has turned black, of course. The New Realists suggest, rather,
that the features of which we are aware in illusion are as much genuine
ingredients of the physical realm as those features that physical objects
are commonly thought "really" to possess. Discussing the case of a single quantity of water seeming to be of different temperatures to each
hand, T. Percy Nunn wrote,

> To me it seems true, not only that both the warmth and the cold-
> ness are really experienced, but also that, under appropriate con-
> ditions, both are there to be experienced . . . I can find no more
> "contradiction" in the simultaneous attribution of the warmth and

coldness to the same water than in the simultaneous attribution to it of warmth and acidity. Only empirical experience can decide what qualities it is possible, and what it is impossible, for a body to wear together, and we must admit that experience shows us that warmth and coldness simply are not among the qualities which exclude one another.[15]

The view that physical objects possess relatively few objective properties—those recognized by everyday common sense (or, indeed, by science)—was stigmatized by the American New Realists as the "brickbat" conception of reality.[16] Jean-Paul Sartre held a similar view.[17] And in the ancient world it was, at least according to testimony of Sextus Empiricus and Plutarch, endorsed by Epicurus: "Every perception is true," he is reported to have beleived.[18]

Now, taken *au pied de la lettre*, a statement such as Nunn's is, of course, absurd. ("Slime and confusion" is Plutarch's judgement on the analogous Epicurean position.)[19] It is not the case that experience alone can decide what properties an object can co-instantiate; we can decide a priori against a contention that is recognizably incoherent or self-contradictory. In particular, the logical relations between genus and species, or between a determinable property and its determinate forms, must be respected in any intelligible characterization of reality—a respect that may seem singularly lacking in Nunn's remarks. It is clear on closer inspection, however, that the New Realists were not simply embracing a mass of self-contradictions. As the slighting reference to the "brickbat" conception of physical objects indicates, such writers were actually engaged in questioning our everyday conception of physical reality, and replacing it with a picture of physical objects as extremely complex systems of variegated views and appearances. Reality is now regarded as being sufficiently rich to allow all the features present in our varying perceptions to be genuine constituents of physical reality. (Sartre suggests that such a "contradiction" in perception "motivates a free choice of true objectivity on my part.")[20]

If our interest in Direct Realism is as a theory that expresses our everyday convictions about the physical domain and our perceptual commerce with it, the present radical defence should have little attraction. Our straightforward understanding of physical objects is replaced in such an account by a bewildering system of properties from which the fairly stable everyday characteristics of things can be abstracted only with great ingenuity. Even such a staunch defender of Direct Realism as Winston Barnes could find such a pan-Realism too much to stomach, referring to "the wilder excesses of realism . . . , in which not only reality but mind-independence was credited lavishly to almost anything that could be named."[21] Barnes also goes on to put his finger on the crucial error involved in such "excesses": on such a view "the world . . . [took] on the appearance of a great museum in which a few of the contents were real operative beings but the vast majority were exhibits only, ready to be produced on the appropriate occasion, but possessed of no other ground of existence." The supposedly physical difference in temperature that my two hands detect in the water in Nunn's example is a difference that makes no physical difference at all. A merely apparent difference is not, to be sure, wholly without possible causal consequences. Such consequences are, however, restricted to causal contexts that involve the psychological realm. I may, for example, be led to withdraw one hand rather than the other because of the felt difference in temperature. The point is that there is no possible non-psychological, merely physical, situation in which the supposedly physical difference of temperature counts for anything. This invalidates the claim that the difference in question is indeed physical.

This consideration of New Realism indicates, however, that our Argument may have to be more selective in the illusions it employs. This is because many of the cases of illusion so far mentioned involve states of affairs that do have physical significance. The difference between a tomato that looks red and one that looks black due to a difference of illumination is one that would show up on a suitably chosen colour film, as would the apparent bentness of a stick half immersed in water. It is therefore open to a less excessive form of New Realism to claim that whenever we are dealing with illusions that have a physical basis, we are dealing with genuinely physical features of the environment. Such a position has indeed been defended in recent times by David Armstrong. "It seems to me," he writes, "that we must admit that a real change in quality occurs at surfaces that, as we say, 'appear to change' when conditions of illumination are changed. I can see no ground for saying that such changes are in any way illusory or merely apparent . . . The sun, or a sodium-vapour lamp, actually *act* on the visible surface, and so it is reasonable to think of them causing different effects at that surface."[22] (It seems that Epicurus actually took this line, but held, mistakenly, that all perceptual states have such physical correlates.)[23] By contrast, when Armstrong considers those changes in colour appearance that are a result of juxtaposing different colours, and that are sometimes called "simultaneous contrast illusions," he admits that because "the differences in colour exhibited by the same surface placed in different environments are not due . . . to the differing causal action of these environments," we have to "treat this as a change in the appearances presented."[24] Such a view does, indeed, depart somewhat from our everyday attitude towards perceptible qualities. In particular, it construes many more of them as relational than everyday common sense would allow: we do not normally think that merely changing a light bulb brings about a real change in the colours of objects, or that walking out into the daylight changes the colour of the tie I have just bought in the shop. Such a revision may well, however, be thought a small price to pay if the only alternative is acceptance of the Argument from Illusion and a wholesale rejection of Direct Realism.

In fact, however, stressing the physical basis of certain types of illusion helps the Direct Realist case not one jot, since there are—especially given sense-datum infection—enough illusions having a more "proximal" location to carry the Argument through to its universal conclusion. For many illusions are purely physiological or psychological in nature: "subjective illusions," as we may call them. As Armstrong himself mentions, the apparent colour of an object changes if it is surrounded by suitably contrasting colours (as does the lightness of an achromatic colour). Such contrast illusions are also found in the realm of touch: a neutral area within a warmer ring feels cold, and within a cold ring feels warm. Again, if the convergence of the eyes is artificially increased whilst viewing an object, that object will appear to decrease in size. And the currently popular books of stereograms are an easily available source of striking subjective 3-D illusions. A particularly intriguing multiple subjective illusion can be created using a "Mach strip"—which, because it is so striking, and because it provides easy access to certain perceptual phenomena that are otherwise difficult to produce, and which I shall have cause to mention later, I shall now describe. Take a sheet of white paper, fold it lengthways down the middle, and place it on a flat surface so that, as you look down on it, it looks like a roof extending away from you. Position it so that more light falls on one side of "roof" than the other. Close one eye and stare at it. When initially viewed, one side of the roof looks shaded, the other not. After a while the roof jumps up, so that it now looks like two pages of an open book standing upright. Not only this, but the less brightly illuminated side now looks a dirty grey, the other a brilliant white. If you now move your head from side to side, the "book" will appear to pivot around its centre, turning wildly from side to side with your gaze. A most striking phenomenon.

A particularly significant type of subjective illusion is that involving negative after-effect due to adaptation.[25] If a moving belt of rough cloth passes over the skin for a while, and is then stopped, there will then occur an impression of movement in the opposite direction, "as clear as if the cloth had been set going backward."[26] If a curved line is fixated, its apparent curvature grows less; and for some little time afterwards, a straight line seen in the same part of the visual field will appear curved in the opposite direction. If you stare at a bright yellow patch for a couple of minutes, the yellowness will sensibly fade; and if you then look at a white surface, it will look slightly violet. This phenomenon of negative after-effect is particularly significant at this point in our discussion since such effects are to be found in *every* sense. Physiological abnormalities also open up a huge field of what in the present context count as illusions. Very short-sighted and colour-blind people do not visually experience the world as others do; and who knows what the limits are to the perceptual effects that may be wrought by tampering with sense organs and sensory channels? By rewiring my optic channels you could, doubtless, make objects of one colour look the way objects of another colour looked to me before the switch. By tampering with my ears you could raise or lower the perceived pitch of notes. And by tampering with the receptors in my skin you could affect my perception of temperature. In short, there are enough kinds of physiologically and psychologically based illusions to sustain the universal applicability of the Argument. For recall that, because of sense-datum infection, we require only one feature of any perceptible object to be subject to illusion for the Argument to go through for the entirety of that object as perceived by that sense. Physiological intervention leading to misperception, in particular, is surely a possibility in relation to every *possible* sense. Since we are dealing with phenomena that have no merely physical significance, a moderate New Realism is incapable of blocking the Argument at its third stage.

It is now beginning to look as if the only way of resisting the Argument is by blocking it at Step Two: by denying the sense-datum inference. There remains, however, one worry that many feel about the overall form of the Argument. The worry is that, while the conclusion of the Argument is that we are not directly aware of normal physical objects at all in perception, the initial premise is to the effect that we do indeed perceive such physical objects, albeit illusorily. After all, this is how illusion differs from hallucination. Winston Barnes has therefore claimed that "not only is the argument fallacious but the conclusion contradicts one of the premises."[27] This worry is settled, however, when we view the Argument as having the form of a reductio ad absurdum of the naive view of our perceptual relation to the world, and specifically of the naive reading of the first premise. Assume, for the sake of argument, that we are directly aware of the objects that appear to us other than they are, and that these objects are realistically construed. The Argument then proceeds, as before, to spell out the implications of one part of this assumption: namely, that such an object appears other than it really is. For, according to the Argument, one implication of this is just what the sense-datum inference tells us: that when an object appears other than it is, we are aware of something that really is that way. And from such a recognition of sense-data as the immediate objects of illusory perceptual states, the Argument proceeds inexorably, via the generalizing step, to the conclusion that some other part of our initial assumption is false: either Realism about physical objects, or the claim to directness in our awareness of them. With this worry settled, our conclusion must be that if the Argument is to be resisted at all, it must indeed be by denying its second step.

There are two ways in which one might demonstrate the invalidity of the sense-datum inference: a laborious way and a swift way. For one way is to present a detailed analysis of perception that involves no sense-data or other perceptual proxies. In subsequent chapters our task will be to investigate such theories as have been devised, to see if any achieve this objective, and if not, to see if we can better them. Another way to dispute the inference is to suggest that it involves some fairly simple mistake; when this mistake is pointed out, the whole Argument collapses. I shall conclude this presentation of the Argument by considering the swift replies to it. I hope to show that none of them is satisfactory. When we have seen the weakness of all such swift responses, we shall have to face up to the serious business of developing a general philosophical account of perception that manages to avoid the sense-datum inference.

SWIFT CRITICISM of the Argument sometimes begins by emphasizing the fact that, since illusion is fully recognized by common sense, there are resources for accommodating it that are unproblematically available within ordinary ways of speaking of the world. For we speak not only of seeing things and their qualities, but of things "looking" a certain way. And similarly with all the senses: we know that sweet things can taste bitter in certain conditions, and so on. Everyday thought allows that things can, in general, *seem* or *appear* other than they are; and this receives expression in everyday language, which embodies what has been called the "language of appearing."[28] What is held to be crucial about such language is that it represents normal, public, physical objects as the entities that appear to us; and, in particular, that since talk of appearing involves no supposition that the object in question actually is the way it appears, a proper appreciation of the use of such language shows the Argument's crucial sense-datum inference to be simply fallacious. For this reason, the sense-datum inference, moving as it does from "appears" to "is," has been dubbed the "sense-datum fallacy."[29]

Can it seriously be thought, however, that all the proponents of the Argument from Illusion have made some silly little slip in moving from "appears" to "is"? The language of appearing is indeed, as its advocates stress, a standard and commonly employed part of ordinary language. Have generations of philosophers simply forgotten, or become confused over, a way of talking that they acquired at their mothers' knees? Let us note, first, that no proponent of the Argument has ever held that one may infer from the fact that some object appears to have some characteristic that the object really does possess that characteristic. The whole point of the Argument is to get us to recognize something other than a normal object as the bearer of the characteristic in question. The inference is always from some object's appearing some way to some *other object* actually being that way. So the Argument at least involves no simple-minded inference from "appears" to "is." No doubt it will be said that the language of appearing warrants no inference to *anything* actually having the feature that something appears to have. But on what grounds can it be claimed that such an inference is not warranted? Simply that naive subjects do not immediately draw it, or that they deny it? Perhaps such subjects have not thought the matter out fully enough. Recall that the Argument claims that common sense *when thought through* undermines itself. One indication that common sense is not as secure in this area as proponents of "ordinary language philosophy" would have us believe is the unsettling effect that exposure to the Argument itself has on most subjects who first encounter it—not to mention the over-reaction of the New Realists.

We begin to see the real force of the Argument, and specifically of the sense-datum inference, when we ask the following question: When, say, something white looks yellow to you, *in virtue of what does it look, specifically, yellow to you?* What, precisely, is it for such a state of affairs to obtain? What are the minimally sufficient conditions for something to appear yellow to you, when nothing relevant is yellow? Typical appeals to the language of appearing have a merely negative import: to say that a white wall looks yellow to me is not to say or imply that anything is yellow. On the ordinary-language inventory of this situation we there-fore find a person and a white wall. No positive account has been given of what constitutes the wall looking yellow, rather than some other col-our.[30] One way of attempting to draw out the inadequacy of such an ap-proach is as follows. If, in the example under consideration, my only in-formation about the colour of the object I am seeing comes from my current perception of it, I shall, other things being equal, take the ob-ject that is in fact white to be yellow. But *why* do I take it to be yellow, rather than any other colour, unless, as C. D. Broad put it, something yellow is "before my mind"?[31] When, in the situation in question, I de-scribe the wall as yellow, I do not just pick a colour term at random. Surely yellowness is appropriate to giving expression to my perceptual state only because that is the colour *I am aware of.* I say "yellow" be-cause I see yellow. When something appears yellow to me, it is, or could be, with me visually just as it is when I veridically see something that really is yellow. The same "sensible quality" is present to con-sciousness in the two cases. For were it not, why should I make refer-ence to the same colour in the two situations? What the Argument from Illusion attempts primarily to achieve is the recognition that *sensi-*

ble qualities can be present to consciousness in perception despite the fact that they do not characterize the normal physical objects we are said to be perceiving. It then challenges us to make sense of this fact. According to the Direct Realist, when the white wall looks yellow to you, you are directly aware of a wall and (we may suppose) nothing else. The thing you are aware of is not yellow, however. So how does yellow get into the picture? The "ordinary language" response will certainly be to say that you speak of yellow because the wall "looks" yellow to you. But if only a negative characterization of such looking is offered, this remark is not satisfying.

There are, however, many uses of such terms as "appears," "seems," and so forth that no one regards as implying that anything must actually be the way that something appears to be. Several critics of the Argument have therefore raised the question why appearances are supposed to sustain the sense-datum inference in the particular context of illusion, though admittedly not elsewhere. So we need briefly to investigate the different uses of the language of appearing to see if we can distinguish in a principled way between those that do and those that do not warrant such an inference.

We need, in the first place, to set aside those uses of the language of appearing that may be called "merely evidential."[32] To say that the economy seems to be improving, or that the military situation looks bad, is not to give voice to the nature of one's perceptual experience at all. I call such uses merely evidential because they simply have the force of "the evidence points to the conclusion that . . ." Such uses are purely judgemental, and typically express a belief that falls short of certainty. They are about as germane to an account of perception as is the use of "I see" to express any act of understanding. Such uses of the language of appearing will ultimately be based on perception, of course, but on perception of items other than the state of affairs that itself is said to appear to obtain—the "focal" state of affairs, as I shall call it. No one, indeed, supposes that in such cases something must actually possess the characteristics that one surmises are realized. If we push the question *why* it appears to someone that the economic situation is getting specifically worse, the answer is immediately forthcoming: since such purely evidential uses of the language of appearing express judgements based on evidence, it is the nature of the evidence that explains the specific nature of the judgement.

We need, then, to restrict our attention to examples of the language of appearing where perceptual appearances themselves are in question: where appearances are not the contents of judgements based on evidence, but our very evidence itself, the actual deliverances of our senses. It has been suggested, however, that even here the language of appearing has the same force of expressing a judgement that falls short of certainty. Anthony Quinton, in an influential paper, suggested that "the mistake [with sense-datum theories] lies in the identification of what appears to be the case with our sense-experience." He continues by suggesting that "a statement of what appears to be the case is rarely a description of our sense-experience and is normally a modified, guarded claim about what is the case, expressing an inclination to believe something about objects."[33] Evidential uses of the language of appearing are, indeed, common even in the context of perception of focal objects. I shall call such uses "perceptual-evidential." "The island looks inhabited," said by a shipwrecked sailor who has noticed smoke in the distance and footprint-like marks in the sand, is in some sense giving expression to his perception of the island, which is the focal object; but, clearly, no one supposes that such a situation entails that the island, or anything else, really is inhabited—least of all a sense-datum. If the sense-datum inference is manifestly out of place in such a straightforward application of the language of appearing to perception, perhaps it is never in place. What a defender of the Argument must do is give a systematic method of distinguishing these admittedly evidential uses of the language of appearing from another use—which we may call the "(truly) perceptual"—and show that the sense-datum inference, although not pertinent to the former, most certainly is to the latter. This can be done.

Whenever we have *any* evidential use, either pure or perceptual-evidential, we have evidence distinct from the focal state of affairs. In the pure evidential cases the evidence is wholly distinct from the focal object itself. In the perceptual-evidential cases the evidence does indeed concern an aspect of the focal object, but an aspect that is *different* from that concerned in the focal state of affairs. In the previous example, there were the smoke and the marks in the sand, whereas the focal state of affairs was the island's being inhabited. In the truly perceptual cases, however, the focus of our judgement is the very evidence of our senses concerning the focal state of affairs. That is why the sense-datum inference has force in these last cases, and not at all in the others. We are not, in the case of the sailor, at all inclined to suppose that either the island or anything else is inhabited, because the crucial question, "Why does the island specifically look *inhabited?*" has a straightforward answer: because of the smoke and the marks in the sand. In the pure perceptual cases, however, there is no such independent evidence to make our judgement intelligible. That a wall looks specifically yellow to you, rather than some other colour, is not something for which you have any independent evidence at all. It just does look yellow.

Quinton himself is alert to these facts, and admits that "there is another use of 'appear' in which no reason can be given for statements containing it and which do report observations." Yet even here Quinton insists that the force of such uses of the language of appearing is to "report observations in a tentative way . . . They resemble ordinary categorical descriptions . . . in subject matter, but differ from them in expressing inclinations to believe rather than full beliefs."[34] The question still remains, however, what it is about the nature of a person's perceptual experience that inclines to such a judgement. Sense-datum theorists at least have their answer to hand: in the perceptual situation just described, the person is aware of something yellow, and, having no collateral information by which to discount appearances, would therefore at least be inclined to believe that a yellow object is being perceived. Quinton (together with the legions of philosophers who have followed him in this) has no answer at all.

In fact, however, such a demand for an explanation of our judgements may be thought to be misplaced. After all, not every belief of ours has an explanation in terms of prior knowledge, belief, or awareness. Some beliefs are, as it is sometimes put, "basic." So why may we not simply find ourselves judging that a certain wall is yellow, or find ourselves inclined so to judge: find that such a judgement, as Price put it, "solicits our belief"? Why does this judgement, or inclination, have to be explained by the wall generating an instance of yellowness of which I am aware, which awareness then leads me to form such a judgement? If an explanation is needed at all, why could it not simply be provided in terms of the object perceived, the nature of the perceptual conditions, and the operation of my senses? Now, many proponents of the Argument have claimed at this point that perception can occur without the making of any judgement at all, and even without any inclination so to judge; so that when perceptual judgement does take place, it is determined by the content of perception itself. This, however, raises big and controversial issues, which an initial presentation of the Argument should not prejudge. In particular, we are approaching what Wilfrid Sellars has stigmatized as the "Myth of the Given."[35] We hardly want to defend the "fallacy" by appeal to a "myth."

It is at this point that we need to turn to another way of drawing out the inadequacy of appeals to the "language of appearing." What we need to do is to insist on *phenomenological adequacy* in an account of what it is for something perceptually to appear to one: to insist that no account can be adequate that fails to recognize certain experiential facts. When a wall perceptually looks yellow to you, it may be with you experientially just as when you veridically see a yellow wall. The experiences are, or may be, qualitatively identical. The Argument claims that the only way to do justice to this fact is to recognize that a veridical and a matching illusory experience have a *shared sensory character*. When a wall perceptually looks yellow to you, a certain sensory quality is realized in your experience whether or not the wall is yellow. It is this fact that is either denied or ignored by appeals to the language of appearing. A proponent of the Argument claims that the fact that a veridical and an illusory appearance of yellow have something *actually* in common is something that is veiled but implied by the truly perceptual use of such language. As Price says: "When I say 'this table appears brown to me' it is quite plain that I am acquainted with an actual instance of brownness. This . . . is absolutely certain and indubitable."[36] No doubt Price's reference here to indubitability raises yet another controversial epistemological issue: the supposed incorrigibility or indubitability of "the mental." And once again, it is advisable not to encumber the Argument with such problems. Let us, therefore, construe Price's remarks as claiming what used to be called "moral certainty" that certain illusions are qualitatively identical to certain veridical perceptions. I think, indeed, that we may go as far as to say that such a fact is about as certain as anything can be.[37]

Daniel Dennett, for one, however, is not so sure even about this. He writes,

> Suppose I am hypnotized and told that the next ice cube I see will be pink. A plain ice cube is presented and I swear to its pinkness. Now perhaps there are two empirically distinguishable hypotheses

about such cases of hypnosis: (a) I have been induced to see the cube as pink, or (b) I have been induced to believe that I see it as pink . . . but what could be offered to persuade us to distinguish (a) from (b)? Not "introspective evidence," so far as I can see, but perhaps there could be good grounds to be found within some "third-person" nonintrospective psychological theory for drawing the distinction. That leaves open the possibility of making a case for a variety of sensing-pinkly . . . , but at the same time pushes the issue, as an empirical possibility, far from the home territory of the obvious.[38]

What is being argued here is that the sheer possibility in principle of my mistakenly judging that I am aware of an actual instance of pinkness entails that, as Dennett puts it, "I cannot tell from my own experience whether or not my experience contains any occurrent pink!" It is somewhat surprising to find a writer such as Dennett echoing a most traditional epistemological move here. For does not this line of argument precisely parallel the following? "Since it is possible for me to believe that I am awake when I am not—for example, when I am dreaming—it follows that I cannot tell from my own experience whether I am ever awake or not." No doubt Dennett will be quick to reassure us that perhaps there could be good grounds to be found within some "third-person" nonintrospective psychological theory for drawing the distinction between dreaming and being awake. Fortunately, it just does not follow from the fact that there are certain circumstances in which I should be mistaken with respect to a discrimination between two states of affairs that in no circumstances can I tell the difference between them; and even less does it support the idea that the very distinction between the two is dubious and awaits scientific validation. A position that denies that, prior to a well-confirmed psychological theory, we have no use for a distinction between being sensorily affected and merely making a false judgement simply does not deserve to be taken seriously. Indeed, Dennett's line of argument leads to a self-contradiction in the very passage in question. For he had earlier admitted "a manifest difference between merely believing-to-be-pink and seeing-as-pink," and allowed that "the latter is sensuous in a way the former is not"; but at the end of the passage no such thing is manifest at all—even as an "empirical possibility." The suggestion that *no* distinction can be drawn between experience and mere judgement or belief is, I suggest, one that can be simply discounted. Such a distinction is, however, all that is needed for the Argument to continue to present a serious challenge to Direct Realism. Illusions are (manifestly) sensory in character. There is a common sensory character to every situation in which a wall perceptually looks yellow to you, whether or not the wall is actually yellow. Sense-data need to be brought in, it is claimed, in order to do justice to this simple fact that perceptual situations can be subjectively identical despite a difference in the physical objects perceived. (And remember that our Argument requires only that such a matching pair of experiences be *barely possible*.)

But why, it may be protested, should the mere subjective identity of veridical and illusory situations—sameness as far as the subject can tell—be an infallible guide to the *actual* state of affairs? Seeing the yellowness of a yellow wall and seeing a white wall that merely looks yellow are two situations which clearly have *something* in common; and what is in common is indeed yellowness; but surely such yellowness does not have to be actually present in both cases. Can we not account for the sensory character of illusory perceptual consciousness in terms of the "intentional" presence of sensible qualities to consciousness, as it is sometimes put? The idea is that, when a white wall looks yellow to you, the wall is represented by you, or by your visual experience, as being yellow. So perhaps all we need say here is that yellowness is simply present *as represented*. Intentionality, whether original or derived, is present whenever we are dealing with representational media. Any representation can misrepresent; and what an object is incorrectly represented as being is something pertaining to the object, not to the representational medium itself. According to Gilbert Harman (among many others) such facts are enough to undermine the sense-datum account of perceptual consciousness: "It is very important to distinguish between the properties of a represented object and the properties of a representation of that object . . . The unicorn is pictured as having four legs and a single horn. The painting is flat and covered with paint. The unicorn is not pictured as flat or covered with paint . . . The notorious sense datum theory of perception arises through failing to keep these elementary points straight." The suggestion that perceptually representing a white wall as yellow involves awareness of some subjective yellow thing is, according to Harman, about as plausible as arguing from the fact that there are no actual unicorns to the conclusion that a painting of a unicorn "is 'in the first instance' a painting of something else that is actual."[39] When I look at the white wall I see yellowness; this, however, is an "intentional seeing," no more requiring a real instantiation of the quality than Ponce de León's searching for the fountain of youth required a real object, mental or otherwise.

Such an approach to perceptual appearances can be implemented in one of two ways. The first I shall call the "divide and conquer strategy." This consists in upholding what I shall call "Naive Realism" for veridical perception, but in accounting for illusory perceptions, in the respect in which they are illusory, in terms of the merely intentional, or represented, presence of sensible qualities in consciousness.[40] Naive Realism draws its strength from the apparent simplicity of perceptual consciousness. You open your eyes, and objects are simply present to you visually. The shutters go up, as it were, and the world is simply there—as if we were "peeping through our sense-organs," as Sextus Empiricus nicely put it.[41] Or someone strikes a triangle, and a sound is simply present to consciousness. The philosophical gloss on this, which I am calling "Naive Realism," holds that perceptual consciousness is, at least when veridical, an immediate registration of a normal physical object, in the sense that the sensory character of your conscious state, that whereby perceptual consciousness differs from mere thought or imagination, is accounted for by the possession by that object of perceptible qualities, together with the fact that you stand in a relation of awareness, or receptivity, to it. One particularly straightforward analysis of perceptual consciousness along these lines is the "act-object" analysis, which we shall be investigating shortly. According to this account, there are no subjective aspects to perceptual experience other than the sheer fact of awareness. All changeable characteristics of such experience are allocated to the *objects* of such experience. One form that Naive Realism can take is to embrace this analysis of sensory awareness, and to claim that at least sometimes we stand to normal physical objects in this relation of "limpid and unstructured awareness," as one writer (who disagrees with the conception) has put it.[42] Perhaps, however, Naive Realism can allow some subjective dimension of variation in awareness. Perhaps, for example, it can allow variations in the *clarity* with which various objects are perceived. What, however, is essential to Naive Realism as I am construing it is the claim that *that which gives sensory character to perceptual consciousness is a public quality of some physical object.*[43] The problem with any such idea is, of course, that it can at best hold only for veridical perceptions. The sensuous character of an illusory perception, in so far as it is illusory, is precisely *not* a characteristic possessed by the perceived physical object. Perhaps the glowing redness that is, as Broad says, "before my mind" when I veridically see a ripe tomato is simply the intrinsic colour of the tomato parading itself before my consciousness; but no such account can be given of the same glowing redness that I may be aware of while looking at a lemon when my optic channels have been re-wired. If this latter redness is an actual instance of redness, however, and if it is attributed to anything other than the lemon, the sense-datum inference has been accepted. Unqualified Naive Realism avoids the sense-datum inference only at the cost of failing to offer any account at all of illusion, or of appealing to wholly unclarified notions of something "merely looking" some way.

The divide and conquer strategy attempts to supplement such Naive Realism by giving illusory perceptual states special treatment. According to this strategy, the same quality is indeed present in a veridical perception and its illusory counterpart, albeit in two different ways: really and actually in the veridical case, merely intentionally in the illusory one. But this will not do at all. For one thing, illusions can be, and typically are, partial: I may misperceive an object's colour, but truly perceive its shape. According to the present strategy, the shape is here sensorily experienced, being *really* present to consciousness, whereas the colour is merely represented. The problem is, of course, that the shape is experienced *as coloured*—for if it were not, it would be invisible. This problem arises because the present reductively intentionalist approach effectively denies the distinctively sensory character of perceptual illusion. In place of such sensory awareness we are offered mere "representation"—mere thinking, to be blunt. Apart from being simply preposterous, this conflicts with the fact that a change in appearances leading to an illusion can be brought about by some merely peripheral physiological change in the subject. A possible re-wiring of my optic channels will lead to my experiencing a certain colour in *precisely* the way I should formerly have experienced some other colour. Such a peripheral change in a sensory system does not abolish sensing and replace it with mere representing; it changes the character of the sensing. The idea that a short-sighted person moves from sensing to merely representing his surroundings when he removes his spectacles is equally absurd. Proponents of the present strategy, recognizing that Naive Realism is incapable of accounting for illusory perception in terms of the actual presence of a public perceptible quality to consciousness, notice that there are certain cognitive states, such as episodes of merely thinking about something, where the object of cognition, together with its qualities, is clearly not actually present to consciousness, but is merely represented. Paradigm cases of such states are, however, those that are *non-sensory* in character. It then proposes to treat illusory perceptions as just like these. But illusory perceptions are a species of sensory perception. The divide and conquer strategy can diffuse the intuitions that lie behind the sense-datum inference only if it construes illusions as *merely* intentional or representational states, as not being sensory in character. But they *are* sensory, as we perfectly well know. Denying that a subject who is suffering a perceptual illusion is in a sensory state of precisely the same kind as may be enjoyed by one who is perceiving veridically, simply on the grounds of the absence of a suitably propertied physical object, is about as plausible as denying, in phantom limb cases, that the subject is really in pain on the grounds that a certain body part is missing. This is not only absurd, but potentially vicious.

As a matter of fact, the majority of philosophers who endorse the present approach to perceptual appearances do not adopt the divide and conquer strategy. They hold, rather, that *all* perceptual consciousness, veridical as well as illusory, should be construed intentionally. We may term this the "uniform strategy." David Armstrong, for example, proposes to account for all forms of perceptual awareness as being simply a matter of acquiring beliefs (of a specified sort) about the environment. Dennett has similarly claimed that the only things of which we have immediate reflective awareness are "propositional episodes," that there are "only featureless—even wordless—conditional intentions-to-say-that-p for us to be intimately acquainted with." Apart from such judgements, "there is—so far as *introspection* is concerned—darkness."[44] More recently Dennett has spoken not of propositional attitudes, but rather of "the sum total of all the innate and learned associations and reactive dispositions."[45] Although there are places where it seems that Dennett's only real target is a strong "first person authority" that amounts to incorrigibility, or infallibility, elsewhere it becomes clear that more than this is being denied. He claims, for example, that "we can have some authority—not infallibility or incorrigibility, but something better than sheer guessing—but only if we restrict ourselves to relational, extrinsic properties like the power of certain internal states of ours to provoke acts of apparent re-identification."[46] A related claim of Dennett's—to the effect that perceptual consciousness is to be understood as a "presentiment" that one's environment is a certain way—elicited what is surely a choice example of understatement from John McDowell: "This suggestion seems phenomenologically off key."[47]

The earlier criticisms of the divide and conquer strategy effectively suffice to deal with this uniform strategy—if only because the latter is even more monstrous. One cannot, to be sure, argue against it by insisting on the common character that is possessed by illusory and veridical perceptions, since the uniform strategy of course offers a uniform treatment of these two. But if reductive intentionalist analyses are incapable of doing justice to the sensory character of illusory perceptions, they are equally bankrupt as accounts of veridical perceptions. At least the divide and conquer strategy, by embodying a limited Naive Realism, attempted to do justice to the obvious fact that when I veridically perceive something, I am aware of an actual instance of a sensuous quality. The uniform strategy denies even this. *No* sensory consciousness is explicitly recognized on this approach, and hence is effectively denied. "Inside" all is "darkness." Indeed, most writers in this tradition end up with the view that there is nothing qualitative in the world at all. This is because most of them accept the primary/secondary quality distinction. So "out there" there is, as far as sight is concerned, just electromagnetic radiation being more or less absorbed by electron shells, and "in here" there are just "featureless" propositional attitudes or dispositions to discriminative behaviour.[48] Such a reductive, or eliminativist, account of sensory experience is astonishingly widespread today. On such a view of perception, all one is allowed to attribute to a conscious subject on the cognitive side of things are thoughts, beliefs, or dispositions toward behaviourally specified discriminations, or "representations." We have here a recrudescence of the "feigned anaesthesia" with which the earlier behaviourists were commonly taunted. By adopting such a position, by failing explicitly to recognize the distinctively sensory character of perceptual consciousness, such people simply turn a blind eye to the challenge presented by the Argument. Such a state of affairs surely calls more for diagnosis than argument.

Rejection of such reductivist accounts of sensory experience does not imply a denial that perceptual appearing is irreducibly "judgemental," "epistemic," or representational in nature. Perhaps nothing can look yellow to you without your being at least inclined to believe that something is yellow. Indeed, perhaps its looking yellow to you is nothing "over and above" your being so inclined. We shall consider the merits of this suggestion later. Even if it is true, however, what cannot sensibly be denied is that some such inclinations and not others *have a sensuous character*. Seeming to see something yellow differs qualitatively, as an experience, from merely having a hunch that there is something yellow before one. We have already seen Dennett admitting that "somehow" this fact must be acknowledged; we have also seen how his positive account wholly fails to acknowledge it, save as a distinction that empirical psychology could possibly make in the future. Perhaps it is even possible, though I doubt it, that a sufficiently detailed functionalist or topic-neutral specification of a certain state will *entail* that such a state is sensuous in character. What must not be overlooked is what it is that is thus entailed: the sensuous character of such states of consciousness. Any account of perception that cannot fully acknowledge the sensuous character of perceptual experience can be simply dismissed.[49]

Now, it may be that being in a sensory state, or even being capable of being in such a state, is not necessary in order to perceive. I think it is an open question, for example, whether insects are at all conscious or sentient; but they clearly in some sense perceive their environment. If so, the Argument from Illusion has no force with respect to insect perception, or to non-conscious perception generally. What must be rejected, however, are all forms of eliminativism, reductionism, and anaesthesia *for us*. By ignoring the existence of phenomenal qualities, one is simply sidestepping the genuine source of the puzzle posed by the Argument from Illusion. No doubt sometimes in philosophy progress can be made by showing how to avoid something that leads to serious puzzlement. The present way out of the Argument is, however, achieved by the famous advantage of theft over honest toil. Russell's well-known quip is not as mild as commonly thought. We should not forget that theft is a form of dishonesty.

I HAVE ATTEMPTED to show that there is a principled way of distinguishing the truly perceptual uses of the language of appearing from those other uses where the sense-datum inference, and anything analogous to it, is wholly to be discounted. When, however, we turn to cases of appearing where what is in question really is the manifest appearance of something to the senses, there are still many cases where the sense-datum inference may appear at least problematic. Consider the following, from George Pitcher:

> Snakes are sometimes said to feel slimy, although usually they are not actually so; must we conclude that something else really is slimy? And what would that be—the person's sense-datum? But what can be made of the notion of a slimy sense-datum? My dictionary tells me that to be slimy is to be "of the consistency of slime; covered or smeared with or full of slime; slippery, hard to hold." Certainly, the sense-datum theorist has a degree of freedom in specifying the nature of sense-data . . . But I cannot think he would want, nor be able, to conceive of them in such a way that any of them could possibly be said to be "covered or smeared with or full of slime."[50]

Further problematic examples are not hard to find. Some things feel wet; do we really want wet sense-data, however? An oar in water may look broken; so are some sense-data literally broken? A person looks sad: a sad sense-datum? Sometimes faint sounds close at hand can be taken for loud noises far off, so if something sounds miles away, is there a sense-datum that literally is miles away from the subject? Something can look heavy; so is there a *visual* sense-datum that is actually heavy? Something can look wooden: wooden sense-data? One object can appear to collide with another and knock it off course; so should we infer mechanically interacting sense-data? These varied examples raise a number of different issues, but none of them has the plausibility of the examples commonly used to inaugurate the Argument. And yet we seem not to be dealing here with evidential uses of the language of appearing; we seem, rather, to be dealing with the simple appearances of things.[51]

It is not uncommon for proponents of sense-data to attempt to handle at least the majority of such cases by claiming that they do, in fact, involve merely perceptual-evidential appearings. It would, for example, typically be held that the look on a face is one thing, sadness—the "focal" state of affairs—another. We do not, it is commonly said, "really"

or "immediately" see someone else's sadness; what we see is a facial expression that "suggests" sadness to us. The face is our evidence, on the
basis of which we *judge* sadness to be present. The extremes to which
philosophers and psychologists have gone along this path are well
known. At its end lies psychological atomism.[52] The excesses of such an
approach have, however, sparked an equally extreme reaction in certain
quarters, especially within the Phenomenological tradition. Merleau-
Ponty tells us that "I hear the hardness and the unevenness of the cobbles in the noise of a carriage."[53] More extreme is Sartre: "It is the sour-
ness of the lemon that is yellow, it is the yellow of the lemon that is
sour; one eats the colour of the cake, and the taste of this cake is the instrument which reveals its shape and its colour to what we could call al-
imentary intuition; conversely, if I stick my finger into a pot of jam, the
sticky coldness of this jam is a revelation of its sugary taste to my
fingers."[54] One does not have to be a psychological atomist to find such
suggestions objectionable.

What is objectionable here is not the emphasis on truly perceptual
accomplishments. What is objectionable is the refusal to draw any distinctions within the area of what is admittedly perceptual. For whenever something is veridically perceived to be *F*, we can always ask
whether it is so perceived *in virtue of our veridically perceiving features of
that object that do not entail that the object is* F. Sometimes the answer to
this is Yes and sometimes No, and this marks an important division
within the objects of perception. The central point here is that for
some, but only some, values of *F*, something can perceptually appear
exactly like something that is *F* when it is not, *even though we are perceiving the thing veridically.* Someone can look sad and yet not be so—
perhaps because he is pretending to be sad and doing it very well. But if
he does thus look sad to us when he is not, this does not mean that we
are misperceiving his face, even if it is solely the face that seems to
manifest sadness. Pretence of this sort does not lead to visual misperception. The face of a person who is not sad can look *exactly like* the
face of one who is, *and visual perception can concern only how things look.*[55]
Feigned sadness is possible because even when we truly see that a person is sad, we do so only in virtue of perceiving some physical attribute.
On the other hand, one does not typically see that an object is red, or
spherical, in virtue of seeing anything other than its colour or its shape.
And if an object does look red or round in this straightforward way, and

one is perceiving this object veridically, it *does* follow that the object really is red or round. Let us call any feature of a physical object of the latter sort a "sensible quality."[56]

We are now in a position to formulate a simple principle that will allow us to discount our recent problematic cases of appearing: *the sense-datum inference is in place only with respect to sensible qualities.* The rationale for this is as follows. If we are dealing with a perceptible feature that is not a sensible quality, we can do phenomenological justice to an object's appearing to have that feature without recourse to a sense-datum inference *involving that very feature.* Since an object appears to have such a feature in virtue of its appearing to have one or more sensible qualities, we meet the demands of phenomenology by insisting on the sense-datum inference only with respect to these latter. Since these latter do not entail that the object possesses the former property, we avoid commitment to the sense-datum inference for all features other than sensible qualities. Of the problematic cases, sliminess and wetness are perhaps the most challenging, since they may seem to have the best claim to be irreducibly sensory in character. They are not, however, "sensible qualities" in the sense just introduced, for something can feel wet when it is not, even though we are perceiving it veridically: powdered graphite is a case in point. My dictionary tells me that "wet" means "consisting of moisture, liquid." This is not true of graphite, even though it feels wet to the touch. We may indeed be misled into thinking that graphite is wet on the basis of how it feels, but this is not a tactile *illusion:* that is how graphite really does feel, how it really is to the touch. There is clearly some sensible quality that we thus detect in graphite, though one for which, as far as I can see, there is no name. This, however, is the quality which the sense-datum theorist should attribute to the sense-data involved in perception of wet things. Then he will not end up with sense-data that are wet. Or slimy.

So I conclude my response to the appeal to the language of appearing as a way of blocking the Argument by pointing out that we have as yet seen no way of blunting the force of the sense-datum inference in relation to *truly perceptual uses of such language in connection with sensible qualities.* (A second, entirely independent way of responding to these problematic cases is presented in the following section.)

AT THIS POINT it should be mentioned that many philosophers who actually accept the Argument from Illusion have held that the crucial sense-datum inference, precisely in the form in which it has been pre-sented so far, is unacceptable. What they propose, however, is not an abandonment of the inference, but a significant modification to it. It has also been suggested, however, that such a modification robs the in-ference of any plausibility it might have had in its original form. In this section I shall argue that even if the modification is accepted, the Argu-ment still goes through.

The way we have so far been construing the sense-datum inference is as follows. As far as perceptions of sensible qualities are concerned, a feature that a normal physical object perceptually appears to someone to have is one that genuinely does characterize a sense-datum of which that person is aware. So if a white wall looks yellow to me, I am aware of a yellow sense-datum. This yellowness is an intrinsic, qualitative fea-ture of my sense-datum. But it is also, or so we have been assuming, one that normal physical objects can also possess. For is it not posses-sion of just this quality that makes yellow objects *yellow?*[57] It is this as-pect of the sense-datum inference that many have objected to. They suggest instead that we should recognize two classes of qualities: those that characterize normal physical objects—such as *physical* colour, and *physical* temperature—and those that characterize sense-data, these lat-ter being merely analogous to the former. Since it is standardly held that ordinary terms for colours, tastes, and other sensible qualities refer to the public features of normal objects, we need to introduce a range of new terms to refer to the range of analogous qualities that are pos-sessed by sense-data. Some today speak in this connection of "primed predicates," a usage I shall follow.[58] So a marigold is yellow; a sense-da-tum is at most yellow'. For a sense-datum to be yellow' is for it to have the quality of which you are immediately aware when something per-ceptually looks yellow to you. Wilfrid Sellars writes of these two fami-lies of qualities as follows: "The various species of visual sensation form a family of resemblances and differences which corresponds to the fam-ily of resemblances and differences which is the system of sensible qualities in the basic sense, the sense which pertains to material things. It is in this way the isomorphism of acts of sense and material things is to be understood."[59] Let us, therefore, from now on reserve the term "sensible quality" for the perceptible qualities of normal physical ob-jects, and "sensory quality" for the intrinsic features of sense-data (if there are such things).

A variety of reasons have been given for the need to draw some such

distinction. It is, for instance, immediately required by anyone who
endorses any form of the primary / secondary quality distinction that
stops short of denying outright that physical objects are red, warm, and
so forth. Physical redness, on such a view, is one thing; the sensory
quality of redness (redness') is another. The latter is *sensuous* in a way
no purely physical feature can be. Physical redness is, on such an approach, frequently conceived as a disposition to cause sensory red'ness
in observers, a disposition realized in physical items that themselves
wholly lack sensuous characteristics. Wittgensteinians, if they recognize sensory qualities at all, would also insist on a strict separation of
them from the sensible qualities of normal objects, on the grounds that
the latter are essentially public features, a grasp of the concepts of
which is governed by public criteria that cannot be constrained by such
subjective features of experience as sensory qualities. Functionalists,
too, will cash out the content of our attributions of sensible qualities to
physical objects in terms of their physical causes and behavioural effects, independently of how these may be realized by sensory qualities
in experience. The possibility of undetectable "spectrum inversion"—
the possibility that when you and I look at the same physical colour in
the same circumstances, the sensory qualities characterizing my visual
sense-datum are different from those characterizing yours, though in
such a fashion that this discrepancy could never be revealed in our behaviour—is commonly taken to reinforce such judgements.[60] I do not
propose to discuss the merits of such suggestions here. I do myself believe that a distinction between sensible and sensory qualities must be
made if Realism about the physical world is true, and I shall so argue in
the final section of this chapter; but the cogency of the Argument does
not depend on the truth of one rather than another of the possible positions that can be taken on this issue. What I propose to do in this section, therefore, is to show that a recognition of the distinction in no
way weakens the Argument. If the distinction is invalidly drawn, the
Argument faces no further problems at this juncture. (Incidentally, if
the distinction *is* drawn, there is a very swift way to deal with the problematic cases discussed in the previous section. There is no problem
with wet or slimy sense-data, since there are none such: there are only
wet' and slimy' sense-data.)

Why recognition of a distinction between sensible and sensory qualities may be thought to weaken the force of the sense-datum inference

is not difficult to see. If you are looking at a white wall, but because of the illusory nature of your visual experience you take it to be yellow, the question "Why do you take it to be specifically yellow, if you are not aware of something yellow?" has a certain force. The question "Why do you take it to be specifically yellow if you are not aware of something analogous to yellow?" on the face of it, however, has very little. Equally, the demand for phenomenological adequacy, on which I have come to place principal weight as a way of motivating the sense-datum inference, also seems to lose its force. The demand to do justice to the possible subjective identity of veridical and illusory perception seems hardly to be met by recognizing a sensible quality in the former and but an analogous quality in the latter.

In fact, however, it is precisely by focusing on this issue of phenomenal identity that we shall retrieve the force of the sense-datum inference, despite the complication of primed predicates. For we have seen that the heart of our Argument is the claim that a veridical and an illusory perception may be subjectively identical. The central point is that we have found no way of doing justice to this fact save by accepting the sense-datum inference. For there may seem but two alternatives to accepting this inference: adopting Naive Realism, and adopting a purely "representationalist" or "intentionalist" construal of illusion; and both of these positions are false. Naive Realism is manifestly so: the sensuous quality that features in illusory perceptual consciousness cannot be a quality of the normal object perceived, precisely because the state is illusory. Naive Realism can survive as an account of veridical perception only if it is combined with intentionalism in the "divide and conquer" strategy. Pure intentionalist or representationalist accounts of sensory experience are also false, however, whether they are restricted to illusory perceptions or uniformly applied to all forms of perceptual consciousness. The former denies that illusion is, or even can be, sensuous in the way that veridical perception is; and that is false. The latter deployment of intentionalism denies that perception is *ever* sensuous, which is even more absurd. By contrast, the sense-datum inference, even when modified, recognizes that illusory and veridical perceptions are sensuous in exactly the same way—a way that involves the *actual* presence of sensuous qualities in experience. Whether these qualities are termed "sensible" or "sensory," whether they are properly signified by primed or unprimed predicates—whether, that is to say, there is a

single class of qualities that can characterize both normal physical objects and sensory states—is, though a matter of some philosophical importance in its own right, of no consequence as far as the force of the
Argument is concerned. This is because the dispute over whether we
are dealing with two families of qualities here is a dispute *over the nature
of physical objects:* a dispute over whether, to echo Locke, they "resemble" what we are immediately aware of when perceiving, because they
possess exactly the same range of sensory qualities as the latter. This
dispute only arises once the presence of sensory qualities in experience,
independently of the presence of normal physical objects, has been recognized. The issue is then whether such qualities are "out there" in
physical objects *as well,* or not. If they are, then the sense-datum inference can revert to its original, unmodified form, and no more needs to
be said. It is only if they are not that the inference needs to be modified.
But then the resulting lack of intuitiveness of the inference is but a reflection of the fact that intuitively we are Naive Realists. The modified
inference is only for those who are no longer naive—only for those
who, in effect, have succumbed to the Argument.

MUST WE therefore conclude that the Argument is unanswerable? That
would be premature. For the only thing that the Argument has demonstrated beyond any shadow of reasonable doubt is that sensory qualities
that are not the qualities of a perceived physical object are really present in illusory perceptual experience, and that these same qualities are
equally present in veridical perceptions. It is, however, perhaps just
possible that we shall be able to develop an analysis of perception according to which such qualities do not function *as immediate objects of
awareness.*[61] Many philosophers have attempted just this, and we shall
be examining their accounts in the following two chapters. Any such
attempt would, however, be rendered impossible from the start if a
certain analysis of sensory awareness that is commonly assumed in presentations of the Argument were accepted. Our final preliminary task
must, therefore, be to examine this analysis of awareness. For if it is accepted, the Argument does indeed proceed inexorably to its conclusion, and we can terminate our enquiry.

The analysis in question is the "act-object" analysis of sensory
awareness, which received one of its most important historical expressions in the classical sense-datum theory as it was developed in the

early years of the twentieth century by G. E. Moore and Bertrand Russell. According to Moore, mental acts are "acts of *consciousness:* whenever we do any of them, we are conscious of something."[62] It is such acts as these, he held, that are the indisputably *mental* items in the world. Such an act is always to be sharply distinguished from the object of which we are conscious. "The entity which is experienced may be of many different kinds," writes Moore. "But, whatever be its nature, the entity which *is* experienced must in all cases be distinguished from the fact or event which consists in its being experienced; since by saying that it is experienced we mean that it has a relation of a certain kind to something else."[63] Similarly, Russell writes that "acquaintance is a dual relation between a subject and an object which need not have any community of nature. The subject is 'mental,' the object is not known to be mental except in introspection."[64] The term "sense-datum" was introduced to stand for the object of any such act of awareness that was sensory in character.[65] They both felt that the term "sensation" was used ambiguously by philosophers and psychologists, but that if it was to be retained, it should be used to stand for the act of being conscious of, or acquainted with, a sense-datum: "A 'sensation' . . . is my *seeing* of the colour, not the colour which I saw . . . I think what we mean by 'sensations' is the experiences which consist in apprehending certain sense-data, *not* these sense-data themselves."[66] They both felt that the traditional notion of sensation was incoherent, because it involves a conflation of consciousness and object.

If the sense-datum analysis of sensory states is adopted, the Argument from Illusion of course goes through and Direct Realism is shown to be false. Such an analysis is not, however, irresistible. Moore felt himself entitled to it in virtue of the following kind of reflection. When I compare a situation in which I am aware of something blue with one in which I am aware of something green, these two situations both differ from one another and have something in common. What they have in common is that in both I am conscious of something. It is the mental act of awareness, Moore claimed, that is identical in both cases. This is in itself characterless or diaphanous, being a pure act of awareness of an object. So what differs concerns the nature of the object *of* which I am conscious: in the one case it is green, in the other blue. Except, therefore, for its character of being a conscious state or event, episodes of awareness *derive all their character from the nature of the objects* of perception.[67] Such a contrast may also be made in cases where something merely looks green or blue—for what we are concerned with here is the nature of the perceptual experience itself, not objective factors in the public realm. The whole of Moore's argument for his sense-datum analysis of experience is contained in the following short passage: "We have then in every sensation two distinct elements, one of which I call consciousness, and another which I call the object of consciousness. This must be so if the sensation of blue and the sensation of green, though different in one respect, are alike in another: blue is one object of sensation and green is another, and consciousness, which both sensations have in common, is different from either."[68]

Such an argument is easily rebutted, however, as C. J. Ducasse soon demonstrated.[69] For its premise does not differ significantly from the observation that dancing a waltz and dancing a tango both have something in common and also something different about them. But do we wish to infer an ontological distinction between an undifferentiated act of dancing, or moving, and a waltz-entity and a tango-entity to which we stand in some relation? Or, moving to the area of the psychological, do we really wish to construe being in a gay mood and being in a depressed mood as a matter of our coming into a relation with an ontologically distinct entity: a mood?[70] The kinds of comparisons that Moore invites us to make simply do not of themselves point to any ontological distinctions; any pair of determinate realizations of a determinable will exhibit the same features.

Not only is Moore's argument for the classical sense-datum analysis of experience extremely weak, the analysis itself is extremely implausible. This emerges when we bear in mind that, although sense-data are typically introduced in connection with perceptual consciousness, the act-object analysis was intended to apply to all conscious states, including bodily sensations. So pains and tingles will be entities distinct from our apprehension of them, so that it is initially an open question whether or not a pain could exist out of all relation to a sentient subject. This is surely unacceptable. Indeed, it worried C. D. Broad, who nevertheless contended that "it seems to me much more certain that, in a sensation of red, I *can* distinguish the red patch and the act of sensing it, than that, in a sensation of a headache, I *cannot* distinguish a headachy object and an act of sensing it."[71] Well, if this is what the game is about, I believe it goes decisively against Broad. I think almost all of us are overwhelmingly more certain that pains are *not* ontologically distinct from us than that the sensuous aspects of our perceptual experiences are so distinct.[72] Indeed, Broad himself was not happy with this position, and finally opted for a mixed account, according to which bodily sensations are analysed as unary—that is, non-relational—states of a subject, whereas perceptual states are given an act-object analysis. In fact, in his later writings Broad even allowed that the act-object analysis was plausible for certain phenomena and not for others even within a single sensory modality, and he came to place increasing weight on how *well-defined* and *definite* the "object" appears.[73] A bee sting is pretty definite, however. But the real problem with this approach is not only that, other things being equal, a uniform treatment of the sensory features of experience would be preferable; it also undermines Moore's *argument* for the sense-datum analysis within the realm of sensory states. Be this as it may, at this stage we do not require a knock-down argument against the sense-datum analysis of perceptual consciousness; all we require to block the Argument is a plausible alternative.

I have introduced problems for the classical sense-datum theory by reference to C. J. Ducasse. Doing so may be thought to introduce problems of its own, however, since Ducasse offered as the alternative to that theory what has come to be known as the "adverbial" theory of experience. Ducasse states the view as follows: "The hypothesis, then, which I present as alternative to Professor Moore's is that 'blue,' 'bitter,' 'sweet,' etc., are names not of objects of experience nor of species of objects of experience but of *species of experience itself.* What this means is perhaps made clearest by saying that to sense blue is then to sense *bluely,* just as to dance the waltz is to dance 'waltzily.'"[74] I say that this may be thought to bring problems of its own because, although the suggestion that the "depth grammar" of such experiential statements is adverbial has been taken up by a considerable number of later philosophers, the suggestion is vigorously rejected in many quarters. Sometimes hostility is based on phenomenological considerations. Panayot Butchvarov, for example, claims that "the adverbial theory is incapable of doing justice to the most obvious and indeed essential phenomenological fact about perceptual consciousness . . . namely, its intentionality, its object-directedness."[75] This response is in some ways similar to Broad's position, since, in marshalling considerations in favour of the sense-datum analysis, Broad placed all the weight on phenomenolog-

ical considerations, albeit in a far from compelling manner. Nevertheless, Butchvarov's remark does present us with a challenge. For there
clearly is *some* phenomenological distinction to be made between perceptual experience and mere sensation. The former does indeed appear to be, in some sense, object-directed in a way that the latter is not.
The challenge is then to explain why this is so. In fact, this will essentially be our task in the following chapters of Part I: to work out an
adequate analysis of perceptual consciousness that can do justice to
its intentionality, its phenomenological world-directedness, while construing the sensory qualities that are present in such consciousness as
intrinsic states of the experience itself, though not as objects of awareness. One indication that Butchvarov's remarks are not a knock-down
argument against adverbialism, but merely a challenge to develop a
theory of perception, is the fact that the adverbial theory is presented as
an account, not specifically of perceptual consciousness, but of sensory
awareness as such, in all its forms. One common suggestion has been
that acts of sensing are not of themselves perceptual or intentional;
they are instead constituents of genuinely perceptual acts, with the admitted intentionality of these acts accounted for by some operation
over and above mere sensing. Investigating such ideas is, as I say, the
topic of succeeding chapters.

A more immediately pressing objection to adverbialism is due to
Frank Jackson, who has argued that adverbial construals of sensory
states are incapable of expressing all the distinctions and logical relations between kinds of experience that we must recognize.[76] I shall
mention just one problem by way of illustration. The adverbs that are
required to express the phenomenal character of sensory states must be
capable of being semantically complex. We cannot, for example, represent an experience of seeing a red triangle as being a matter of sensing
(red-triangle)ly—where "red-triangle" expresses an unstructured concept—for then we shall not be able to infer from this, as we can, that
the experience is as of a triangle. If a hyphen is used, it must have the
status of conjunction. No simple conjunctive account can work, however, since sensing redly and triangularly is not the same as having an
experience of a red triangle, since the former holds for someone who is
seeing anything red and anything, perhaps another thing, that is triangular. Mere conjunction is too weak to express the *co-presence* of features that characterize a single object of awareness.

Adverbialists have not been slow to offer answers to such objections. Michael Tye in effect replaces conjunction with an operator expressing co-presence, and Wilfrid Sellars has pointed out that his own influential form of adverbialism has never been to the effect that the relevant adverbs are such as "(red and triangular)ly" but, rather, such as "(a red triangle)ly"—a locution that unlike the former succeeds, as he puts it, in "collecting" the colour and the shape.[77] I regard such replies, taken as a whole, as satisfactory. But a more important point, perhaps, is that all of Jackson's objections to adverbialism are premised upon a wholly questionable assumption: namely, that sensing is not just unary, or non-relational, but *unitary*—entirely devoid of any constituents, at least sensing constituents. But why should anyone suppose this to be the case? Is it not obvious that your visual sensing of this page is but a part of your total state of visual sensing—that which constitutes your entire "visual field"? It is true that certain philosophers are motivated to embrace adverbialism at least in part by a desire to establish an austere ontology that does not "countenance" mental states and processes.[78] No such ontological reform is being suggested here, however. *Of course* there are such states and processes; the only issue of concern to us at the moment is whether they are to be analysed in terms of a relation holding between either the subject or the subject's mental states and processes *and a distinct entity*—the "object." That experience involves some kind of relation between the subject and the subject's experiences is not here in question.

Why, in any case, should it be thought that a rejection of the classical sense-datum theory's act-object analysis of sensory experience must take the form of an *adverbial* construal of such experience? After all, the sense-datum analysis of experience was originally presented by Moore and Russell, quite rightly, as a *novel* account—one at odds with all traditional talk of "sensations," "ideas," and so on. And yet we hardly ever find earlier, pre-sense-datum accounts of sensory experience attempting adverbial construals of sensory experience.[79]

I conclude, therefore, that an irresistible case for the act-object analysis of sense-experience has not been made. This does not, however, clearly weaken the force of our Argument. Although the truth of the act-object analysis of sensory experience would have clinched the Argument, its rejection does not by itself indicate a way to rebut it. For even if sensory qualities are inherent qualities of sense-experience itself, it is far from clear how we can avoid the conclusion that we are *aware of them* as objects whenever we are perceptually conscious, or that we are immediately aware of the experience itself that exhibits such qualities. On such a view perceptual experience would be *self-presenting*, and the upshot of the Argument would be that we are only ever aware of our own experiences, with such experiences themselves constituting the "veil of perception." That this is indeed a possibility to be taken seriously is indicated by the history of the sense-datum theory itself. In expounding the views of Moore, Russell, and Broad, I sometimes referred to the "classical" sense-datum theory. This is because, subsequently, although the term "sense-datum" was often retained, the original accompanying act-object analysis of experience was soon almost universally dropped. As early as 1919, Russell himself wrote: "I have to confess that the theory which analyses a presentation into an act and object no longer satisfies me. The act, or subject, is schematically convenient, but not empirically discoverable . . . The first effect of the rejection of the subject is to render necessary a less relational theory of mental occurrences . . . A sensation in particular can no longer be regarded as a relation of a subject to a sense-datum; accordingly the distinction between sensation and sense datum lapses."[80] H. H. Price was at least non-committal on the nature of sense-data: "But, it will be said, the Sense-datum Philosophers claim to have discovered a new set of *entities* . . . I agree that some of them may have made this claim in moments of exaltation. But in a cool hour, I believe they would claim something much less specific. They would claim to have discovered (shall I say?) a 'feature of our experience.'"[81] And A. J. Ayer, perhaps the most notable latter-day advocate of sense-data, never held the act-object view.[82] The fact that denying the act-object analysis of sensory consciousness does not by itself blunt the force of the Argument is clearly recognized by the later Russell in the following passage: "According to some authors—among whom I was formerly included—it is necessary to distinguish between a sensation, which is a mental event, and its object, which is a patch of colour or a noise or what not. If this distinction is made, the object of the sensation is called a "sense-datum" or a "sensible object." Nothing in the problems to be discussed in this book depends upon the question whether this distinction is valid or not. If it is not valid, the sensation and the sense-datum are identical."[83]

What all such writers subscribe to, and what I regard as definitive of

anything that deserves to be called a "sense-datum" account of perception, is the following pair of theses: that sensory qualities are *really*, not
merely intentionally, involved in all perceptual experience, and that
they feature in all such experience as (immediate) objects of awareness.
The fact that they are not regarded as being ontologically distinct from
the experiencing subject in no way shows that they are not themselves
objects of awareness. In fact, it is far from immediately clear how they
could fail to be. After all, although a headache is not ontologically distinct from me, it is certainly an object of awareness. Indeed, it stub-
bornly draws attention to itself. The task that falls to us if we are to
withstand the Argument is, therefore, no mean one. We need to develop an analysis of perception that recognizes the real, unreduced
presence of sensory qualities in perceptual experience as inherent features of such experience, and yet in such a way that we can deny that
such qualities are objects of awareness. It is to accounts of perception
that attempt to meet these conditions that we turn in the next chapter.

Since this is our task, I shall no longer refer to sensory qualities as
sense-data, or as the qualities of sense-data. That would, in effect, be to
capitulate to the Argument. The term "sensory quality" itself is indeed
serviceable, but it leaves wholly undetermined what the bearers of such
qualities may be. They might, for example, be sense-data. This same
problem attaches to the currently popular term "quale," since qualia
are universal characteristics, not entities. In order to underline the fact
that we need, at least, to reject the novel act-object analysis of sense-experience if Direct Realism is to be vindicated, I shall revert to the traditional term "sensation." Perception is sensuous in a way that mere
thought is not because it involves *perceptual sensation.* Our problem is,
therefore, to see how such sensations can fail to be our immediate objects of awareness whenever we perceive. Perhaps the appropriateness
of this term itself will eventually have to be questioned, but it at least
has the merit, at this stage of our enquiry, of opening up the abstract
possibility of a defence of Direct Realism in virtue of regarding sensory
qualities, or qualia, as inherent features of sense-experiences themselves, rather than of some *object*—a sense-datum—of which we are
aware.

BEFORE PROCEEDING to our principal task of developing a general philosophical theory of perception, I feel that I ought to spell out a perhaps

non-obvious implication of our recent findings—one that is not only both surprising and important in its own right, but one that will acquire some argumentative significance in Part II. The implication in question is that if we are to be Direct Realists, we must endorse the traditional distinction between primary and secondary qualities.

Although we have not yet passed judgement on the cogency of the Argument from Illusion, we have already seen that it does succeed in proving, or in drawing our attention to, one thing: that the very same sensory qualities that are actually present to consciousness when we veridically perceive a normal physical object may also be present to consciousness when we suffer illusion. In the latter type of case such sensory qualities must qualify something other than a normal physical object; and I have just suggested that, if Direct Realism is to have a hope of being defended, they must be taken as qualifying sensations or sense-experiences themselves, rather than classically conceived sense-data. Now, the denial of the traditional primary / secondary quality distinction amounts to claiming that such sensory qualities characterize normal physical objects.[84] In other words, the denial amounts to holding that a single range of sensory qualities characterizes *both* sensory experience itself *and* normal physical objects, and rejects the idea that we must recognize two families of qualities—"primed" and "unprimed"—to allocate to the ontologically diverse categories of experiences and physical objects. The very same sensuous redness that characterizes my illusory perception of a green apple when it looks red to me is to be found in the physical surface of a genuinely red apple. As Locke put the matter, physical objects "resemble" our experiences of them.

Now, if the bearers of sensory qualities were sense-data classically conceived, rather than sensations or sense-experience itself, then, other things being equal, there would be less motivation to recognize a special class of "primed" predicates, different from and merely analogous to the sensible qualities possessed by normal physical objects. For given that sense-data are not "mental" in nature, there is perhaps little need to deny them the perceptible qualities that similarly non-mental physical objects are taken to possess. If, however, the bearers of sensory qualities are such paradigmatically psychological items as sensations or experiences, there is a problem with recognizing but a single family of qualities. For the sensuous qualities that are in question here are the "proper sensibles": those that go to define our different sense modalities. They so define the different senses because they are inherent qualities of experience, and their very instantiation *entails* that a certain sort of experience is occurring. So how could sensuous redness, for example, possibly characterize an insensate physical object? We are not dealing here with some merely formal property that, like temporal duration, doubtless can univocally characterize such radically diverse entities. We are dealing here with qualities that intrinsically make experiences the kind of experiences they are. Such qualities have the same status as the various qualities of bodily sensations. So there is as much chance of a physical object being sensuously red as there is of a pin that is stuck into my body possessing the same quality as my resulting pain. The only way that we could make any sense of this latter idea is by supposing that such a pin should itself be feeling pain. Analogously, the only way we can make sense of a physical object possessing any sensuous characteristic is by supposing that that physical object itself enjoys sensory experiences of some kind—for only so can any sensuous quality be realized. The view therefore requires some form of panpsychism. And even this will not deliver what is required by opponents of the primary / secondary quality distinction in its traditional form. For what opponents of this distinction suppose to be possible is that, for example, the round mass that constitutes the body of a ripe tomato, or at least the surface of that mass, should itself be characterized by some sensuous quality. Merely supposing that the tomato has visual experiences hardly entails that. The only way to support such a view, given that sensory qualities can only characterize experience, would be to propose a particularly astonishing version of the mind-body identity theory, according to which something like a tomato, or a tomato's surface, could be identical to a sensory experience. I think we can afford to forgo the exploration of such a suggestion.

What is particularly surprising about this finding is that the denial of any sensuous character to brute physical objects has been forced on us *by an attempt to defend Direct Realism*, whereas the primary / secondary quality distinction is commonly thought to be at odds with this position. We are now in a position to see matters differently. For if the indisputably true conclusion of the Argument from Illusion—that the sensuous character of illusory perceptual experience is to be accounted for by the real presence of sensory qualities in experience—is supplemented by an act-object analysis of the way in which such qualities so feature, the Argument from Illusion as a whole goes through, and Direct Realism is refuted. The *only* way to avoid this is to construe sensory qualities as real qualities of experience itself. In this way alone may it be possible to construe them as not objects of awareness. If this is so, however, then the realization of such a sensory quality entails the occurrence of a sensory experience that intrinsically has such a quality. Since brute matter enjoys no such experiences, it must be devoid of such qualities.

There is a long history of philosophers from Berkeley, through Whitehead, to the present day who have railed heatedly against the primary / secondary quality distinction's denuding our world of its familiar, loveable, character. Indeed, even in the ancient world we find Plutarch lambasting Democritus for presenting a philosophy by which no human could *live*.[85] If such a position is indeed intolerable, we should be clear what is involved in rejecting it: that we must reject Realism about the physical world as such. For even *Direct* Realism, in its only viable form, entails the distinction.

Three Theories
of Perception

2

THE ARGUMENT FROM ILLUSION compels the recognition that in a veridical perception and its perfectly matching illusion, the same sensory qualities, or qualia, are present in consciousness in exactly the same way. This, and no more, has been proved. It has not been shown that we are infallibly knowledgeable about these qualities; that they are to be characterized in terms of the traditional schema of "meaningless sensations" that are "given" independently of any "interpretation"; that they serve as the foundations for all subsequent cognition; or that they are themselves intrinsically non-cognitive or non-representational. All of this may be true or none of it may be true; we have yet to see. The challenge to Direct Realism posed by the Argument is serious, and in need of a considered response, even without reliance on any such controversial theses. For a real Problem of Perception is posed by the sheer fact that typical perception, whether illusory or not, is intrinsically sensory in character, and that this sensory feature of perceptual consciousness is adequately accounted for by neither Naive Realism nor reductive intentionalist accounts of sensory experience. We have also seen that the only possible way forward toward a defence of Direct Realism requires that we conceive of such qualities not as characterizing sense-data—entities to which, by definition, we stand in the relation of *being-aware-of*, or "acquaintance"—but as intrinsically characterizing psychological states, or the flow of experience as such. For this reason I have chosen to speak of "perceptual sensations." Even if this line is taken, however, Direct Realism still faces a serious problem, since the things that we commonly regard as sensations—"bodily" sensations—are most certainly themselves objects of awareness. So, if perceptual sensations are always somehow present to, or in, consciousness whenever perception occurs, how can we avoid saying, equally, that we are aware of *them*, and hence but indirectly aware of normal physical objects, whenever we perceive? The only way to preserve Direct Realism is to make a distinction between being present to consciousness in the way that (perceptual) sensation is, and being present—and directly present—to consciousness in the way that the immediate object of perceptual awareness is. This is, to say the least, a subtle distinction; but on it hangs the fate of Direct Realism. In the rest of the first part of this book we shall, in effect, do nothing more than explore the possibility of making such a distinction.

We can therefore state what has emerged at the very heart of our Problem by asking: *How does perceptual consciousness differ from merely having sensations?* For what the Argument from Illusion brings out is that perceptual consciousness and mere sensation have something in common. Both are experiences possessing an irreducible sensory character. There is a presentational immediacy in both. We can contrast merely thinking about pain with suffering it, just as we can contrast merely judging a coloured object to be before us with actually seeing (or perceptually seeming to see) one. But how, then, do perceptions and sensations differ? According to Hume, "Every impression, external and internal, passions, affections, sensations, pains and pleasures, are all originally on the same footing."[1] If this is so, we need to see how perception eventually emerges as a distinctive cognitive phenomenon; if it is not, we need to see why not. Making out such a distinction is mandatory for a Direct Realist, since all change in the experience of a sensation must be attributed to a change in the character of the sensation itself—a change either in quality, intensity, extensity, or location—just as the sense-datum theory claims. On the other hand, it is of the essence of perception that there can be changes in the character of the perceptual experience of an object that do *not* involve changes in the object of perception at all—as any illusory appearance of change in an object testifies. In short, a notion of *objectivity* applies to perception in a way that it does not to sensation.

To say that the objects of perception are "objective" is to make all of the following claims. First, the objects of perception have an existence that is not dependent, causally, conceptually, or in any other way, on perceptions of those objects: in short, objects of perception can, and often do, exist unperceived. They therefore can, and typically do, have a relatively enduring, continuous history, in contrast to the episodic nature of those perceptual experiences that are "of" them. So objects of perception are in principle re-identifiable. Secondly, objects of perception are, to use Russell's useful term, "public": one and the same object is in principle perceivable by more than one subject. Thirdly, and relatedly, such public objects are in principle perceptible by more than one sense.[2] Finally, there is a distinction between sensory appearance and reality. None of this, as a quick survey will confirm, applies to sensation.

For this reason, a firm distinction between sensation and perception has commonly been drawn by psychologists and philosophers. As Dugald Stewart put it, "It is necessary to attend to the distinct meanings of the words Sensation and Perception. The former expresses merely that change in the state of the mind which is produced by an impression upon an organ of sense; (of which change we can conceive the mind to be conscious, without any knowledge of external objects;) the latter expresses the knowledge we obtain, by means of our sensations, of the qualities of matter."[3] A long and distinguished line of philosophers and psychologists have taken it as obvious that such a distinction can be accounted for only by supposing that, in perception, sensation is *supplemented* by an additional, distinctively cognitive, act of the mind: that, in the words of Thomas Brown, the "objective reference" of perception is "unquestionably something superadded to the original sensation itself."[4] On such a view, sensation does indeed occur when we perceive: that is why perception has the sensory character that it typically has. Such sensation is, however, accompanied in perception by another element that determines its character as genuinely perceptual, and that thereby accounts for the applicability to perception of the notion of objective reference, or "transcendence" as it is sometimes called. This crucial second element in perception, over and above sensation, is *thought*, or the employment of *concepts*. Without this, sensation, of whatever kind, is "meaningless" or "blind." Because it views perception as an amalgam of two radically different psychological operations, I term this approach the "dual component" theory of perception.

I believe that we can immediately discount one characterization of this distinctive cognitive element in perception, despite the fact that it has had, and continues to have, many distinguished adherents. (It appears, for example, to have been orthodoxy throughout the nineteenth century.) It is to the effect that, as T. H. Green succinctly put it, "The reference of a sensation to a sensible thing means its reference to a cause."[5] By this he means not merely that in perception sensation is "referred to" what is *in fact* a (distal) cause of the sensation. What Green means is that in perception sensation is referred to a physical object *as* the cause of the sensation. Indeed, it is precisely such thinking in causal terms that establishes and explains the "transcendent" reference of perception and its phenomenologically perceptual character. I shall refer to such a view as "causalism." Perhaps the most insistent philosophical advocate of causalism was Schopenhauer. "What a meagre thing . . . is mere sensory experience!" he writes.[6] What liberates us from this cognitive poverty is the understanding's grasp of causality: "The first, simplest, always present expression of the understanding is the perception [*Anschauung*] of the real world: this is wholly knowledge of the cause from the effect . . . [T]he understanding, through its one simple function, at *one* stroke transforms the dull mute sensation into perception. What the eye, the ear, the hand experiences is not perception: they are mere data. The world first stands there in so far as the understanding passes from the effect to the cause."[7] Essentially the same account of the distinction between sensation and perception is to be found in the later, and perhaps even more influential, writings of Helmholtz.[8] Here is a typical passage: "We can never escape from the world of our sensations to the idea [*Vorstellung*] of an outer world, except by an inference from the changing sensation to outer objects as the causes of this change."[9]

I say that such a theory may be discounted; this is for two reasons. The first is a conditional rejection: any such position is incompatible with Direct Realism. If, as Schopenhauer says, the perceptual operation "grasps . . . the given sensation . . . as an effect"; if, as he also says, such effects are "*immediate objects* for the subject"; then such an account involves the subject being *immediately aware of a mere sensation as an object*, and recognizing it as being caused from outside.[10] Helmholtz, at least, was fully aware of this implication of his views: "We never perceive the objects of the external world immediately, rather we perceive only effects of these objects."[11] The position, in other words, is indistinguishable in essence from that propounded in such a locus classicus of Indirect Realism as Russell's *The Problems of Philosophy:* "Thus what we directly see and feel is merely 'appearance,' which we believe to be a sign of some 'reality' behind."[12] Any such causalist account of the distinction between sensation and perception can amount to no more than Indirect Realism at best—and not even that in Schopenhauer, of course—because of the way in which an awareness of sensations as effects is written into the very content of perceptual consciousness.

The second and unconditional criticism of causalism is simply that it is false—phenomenologically false. For when we perceive, we are not necessarily aware of a causal interaction between us and the world. There are, perhaps, the makings of a case for such a view in relation to the sense of touch: feeling and manipulating objects is both a mechanical, interactive operation and appears as such. But sight, hearing, or smell? Do the perceived objects of these senses really appear to be affecting our eyeballs, eardrums, and nasal passages? Or causing sensations in us?[13] Whatever may be said about Naive Realism, it can certainly claim to draw some support from the deliverances of untutored consciousness. Perceived objects do appear simply to be there. *For consciousness* they have an unmediated presence.

Let us therefore turn to what I shall regard as the orthodox form of "dual component" accounts of perception, and that from now on shall alone be intended by this term. What distinguishes the orthodox theory from the causalist version is that, although perceived physical objects are commonly regarded as causes of perceptual experience, the distinctively cognitive element in perception is not seen as a conceptualizing of such objects *as* causes of our sensory states. Rather, it simply represents a perceived physical object as a certain kind of physical thing.[14] This theory and the sense-datum theory are the two modern, classic accounts of perception. Since the sense-datum theory is incompatible with Direct Realism, we may regard the dual component theory as the classic modern form of Direct Realism. Given this status, it is surprising how little explicit and detailed consideration this theory receives in works on perception. As a result, some of the most significant attempts at a Direct Realist theory of perception in the history of our subject tend to get overlooked. Partly in order to remedy this situation, but partly because of the intrinsic interest and influence of their writings, I shall present the dual component theory by considering two of

its principal advocates. In our own times, the most detailed and extensive development of the theory is to be found in the writings of Wilfrid
Sellars, who almost single-handedly established it as orthodoxy, at least
in the United States, for a generation.[15] I take him as one of our two
representative figures. The radical separation between sensibility and
understanding, which we have already noted to be a feature of this approach, together with the claim, effectively entailed by this, that sensibility is of itself "blind," is of course central to all Kantian approaches
to perception—as is the related scheme of "content" and "interpretation." I shall not, however, focus on Kant: partly because Kant exegesis
is so fraught with controversy, partly because he is not a Direct Realist,
and also because what he is primarily interested in is "experience"
(Erfahrung), not perception.[16] Shortly before Kant, however, the theory was propounded by Thomas Reid, whom I shall take as my second
authority. I choose Reid partly because his is one of the earliest, and
one of the clearest, extended presentations of the theory;[17] partly because until quite recently Reid's theory did not receive the attention
that it deserves; and also partly because this state of neglect has recently
been remedied, though in a most unfortunate way. For several works
are now available that present Reid as having, in effect, solved the
Problem of Perception. As we shall see, he achieved no such thing. Indeed, I hope to show that no possible form of the dual component theory can satisfy us.

Reid defines perception as follows: "First, Some conception or notion of the object perceived. Secondly, A strong and irresistible conviction and belief of its present existence. And, thirdly, That this conviction and belief are immediate, and not the effect of reasoning."[18] In
short, perception is a matter of occurrently having, or acquiring, immediate (that is, non-inferential) beliefs about the physical world. Perception is judgement.[19] This may remind us of the reductivist and
eliminativist accounts of perceptual experience noted in the previous
chapter. Reid was, however, far from denying the presence of irreducible sensory features in perception in the manner of a Daniel Dennett.
Ordinary perception involves, for him, the having of sensations in
addition to the earlier-mentioned cognitive functions: "The external
senses have a double province; to make us feel, and to make us perceive.
They furnish us with a variety of sensations . . . ; at the same time they
give us a conception, and an invincible belief of the existence of exter-

nal objects."[20] Such sensations, however, accompany, or occasion, perception, rather than helping to constitute it. More precisely, they feature in a quasi-causal chain leading from the object perceived to the
perception of it.[21] Impressions are made by an object on our sense-
organs, which in turn cause some modification of the brain; such a cerebral effect gives rise, in a regular way, to sensations, which in turn account for our perceptions—that is, our non-inferential beliefs about
our environment.[22] Such orderly dependence both of sensation on
physical impressions, and of perception on sensation, leads Reid to an-
ticipate the currently popular emphasis on the way in which perception
embodies *information* about the environment.[23]

One reason why Reid excludes sensation from the analysis of perception itself is that, although *for us* perception follows sensation—indeed,
is "suggested" by it—this is, according to Reid, but a contingent fact:
"For anything we know, we might perhaps have been so made as to
perceive external objects, without any . . . of those sensations which in-
variably accompany perception in our present frame."[24] So we are, indeed, in sensory states when we perceive; but a precise philosophical
analysis of perception as such need not advert to them.[25] One can, however, say that sensation is an ingredient in the total perceptual situation
for us humans, with our given frame. *We* perceive in our characteristic
way only because we enjoy sensations, and which perceptions we have
is determined by which sensations we experience. What is distinctively
perceptual, or cognitive, about such a situation is, however, accounted
for by "conception and belief."[26] Reid goes so far as to say that "as the
confounding our sensations with that perception of external objects,
which is constantly conjoined with them, has been the occasion of most
of the errors and false theories of philosophers with regard to the
senses; so the distinguishing these operations seems to me to be the key
that leads to a right understanding of both."[27] This leads Reid to say of
Berkeley that he takes "one ingredient of a complex operation for the
whole."[28]

What underlies Reid's whole theory of perception is the claim that
perceptions, unlike sensations, have "objects distinct from themselves."
There is, he says, "no difference between the sensation and the feeling
of it; they are one and the same thing. It is for this reason that we before observed, that, in sensation, there is no object distinct from that
act of the mind by which it is felt; and this holds true with regard to all

sensation." By contrast, "He that perceives, must perceive something; and that which he perceives, is called the object of his perception. To perceive, without having an object of perception, is impossible. The mind that perceives, the object perceived, and the operation of perceiving that object, are distinct things."[29] This is, in fact, but an implication of certain other aspects of Reid's theory. For he has analysed perception in terms of "conception and belief," and both of these are intrinsically and essentially directed towards objects. "Belief must have an object. For he that believes, must believe something; and that which he believes is called the object of his belief." And as for conception, "When we conceive any thing, there is a real act or operation of the mind . . . ; but every such act must have an object; for he that conceives, must conceive something."[30] As a later age will put it, sensations are not *intentional*, whereas perceptions are. The fundamental reason for this, according to Reid, is that "no sensation can give us the conception of material things."[31]

Wilfrid Sellars is as certain as Reid that perception involves a distinctively "cognitive" element. He repeatedly points out that perceiving involves what he likes to call a perceptual "taking," a representation of the world as being thus and so, claiming that "whereas we often contrast perception with thinking, there is, nevertheless, a proper sense in which perceiving essentially is or involves *a thinking*"—specifically, a "thinking in presence."[32] Hence perception can be characterized by him as "successful conceptual activity."[33] He is, however, equally insistent that that no purely cognitive analysis can be adequate to ordinary human perception. "It is clear," he writes, "that, phenomenologically speaking, there is . . . a non-propositional component" to perceptual experience.[34] More particularly, he says that "what I have so far referred to as *the* explication of the perceptual taking of a red triangle, namely its construal as a believing *in* a red triangle, is but one aspect of a more complex state that also includes a *sensing* of a red triangle."[35] So, as with Reid, sensation is brought in to do justice to the sensuous character of perceptual experience: "Phenomenologically speaking, the descriptive core consists in the fact that something in some way red and triangular is in some way present to the perceiver other than as thought of."[36] Such sensations, or sensings, or sense impressions are not, as Sellars puts it, "epistemic": they do not by themselves constitute an awareness of anything.[37] Awareness, for Sellars, is always an awareness of something *as* being something or other; and the "as" is taken by him to be "an index of conceptuality," whereas "sense impressions are non-conceptual states of consciousness."[38] The only sense in which a sensation can be "of" a red triangle is that it is standardly brought about in normal subjects in normal perceptual situations by red triangles and only red triangles. Here the "of" is causal, rather than epistemic.

With all these pieces of the dual component theory in place, we are now ready for the claim that is central to our own concerns. It is to the effect that the object—the immediate object—of perceptual awareness is that which is the object of the cognitive element in perception: the object of the perceptual belief or judgement. That this must be so for Reid is immediately implied by his *defining* perception in terms of conception and belief. Sellars similarly asserts that "what we are aware of in perception is what we perceptually take there to be, what . . . we perceptually *believe in*."[39] Since, of course, what we typically so believe in are normal physical objects, these are what we are perceptally aware of: "The *objects* of perceptual knowledge are the objects referred to in the propositional component of the perceptual experience, and these are physical objects, not private, subjective . . . items."[40] It is in virtue of this last claim that the dual component theory has a claim to be considered a version of Direct Realism.

WHAT MUST our judgement be on such a theory? The relation between perception and belief is far from the simple matter that Reid and Sellars present it as being.[41] Indeed, in numerous publications Fred Dretske has argued that belief is irrelevant to the proper analysis of perception.[42] No doubt, however, the dual component theory could be formulated so as to be consistent with any position we should ultimately adopt on this issue.[43] It is the role of conceptualization that is critical. In the next chapter I shall argue that allocating an essential role to conceptualization in perception is, depending on how it is understood, either simply mistaken or so empty and unilluminating as to fail to sustain any response to the Argument from Illusion. There are, however, additional problems attending the dual component analysis of perception—problems that all stem from its specifically dualistic character. In fact, there are at least the following four reasons for thinking that any such theory must be rejected in toto, reasons that I present in an order of increasing seriousness. We can, I believe, learn something of importance, if only it be of negative import, from clearly seeing the shortcomings of this perennially attractive theory of perception.

First, can we really do phenomenological justice to perceptual consciousness by allocating to sensation a merely causal, or "occasioning," role in relation to perceptual judgement? Would it really be unfair to say that on such a view we do not really see (or hear or feel) objects in our environment, but are merely brought to *think* that various physical items are present?[44] But a headache could make me think of my mother. Indeed, it is presumably possible that a headache should cause me to believe that my mother is present. I should not, however, thereby be perceiving my mother—even if she were indeed present, and even if she had somehow caused the headache.[45] On the dual component theory, perceptual judgements are not perceptual because they are based upon, or derive from, or are caused by, perception. They derive, rather, from mere sensation. Nor are such judgements perceptual in their own right: in themselves they are just judgements as to what is the case, differing from any non-perceptual judgement simply in their aetiology. It is hardly a satisfactory reply to this general objection to be told by Sellars that the distinctively cognitive achievement in perception is guided "from without," causally, by sensations[46]—for that applies to the earlier belief in my mother's presence. We need, in short, to do justice to the *immediate sensory presence* of physical objects to us in perception. We do not achieve this by making our relation of awareness to the world wholly a matter of judgement, and by throwing in some sensory items to try and make good the phenomenology.

As Reid fully recognized, any such account has to settle for an ultimate unintelligibility at the heart of perceptual consciousness. Although, for him, sensations are *signs* that *suggest* conceptions of the surrounding world—he even speaks of them as constituting a kind of natural language—the manner in which they operate is so much beyond our comprehension that he can speak in this connection of magic: "A third class of rational signs comprehends those which, though we never before had any notion or conception of the things signified, do suggest it, or conjure it up, as it were, by a kind of natural magic, and at once give us a conception, and create a belief of it."[47] This third class comprises perceptual sensation. He suggests, rather lamely, that we refer this operation to an "original principle" of the human mind, and, on one occasion, to "the inspiration of the Almighty."[48] Speaking of a person's knowledge derived from perception, he says that "he is led to it in the dark, and knows not how he came by it."[49] Michael Ayers states the problem here concisely, in relation to both Reid and Malebranche: "In separating 'perception' and 'sensation' as different sorts of mental occurrence, they made the connection between them unintelligible."[50] By contrast, Ayers is surely correct in stressing the distinctively *transparent* character of perceptual belief, which separates it, as by a gulf, from any mere hunch or Dennettian "premonition."[51] Reid, as we have seen, is no Dennett; he fully recognizes a sensory aspect to perception. What he effectively offers us, however, is such a sensory element *giving rise to a blind hunch*. There has surely got to be something awry here—something that stems from the theory's dualistic nature.

Secondly, the dualism of the theory would seem to render it incapable of giving an acceptable account of the distinction between illusion and veridical perception. We all know that despite seeing something, even veridically, we can acquire a false belief about it—even about its perceptible aspects. Imagine, for example, that you are the referee of a snooker game, and that you are called upon to declare whether the white ball has just hit the yellow or the green ball first. It is quite possible, especially if there was but a split second between the two impacts, for you to be wholly convinced that it hit the green one first, even though you *saw* it first hit the yellow ball. What, however, can it mean to say that, despite your judgement to the contrary, you really did see the white ball hit the yellow one before the green? One possibility is that you misperceived the scene: for whatever reason, it really did look, from where you were standing, as though the white ball hit the green one first. That, however, would be unusual. What normally happens in such cases is that, despite your belief to the contrary, not only did you see the white ball hit the yellow one first, but the scene visually appeared to you that way. When we make such mistakes—and they are far from uncommon, especially with brief events, or when pinpoint accuracy is called for, and generally under conditions that stretch our perceptual capacities—we do not typically suffer an *illusion*, even in the wide sense of this term that is operative in these pages. Other things being equal, what you see is determined by what unfolds in your visual field, in the flow of visual sensation. In such situations, your *senses* register the scene *accurately*; it is your "cognition" that is at fault. If we could have a slow-motion re-run of our perceptual experience, we like to imagine, we should be in a much better position to state what it was we really saw. Now, in slow motion, you clearly see the white ball touch the yellow ball first before rebounding on to the green. When it all happened so fast, however, you acquired the wrong belief. On the dual component theory, however, sensation is of no cognitive value whatever except in so far as it occasions a judgement, which alone can be accurate or inaccurate.

The following, related problem also arises. Consider a case where, as before, you acquire a false belief concerning what took place in your field of vision, but where *you also suffer an illusion:* the white really did hit the green first, but because of trick lighting, mirrors, time delays, or what have you, your visual sensations are the same as if you were seeing it hit the yellow first. Here we have a case where you perceive a scene, make a correct perceptual judgement about it, and yet misperceive it. What both these examples show is that we need to be able to make sense of the distinction between illusion and veridicality in perception prior to any post-sensory judgement. On the dual component theory, however, that will take us to the level of mere sensation where, since this level is pre-perceptual, such notions can get no purchase.

Thirdly, the dual component theory does not even succeed in the crucial task of sustaining Direct Realism. One fact that should immediately raise our suspicions is that what is essentially a dual component account of our perceptual transactions with the physical world has been explicitly promulgated by many writers as a form of *Indirect* Realism. Indeed, from Sir William Hamilton's detailed commentary on Reid through to recent responses to Sellars, there has been a sustained complaint that, whatever its possible merits, the dual component approach to perception fails to be a form of Direct Realism.[52] In particular, Reid's contention that sensations are "signs" that "suggest" conceptions of physical objects to us does not serve to distinguish his position from Indirect Realism. In the *Problems of Philosophy* Russell asks, "Granted that we are certain of our own sense-data, have we any reason for regarding them as signs of the existence of something else, which we can call the physical object?" And later in the same work he writes that "over and above the sensations of colour, hardness, noise, and so on, which make up the appearance of the table to me, I assume that there is something else, of which these things are appearances."[53] These remarks are part of a classic exposition of Indirect Realism, and what they express is—

except for the epistemological worry present in the first quotation—identical with Reid's position. (Indeed, it is one of the greatest ironies in the history of the philosophy of perception that Russell's work on the *Problems of Philosophy*, one of the classic Indirect Realist texts, involved a close study of Reid's writings!) Moreover, it is worth recalling that the notion of suggestion, which Reid took over from Berkeley, was used by Berkeley, quite reasonably, only in cases where we *lack* "immediate" perception. For Berkeley's principal use for the notion of suggestion was to define, by its absence, the notion of a "sensible thing," and, equivalently, of an object that is "immediately perceived." Despite Reid's intentions, this feature of suggestion carries over into his own theory. We have need of suggestion only where we have not been given the thing itself.[54]

Some commentators have attempted to extricate Reid from this disastrous position by pointing out that for him the relation of signification is causal in nature.[55] It is certainly true that the move from sign to signified reality is not *inferential* for him—as it was for Helmholtz and many other leading Indirect Realists.[56] This, however, hardly saves the day. For one thing, since self-styled Indirect Realists who appeal to inference typically claim that it occurs unconsciously, it is far from clear how significantly different Reid's talk of suggestion really is. For another, it is not the case, contrary to what many writers suggest, that Indirect Realism simply amounts to being a Realist and recognizing such inference. Perhaps inference here entails indirectness, but the converse is certainly not the case. Consider David Hume. He was an Indirect Realist; and yet no inference is involved in perceptual consciousness on his view.[57] Rather, we *mistake* our perceptions for physical objects, attributing to our perceptions an independence from sense that they do not have. H. A. Prichard was of the same opinion: "What we call seeing or feeling a body consists in genuinely mistaking certain sensa for a body."[58] Perhaps, however, Reid's talk of signs and suggestion was but an unfortunate choice of vocabulary. Certainly, we find no such language in Sellars. Nevertheless, the suspicion that the dual component account of perception fails to amount to Direct Realism will fail to be justified only if its proponents can convince us that sensations do not function as objects of awareness. This they have never been able to do.

In Sellars, for example, we find little more than bare assertion on this point: the object of awareness is the object of the distinctively cognitive element in perception, and there is no other. He does, to be sure, attempt to derive this conclusion from his insistence that the role of sensations in perception is causal rather than "epistemic": "The direct perception of physical objects is mediated by the occurrence of sense impressions which latter are, in themselves, thoroughly non-cognitive. Furthermore, this mediation is causal rather than epistemic. Sense impressions do not mediate by virtue of being known."[59] A perceptual taking is a "conceptual *response* to a *stimulus*."[60] Because of this, "the sensation of red is not a *reason* even for *I am seeing red*. Having sensations is having *causes of* judgements, not *reasons for* judgements."[61] Indeed, he can say, as we have seen, that sense-impressions guide conceptual activity "from without." Such an emphasis on the distinction between a reason and a cause is not convincing, in relation to our present concern, however, because an Indirect Realist need not hold that an awareness of sensations provides a *reason* for believing in the existence of "external" objects. Recall Hume and Prichard. Even if an awareness of sensation merely causes us so to believe, if what functions causally here is indeed an *awareness of a sensation*, perception is "epistemically" indirect. If we ignore this false trail, we are left, as I say, with brute assertion on Sellars's part. We have seen that the crucial problem for Direct Realism is how perceptual sensation can be *in consciousness and yet not be an object of awareness*. I cannot see that any real light is thrown on this problem by Sellars's writings.[62]

Reid, however, is somewhat more sensitive to the problem, and throughout his writings repeatedly claims that we *do not pay any attention to our sensations*.[63] Sensations are indeed states of consciousness, but in perception we are not conscious *of* them. Reid points out, for example, that most of the objects we see at any time—all those before or beyond the point at which we are focusing—are seen double; but this fact comes as a surprise to most people. And in general, "besides the sensations that are either agreeable or disagreeable, there is still a greater number that are indifferent. To these we give so little attention that they have no name, and are immediately forgotten, as if they had never been; and it requires attention to the operations of our minds to be convinced of their existence."[64] Because of this, "though all philosophers agree that in seeing colour there is sensation, it is not easy to persuade the vulgar, that, in seeing a coloured body, when the light is not too strong, nor the eye inflamed, they have any sensation or feeling at all."[65] Matters are, however, far from so straightforward. The fact that the "vulgar" do not recognize the existence of perceptual sensation cuts no ice, since they are Naive Realists—a view we have seen to be false. It does not follow from their ignorance that in perception they are not aware of what is in fact, as philosophers or psychologists are in a position to recognize, a sensation. Perhaps, as Hume suggests, the vulgar "confound perceptions and objects."[66] Moreover, Reid's claim that we overlook our perceptual sensations is plainly false. That there are perceptual sensations that we do overlook hardly needs arguing.[67] But that *all* are overlooked is a claim that is quickly seen to be false when we recall that sensations have been introduced by the dual component theorist so as to account for the sensuous nature of perceptual experience. Literally to overlook our sensations would be to overlook the fact that perceptual experience is sensuous at all—to overlook the fact that we are *perceiving*, rather than merely thinking. That we do not, at an unreflective level, explicitly recognize them *as* sensations is, for the opponent to Direct Realism, a matter of no moment. In particular, Reid's claim makes nonsense of the phenomenon of perceptual attention. Consider what happens when we hear a sound, for example. Out there in the physical world there is, as Reid would be the first to admit, simply vibrating air. When we hear something, our attention is focused by a phenomenon having an auditory quality, which is, according to the present theory, that of sensation. To overlook such a sensation, or not to attend to it, would be to overlook, or not to attend to, the sound itself. It is through such sensation that we are alert to perceptible aspects of the physical world. When such cases are under consideration, how are we to resist Helmholtz's claim that "the . . . grasp of the object shows that the sensation in question has been perceived and employed by consciousness"?[68]

In fact, when Reid turns to detailed consideration of the various senses, he is forced to face up to this fact. "Three of our senses," he writes, "to wit, smell, taste, and hearing, originally give us only certain sensations, and a conviction that these sensations are occasioned by some external object."[69] Because of this, our very conception of such "secondary qualities" involves reference to a type of sensation. Sensations relating to secondary qualities "are not only signs of the object perceived, but they bear a capital part in the notion we form of it. We conceive it only as that which occasions such a sensation, and therefore cannot reflect upon it without thinking of the sensation which it occasions. We have no other mark whereby to distinguish it. The thought of a secondary quality, therefore, always carries us back to the sensation which it produces."[70] In other words, Reid endorses the primary / secondary quality distinction on two levels. Not only does he hold that as a matter of fact the sensuous qualities of perceptual experience are qualities of sensation that bear no resemblance to configurations of inert, insentient, physical matter; he also holds that this distinction is embodied in perceptual consciousness itself, as a distinction between the different sorts of conceptions that are found in our perceptions of primary and secondary qualities: "They are distinguished by this, that of the primary we have by our senses a direct and distinct notion; but of the secondary only a relative notion, which must, because it is only relative, be obscure; they are conceived only as the unknown causes or occasions of certain sensations with which we are so well acquainted."[71] Hence he can say, quite explicitly, that "the sensations belonging to secondary qualities are an object of our attention."[72] By contrast, our conceptions of primary qualities are clear, intelligible and non-relative. In fact, much of what Reid says about our perception of primary qualities and the fundamental role they play in constituting our awareness of an objective world has at least an element of truth in it—one that I shall attempt to incorporate into a viable theory of perception in the final chapter of Part I. The suggestion that sensations are overlooked in perception is at its most plausible in the case where we feel an object to discover its shape. As we pass our hands over a solid object, feeling its sides and edges, we have a succession of fleeting tactile sensations, but a steady conviction of a single coherent body with a determinate shape. The discrepancy between sensations and perception is clear here because of the serial nature of the tactile sensations that subserve the perception of an unchanging persistent body. If, however, such observations can be put to the service of Direct Realism, they are, in Reid's own theory, wholly subverted by his account of the perception of secondary qualities—those that involve, on Reid's own admission, attention to sensory features that are themselves qualities of sensation. For given that every perceptible physical object has some sensuous (or "secondary") quality or other, we end up with Indirect Realism, at best, across the board, in virtue of what, in Chapter 1, I called "sense-datum infection."[73] This inability of the dual component theory to sustain Direct Realism stems ultimately from the very dualism that is its essence. If sensations are brought into consciousness *in addition* to a distinct cognitive act that supposedly achieves perceptual "transcendence" to the world, such sensations, given that Reid's suggestion that they are simply overlooked is plainly false, are going to be sensory items of which we are aware whenever we perceive. Minor details apart, there is nothing in the dual component theory with which H. H. Price, C. D. Broad, or Bertrand Russell would disagree. This theory does not give us Direct Realism.

The final, and most important criticism of the dual component theory, however, is that it is incoherent. This fact emerges when we enquire more precisely into the *content* of the judgement that is seen as being at the heart of perception. According to Reid, perception involves a conception of an object and a "belief in its existence." Now, what is the force of this "its"? If Direct Realism is to be sustained, "it" had better be the physical object perceived. So this is the thing that needs to be "conceived" when we perceive. The ultimate test for the dual component theory is whether it is able to make sense of this ability to conceive or think about *individual objects* in the environment. Reid wholly fails to see that there is even a problem here. Perhaps it is simply to be accepted that when something red and round gives rise to characteristic visual sensations in me, I come to believe that a round, red object is present. What cannot be left wholly in the "dark," however, is how I am supposed to come by a conception *of the particular object* that is responsible for the sensations. The problem is not so much how "round" and "red" pop into my mind, as how I can come by a conception of *this* red and round object.[74] Sellars at least recognizes, indeed stresses, that perceptual judgements are thus *demonstrative* in character: the objects of perceptual "takings" are, as he puts it, *this-suches*.[75] Not only is this insistence incompatible with central elements in Sellars' account of perception, however, but doing justice to the distinctively demonstrative content of perceptual judgement undermines any possible form of dual component theory, since it is incompatible with the dualism of sensation and perception that is definitive of that theory.

In order for me to see, say, a red triangle that is before me, it is not necessary that I be visually caused to believe that there is a red triangle before me.[76] This is simply demonstrated by the possibility of illusion. If the red triangle looks green to me, I shall not non-inferentially believe that it is red, and yet I see it. Although Sellars recognizes *this* fact, he not only failed to see that I can *wholly* misperceive an object—misperceive it with respect to each of its perceptible qualities—but made his theory incompatible with such a possibility. For he spells out what it is for a perceptual taking to be of a certain object in terms of that belief *correctly representing* at least certain aspects of the object. If I mistake the red triangle for a green one, I can still be credited with seeing it, he suggests, if I at least take it to be a triangle; and if I am wrong about this, I can be credited with seeing it if I at least correctly believe that it is *over there*, in a certain direction from me.[77] I can, however, get all of this, even this last positional fact, wrong, and still see that triangle. Visually I can misperceive not only an object's colour, but also, and at the same time, its shape, size, location, and direction. Just think of the effects of distorting lenses.

When Sellars characterizes such cases of misperception in terms of "limited referential success," he effectively indicates that he is basing perceptual directedness on a semantical notion of reference derived from Russell's theory of descriptions.[78] Indeed, Sellars in effect endorses what Gareth Evans used to call "the bad old Philosophy of Mind": the view that we can be cognizant of at least any "external" object only in virtue of entertaining some description that that object uniquely fits, or "satisfies."[79] In other words, we supposedly perceive objects in virtue of *correctly representing* or *depicting* them. So the issues here are closely analogous to those that have been extensively thrashed out in connection with the "Descriptive Theory of Names" in philosophical semantics over recent years[80]—though the verdict is, if anything, even more clear-cut against any attempt to give a descriptive analysis of perceptual reference: for the possibility of illusion immediately invalidates any such idea.[81] Even a weakened, and somewhat more plausible, claim to the effect that the object of a perception is that object which, of everything in the world, *most closely* fits the perceptual "conception" is untenable. Even if we stress, and indeed place all the weight upon, the fact that the perceptual conceptions in question embody a specification of an object's spatial location in relation to the perceiver, as Sellars often did, we shall get the wrong answers concerning which object is perceived in various situations. Suppose, for example, that I see a white piece of paper that looks yellow, but that precisely covers an exactly congruent piece of paper that *is* yellow. We cannot perceptually distinguish between something being, say, ten feet and being ten feet and one hundredth of an inch away from us. So the occluded yellow paper would win the contest for closest fit, since it is at least yellow. Even if we allowed perfect spatial discriminations into perceptual conceptions, we should still have problems. Suppose, to rehearse a familiar scenario, that when I take myself to see the piece of paper before me, there is, unknown to me, a mirror in front of me, and the paper that is responsible for my perception is off to one side, out of my direct line of vision but reflected in the mirror; let us also suppose, however, that there is an exactly similar piece of paper behind the mirror just where I seem to see one.[82] The idea that perception is of the object that matches a conception inherent in the perception would have it that in this situation I see the piece of paper that is located behind the mirror. But that, of course, is false; I cannot see through mirrors. Similar remarks apply to the other senses: I do not hear the quartet that is playing before me if my auditory experience, even if identical to what I should enjoy if I were really hearing that quartet, comes to me through earphones from a recorded source. Indeed, Sellars's very phrase "limited referential success" should set alarm bells ringing. For recall that what is supposedly explicated here is *what we are aware of in perception*. I do not, however, have but a limited success in being aware of a red triangle when it looks green to me.

Perceptual judgements are what these days is commonly termed *"de re."* Sadly, the now considerable literature on this topic is, as a whole, in something of a state of disarray. There is, for example, little consensus over whether the *de re* is characteristic of certain cognitive states or only of attributions of such states to subjects; whether it requires identifying knowledge; whether the *de re* can be reduced to its supposed complement, the *de dicto;* whether the distinction can be analysed in terms of "scope"; and how widespread the phenomenon of the *de re* is. Indeed, one leading contributor to the debate is perhaps not going too far when he describes the relevant literature as a "disgusting mess."[83] For the purposes of the present investigation, however, it is most helpful to understand the *de re* negatively as that which is *not descriptive*, in the sense of not securing reference to an individual object in virtue of correctness, or accuracy, of depiction—even when this is weakened so as to be a matter of "closest fit." This is not a matter of the ways in which we attribute cognitive states to perceivers, but a matter of the nature of states of perception themselves. Perceptions are not of objects in virtue of perceptual judgements (more or less) accurately depicting or representing those objects. The of-relation holding between perceptual states and physical objects needs to be accounted for in some other way. Sellars, as I have said, recognized that perceptual judgements are indeed demonstrative in form; what he failed to realize is that this is incompatible with his effective adherence to the "bad old Philosophy of Mind."[84] Perception puts us in a *de re* relationship with an object because it embodies information about that very item. One form that information can take, however, is *misinformation*. When I misperceive a white object as yellow, I am misinformed *about it*. Correctness in depiction is not a condition for the holding of such an informational relationship. So neither Reid nor Sellars can be our guide towards a proper understanding of perceptual judgement. In fact, however, this problem is not remediable within *any* dual component approach to perception—within any theory according to which sensation can at most, as Sellars says, guide perceptual judgement "from without," as we shall now see.

The reason why perceptual judgements are indisputably *de re*, at least if Direct Realism is true, is that in perception we are, to use Russell's term, *acquainted* with a physical object. Russell himself, of course, held that we could be so acquainted only with sense-data.[85] What the Direct Realist needs to do is to respect something like Russell's distinction between acquaintance on the one hand, and cognition that is achieved by description on the other, while yet insisting, against Russell, that we can be acquainted with normal objects in the physical world. As I mentioned above, there is some debate over the range of the circumstances in which we can have *de re* cognitions. There is debate, for example, over whether we can think *de re* of objects on the basis of the testimony of others, or whether we must ourselves be in possession of some more direct cognitive access to such objects, through perception or memory.[86] The *de re* character of perceptual judgement is, however, beyond question precisely because it constitutes acquaintance with objects.

The crucial problem with the dual component analysis of perception can now be stated: according to this theory, a perceptual judgement *does not occur in a context in which we are acquainted with a physical object*. It occurs, rather, in a situation in which we are caused to have an objectless sensation that by itself does not constitute acquaintance with an object. I can judge of a sound that it is, say, like the sound of a high-pitched trumpet, and that it is coming from over there, even though it is really neither of these, only if I am already acquainted perceptually with the sound, so that none of these mistaken predications counts against the "referential success" of my judgement. On the dual component account, however, there is no acquaintance with physical objects prior to the this-thinking which goes to constitute the perception. This is incoherent, because it presupposes that a this-thinking has an object, while making the occurrence of that very thinking constitutive of the awareness of the object that itself alone gives cognitive access to the object in the kind of contexts that are in question. For a perceptual this-thought to succeed referentially, *our senses themselves must provide an object.* On the present analysis sense provides no objects, but merely objectless sensations. In short, perceptual judgement comes on the scene too late to be of any cognitive use. We need the senses themselves to acquaint us with objects. The dual component theory is incapable of recognizing this fact.

The problem here arises from making perceptual sensation *external* to the perceptual judgement that supposedly confers cognitive status on perceptual consciousness. If sensations merely "guide from without," they are at best the occasions of independently specifiable judgements, whereas, if Direct Realism is true, the particularity of perceptual judgement must result from the particular relation in which such sensations stand to particular objects. This problem surfaces clearly in P. T. Geach's rare foray into the Philosophy of Perception. "The content of the [perceptual] judgement," he writes, "is always intelligible and conceptual—acquaintance with a particular sensible thing is no part of the judgement itself—but an act of judgement performed in a particular sensory context may thereby be referred to particular sensible things. It is clear, indeed, that the act of judgement must bear a closer relation than mere simultaneity to the context of sense-perception that gives it its special reference to these particular sensible things; I am not prepared to characterize this special relation."[87] What I am suggesting is that even supplementing mere simultaneity by causal dependence, as Sellars does, fails to sustain any genuine perceptual acquaintance with the world. Since such causal relations are the most that the dual component theory can offer by way of bringing sensation and judgement closer together without abandoning the radical "Kantian" separation of sensibility and understanding that is definitive of it, this theory is unacceptable. We need to deny that sensation is external to the cognitive achievement of perception. If Direct Realism is true, it can only be because it is perceptual sensation itself that guides cognition to the physical world—from within.

This final criticism of the dual component theory may, however, seem to be premised on a questionable assumption: that if sensation is but externally, causally related to a judgement that constitutes our first cognitive contact with the world, such a judgement must have a content that is specifiable independently of such causal antecedents, and thus fail to be *de re*. Now, if Geach were correct in holding that the content of even perceptual judgement is wholly "intelligible and conceptual," this would no doubt be the case; but this is precisely what the most influential recent account of the *de re* denies. The account in question derives from Tyler Burge. He specifies a *de re* belief as one where the subject stands in "an appropriate nonconceptual, contextual relation to objects the belief is about."[88] This is, as far as it goes, doubtless correct, as is his corresponding denial that a *de re* belief has a content "all of whose semantically relevant components characterize elements in the believer's conceptual repertoire"—*if*, that is, this means that *de re* belief-contents do not secure reference descriptively, by objects matching our representation of the world. This is not, however, all that Burge means, for he concludes that there is nothing in the content of a *de re* belief *functioning as subject term*. What this in effect means, however, is that there is no such thing as acquaintance with an object. Attributions of *de re* belief, we are told, "are about predication broadly conceived," dealing with "a relation between *open sentences* (or what they express) and objects." But any such representation of a perceiver's mental state would contain a conspicuous gap where acquaintance with the world should be. What determines perceptual reference is "not part of the mental . . . repertoire of the believer."[89] Burge holds that perceptual judgement about a certain object "depends not only on information the thinker has about it but on his nonconceptual contextual relations to it" because of the "incompleteness of information" we have about the objects we perceive.

In a number of subsequent papers, Burge has implicitly applied this perspective to a number of topics in a way that has convinced many.[90]

And perhaps such an account of *de re* judgement is applicable in certain contexts. It is, to take one of Burge's most famous later examples, perhaps not wholly implausible to suppose that someone could be in the same "narrow" psychological state as I am in when I think of arthritis, and yet not be thinking of arthritis, but of some distinct complaint, simply because this other person is located in a different linguistic setting. Any such suggestion is, however, totally implausible when we are dealing with perception, precisely because perception involves an *awareness* of objects. Perceptual judgement is judgement about what we are sensorily aware of. Without doubt, contextual, non-conceptual relations are involved in the perception of any normal object, but such relations help put us in a situation in which we can receive information from the world in a way that is sufficient for acquaintance with objects in it. This, at least, is what the Direct Realist will insist. Burge's position, in some ways the polar opposite of Geach's, is, if anything, even more inadequate for the purposes of Direct Realism than the latter. When Burge tells us of the contextual relations that need to be in place for a *de re* perceptual judgement about an object to be possible, he tells us that it must be the case that the subject's "sense organs are affected by" the object. Perhaps this is necessary, but it is hardly sufficient, even when taken together with the entertaining of "open sentences." What, in particular, is needed is that the subject *perceive* the relevant object. Burge's account of the perceptual *de re* cannot do justice to this obvious truth. At the very best, Burge's account of *de re* judgement in its specifically perceptual form *requires* a theory of perception: it cannot, by itself, form even part of such a theory.

Kent Bach has seen the need to modify Burge's approach, noting that "predicates or open sentences won't do, for they do not give complete contents."[91] Bach proposes to supplement the open sentence in a perceptual judgement with a "percept." This is a move in the right direction on two counts. First, we are not left with an incomplete mental content that does not even begin to answer to the requirement of perceptual acquaintance. And secondly, we locate the subject-constituent of the content in perceptual experience itself. The problem with Bach's analysis is that his "percepts" are Sellarsian objectless sensing-events.[92] So the content of perceptual judgement remains an open sentence, merely one slightly more complex than we find in Burge.[93] Although there is no longer, as there seemed to be in Burge, a cognitive gap in perceptual belief, acquaintance has once again disappeared from perceptual consciousness. As Bach says quite openly, perceptual beliefs have contents that are "not complete representations," they do not contain "any element that identifies the object being represented." But perceptual consciousness, if it is to give us acquaintance with normal objects, as Direct Realism requires, needs to be *completely* "representational" (if that is the right term). But if so, what functions in consciousness as the subject-term of such judgement? Suppose I hear a shrill noise. I am, according to the Direct Realist, thereby acquainted with a physical phenomenon, related *de re* to an element in the physical world. In the absence of any prior information, I should not have been cognitively so related unless my senses were informing me of the world. Perception typically puts me in a position to make *de re* judgements that would otherwise be unavailable to me.[94] How is this possible? Certainly not, as Burge suggests, simply in virtue of my mentally entertaining the predicate "ξ is shrill" while my eardrums are caused to vibrate. Bach at least sees that this phenomenological gap needs to be filled. What it is filled by is, of course, perceptual sensation. But we have also seen that if Direct Realism is not to be abandoned, this sensation must *itself* function as a *de re* mode of presentation of a physical object. It is the particularity of sensation that confers *de re* particularity on perceptual judgement. But this means that sensation is *not*, as against the dual component theory, external to the perceptual judgement that alone is supposed to be truly cognitive.

I have suggested that I have to hear that shrill noise if I am to be in a position to make a *de re* judgement about it (given that I am not otherwise informed about it)—as if perception had to be in place *first* for a *de re* judgement to be possible. But is this really necessary? Consider, again, our hypothetically non-conscious insect from Chapter 1. When, on the basis of seeing this insect pushing along a morsel of food, we attribute perception to the creature, we do not attribute to it an inner representation the content of which is merely that some morsel of food or other is in the vicinity, but a representation of *that* morsel. It is only because of this that the creature can act on it. Surely there is some functionalist story to tell here about this insect's causal involvement with that particular bit of food, one that allows us to attribute *de re* "attitudes" to the insect, entirely in the absence of any sensation, or indeed consciousness. Here, surely, we have no inclination to insist that the insect must *already* perceive the morsel if it is to be in a position to be in any cognitive state that relates to it *de re*. So why may not some such story apply to us—except that, in our case, sensation occurs in the causal chain just before the eventual *de re* belief? The problem with such a suggestion, however, is that, since our insect is wholly insentient, by applying the insect story to ourselves we are suggesting that even typical human perception is, in itself, non-conscious. This may seem unfair. After all, it may be replied, the human story features a sensation, which is a conscious sensory state. The problem is, however, that this state is supposed to occur *before the perception itself.* On such an account, there is really no such thing as truly perceptual consciousness. What we are offered, rather, is a conscious state that consists in the occurrence of "meaningless" sensation, and which is not, therefore, of itself perceptual, followed by the supposedly truly perceptual stage that is not itself conscious. The only form of consciousness that is allowed on such a view, therefore, is that of blind sensation that fails to be world-directed, and that therefore fails to embody any notion of a sensory awareness of a world. Hence, in so far as there is any awareness at all in perception, it must be awareness of sensation.

This criticism is damning, however, only if sensation is presented by the dual component theorist as the only conscious episode in any perceptual situation. Now, although this is doubtless true of Sellars's version of the theory (along with most other modern accounts of perception that fall into this tradition), it is not true of Reid's account. For when he says that we could have had all the perceptions that we do without any perceptual sensations, he was not picturing a situation in which we should have been wholly non-conscious perceivers of the world. Belief itself was, for him, a conscious act, for he followed Descartes in rejecting the Aristotelian claim that all cognition must involve some sensory state or other (be it only a "mental image," rather than a full-blown sensation). He recognized, in other words, what we may call "pure thought." The idea is that you can think of something without perceiving it, without remembering it by way of forming any image, without imagining it, without any words or other symbolic representations running through your mind, and without any attendant bodily sensations whatever. One does not have to be a card-carrying Empiricist to find this idea fanciful. (Leibniz, for instance, explicitly rejected the possibility.) Let us not stop to criticize the idea, however, but see

what account of perception emerges for a dual component approach if
it is accepted. What we find is something that is surely as disturbing as
the earlier proposal: for perception now emerges as featuring *two distinct episodes of awareness.* This is phenomenologically absurd.

In my initial discussion of Reid, I interpreted him as holding the
view that perceptual belief is occasioned by sensation. Some, however,
have interpreted him as having moved toward the view that such belief
is occasioned directly by the input of our sense-organs to the brain.
The suggestion is that such cerebral events immediately cause *both* our
perceptual beliefs and our perceptual sensations. On this view sensation merely accompanies belief, and is epiphenomenal to the cognitive
order. Whatever the merits of this as an interpretation of Reid, we need
to consider the suggestion in its own right, not only because such an
idea has many current followers, but also because it may seem to avoid
preceding criticisms.[95] In fact, it fares no better than the two suggestions just considered. If the belief is non-conscious, it falls prey to the
problems of the former; if it is conscious, then again we have two states
of awareness and not one. The fact that these two states occur at the
same time may somewhat diminish the implausibility of the suggestion,
but such a view has the following unnerving consequence: it implies
that if you were not now enjoying any visual sensations at all (because
that effect of the relevant brain process was inhibited), you could still
be perceiving this page, and *consciously* perceiving it, so long as the
other, belief-inducing, effect of the brain process remained intact.
Even if we do not simply discount the possibility of a conscious belief
entirely lacking sensory character, introducing such a thing into the
analysis of perceptual consciousness would wreak phenomenological
havoc. Just try and envisage what such a belief would be like consciously. It would have to be some kind of blind hunch, or one of
Dennett's "premonitions." When we bear in mind that the onset of
such a belief is, on the current proposal, quite independent of the occurrence of sensation, we end up with a bizarre view of perceptual
awareness as involving a blind hunch accompanied by a sensation. As
an account of ordinary perceptual consciousness, this is barely intelligible.[96]

SINCE ALL of the problems with the dual component analysis of perception that we have just surveyed ultimately derive from the spe-

cifically dualistic character of the theory, from its radical separation of cognition from sensation, a simple, albeit fundamental, modification to such an account may now naturally suggest itself. For perhaps we can give a more than merely ancillary role to sensation in perception by regarding such sensation as *itself* constituting the world-directed judgement that the dual component theory sees as the distinctively cognitive, intentional element in perception. If perception is both sensory and cognitive, but if, also, a dualistic view that regards perception as a compound of two separate functions is unacceptable, perhaps we should simply *equate* these sensory and cognitive aspects of perception. What naturally suggests itself, in short, is a monistic replacement of the dual component approach. Such a view would, of course, mean rejecting Reid's characterization of sensation as essentially lacking an object distinct from itself, and, in general, rejecting the traditional characterization of mere sensation as "meaningless." Perhaps this is true of some sensations—bodily sensation, for example; but perhaps it is not true of perceptual sensation. That, perhaps, is why such sensations are indeed perceptual. The idea would be that for sensation to be perceptual it must be *intrinsically* intentional, or world directed. Because of this I shall sometimes refer to the proposed account as "intentionalism." The position in question may be seen as a non-reductive, non-eliminative version of accounts of perception, such as those of David Armstrong and Daniel Dennett, which we considered in Chapter 1. Edward Craig, for one, sees things in this way. "Sensory experiences actually are judgements about our environment," he writes, "or, to put the point slightly more accurately, having a sensory experience is making a judgement about the environment." He continues, however: "I do not thereby intend a contrast with theories which make use of the notion of sensory experience in their account of perception—I do not intend to substitute judgement for sensory experience, as some . . . seem to wish to do."[97]

If it is true to say that until recently the dual component theory was philosophical orthodoxy, at least for Direct Realists, the identification of sensation and judgement appears of late to have taken over this position. And the advantages that such an account would have over a dual component approach are not hard to see. For one thing, the problem of how sensation, as a state of consciousness, can fail to be an object of awareness (as Direct Realism requires) receives a simple solution: since sensation is now viewed as being intrinsically intentional in character, it poses no more of a problem on this score than does thought. For thoughts too, are conscious states; and yet their immediate objects are simply whatever we are thinking of. Again, the *de re* character of perceptual judgement, judgement that achieves particular reference in virtue of the occurrence of particular sensations, is naturally accounted for.

These points are perhaps most clearly seen in the monistic account of perception by Romane Clark, who in several papers has developed ideas to be found in the writings of Everett Hall into what is perhaps the most well worked out version of such a theory.[98] Clark develops an analogy between perceptual experience and linguistically formulated judgement. We are to construe perceptual sensations as *natural predicates:* a red (or red') sensation has the cognitive force of ". . . is red." The natural analogue of the referential component of a judgement is the *occurrence* of the sensation itself, which constitutes indexical—more precisely, demonstrative—reference to the world. Hence the occurrence of a red' sensation has the cognitive force of "This is red." As he says, in conscious opposition to Sellars, "Acts of sensing are not mere causal concomitants of acts of perception. They are literal constituents of them. To perceive is sensuously to judge. It is to judge with its constitutive acts of sensing functioning as the vehicles of the demonstrative reference involved in seeing what is the case, and with the sensuous character of the acts functioning to provide the particular ascriptions made."[99]

What are we to make of such an account? In Chapter 4 I shall argue that the dual component theorists were at least right about one thing: no type of sensation is, as such, necessarily directed to normal objects. So if the present proposal is, as some of its proponents seem to imply, that some types of sensation *necessarily* constitute world-directed judgements, it is simply false. If, however, it is allowed that, although some sensations constitute such judgements, some do not, we are faced with the task of explaining this fact. None of the proponents of the present proposal have attempted this task (perhaps because they do indeed mistakenly believe that sensations are necessarily judgements). A more immediate, and crushing, objection, however, concerns what the present proposal shares with the dual component theory. For it continues to hold that the only way in which we can understand the world-directedness of perceptual consciousness is by reference to the exercise of concepts. I believe this to be fundamentally mistaken. We need to turn our attention away from philosophers' perennial concern with concepts if we are properly to understand the nature of perceptual consciousness. It is the task of Chapter 3 to explain why this is so.

Perception and Conception

3

WHAT ALL THE ACCOUNTS of perception discussed in the previous chapter have in common is an appeal to conceptualization, or thought, in order to explain the intentionality of perceptual consciousness. In this chapter, I argue that any such appeal is fundamentally misguided. More precisely, I shall argue that the idea that perception essentially involves the exercise of concepts is either entirely false, or at best unhelpful (that is, bluntly, worthless) in relation to our attempt to withstand the Argument from Illusion. Whether the claim is false or unhelpful depends on how one is to construe what it is to be in possession of a concept and to exercise it.

I shall term the target of the present chapter "conceptualism." A natural way of stating it would be as the claim that every perception, as such, necessarily involves the exercise of some concept, and that it is only in virtue of this that perception is anything more than mere sensation. This may sound a strong enough claim, but in the context of our present enquiry conceptualism needs to be even stronger. It needs to claim that *every sensory element* in perceptual consciousness involves the exercise of a concept. This is true whether conceptualism is proposed in the context of a dual component or a monistic account of perception. For although the dual component theory recognizes non-conceptual, sensory elements in perception, in so far as these are elements *in perception* they must give rise to a "cognitive" representation of the world. Every change in perceptual sensation, no matter how small, and every

degree of quality and intensity, must be conceptualized, for otherwise
they would not be functioning perceptually. The point is even more
obvious in relation to the monistic transformation of this view, since
here all perceptual sensation is *identified* with a conceptual representation. It will, therefore, suffice to discredit either approach to show that
this stronger claim is false—something that a number of recent writers
are content to do. In this chapter I shall, however, contest even the
weaker claim. Indeed, I shall contest an even weaker one yet: that in order to perceive you need to possess at least one concept. Concepts are
simply irrelevant to perception as such.

In saying this, I in no way contest the enormously important role
that conceptualization plays in the perceptual lives of adult human beings. Perception, for us, is indeed typically "suffused with concepts," as
it is often said. For all that is to be said in these pages, it may be that *every* adult human perception is so suffused. Nor shall it be denied that
possession of a concept, or of even a recognitional ability, may affect
the way something perceptually appears to you. Claims for "familiarity
effects" and the effects of "set" on perception have been made for a significant number of perceptual situations.[1] Although at least some of
these are plausibly seen as involving effects on judgement, rather than
on sensory experience itself, some are not.[2] Perhaps the clearest examples concern the organization of the perceptual field. Consider, for example, the case of "hidden pictures": drawings that only with extended
viewing take on the appearance of depictions of familiar objects. One
such, for example, at first appears as but a meaningless array of marks,
but on prolonged viewing suddenly takes on the appearance of a depiction of a Dalmatian dog on a leaf-strewn path. It may well be that such
re-organization is possible in this case only for subjects who are familiar with the sight of dogs and paths. If so, a certain kind of genuinely
perceptual phenomenon would be concept- (or at least recognition-)
dependent. Such genuinely perceptual, concept-driven effects are, in
fact, somewhat limited in scope;[3] but even if they were widespread and
dramatic, such a fact would have no bearing on the issue of conceptualism as it arises at this stage of our enquiry. For when I say that concepts
are irrelevant to perception, what I mean is that they are irrelevant to
what it is that makes any sensory state a perception at all: they are irrelevant
to the intentionality of perception, to its basic world-directedness.

Can one perceive, say, a typewriter, if one does not possess the concept of a typewriter? Especially around the middle of the last century, one can find many writers who were at least loath to give a simple affirmative answer to such a question.[4] "While Tycho sees a mere pipe," wrote N. R. Hanson, "Kepler will see a telescope."[5] In certain contexts such an "intensional" use of perceptual verbs doubtless has a point. It would, however, be foolish to insist that *only* such usage is to be allowed, for that would not allow us to give expression to certain indisputable perceptual facts. Show a typewriter to, say, a primitive tribesman in Borneo, and *of course* he will be able to see (and feel) it. If he could not, he would not be in a position to wonder, as almost certainly he would, what on earth it was. Saying that he would, or at least could, see "it," means that he would see *the very same physical object* as you. No doubt the tribesman will not perceive the object "as" a typewriter; but that simply shows that you can perceive a typewriter without perceiving it as a typewriter. Hanson, for one, certainly denied no such thing: "Naturally," he says, "Tycho and Kepler see the same physical object." What he does, rather, is to ask which use of perceptual verbs is the more "illuminating," and plumps for the intensional use. Now, I do not myself approve of such an intensional use of perceptual verbs in a theoretical context such as the present one. Everything that can be said in this manner can be equally well expressed by saying such things as that Kepler saw the telescope *as* a telescope, or that he *recognized* it to be a telescope, whereas Tycho did not, even though he, too, saw a telescope;[6] and if we condone two uses, it may be unclear in various contexts what is being intended. Be this as it may, in the present context the "extensional" use of perceptual verbs is, if not the more illuminating, at least the more serviceable, since what we are interested in is what is involved in perceiving any physical object at all. That Tycho and Kepler see the same physical object is a fact that would, no doubt, be of little significance in many contexts. What makes possible such a humble fact is itself, however, a problem for us. Strict adherence to the intensional use of perceptual (and "comportmental") verbs is also found in Heidegger's writings (and, in large part because of this, in almost all subsequent "continental philosophy"). This leads him to say of a case like the one involving you and the Borneo tribesman that the native's perception is "fundamentally different" from yours.[7] But that the two of you will be able to see and feel the very same physical thing surely constitutes a "fundamental" sameness. The differences between the two of you are, of course, highly significant in relation to possible actions, reactions, beliefs, desires, intentions, and evaluations; but there is, or need be, no *perceptual* difference. In fact, as I have pointed out, the acquiring of a conceptual ability does not generally affect the appearance of things. But even if it did, universally, the change would not be one from having an array of meaningless, subjective sensations to perceiving an objective world.

Although there are signs that it is waning, conceptualism is and has been rampant in the Philosophy of Perception.[8] We find T. H. Green in the last century writing, almost as an aside, and as if there could be no dispute on the matter, that perception is possible "only because we do more than feel—only because we think in feeling, and thus feel objects."[9] And closer to our own day Wilfrid Sellars could claim that "it is, I suppose, as non-controversial as anything philosophical can be that visual perception involves conceptual representations."[10] This leads Sellars consistently to take propositional acts of perceptual judgement ("perceives that p" rather than "perceives x") as central and paradigmatic in his account of perception, suggesting that all perceptual situations are ultimately analysable into perceptual judgements. Perception "is not a mere matter of selecting or referring to an object. It involves the 'judging' or 'affirming' that the object has such and such properties and stands in such and such relations . . . Indeed, even the selection of the object presupposes the ability to classify and relate."[11] According to Sellars, perception is a "classifying awareness," and therefore involves the employment of a conceptual scheme.[12] I believe that all of this is mistaken.

It is not, however, difficult to see certain attractions in invoking thought and concepts to elucidate the intentional character of perception. When I think of my mother, it is far from plausible to suggest that I do so only as a result of inspecting some mental item that stands proxy for her; rather, I quite straightforwardly think of the lady herself. We may say that, when I think of her, I have an "idea" of her. But this idea or conception just is my act of thinking, or the content of such an act, or my capacity to have such a thought; it is not plausibly seen as the *object* of such a thought. Such a thought surely has only one object, and that object is my mother. There is nothing analogous to the Argument from Illusion for thought.[13] Thought appears, in short, to possess those very features of objectivity and transcendence that we are trying to find in perception itself. Thomas Reid, for one, supported his account of perception by emphasizing such facts: "For whatever the object be, the man either thinks of it, or he does not. There is no medium between these. If he thinks of it, it is an immediate object of thought while he thinks of it. If he does not think of it, it is no object of thought at all. Every object of thought, therefore, is an immediate object of thought, and the word *immediate*, joined to objects of thought, seems to be a mere expletive."[14]

A second source of conceptualism is the idea that all perception is perception of something *as* being thus and so. To see anything, it has to look a certain way to you; to hear anything, it must sound a certain way to you, and so on. So perception is not of objects *simpliciter*, but of states of affairs. The representation of a fact, however, is propositional; and all propositions involve concepts. So nothing can appear to be *F* to you unless you possess the concept *F* and are exercising it in the perception.[15] As Wilfrid Sellars neatly puts it, "Predicates cannot be in sense unless judgement is there also."[16]

A third attractive feature of conceptualism can be seen by focusing on the issue of identity amidst difference. At around the same time as Reid, Kant propounded a dual component theory of perception that focused on this particular fact. In the Transcendental Deduction(s), Kant is exercised by the unity of an "intuition" that is implied in speaking of "the object" of such a representation: "In so far as [our cognitions: *Erkenntnisse*] are to have reference to an object, they must also necessarily agree amongst themselves in relation to it, i.e., they must have that unity which makes up the concept of an object."[17] Kant tells us that the word "concept" stands for "a consciousness . . . that unites in one representation [*Vorstellung*] the successively intuited and then reproduced manifold."[18] If there is indeed unity amidst diversity in perception—the continuing appearance of a single object despite, indeed through, its manifold appearances—this can only be due, it is suggested, to concepts.[19] Such conceptual unification is supposed to be at work not just in the articulation of human knowledge, but also in simple acts of perception, since it is such conceptualization alone that gives unity to the manifold of a "given intuition."[20] Although there are other, pre-conceptual syntheses at work in perception, it is not until we have "recognition in the concept" that we have *unity*—the unity demanded by talk of "the" object of a perception.[21]

A long-held related idea is that, since the senses register only a thing's sensible attributes, the reference of such attributes to a substance must be the work of the intellect. Sextus Empiricus, for example, wrote that sight "is receptive [*antilēptikē*] of figure and size and colour, but the substance [*onkos*] is neither figure nor size nor colour, but, if anything, is that in which these coincide [*symbebēken*]; and because of this, sight is incapable of grasping [*labein*] the substance." It is, in particular, the reference of several distinct qualities to a single subject that is supposed to be beyond the capacity of the senses: "This putting together of one thing with another, and apprehending [*lambanein*] a certain size with a certain figure belongs to a reasoning power [*logikēs dynameōs*]. For sight is non-rational [*alogos*]."[22]

If there are at least these three initial considerations in favour of analysing perception as involving a conceptual dimension, there is also, for many of us, a strong initial reaction against the whole idea. The reaction is quite simply that construing perception as involving something analogous to thought over-intellectualizes what is but a function of the senses, a fairly basic animal endowment. For the idea would seem to be, to put it bluntly, that you cannot perceive unless you can think; but thinking and conceptualization are relatively sophisticated achievements. We quite happily talk of cats and dogs as seeing and hearing things; we do not quite so easily attribute thoughts and concepts to them. Traditionally, perception was believed to be the province of the senses, thought that of the intellect. Was tradition really so misguided on this matter? I believe that it was not, and that it is a serious mistake to attempt to overthrow the traditional distinction between *aisthesis* and *nous* that is echoed in Schopenhauer's remark that "the animal experiences and perceives; man, in addition, *thinks*."[23] Schopenhauer goes on, indeed, to refer to this as "the unanimous opinion of all times and peoples." Sadly, this is not true, as we shall soon see. Note that this resistance to conceptualism does not rest on the assumption that of all the creatures that inhabit the Earth, man alone possesses concepts. That may or may not be true.[24] Given that we are concerned with an attempt to analyse perceptual consciousness as such, all that is required in order to refute conceptualism is that there *possibly* be one perceiving creature that lacks concepts.

This intuitive objection to conceptualism will be serious to the extent that it involves what we may term a "high" account of thought and conceptualization. Only then will it be unacceptable to postulate their necessary presence in the most primitive of all cognitive capacities. Later we shall explore the possibilities of developing a "low" account of what it is to possess a concept. It is worth emphasizing, however, that legions of philosophers have espoused a specifically high form of conceptualism—and not only in the dusty annals of philosophy's history. Wilfrid Sellars is one of them. This is demonstrated by, among other things, his "coherence theory of meaning," according to which conceptual schemes have a holistic character: "One can have the concept of green only by having a whole battery of concepts of which it is one element . . . [T]here is an important sense in which one has *no* concept pertaining to the observable properties of physical objects in Space and Time unless one has them all—and, indeed, as we shall see, a great deal more besides."[25] Basic observational concepts presuppose a grasp of "general truths about material things and our perception of them."[26] The full extent of the necessary preconditions for conceptual activity emerge when we explore Sellars's view that all thinking is a *symbolic process*. He denies that "there is any awareness of logical space prior to, or independent of, the acquisition of a language." Moreover, "One must, therefore, have the concept of oneself as an agent . . . To be a language user is to conceive of oneself as an agent subject to rules."[27] Symbolic activity is norm-governed, and to think is to be aware of being so governed: "To be a being capable of conceptual activity, is to be a being which acts, which recognizes norms and standards and engages in practical reasoning."[28] Now, there is perhaps not much to object to in all of this. Indeed, I have bothered to lay out such details of Sellars's views on conceptual activity because I believe them to be far from implausible. What is intolerable, however, is the suggestion that conceptual activity, so understood, is a necessary requirement in order to perceive. "To characterize S's experience as a *seeing* is, in a suitably broad sense . . . to apply the semantical concept of truth to that experience," claims Sellars;[29] and it is quite clear that he takes this to imply all of the complex stage-setting just rehearsed. But can we really suppose that in order to notice a light coming on, or to feel a kick in the pants, one must be able to engage in all of these sophisticated self-referential and linguistic conceptual episodes? Moreover, such a claim would seem to deny awareness of the environment to all non-linguistic creatures.

Sellars in fact expresses awareness of the intolerable position that his high conceptualism seems to have got him into. "Before continuing," he writes at one point,

> I must qualify the above remarks lest the animal lovers among us take them as libel and calumny. I count myself in their ranks and therefore hasten to add that of course there is a legitimate sense in which animals can be said to think and hence to be able . . . to see . . . Not all "organized behavior" is built on linguistic structures. The most that can be claimed is that what might be called "conceptual thinking" is essentially tied to language, and that, for obvious reasons, the central or core concept of what thinking is pertains to conceptual thinking. Thus, our common-sense understanding of what sub-conceptual thinking—e.g. that of babies and animals—consists in, involves viewing them as engaged in "rudimentary" forms of conceptual thinking. We interpret their behaviour using conceptual thinking as a model but qualify this model in *ad hoc* and unsystematic ways which really amount to the introduction of a new notion which is nevertheless labelled "thinking."[30]

In fact, it was not until his last years that Sellars explicitly turned his attention to what he came to call "animal representational systems."[31] Such systems are pre-linguistic, though not pre-symbolic. We shall consider this account shortly—and discover that even such a proto-linguistic system of representation is inessential for perception. What is immediately striking, however, is not only that Sellars could have spent the best part of his career propounding a theory of perception that, by his own admission, is simply not true of perception as such—a situation that also applies to Thomas Reid[32]—but also, and more importantly, that even from the perspective of his later writings, we can attribute perception to non-linguistic animals only in so far as we can see them as engaging in something analogous to linguistic activity. But is our attribution of perception to a baby on seeing it grasp its rattle, or to a dog on seeing it chase a cat, really dependent upon our viewing such creatures as proto-language-users? Animal perception, and our recognition of it, is surely not in *any* sense derivative or secondary.[33] Moreover, bearing in mind that much of what Sellars has argued to be essential to our core concept of thinking—language, self-awareness, grasp of norms, meta-language—seems to be *entirely* absent in languageless creatures, any such recognition by analogy would at best be shaky; whereas it is as clear as daylight that some pre- and non-linguistic animals perceive their environment. This strongly suggests, at least if Sellars's account of our core concept of thinking is at all on the right lines, that in focusing on thinking and concepts we are missing the essence of perception. Having to view young infants and animals as perceivers only on the strength of some analogy between their inner states and language use is one possible price of pairing a high account of conceptuality with the claim that such is essential to perception.

There is, however, another, more heroic reaction to the apparent problem with conceptualism—one that is also to be found among contemporary philosophers. John McDowell, for example, also espouses a "high" account of concepts. To possess a concept is not, for him (any more than for Sellars), merely to have a discriminatory capacity: a genuinely conceptual capacity must be able to be exercised in non-perceptual contexts, it being "essentially something that can be exploited in active thinking—thinking that is open to reflection about its own rational credentials." Indeed, concepts must "be rationally linked into a whole system of concepts and conceptions within which their possessor engages in a continuing activity of adjusting her thinking to experience." Hence, concept possession "implies self-consciousness on the part of the thinking subject."[34] He is a conceptualist in our sense since he, too, insists that concepts are essential for perception: "Experiences have their content by virtue of the fact that conceptual capacities are operative in them."[35] Saddled with the same pair of theses as Sellars, McDowell takes the most un-Sellarsian route of refusing to credit non-linguistic creatures with "experience, in a strict sense."[36] Such creatures do not have "outer experience" or "experience of objective reality." He does, indeed, credit them with a "perceptual sensitivity to the environment," but this does "not amount to awareness of the outer world" and is not "world-representing."[37] Indeed, by implication, no animal has as much as a "glimpse of the world."[38]

One's initial reaction to these apparently outrageous statements should certainly be tempered by noting that in such passages McDowell is echoing Gadamer's distinction between *Welt* and *Umwelt*, "world" and "environment";[39] and so it may be thought that his remarks are not meant in the extreme way I have taken them. Perhaps all that is meant is that animals have no appreciation of the kind of highly structured and meaningful environment that he chooses to call specifically "world." In fact, however, the originally Heideggerian perspective that lies behind Gadamer's distinction between world and environment is simply of no use in the present context.[40] Although there is for Heidegger, as for Gadamer, an enormous difference between us and mere animals, an equally fundamental distinction is that between those entities that merely crop up in the world, like sticks and stones, and those entities that are *alive*. In an early discussion, Heidegger seems, indeed, to imply that the latter is the *more* fundamental distinction: everything that is alive fares *(befindet sich)* somehow, and such "faring" (or "disposition" as it is commonly translated) serves to define the phenomenological sense of being-in-the-world.[41] What is significant here for our purposes is not contradicted by Heidegger's later and more extensive treatment of animal life, in which he distinguishes between sticks and stones as being *weltlos* (worldless), animals as being *weltarm* (poor in world), and humans as being *weltbildend* (world-forming), even though he here states that animals are separated from us by an "abyss," and even questions the propriety of speaking of an animal "*Um*welt" at all, because of its suggestion of "*Welt.*"[42] For despite a possible shift of emphasis, what is consistently presented by Heidegger is an account of a single form of distinctively animal, non-human, lived relatedness to an environment that is possessed *by every living being*, including unicellular organisms.[43] Gadamer, too, ascribes an environment to "everything that is alive."[44] In other words, the issue of consciousness, specifically in the form of the relation between sensation and perception, is not so much as broached. We do not make any progress towards solving the Problem of Perception—a problem, as I emphasized in Chapter 1, that solely concerns conscious, sensory perception—by attributing an environment to an amoeba.[45]

That there is an enormous gulf separating us cognitively and existentially from the lower animals is not to be contested. That we share perception with them, and conscious perception with many of them, also cannot be reasonably denied, however. Heidegger does effectively deny it: "But at bottom the animal has no perception," he writes.[46] Now, doubtless one reason for this claim is that the standard German word for perception is "*Wahrnehmung*"—literally "taking for true"; and there is no *truth* for the animal, according to Heidegger. The fundamental difficulty for his account, however—apart, that is, from his side-step-ping the issue of sensory consciousness—is that Heidegger institutes such a radical separation between human and animal cognition that it is difficult to make any sense of a human being and any animal *perceiv-ing the same physical object*. For whereas we humans have a "comport-ment" *(Verhalten)* towards a "world," animals merely exhibit "behav-iour" *(Benehmen)* in relation to what he eventually characterizes as an encircling "ring" constituted by animal drives.[47] Nothing in the *world* can be an object for any animal. Heidegger does, indeed, distinguish world from "nature": although we encounter nature within the world, inner-worldliness does not belong to the being, or the essence, of na-ture, but is something that devolves upon it when we encounter a world as having a natural stratum—when nature is *revealed*.[48] So although not world, at least nature can exist whether or not *Dasein*—the distinctive sort of being that we humans possess—exists.[49] And, more generally, Heidegger allows an ontical independence of what is *(das Seiende)* from *Dasein*. For although "there is being [*es gibt Sein*]" only when a world occurs meaningfully for *Dasein*, beings themselves *are* whether or not *Dasein*, and hence a world, exists.[50] So perhaps animals can be said to "perceive" the same elements of nature, or the same beings, as we can. Not so. Heidegger's insistence on treating all perceptual, comport-mental, and behavioural contexts as intensional precludes him from al-lowing, or even being able to express, any such thing. Heidegger takes the primary objects of human perception, and, indeed, of all human comportment, to be meanings, or at least meaningful things. Heideg-ger follows Husserl in taking the world to have phenomenological pri-macy over the individual objects that may be encountered within it—quite rightly, in my view. In Heidegger, however, this is interpreted as implying that what is primary is "the meaningful" *(das Bedeutsame)*.[51] All human experience, perception included, is informed by "under-standing," in such a way that everything encountered is taken *as* some-thing that *is (ein Seiendes)*. It is because of this, indeed, that "fundamen-tal ontology" takes the form of a "hermeneutic" of *Dasein* (something that is the primary emphasis in Gadamer). None of this is true of the animal, since nothing is taken *as anything* by them, and least of all as something that *is*.[52] Not surprisingly, Heidegger is not wholly consis-tent in his intensional usage of perceptual verbs. He can speak of ani-mals relating to "the sun," for example, and of something being present

to an animal *as* a mate, or prey.[53] Heidegger does not have the where-
withal within his philosophical framework to make sense of such inevitable judgements.

Heidegger's problems here all stem ultimately from his refusal to accept that there can be any philosophically significant account of human
perception that dips below the level at which human life is distinctively
meaningful. "When things appear," he writes, "we never . . . originally
and really perceive a crowd of sensations—tones and noises, for example; rather, we hear the storm whistling in the chimney, we hear the
three-engine aeroplane, we hear the Mercedes in its immediate contrast with the Volkswagen. Much closer to us than any sensations are
the things themselves. We hear the door slam in the house, and never
hear acoustic sensations or mere sounds."[54] Few would disagree with
what is explicitly said here. The primary thing you will probably notice
about, say, a hammer that you see, is, indeed, that it is *a hammer*—
rather than some mere physical arrangement of matter.[55] Nevertheless,
an important error is being implicitly made. For what is being suggested is that the only way in which sense-experience can be more than
the having of sensations is if it is "suffused" with concepts.[56] Heidegger
contrasts this natural, everyday, "proximal" mode of perception with
what he calls a mere "perceptual cognition" *(vernehmendes Erkennen)*,
which he takes to be the traditional picture of perception, and which he
characterizes as *"ein starres Begaffen"*: a fixed staring, or gawping, at the
world.[57] Heidegger proposes in opposition to this traditional, "theoretical" view of perception an account according to which perception is a
mode of our fundamental *concern with* the world. The objects of such
concern are, however, defined as "gear" *(Zeug)*, which makes sense only
in relation to activities such as manipulation, production, and arrangement that embody references beyond themselves in the form of the "in
order to . . ." In short, our primary relation to the world is seen in terms
of *instrumentality*.[58] Heidegger allows us to say *nothing* about perception that would prescind from such a "circumspect," means-end assessment of situations. There seems to be no medium, for Heidegger, between treating things as "gear" and gawping at them in a wholly passive
manner. Moreover, the latter "perceptual cognition" is seen by him as a
non-original modification of an instrumental involvement with gear.
But must we not already perceive things in order to wonder what use to
put them to? Heidegger poses himself this very question, and retorts

that we must at the very least take things as gear to which we have yet to devise a use[59]—though how we are supposed to try and think of a use for a bird flying through the air, or a star in the sky, is less than evident.[60] I shall not, however, dilate upon the absurdity of all this, but make just two comments. First, there is no reason to deny that traditional accounts of perception have indeed tended to adopt a view of perception as a mere registering of the passing show, nor that such a view is inadequate to the facts. Perhaps, as Heidegger insists, every perceived object is perceived as having some significance or value in relation to the perceiver's life, even if it is only as being irrelevant to a creature's vital concerns. There is certainly no reason to deny that we come into the world innately disposed. Perhaps it is even true, as Heidegger also suggests, that no perception is possible in the absence of some "affect" relating to the object, even if that affect is only a sense of things being unremarkably as they should. The point is that it is not *because* of this that perceptions are perceptual at all. Even if all perception is essentially "engaged," this affords no illumination on how it is that experience can present us with a world with which we are engaged. No such Heideggerian observations achieve, as Heidegger himself believed, the displacement of perception from its *fundamental* role in cognition *or* "comportment" with respect to an objective domain. To the extent that they are correct, they indicate how perception itself is properly to be understood. Secondly, the "hermeneutic" approach to perception not only abolishes the possibility of making any sense of how an animal and I may perceive the same physical object, but also leaves entirely obscure how our supposedly originally all-consuming instrumental interest in things is directly about real physical things at all. We are not primarily aware of auditory sensations when we hear things, I earlier quoted Heidegger as saying. No doubt this is true, if Direct Realism is true; but we shall find no illumination in Heidegger as to how it can possibly be true.

McDowell is in the same predicament. For although he may appear to be less extreme than Heidegger when he writes that "if we share perception with mere animals, then of course we have something in common with them," the common element emerges, on closer inspection, to be nugatory.[61] For he characterizes as a "temptation" the thought that "it must be possible to isolate what we have in common with [animals] by stripping off what is special about us, so as to arrive at a residue that we can recognize as what figures in the perceptual lives of mere animals."[62] Now, one may well have reservations about such an operation of "stripping"; but that there is a common core to human and animal perception must be recognized. If any mere animal is ever a sensing perceiver of the same physical object that we perceive, the intentionality of *their* perceptual experience cannot be dependent upon the exercise of concepts, since, according to McDowell, they lack them. So concepts are not required for the intentionality of conscious perception as such. Now, can it seriously be supposed that the intentionality, the mere world-directedness, of perception in us higher animals has a wholly different basis? That in our case alone it is concepts that ground and explain our ability to hear and see things in the world? Even if every human perception were shot through with concepts, so that any "stripping" would falsify the phenomenology, it still wouldn't be this conceptual dimension that explains how we are able to perceive physical objects *at all*. But that is what needs explaining in the context of our present enquiry. Doubtless my experience of seeing a cat is different from a dog's experience of seeing the same cat; but what makes them both conscious visual perceptions of an entity in the physical world is the same. It is not in virtue of what distinguishes us from mere animals that we are able to perceive normal physical objects at all. It is not because we are spiritual beings that we can perceive, but because we are sentient.

In fact, it is far from clear that McDowell accepts that there is such a thing as true animal sentience at all—any genuine awareness of even an "environment." The only notion of "what it is like" to be such an animal that McDowell allows is one that is exhausted by a merely functional account of an animal's life in terms of biological imperatives and behavioural responses to the environment: "These accounts capture the character of the proto-subjectivity of the creatures in question."[63] From the fact that "we are familiar 'from within' with what it is like to see colours," it is tempting, says McDowell, "to think that this equips us to comprehend a fully subjective fact about what the colour vision of cats is like." This, however, is "just another form of the Myth of the Given," he claims.[64] But it is not. It is just Realism, a rejection of reductive behaviourism, with respect to animal sensory experience.[65]

It is, in fact, astonishing how widespread the at least implicit denial of merely animal consciousness is in current philosophy. It can even be found among philosophers who recognize the non-conceptual nature of perceptual content. For certain philosophers find it impossible wholly to divorce such non-conceptual content from conceptual abilities. Much of the discussion of "non-conceptual content" that has recently taken place in Britain stems from the work of Gareth Evans; and yet he claimed that "our intuitive concept [of conscious experience] requires a subject of experience to have *thoughts* . . . [W]e arrive at conscious perceptual experience when sensory input . . . serves as the input to a *thinking, concept-applying, and representing system.*"[66] Once again it would seem to follow that we cannot attribute conscious states to "brutes" (as non-linguistic animals are often termed by philosophers), since few of us are willing to attribute to them concept application and thought. That is what makes them "brutes." Our common conception, as expressed by Schopenhauer, is, by contrast, that such creatures are sentient, and yet pre-conceptual; they are possessed of *aisthesis*, yet lack *nous* and *dianoia*. Most of us believe that brutes perceive and feel, without them needing more highfalutin mental machinery waiting to be caused to operate. Contrary to Evans, it most definitely is *not* an "intuitive concept of conscious experience" that "requires a subject of experience to have thoughts."

There is one concept in particular that a great many philosophers find it impossible to dissociate from perceptual consciousness and, sometimes, sentience. This is the concept of *self.* The fundamental idea here derives ultimately from Kant. As was mentioned in the initial survey of reasons why one might embrace conceptualism, Kant's principal interest in this area was in the synthetic unity of perceptual consciousness. Without the unifying force of concepts exercised in judgement, perceptions "would be . . . without an object, and nothing but a blind play of representations—that is, less than a dream."[67] On closer inspection it turns out that the unifying effect of conceptualization derives from the unity of self-consciousness: "For this unity of consciousness would be impossible if the mind, in cognition of the manifold, could not itself become conscious of the identity of the function through which it synthetically connects it [namely, the manifold] in one cognition."[68] Such synthetic activity, in order to confer unity, must "have before its eyes the identity of its operation."[69] In other words, there can be no perception without self-consciousness.[70] Immediately after Kant this idea was taken up and emphasized even more by Fichte, and it can be seen to run throughout German Idealism and the various later schools of neo-Kantianism and neo-Hegelianism.[71] Here, for example, is T. H. Green again: "Primitive experience . . . involve[s] consciousness of a self on the one hand and of a thing on the other, as well as a relation between the two . . . The idea is a perception, or consciousness of a thing, as opposed to a sensation proper or affection of the bodily organs. Of the perception, again, there is an idea, i.e. a consciousness by the man, in the perception, of himself in negative relation to the thing that is his object, and this consciousness . . . must be taken to go along with the perceptive act itself. No less than this indeed can be involved in any act that is to be the beginning of knowledge at all. It is the minimum of possible thought or intelligence, and the thinking man, looking for this beginning in the earliest experience of the individual human animal, must needs find it there."[72] Well, if this is what thinking and judging involves, we can dismiss the suggestion that they are essentially involved in perception. The idea that mere perception presupposes a capacity for such sophisticated conceptual activity, that *self-consciousness* is required for it, is just too paradoxical to be worth exploring. It is, as Williams James says, "a perfectly wanton assumption, and not the faintest shadow of reason exists for supposing it true."[73] Mere animals, or some of them, are conscious, but not self-conscious. At the very least it is a metaphysical possibility that this should be so.[74]

THE PRECEDING line of argument against conceptualism will perhaps be criticized in two contrary ways. The first is that considerable weight has so far been placed on the supposed fact of animal consciousness. But is this really a sufficiently hard datum on which to base the entire case against conceptualism? There certainly are not wanting numerous philosophers who more or less explicitly contest it. Now, although I do feel that the denial of conscious perception to a creature such as a dog is sufficiently preposterous to be of dialectical weight, I do not wish to base the entire case against conceptualism on this point. For reflection shows that perception is more primordial than conceptualization even for normal, adult human beings. The world is already there for us perceptually before we engage in anything that might reasonably be called conceptualization. So I shall argue.

The other objection is that the resistance to conceptualism that has been expressed so far has been focusing on excessively exalted accounts of conceptualization. Perhaps we can agree on a sufficiently "low" account of concept-possession, so that it would be far from implausible to suggest that even perceptual experience, in all its forms, essentially involves the exercise of concepts. For do not animal psychologists commonly attribute certain concepts and powers of "abstraction" to various species of animal? If there is anything to such research, surely there is a "lower" account of conceptualization in the offing that can be appealed to at this point. I shall argue that "low" versions of conceptualism are, depending on what precise form they take, either incoherent, or empty and unilluminating. In either case, they cannot serve to buttress Direct Realism. Since any such "lower" account, being weaker than any "high" theory of conceptualization, is entailed by the latter, this negative judgement rebounds back on to any such "high" theory *even when restricted to mature human beings.* In short, conceptualism in any form is either false or worthless.

The only "low" account of what it is to possess a concept that I think it worth discussing is one that views it as simply a matter of possessing a recognitional capacity.[75] Brian Loar has recently put the matter as follows: "Given a normal background of cognitive capacities, certain recognitional or discriminative dispositions suffice for having specific recognitional concepts, which is just to say, suffice for the capacity to make judgements that depend specifically on those recognitional dispositions. Simple such judgements have the form: the object (event, situation) *a* is *one of that kind,* where the cognitive backing for the predicate is just a recognitional disposition, i.e. a disposition to classify objects (events, situations) together."[76] In this passage the terms "discriminatory capacity" and "recognitional capacity" are treated as equivalent. It is, however, useful to distinguish between the two. For perception affords us extraordinarily acute powers of discrimination. There are, for example, hundreds of thousands of different colours that average human beings can differentiate (where a difference in "colour" is taken to be any difference in hue, saturation, or brightness). Such powers of discrimination far surpass powers of *recognition.* I can, for example, distinguish two shades of red on a certain occasion, and yet be wholly unsure, when shown one of them again very shortly afterwards, which of the two shades I am again perceiving.[77] I have claimed that conceptualism is either false or empty. The suggestion that conceptualization is no more than a discriminatory capacity constitutes an empty trivialization of the notion of a concept. If *this* were all that is meant by saying that perception involves concepts, no one would ever have contested the view—since, obviously, you have to be able to discriminate some things if you are to perceive at all. Moreover, this meagre claim will not help us to sustain Direct Realism. If the conceptualist approach to perception is to be sufficiently interesting to warrant our attention, it must hold that the exercise of a concept is at least the exercise of a *recognitional* capacity—that to possess a concept is to be in a position to *classify* objects. Concepts relate to *kinds*, and to possess them we need a distinctive sensitivity to the fact that a thing falls within that kind. So, from now on, we are to understand conceptualism as appealing to recognitional capacities.

Although at the beginning of this chapter I said that I would be attacking conceptualism even in its weakest form, it is worth noting that the present suggestion fails to embody the strong form of conceptualism that is actually required at this stage of our enquiry: namely, that every element in perceptual awareness involves conceptualization. For the distinction between discrimination and recognition shows that there are determinate aspects to perception that escape the conceptual (or recognitional) net. The "just noticeable difference," as psychologists call it, between two adjacent shades of colour so escapes, for example. John McDowell has contested this, by claiming that we always have at our disposal concepts of wholly determinate *shades* of colour.[78] McDowell thinks that although our grasp of such concepts is very short lived, they enable one "to embrace shades of colour within one's conceptual thinking with the very same determinateness with which they are presented in one's visual experience." Now, although we do indeed possess concepts of absolutely determinate shades of colour, these are not recognitional capacities, for every one of them requires, for its exercise, that it be "anchored" by the presentation of a determinate shade of colour in one's current experience. Such anchoring is lost with the loss of the presentation, because recognitional capacities are less finegrained than discriminatory ones. So grasp of the absolutely determinate content afforded by the former is not even "short lived," if this means, as it must, having a short life beyond actual perception of the anchoring shade. Staring at a ripe tomato, I can, no doubt, exercise the concept of *this very shade* of red. Such a concept is, however, qua concept, useless. Take away the tomato, and I cannot exercise it, since I shall have lost the absolutely determinate grip on the shade in question. It is also the case, of course, that not every perceiver, indeed not every normal adult human perceiver, necessarily possesses the concept of a shade of colour.

Returning to our weaker target, an immediate problem with the suggestion that perception essentially involves the exercise of recognitional capacities is that, taken at face value, it is simply false. We can perceive something and wholly fail to classify it, fail to perceive that it is any particular *kind* of thing at all. Striking instances of this are provided by patients suffering from certain forms of agnosia.[79] When shown everyday objects and asked to identify them, such patients commonly express ignorance. One patient, for example, replied either "Not sure" or "I don't know" when shown a cigarette lighter, a toothbrush, a comb, and a key.[80] Another patient, when shown a picture of a carrot, replied, "I have not even the glimmerings of an idea. The bottom point seems solid and the other bits are feathery. It does not seem to be logical unless it is some sort of a brush."[81] These patients could certainly *see* the objects in question; for one thing, they could produce fairly accurate drawings of them. Moreover, the disabilities of such subjects are not merely verbal, since unlike aphasics they are unable to give any non-verbal, gestural indication of the kind of object perceived. These people simply do not recognize the objects they see. As H.-L. Teuber has put it, they have "a normal percept that has somehow been stripped of its meaning."[82] Hermann Munk, one of the early investigators of the phenomenon, termed it "Seelenblindheit": mind-blindness. We do not, however, need to turn to such unusual cases in order to make the point. For to deny that we can perceive something without classifying it is to deny that a question such as "What is that?", uttered in a perceptual context, can ultimately have any meaning. Such conceptual ignorance can, for any of us, concern even the perceived object's most fundamental nature. I can see something and be wholly unsure whether it is even animate or inanimate. When you think about it, the suggestion that you have to recognize (or seem to recognize) everything you perceive is absurd. Indeed, it is incoherent: what about the *first time* you perceived a certain sort of thing?

Perhaps, however, it will be suggested that we are looking towards the wrong kind of concepts here. The foregoing criticism, it may be said, does little more than repeat the point made at the beginning of this chapter, that someone can see a typewriter without possessing the concept of one. Conceptualism does not need to credit a perceiver with conceptual appreciation of the essential kind to which an object belongs. A much more plausible claim is that a perceiver needs only to conceptually represent the *perceptible features* of any object that is perceived. Such a suggestion fares little better, however. For classifying as such presupposes not only that there are things to classify, but also that such things are already cognitively available to us. Conceptualization is not required for perception since *it is perception that vouchsafes to us the original cognitive access to the entities in the world on which we can exercise such classificatory abilities.* I do not possess (or fully possess) the concept *vermilion,* for I do not possess the ability to distinguish vermilion from non-vermilion things.[83] All this word means to me is some shade of red, and if I were to attempt to identify vermilion-coloured things, doubtless I should include a number of scarlet items. The best I can do, indeed, is exclude things that are not red. It is not just that I am not a master of the *word* "vermilion." I am, rather, simply not attuned to that particular shade of red. No doubt I could come to acquire this concept. But if so, it is only because I can now already see vermilion things and because vermilion things already now *look different* to me from things, even red things, that are not vermilion. Perhaps, at the moment, I do not see vermilion things *as* vermilion; but if so, I can see vermilion things that look vermilion to me without seeing them "as" vermilion. Possessing a concept is a matter of being attuned to relevant samenesses and differences, but lacking such attunement in no way means that such differing features are not perceptually registered. Indeed, they must be so registered if we are to be in a position to classify anything.

It is, to be sure, possible to train subjects to classify types of object even when the basis of classification is unknown to the subjects themselves. Chicken-sexers are a famous example of this—though an extreme and unusual one, since here it seems that it is impossible perceptually to isolate and recognize the features of chicks that are the basis of the discrimination. (No doubt this is why the chicken-sexer's ability is far from accurate.) In more typical cases, those features, the presence and absence of which determine the classification, are apparent and could in principle be attended to. It is just that they are non-obvious, and so are not in practice used consciously as classificatory indices.

What such cases indicate is that it would be too strong to claim that, universally, if a perceptually based recognitional or classificatory capacity can be acquired, items in the relevant class must already appear different to the subjects from items that fall outside the class. Such a concession does not, however, undermine the point that is here at issue, which is not that any perceptually based classificatory capacity must relate to features that are anyway perceptually evident to the subject, but that a classificatory capacity is brought to bear on objects that themselves are already perceptually available.[84] You need already to be able to perceive things in relation to which you are going to develop a perceptually based classificatory, or even recognitional, capacity. Did you recognize and classify the *first* sound, or colour, or smell you ever perceived? And in virtue of what? Some kind of anamnesis?

This fact undermines Wilfrid Sellars's eventual attempt, alluded to above, to de-sophisticate his account of perception by focusing on the notion of an animal "representational system." Sellars quite rightly sees that if an animal is to be credited with even an analogue of a concept, it must be on the basis of more than mere discriminatory behaviour—for otherwise the essential classificatory aspect of conceptualization would be wholly lost. So, for one thing, a representational system is a *system* of representation. This leads Sellars to say of a rat that has been trained to jump at panels with varieties of triangles painted on them—the sort of experiment that psychologists discuss in terms of "abstraction"—that "we should be careful about concluding that simply by virtue of its training the rat has acquired an ur-concept of a triangle . . . [A] much greater degree of integration of responses to triangles *as* triangles into the rat's [representational system] is required before we can appropriately say that the rat has even the most primitive concept of a triangle. Primitive inference would also be involved."[85] Doubtless this is true; but the problem is that even if the rat has only reached the stage of jumping at panels exhibiting triangles, it must be able to *see* the panels and the triangles. Indeed, it must have been able to see them before even that training. Such training hardly improves a rat's vision!

Am I then suggesting that a subject can perceive something and yet not perceive it *as* anything? In fact, although the "perceiving-as" locution has, at least since an influential paper by Godfrey Vesey, become something of a term of art among philosophers, its precise meaning is far from settled. If all that is meant by the slogan "all seeing is seeing as" is that in order to see something it must look a certain way to the subject, the proposition is indeed easily accepted. More, however, is often packed into the notion—specifically the idea that "seeing as" involves "recognizing as," "classifying as," "conceptualizing as." We have ourselves already seen the slide in Sellars from perceiving, to perceiving as, to perceptual taking, to perceiving-that and conceptualization (or, at least, ur-conceptualization). But this is a mistake, as Sellars's rat shows. Fred Dretske, who has done as much any anyone to combat conceptualism over recent years, also points out that many species of animal that can be led to "abstract" the *larger than* relation holding between two objects find it impossible to abstract the *intermediate size* relation between three objects. But this can hardly mean that such an animal cannot see three differently sized objects in such a way that they look differently sized to it.[86] If all that is meant by saying that a subject sees a certain rectangle as intermediate in size is that it looks smaller than one and larger than another rectangle, then the rectangle is indeed seen "as" intermediate; but for this no concept is required—not even the concepts larger and smaller, since such objects must first look differently sized if any classificatory ability is to have a chance of being developed. The notions of perceiving, and of things appearing in determinate ways, have work to do at this pre-conceptual level. This is brought out nicely by an example of Michael Ayers. If we consider two subjects looking at a trapezium, one of whom does not possess the concept of a trapezium, we need to be able to express the fact that the trapezium may *look* exactly the same to the two of them, that it may, indeed, look trapezoid to both of them.[87] We need to be able to do justice to this fact because we need to be able to distinguish both of these observers from a third who *misperceives* the same object so that it does not even appear trapezoid to him. As Ayers says, such cases "very well illustrate the worthlessness of the notion of 'concepts' to a philosophical account of what perception is."[88]

At this point it may be objected that the claim that perception essentially involves a recognitional capacity does not necessarily mean that I recognize everything I perceive. A more plausible claim is that every perception at least *gives* me such a capacity if I do not already possess it. Although I did not recognize the first colour I saw, in seeing it I acquired the ability to recognize it again. Now, the idea cannot be that I acquired the capacity *as a result* of perceiving—for that would leave the initial ability to perceive as obscure as it ever was. The idea must be, rather, that perception itself *constitutes* your acquisition of the capacity, if you did not possess it before. Although I may see something vermilion and not acquire a recognitional capacity specifically with respect to that shade of colour, surely there must be *something* in what I perceive of the object that I can recognize on some future occasion. Moreover, the claim would go, my acquiring such a ability was partly constitutive of the experience being perceptual. In order not to rule out unusual but presumably possible cases of perceivers with *extremely* bad memories, such recognitional capacities had better be possibly very short-lived—and, because of the "drift" involved in recognition, as opposed to discrimination, somewhat course-grained. But that said, the idea is not that implausible. This suggestion in effect brings us back to the third, Kantian reason in favour of conceptualism that was mentioned at the beginning of this chapter, and it deserves serious consideration.

One of Kant's signal achievements was to point out something that in retrospect cannot but seem a glaring omission in earlier, and especially empiricist, accounts of experience—an omission that is equally glaring in certain more recent accounts that, like the sense-datum theory, are effectively uninfluenced by Kant. The omission consists in failing to address the question of what is involved in being aware of something *through time*. Although Locke raised questions about the nature of the personal identity that relates us to our more or less distant experiential past, and although Hume worried over the nature of the bond that bundles impressions and ideas together to form a self, each took the notion of "perceiving" an idea or impression as being simple and unproblematic—as simple, indeed, as the ideas and impressions themselves. The problem of the *temporality of experience* as such simply did not surface for them. For experience is temporal in a way that goes beyond the way in which something like a stone may be said to be temporal—that is to say, merely existing in time and persisting, albeit perhaps only briefly, through time. With experience we need to recognize the wholly distinct fact of *lived* or *phenomenological time*. Kant put his finger on this vital issue in the following well-known passage:

> Now it is clear that when I draw a line in thought, or think of the time from one morning to the next, or even if I only represent a certain number to myself, necessarily I must first grasp one of

these manifold representations in thought after the other. If, however, I always let the preceding one (the first part of the line, the preceding part of the time, or the unities represented one after another) drop out of the thoughts by forgetting them, and never reproduced them while proceeding to the following ones, no whole representation, and none of the aforementioned thoughts, indeed not even the purest and primary fundamental representations of space and time, could ever arise.[89]

He goes on to claim that even this is not enough for the unity and coherence implied in awareness of an object: "Without consciousness that what we are thinking is the very same as what we were thinking a moment before, all reproduction in the series of representations would be futile . . . If, in counting, I were to forget that the unities that now hover before my senses have been added together by me one after another, I should not recognize the production of the quantity through this successive addition of one to one, and nor, therefore, the number; for this concept consists simply in the consciousness of this unity of the synthesis . . . For it is this consciousness that unifies the manifold that has been successively united and then reproduced." Even though Kant is here arguing for conceptualism, and is primarily interested in theoretical thought rather than simple perception, and despite the fact that the details of the story are doubtless unacceptable, Kant here shows up the naiveté of most empiricist accounts of experience.[90] The philosopher who above all has taken this Kantian point seriously, while yet avoiding conceptualism and intellectualism, is Edmund Husserl. For although early in his career Husserl could fall into treating the synthetic achievements involved in experience in a "Kantian," intellectualist way, patterning his theory on his own account of linguistic comprehension, he increasingly came to see the need to distinguish what he calls "active synthesis"—that which is indeed an expression of the "spontaneity" of conceptual understanding, and which alone Kant recognized—from *passive synthesis*.[91] It is the latter we need to understand if we are to give the distinctive intentionality of perception its proper due.[92] Husserl speaks of the experienced present moment as being constituted in part by "retention" and "protention."[93] Retention is not recollection—the recuperation of a past that has slipped from our grasp—nor is it strictly perception. It is, rather, a quasi-perceptual awareness of the immediate past as slipping away behind us—a slippage that is correlative to the lived present pushing forwards into the future. Such a future is opened up phenomenologically by protention, which stands to anticipation as retention stands to recollection, and is a sheer openness to the new. Such retentions and protentions are not mere adjuncts to an otherwise integrally constituted present; for such a present, as a lived present, is possible only in virtue of such retentions and protentions, because of the necessity that any experience have temporal *breadth*. Indeed, it is because of this fact that one may have reservations about the appropriateness of the term "synthesis" in this connection. For a synthesis is usually thought of as a bringing together of things that may otherwise exist apart. This is precisely what is not true here. We are not dealing here with mere association as we find it, for example, in Hume. Rather, the whole approach embodies the recognition that a Humean "impression," construed as both wholly self-subsistent, atomic, and yet given to consciousness, is a nonsensical notion.

The crucial point to recognize in all this is that *a succession of appearances does not of itself amount to the appearance of succession*—for any point in the latter presupposes that we in some sense retain a grasp of what has just occurred in the unfolding succession. If such a grasp is lost, there would be no experience of a succession as such. Even when we consider not a succession of objects, but the continuous perception of a single unchanging one, the same point holds. For just as a changing appearance does not entail an appearance of change, a persisting appearance does not entail an appearance of persistence—for once again the experience of the elapsing of time has been entirely omitted from the account. We need to do justice to these facts. Moreover, it seems that this cannot be done without crediting the subject of experiences with at least a minimal grasp of samenesses and differences in sensory fields through time: in other words, with recognitional capacities.

I do not believe that this claim can be gainsaid. One may well have reservations about the appropriateness of regarding the minimal cognitive achievements that are here in question as exercises of *concepts;* but that is perhaps a matter of no great moment. Of much greater significance is the fact that, even if all the earlier claims are accepted, it sheds no light at all on the intentionality of perception. This is because the kind of passive synthesis in question here is necessary *for any experience as such*, whether it takes the form of perceptual consciousness or the mere having of sensations. A literally punctual experience is inconceivable. Any experience, however brief, must occupy some span of time—indeed of lived time. It is not that we need a present retention of the immediate past only for such relatively sophisticated operations as addition; we need it for the very possibility of any experience, however rudimentary. Even the most obscure feeling, even the least "objectified" sensation, in so far as it possesses experienced duration, requires a synthetic grasp of the flowing away of the immediate past of experience. So the trouble with our latest version of conceptualism, construed as appealing to recognitional abilities, possibly acquired through sense-experience itself, is not so much that it is false, as that, if it is true, it will apply to the mere having of sensations. The sort of passive synthesis that is required for the lived temporality of experience does not suffice for that experience to be as of an objective realm. Perhaps my first experience of pins and needles put me in a position to recognize that type of sensation again; but that does not render the experience perceptual, whereas we have turned to conceptualism to elucidate the intentionality of perceptual experience.

There is, however, one final form that conceptualism can take—one that is also essentially Kantian in inspiration. For all the concepts that we have considered so far have been *empirical* concepts. Perhaps what we need to recognize is the operation in perception of *categorial* concepts: those definitive of objectivity. Wilfrid Sellars, for one, finally endorses this view. "In a limiting case," he writes, "the sortal is simply *physical object.*" He continues:

> To eliminate *specific* implications concerning what is not perceived *of* an object need not (and, indeed, cannot) be to eliminate *generic* or *categorial* implications. This, of course, was Kant's brilliant insight. Thus, the perceptual taking *This now occurring yellow flash over there* where "flash" does not carry with it the specific sortal "of lightening", has no *specific* implications concerning future developments . . . Even so, it implies that *something* has happened *before now* and that *something* will happen *after now*, in places other than *there*. Indeed, if Kant is right, it implies that the flash belongs to a world of changing and interacting things, a spatio-temporal-causal system. In the absence of Kant's insight, the categorial sortal (physical) object (or event), which remains after all the

above pruning, is treated as though it were the mere notion of a *something* (I know not what?), or, as I shall put it, an *item*, that has sensible "qualities". Thus the idea that perceptual takings can be appropriately *minimal* and yet carry rich categorial commitments was lost to the empiricist tradition.[94]

Even agnosics and neonates will, therefore, conceptualize their environment in terms of objectively existing entities; and since such categorial concepts will presumably be deemed innate, no incoherence is involved in the suggestion that they are omnipresent in perception. All problems for conceptualism seem to have been solved.

I said at the beginning of this discussion that the idea that perception essentially involves concepts would be found to be either false or empty. This Kantian suggestion is empty. For all it does is assert that perception, unlike mere sensation, is objective. We have as yet been given no understanding of how this can be so. We want to know what it is about perceptual experience that allows spatio-temporal physical objects to appear to us. For Kant himself, this was a function of understanding, a faculty that animals lack. And the argument for the necessary applicability of categories of understanding rests crucially on our ability to think of ourselves as subjects, again something not true of animals. This at least is a positive account, though false. In the absence of some such account, the suggestion is wholly empty. We have, in effect, returned to Reid's natural magic. Rather than talking airily about the exercise of concepts of objectivity on the occasion of sensory experience, what is required of an illuminating perceptual theory is that we pay attention to the specific sensory character of perceptual experience to see how it differs from the mere having of sensations. *In virtue of what* does perception exhibit its admitted objectivity? This fundamental question will be addressed in the final two chapters of Part I.

What, in the light of these considerations, are we to make of the three reasons for thinking that concepts must be implicated in perception, given at the beginning of this chapter? Two of them—the Kantian one concerning synthesis, and the idea that perceiving "as" involves concepts—have been covered. The only remaining one—that thought does seem to be immediately directed to its objects, so that if perception features such cognitive directedness, it too can be seen as immediately directed to normal objects in the environment—is at most a recommendation to explore an idea further. It suggests one way in which Direct Realism might be true. If, however, the suggestion founders upon closer inspection, as it has, it must be rejected. Indeed, the very idea that we shall learn much about perception by turning to the distinctively different cognitive achievement of thinking, hoping to learn about *aisthesis* from a consideration of *dianoia*, is, on reflection, bizarre. Such a proposal almost guarantees that we shall lose sight of what is distinctive about perception.

Taking Stock

4

OVER THE PAST couple of chapters we have covered a considerable amount of ground in our search for an acceptable account of the nature of perceptual consciousness. In terms of our single, central interest in discovering a way of answering the Argument from Illusion, however, we must recognize that we have got precisely nowhere. The possibility that sensory experience should give us a direct awareness of the physical world is as opaque as ever. About all we have achieved so far is a recognition of how *not* to analyze perception if we are to defend Direct Realism. Nevertheless, we can put these negative findings to use by fashioning from them certain fundamental criteria that any acceptable analysis of perception must meet. We must, in the first place, find an account of perceptual consciousness that does not, like the dual component theory, attempt to do justice to its intentional, world-directed character by bringing in some cognitive faculty external to sensory experience itself. Secondly, we need an account of perception that makes no essential reference to thinking or conceptualization in order to clarify the possibility of direct perceptual contact with the physical world, even if this does not take the form of a dual component analysis of perception. Thirdly, an acceptable account of perceptual consciousness will not represent it as essentially embodying an appreciation of some causal interaction between the subject and the environment. This third criterion is actually distinct from the second. For although at the start of the previous chapter I presented "causalism" as a particular form of the dual component approach to perception, thereby construing the supposed causality-invoking element in perceptual consciousness as taking the form of thinking about, or conceptualizing, our experience as being caused in a certain way, it is possible to analyse perception as involving some sort of non-conceptual appreciation of causality. For although T. H. Green, one of the causalists considered earlier, can characterize perception as "a complex work of thought, successively detaching felt things from the 'flux' of feelings," Schopenhauer, by contrast, stressed that the appreciation of causality in perception is not one that is "discursive, reflective, *in abstracto*, by means of concepts and words . . . ; but one that is intuitive and wholly immediate."[1] And in our own day John Searle and Michael Ayers have followed a similar line.[2] Given the findings of the previous chapter, this is doubtless to be seen as an improvement on the overly intellectualistic form that causalism may take. Nevertheless, my earlier treatment suffices, I believe, to discredit causalism in whatever form it may be presented. For it is simply phenomenologically false that perceptual consciousness, in all its possible forms, necessarily involves any "appreciation" of our causally interacting with an environment, conceptual or not. The following therefore emerges as the necessary form that any acceptable analysis of perception must take: Certain sensory states are internally, intrinsically directed to normal objects, prior to the offices of conceptualization, and independently of an appreciation of causality. There is something about the character of certain sense-fields themselves that sustains such a non-conceptual intentionality. It is our task to discover what this something is.

That an acceptable theory of perception should meet these criteria of adequacy is hardly a new view in the history of our subject. Indeed, it was philosophical orthodoxy before the rise of the "New Way of Ideas" in the seventeenth century. St. Thomas Aquinas's account of perception, for example, the general form of which dates back to Aristotle— according to which one is intentionally directed to worldly objects by a sensory image that immaterially embodies a sensible "form" or "species"—self-consciously abides by these constraints.[3] When St. Thomas writes, for example, that "sense is cognitive because it is receptive of species without matter," he implies that our senses *themselves* are competent to direct us intentionally to the world, independently of the offices of the understanding or intellect.[4] Understanding is required only for that more sophisticated cognitive achievement, *intellection*, which among animals is unique to man, and which has kinds or universals as its objects. By the senses we are acquainted only with individuals.[5] Moreover, sense-experience is supposed by St. Thomas to give us direct awareness of physical individuals. A sense-image is not *what (quod)* we experience, but that *by which (qua* or *secundum quam)* we experience perceptible objects in the surrounding world.[6]

The philosophical context in which such a medieval attempt at a Direct Realist theory of perception was fashioned is, however, one that is separated from us by what is arguably the single most radical switch of perspective that philosophy has ever seen—a switch that took place in the seventeenth century and had a profound influence on accounts of perception. For a medieval philosopher, the most fundamental metaphysical opposition was between matter and form.[7] From the seventeenth century onwards that opposition was replaced, for all but a few materialists, by that between matter and mind (or "spirit"). This later view, working as it does with a simple opposition between two distinct substantial natures, has an immediate consequence for cognition: only that which is, or at least involves, an operation of an immaterial mind is in any sense cognitive. The view that holds matter and form in opposition, however, can make sense of different levels of immateriality, since matter is not, on this view, a substance, or a nature, but an indeterminate potentiality. The nearest equivalent to the modern idea of matter that we find in the Middle Ages is that of a corporeal substance whose qualities are limited to those definitive of the four elements. Many corporeal things, however, have "active principles" that cannot be accounted for in terms of the qualities of such "inferior bodies," which are, in general, "material dispositions for the substantial forms of natural bodies."[8] There is thus a hierarchy of forms, and "the nobler the form, the more it dominates corporeal matter, and the less it is immersed in it, and the more it exceeds it by its operation or power."[9] This is relevant to the philosophy of perception, since sense-perception was viewed as involving the *immaterial* reception of form in *corporeal* sense-faculties: "Sensitive powers . . . receive the forms of things in a bodily organ."[10] It was in this way that the medievals attempted to embody in their theories a recognition of the intentional directedness of the senses themselves, prior to any activity of the intellect. After the seventeenth century, however, such a notion of an immaterial operation of a material organ could not but seem unintelligible, something that is demonstrated with particular clarity by writers of this time who, while profoundly influenced by Descartes, yet retain an essentially Aristotelian approach to cognition—such as Kenelme Digby and John Sergeant. To the extent that the view that sense-perception is a function of corporeal faculties lived on in the seventeenth century—as indeed it did[11]—the following conclusion was unavoidable: the senses, of themselves, are thoroughly non-cognitive. "For phantasms beasts may indeed have," wrote John Sergeant, "they being no more but effluviums emitted from other bodies, and received by the portals of the senses into the brain; where the animal spirits stand readily waiting to move the brute, according as those tinctures are agreeable, or disagreeable to the compound."[12] The result is that for perception, which is genuine cognition of the world, we need to bring in a different, specifically mental operation to supplement the mere play of sensory images. *What we find, in short, is the birth of the dual component theory.*[13] It will come as no surprise, therefore, to find sensations now spoken of as "signs" that the mind has to interpret in order for perception to occur: "If we will compare the notion in our understanding," writes Digby, "with the signs which beating in our fancy do beget those notions; we shall find, that these are but barely signs: and do not in their own nature express, either the notions they raise, or the things they are signs of."[14] One could hardly wish for a clearer anticipation of Thomas Reid's account of perception and cognition. The idea that thought, or conceptualization, is necessary for even perception of the physical world is now firmly in place; and even the monistic variant of conceptualism that we considered in Chapter 2 emerged as a possibility only after this time. In either form, the appeal to conceptualization to explicate the intentionality of sense-experience is a modern phenomenon, and, as I have suggested, totally wrong-headed. What all this indicates is not, to be sure, that we should simply return to some medieval theory of perception. It does indicate, however, that if we are to vindicate Direct Realism, we need to return to the general view that the senses themselves are intentional, and to fashion anew an account of how we can be acquainted with the physical world by the senses.

This is no mean task because of the following fact: *sensory experience is not necessarily intentional in character.* The dual component theory was at least right about that. If sensations necessarily gave us an awareness of normal physical objects, and if we could understand why this was so, our search for an adequate account of perceptual consciousness would be at an end. If, however, there is no such necessity, we are faced with the following perplexing task: to explain why sensory experience is sometimes intentional and sometimes not, without bringing in the offices of some distinct, non-sensory faculty—without, in short, reverting to the dual component theory. Sense-experience itself must be capable of being intrinsically, and yet not essentially, intentional in character. In Chapter 5 I shall present an analysis of perceptual consciousness that attempts to meet this demand. In the rest of the present chapter, I shall argue for the premise that is now causing us such problems: that sense-experience does not necessarily constitute even putative awareness of normal objects.

One class of sensations that are commonly regarded as being non-intentional is that of bodily sensations. These are not, it is commonly held, "of" anything: they have no object distinct from themselves. If this view is taken, then, if "perceptual" sensations are supposed to be intrinsically intentional in character, we have a radical bifurcation within the class of sensations that cries out for an explanation. Perhaps, however, such a view of bodily sensation, though common, is mistaken. Indeed, in recent years an increasingly large number of philosophers have held that even bodily sensations are intentional and object-directed. Such sensations are not, indeed, directed towards the environment, but they are directed towards the "external world" as philosophers usually understand this term: for they are directed towards our bodies. To suffer pain, on this view, is to be aware of a part of one's body being disordered or damaged in some way. Michael Ayers, for example, asserts that "to have or feel a pain in the left foot is to have a certain sort of sensory awareness of one's left foot."[15] Echoing Clark's account of perceptual sensation, we could say that the objective reference is achieved indexically in virtue of the occurrence of the sensation in a certain part of our "body image."

Now, this suggestion cannot sensibly be that in having bodily sensations we are aware of our body as possessing a feature in a way that is specifiable independently of the sensations themselves. It is not that having, say, a toothache necessarily involves us being aware of our tooth in a way that we could be even if we had never had toothache. In order to have any plausibility, the idea must be, rather, that the toothache itself may be our first cognitive access to our tooth, and that what it reveals of the tooth, or at least how it reveals it, is different from any non-sensory representation of some state of disorder. But what exactly is attributed to our tooth when we experience a toothache? The suggestion that it is *damaged* attributes far too sophisticated a notion, and one that is, moreover, independent of what it is like to feel toothache. We require an attribution that does not go beyond the felt character of that sensation. Perhaps it is some sort of intuitive awareness of something being amiss or untoward. But what, then, should we regard as being revealed by the enormous variety of bodily sensations that are not painful? What is it about our bodies that we aware of when we feel pins and needles, nausea, light-headedness, and so on? In fact we are on a wild goose chase here. What, if anything, it is about the tooth that we are aware of when we feel toothache is just that it hurts! Phenomenologically it is the pain itself that is attributed to a part of the body, just as it is phenomenal colour that we naively attribute to physical objects. Nevertheless, the suggestion remains that such experiences constitute a form of perception. Even if what is attributed is pain itself, what it is attributed *to* is our body—which, as a physical object, counts for philosophical purposes as part of the "external world." Bodily sensation is perception of our own bodies "from within."

Whatever the merits of this suggestion, it does not, at least without considerable supplementation, help us in our current project. For although bodily sensation may have an intrinsic reference to the "external world" in the form of our physical bodies, it does not have a reference to the environment. So even if sensation does not divide inexplicably into intentional and wholly non-intentional varieties, it does inexplicably divide into those that are and those that are not directed to the physical environment beyond our bodies. If we are not to settle for Reid's natural magic, we need to be told more. Moreover, and perhaps more significantly, even if bodily sensations give us an immediate awareness of our bodies, we do not attribute "continued existence" to the bodily states of affairs that are thereby revealed. This would be true only if what we attributed to the body were some disordered state that could persist even though we ceased to feel it. This would, however, mean attributing to any subject that can feel pain a grasp of a notion of disorder that is independent of pain itself—one that would, therefore, be conceptual, not peculiarly sensory, in nature. Because of this, bodily

sensations must still be seen as failing to present their objects as possessed of any of the characteristics definitive of objectivity that were
spelt out at the beginning of Chapter 2. How, then, do so-called perceptual sensations manage to achieve this?

One difference between perceptual and bodily sensation may, however, suggest itself as obvious. This is a difference for which there is no
commonly agreed term, but which is phenomenologically evident: the
fact that bodily sensations, unlike perceptual sensations, have a certain
"feel" to them. There is a great oddity, to say the least, in speaking, as is
common in certain quarters, of all sensations as "raw feels"; for it does
not literally *feel* like anything to have a visual experience of something
looking red. It is, to be sure, "like something" to enjoy such an experience; but it is hardly a "feel." So, the suggestion is that bodily sensations are feelings, perceptual sensations are not.[16] In fact, however, this
criterion fails to serve its intended purpose, for we *perceive* heat and
cold, and yet the sensations involved here, though perceptive of things
beyond our bodies, involve "feeling."[17]

However we may eventually distinguish bodily from perceptual sensations, the most important point to see at this stage is that neither is
necessarily intentional in character: "bodily" sensations do not necessarily give us an awareness of our bodies, and sensations of the type that
can be perceptual are not necessarily so. Let us begin with "bodily"
sensations. We shall be exploring this topic in greater detail in the following chapter, but for the present just consider a subject who, although he experiences "bodily" sensations, is totally paralyzed. Such a
subject would, I shall later argue, not have any appreciation even of his
own body. And so no sensation, however much of a genuine "feeling" it
is, would appear to such a subject to be "in" its body.[18] That *we* know
that a creature that was confined to experiencing bodily sensations
would be registering states of its own physical body does not mean that
those sensations are intentional. Intentionality is not just a matter of
informational relationships, even when the information is embodied in
a conscious state. It is also a matter of phenomenology, and of how the
subject responds to, or "takes," what he is presented with. Since the occurrence of a "feel" of itself entails no awareness of one's body as such,
we are left with the question why, when such sensations *are* attributed
by us to our body, they are so attributed.

This gaping explanatory hole is also to be found when we turn our attention to types of sensation that are typically perceptual in character. For even such sensations as these are not *necessarily* perceptual. Consider darkness, for example. This a genuine visual phenomenon. Some of our senses simply cease when they receive no input. But when a conscious, visually normal subject is receiving no optical input, visual consciousness does not simply cease, for we are then conscious of "darkness."[19] Indeed, the nature of this darkness can be considered and compared with other kinds of visual experience: it is, for example, not an experience of blackness, but of what psychologists call "brain grey." And even if it were a case of pure blackness, that, too, would be a visual quality, one originally appreciable only by a subject with visual experience. As Edmond Wright says, "If you are doubtful about darkness . . . as a positive state of the registering field, consider a human being born *without any visual cortex* but who has healthy eyes and the remnant of a healthy optic nerve, but one that goes nowhere. [*H*]*e does not even register darkness.* There are persons with brain damage to the occipital cortex who have lost a part of the visual field, and this part is *not replaced with darkness:* the field itself has just shrunk."[20] Analogously, although if you close both eyes you will experience darkness, if with eyes open you turn them to the extreme right, you will not experience a dark area encroaching at the left-hand side of your visual field. The field simply recedes. If, though, darkness is a state of visual experience, we have a demonstration that sensation is not necessarily intentionally directed to anything: we simply consider a subject whose *first* experience is of "inner darkness." In the absence of any other, prior experience of the world, it will clearly not appear to such a subject that all the lights are out, that it is dark, that the world is empty, that there is nothing there, or any such thing. Such an impoverished subject would not, as yet, be in a position to relate perceptually to an environment at all. Moreover, not even chromatic visual experience is necessarily intentional: just consider the visual experiences we have with our eyes closed when we press our eyeballs—those that led the ancient Greeks to think that some sort of light or fire resided within the eye. Such an "inner lightshow," if I may so call it, is even for us a matter of pure visual sensation. If I press my eyeball and experience a faint glowing light, I am not even tempted to suppose that a light has come on in the outside world. It is not merely that, knowing that I have myself induced the experience, I override an intuitive appearance of such a thing; the experience simply does not present itself as of anything external to consciousness. If this is doubted, perhaps on the grounds that for someone who does ordinarily perceive the world visually *any* visual sensation must carry some sort of reference to the surrounding world, it surely cannot be doubted in relation to a creature who has never perceived the world visually: a creature whose *first* visual experience was of such an inner light-show. It is thus not true to write, as does Michael Ayers, that a sensation of yellow "is not something we could conceivably have except as an aspect of our sensory awareness of things, the appearance to us of space and things in space."[21] We therefore have a serious problem. For there is clearly a community of nature between all visual sensations. If intentionality can sometimes be present and sometimes absent even within the class of sensations belonging to a single sense, how are we to account for this except on the supposition that some of these sensations are, and some are not, accompanied by a distinct, because separable, cognitive act— thereby returning us to the dual component approach?

Richard Aquila has attempted to answer this problem. He fully recognizes the essential shortcoming in any position that regards sensation as such as intrinsically intentional, and also recognizes the need to introduce an intentional element, over and above the purely sensory aspect of sensation, in a way that does not simply constitute a reversion to the dual component theory. What he attempts to establish is that "it is possible to grant that such a non-sensuous element is an element which might be exhibited by sensory states *themselves*, and not merely by some appropriately related non-sensory state."[22] It is precisely the presence and absence of this non-sensory feature that determines whether sensation is perceptual or not. I believe this to be exactly right, and we shall be exploring this possibility in Chapter 5. I cannot, however, find much illumination in Aquila's positive account of the matter, for we are told next to nothing about these non-sensuous elements. They may be, Aquila says, "a matter of the 'context' in which sensory states occur, or a matter of the *way in which* sensory content is present in experience. (If, for example, sensory states are brain-states, then what would be semantically significant would be at least some of the various ways in which the same sensory brain states might occur in the brain)."[23] This, of course, is sheer and indeterminate speculation, which does no more than direct us to the abstract possibility of sensory states possessing non-sensuous features as a way of avoiding any form of dual component theory. In this, as I have said, I believe him to be wholly correct; but we certainly need to be told more about these crucial features in virtue of which sensations themselves become intentional. Failing this, we simply have the brute assertion that some sensations are intentional and some are not in virtue of something we know not what.

Nor can the currently popular emphasis upon *information* as central to an understanding of perception help us at all in our search for a solution to our Problem. The claim that perception embodies information about the environment is certainly one that cannot sensibly be denied. Moreover, since information need not be "encoded" conceptually, the following may be thought to be a suggestion worth taking seriously: that sensation is perceptual when it embodies information about our environment, whereas "mere" sensation does not provide such external information, but at best gives us information about the state of our own bodies. One thing that has suggested such an idea to some writers is the fact that certain sense-modalities can be so harnessed as to enable us to perceive the environment in wholly novel ways.[24] For example, although we normally detect only sounds and not the shapes of physical objects by hearing, this fact is not entailed by the nature of auditory sensation itself. A number of years ago, W. C. Clement argued persuasively that if a few contingencies associated with hearing were different, we should be able to say that we "heard the surfaces of objects."[25] Since then, Stuart Aitken and Tom Bower have devised the "sonicguide," an instrument that emits ultrasonic sound that bounces off surrounding objects and upon returning to the machine is converted into audible sounds that are fed into a subject's ears through headphones. The distance of an object is correlated with the pitch of the sound, its size with loudness, texture with timbre, and direction with time of arrival of the two signals at the ears, as in ordinary hearing. Although older subjects adapt poorly to the device, infants from about five months of age who are congenitally blind exhibit all the signs that they have acquired an auditorily based "distance sense" akin to vision: they reach out for approaching objects, track moving objects, and so forth.[26] So perhaps all that is necessary for perceptual consciousness is that the sensory manifold be structured in a way that is dependably isomorphic to certain features of the environment that serve as input to the sensory system.

Such a suggestion will not do at all, however. For the course taken by the various sensations in my leg during a certain period could conceivably be isomorphic to the positions of clouds overhead. Even if, bizarrely, the course of my sensations were *caused* by the positions of the clouds, even if I were in a context where such sensations would occur *only if* there were clouds moving in a determinate way above my head, my sensations would feel just as they ordinarily do, and would remain mere bodily sensations. Isomorphism, and even a causally grounded informational relationship, is a matter of external relations between two terms, whereas what we are interested in is what is internally constitutive for the phenomenology of perceptual consciousness. The present suggestion is hardly any better, on this count, than Richard Aquila's proposal. Precisely because of its phenomenological irrelevance, the present suggestion is also wholly unhelpful in the context of a search for a defence of Direct Realism—for the simple reason that an Indirect Realist can happily accept the suggestion. Of course perception embodies information about the physical world, such a Realist will say; but it does so because it features an immediate awareness of sensation that is itself informationally related to the objects in our physical environment.

What has therefore emerged as our first task, in the development of an acceptable theory of perceptual consciousness, is to show how some sensation can be intrinsically world-directed (or even just body-directed), thereby avoiding the dual component theory, while yet recognising that no type of sensation is necessarily so directed. Something other than thought and conceptualization can be sometimes present and sometimes absent, in such a way that the distinctive intentionality of perceptual consciousness is thereby installed. It is to this task that we turn in Chapter 5.

The Nature of
Perceptual Consciousness

5

IT IS HIGH TIME that we put the standard accounts of perceptual consciousness behind us, along with aprioristic assumptions about what such consciousness "must" be like, and turn, as Husserl put it, to "the things themselves." What we need is a careful phenomenological appreciation of the lived character of perceptual experience. As we have seen in the last chapter, if Direct Realism is true we should be able to discern a non-sensuous aspect to such experience, though one that is not a matter of the exercise of concepts. Let us, therefore, take a fresh, unbiased look at perceptual consciousness, to see if we can discern anything that makes it, simply qua mode of sensory consciousness, distinct from sensation.

One fairly obvious initial suggestion is that what distinguishes perceptual consciousness from the mere having of sensation is the *phenomenal three-dimensional spatiality* that attaches to the former. Is it not the case that all and only *perceptual* sensations present us with objects that are ostensibly located in three-dimensional space? Such phenomenal spatiality is not plausibly seen as a matter of conceptualization, but seems, rather, to be a matter of the intrinsic character of certain sense-fields—though hardly a matter of their "qualitative" character. Phenomenal *three*-dimensionality would be essential to the suggestion. Arguing merely that some sensations form a two-dimensional array would not suffice to justify treating them as perceptual, since some mere sensations—such as the "inner light-show"—are so arrayed.

Moreover, if William James is right, and every kind of sensation is possessed of what he termed "voluminousness," then the requisite phenomenal three-dimensionality will have to be more than this.[1] But that granted, the suggestion may seem straightforward.[2] Nevertheless, this suggestion will not be even initially plausible unless we introduce a closer determination of what "spatiality" means here. For are not even bodily sensations in some sense spatially arrayed, even three-dimensionally? A pain felt in my hand is phenomenally separated from a tickle in my foot; and with four movable limbs it is easy, if we experience a sensation in each one, to be aware of four sensations occupying positions that cannot be located in a plane. The more precise notion of spatiality that we require, therefore, is one that essentially involves not just the spatial relationships between the objects of awareness, but the spatiality of the relationship between any such object and ourselves—more specifically, a part of our body. In vision, for example, objects are characteristically seen, when genuine perceptual consciousness is involved, as more or less distant from us—specifically, from our eyes (or eye). And sounds are heard as being at varying distances from us—specifically from our ears (or ear). Although sight and hearing, unlike touch, are standardly regarded as "distance senses," the same kind of spatiality is also found in touch. Although when we feel an object that object is usually felt as being in contact with us, we feel it to be a three-dimensional solid body localized beyond our body's surface. What is crucial is precisely this spatial *over-againstness* with which perceptual objects are given to awareness: an over-againstness which involves a part of our body functioning as *sense-organ*. Perception concerns the "external world." The suggestion is that this is, in essential part, because perceptual experience presents such "external" objects as *literally* external—to our bodies. A bodily sensation such as a headache is experienced as *in* your head; it is not perceived as an object *with* your head. When, by contrast, you look at your hand, although the object seen is not spatially separated from you (since it is a part of you), it is, nevertheless, spatially separate from the eye with which (and from where) you see it.

The "spatiality" of perceptual consciousness (which in what follows is always to be understood as shorthand for the phenomenal, three-dimensional locatedness of the objects of awareness in relation to a sense-organ) underlies an essential feature of the perceptions of at least the majority of objects of perception: of "physical objects" in the narrow sense, or "bodies," as opposed to what I have sometimes called physical "phenomena," such as sounds, shadows, and radiant heat. This feature is that there is more to such an object than is directly registered in sensation, and that we appreciate this fact. Bodies are always perceived only from one side, so that they hide from us aspects of themselves that may be further explored. As we watch a vase rotating on a revolving plinth, for example, our changing visual experience is immediately taken as embodying merely differing perspectives on a single, intrinsically unchanging object. What we discover as the vase begins to turn is *more* of this self-same object, discovering formerly hidden parts that belong integrally to it along with the portions perceived earlier. None of this holds of mere sensation: *there are no perspectives to be had on our sensations*, and so they have no further aspects that transcend our current awareness of them. We can attend more fully to a sensation, but we cannot turn it over and contemplate its different aspects—not even in our mind's eye. A sensation has no hidden sides because we are not aware of it through the exercise of a sense organ spatially distinct from it. Where there is the possibility of different perspectives on a single object, we have genuinely perceptual experience rather than mere sensation.

Not all perceptible objects have hidden sides, of course; shadows don't, for example; nor do sounds. We can, however, albeit to a more limited extent than with bodies, have different perspectives on them. We can move from viewing a shadow face-on to viewing it from one side, with a consequent change in visual experience; and we can get different "perspectives" on a sound by moving in relation to it. These are hardly cases of discovering hidden sides, or even aspects, of the object; but we do learn how the self-same thing looks, or sounds, from here rather than there. Indeed, not only can we achieve different "views" of such objects, but, as Husserl and Merleau-Ponty stressed, there is involved in our perceptual commerce with the world a sense of getting *better* or *worse* perspectives on objects.[3] We can discover how loud a distant sound really is, or how hot a fire really is, by moving closer to them. If we want to hear the ticking of a pocket-watch "properly," we put it close to our ear; we behave very differently when it is a matter of hearing a cannon fire. All of this is absent only for the simplest operations of the "contact senses"—as with taste and the perception of surface temperature. And it is, of course, wholly absent from the realm of mere sensation.

It is, at first sight, difficult to see how phenomenal spatiality could fail to suffice for perceptual consciousness. For what more could be required for this than that one be ostensibly presented with an object *out there*, spatially separate from oneself, even if in contact with you? Surely no such object could be intuitively taken to be a sensation? The well-known phenomenon of a phantom limb should not be thought to constitute a counter-example to this idea.[4] For although, in such a case, the subject feels a mere sensation to be at a point in space that is in fact beyond his body, it is not felt to be beyond his body; it is, rather, that the body itself is felt to be beyond a point at which it objectively terminates. The only case I know of that might be thought to cast doubt on the sufficiency of spatiality for perceptual consciousness is due to Georg von Békésy. In his investigations into the surprisingly close similarities between the way the skin and the ear respond to vibrations, he found that something analogous to stereophony can be produced by placing vibrators, slightly out of phase with each other, on two parts of a subject's skin. When the ends of two adjacent but separated fingers are thus excited, the feeling of vibration can be made to move from one finger *through empty space* to the other. With other apparatus, subjects were induced to locate such feelings up to three feet outside their bodies.[5] Unfortunately, von Békésy does not give a sufficiently detailed phenomenological account of what the subjects experienced. For although he speaks of "sensations" being felt outside the body, he both fails generally to observe any distinction between sensation and perception, and also likens the phenomenon to someone's poking at an object with a stick and feeling resistance and solidity at the other end of the stick—which suggests perception rather than sensation. It is, however, only the former reading, according to which the subjects feel "bodily" *sensations* outside their bodies, that would cast doubt on the present claim to sufficiency; and such a reading is certainly puzzling. Perhaps we should regard the present case as but an extreme example of something akin to the phantom limb phenomenon: a case where "bodily" sensations are felt, not only at a point beyond the subject's objective physical body, but at a point that is beyond even the normal extent of the body. If it is objected that one surely cannot feel one's body to be up to three feet beyond its natural extent, one should recall the possibility, mentioned in Chapter 1, of feeling one's nose to be over a foot long. Perhaps, in the present case, one would have to go as far as saying that one's body was felt to be subjectively discontinuous; for when subjects feel these vibrations as being up to three feet away, there is no suggestion that they feel that their bodies have expanded, and this may well be thought to be bizarre. But is it any more bizarre than suggesting that sensations are felt outside one's body altogether? In fact, however, the suggestion is not at all bizarre. We shall be examining shortly the cognitive relation in which we stand to our own bodies in some detail, but for the moment, simply imagine a subject with a permanently paralyzed leg in which no sensation has ever been felt. Now, for the first time, a sensation is felt "in the foot." Would there be any less of a "discontinuity" here than in the von Békésy case? For we should certainly not think of our "body image" as a continuous, body-shaped field of sensation. That, as Brian O'Shaughnessy has argued at length, is just a myth.[6]

In any case, what finally disposes of such extra-bodily sensations as a counter-example to the sufficiency claim is the fact that they do not involve the precise form of three-dimensional spatiality that is here at issue. For one thing that is implied as a possibility by the kind of spatial over-againstness which we are exploring—an over-againstness in relation to an organ of perception—is that something should interpose itself between ourselves and the perceived object so as to *occlude* it, or to obstruct our perception of it. The notion of occlusion applies literally only to the sense of sight, where the possibility is obvious. Nevertheless, something analogous to occlusion holds for touch, despite its being a "contact sense." For while you are touching something, a thin rigid object can always in principle be interposed between your body and what was being touched, so that you feel it obstructing your perception of the latter. Similarly with hearing, for a nearby sound can impede your perception of a more distant sound even though it is no louder than the latter. No such thing seems intelligible with von Békésy's sensations. Even if he could produce serried rows of such sensations, the nearer ones could hardly obstruct awareness of the more distant ones *if they genuinely are mere sensations.* Differently located sensations do not "occlude" one another.[7] When the possibility of such occlusion is taken into account, it surely becomes evident that the precise kind of spatiality that is in question here suffices for perceptual consciousness.

Although spatiality looks as if it suffices for perceptual consciousness, if it is not universally, indeed necessarily, present in perceptual consciousness as such, we shall not have attained a wholly satisfactory account of such consciousness, since we shall be left in the dark about how genuine perception is possible in its absence. So if phenomenal spatiality is, as at present, our only way of distinguishing between perception and sensation, we need to ask if it is necessary as well as sufficient for perceptual, as opposed to merely sensory, consciousness. This presents us with a problem, because it is not.

Sight, hearing, and touch we have already seen to exhibit spatiality. But what of taste and smell? The latter may indeed possess James's "voluminousness"; but that is not what we are concerned with. Still, it may seem to you that you can, standing in a well-stocked florist's, smell the odours of the flowers filling the room. On reflection, however, we realize that this is not really so. A single, strongly perfumed and variegated bunch of flowers under your nose could lead to the same perception. Blindfolded, you would not be able to tell the difference. Now, as a matter of fact it is not true that smell is merely "voluminous." Georg von Békésy has demonstrated our ability, in finely controlled contexts, to smell the precise lateral location of an odour under our nostrils. Indeed, he showed how time delays in the output of two fine perfume sprays, one positioned under each nostril, can determine the subjective localization of the smell in a way that is analogous to the way in which discrepancies in the time of arrival of a sound at our two ears determine our radial localization of sounds.[8] Were our nostrils farther apart, we should be even better at this than we are: as von Békésy points out, that champion truffle-hunter, the pig, has nostrils set relatively widely apart. Even in such a case, however, *distance* is all but non-existent for the sense of smell—though perhaps it gets some foothold with the pig. We should not misinterpret the fact that certain male moths can detect the pheromones of a possible mate that is several miles away; or, to take a less dubious case of sentiency, the fact that polar bears can smell a seal at comparable distances. For a polar bear does not smell a seal *as being* several miles away, or smell the odour either as at, or as coming from, such a distance: the bear is phenomenally presented only with changes in the intensity of the smell and, apparently as a result of the detection of air-flow, a direction. Such a creature, like a dog, has to *follow* a scent. The reason for this is that, as things stand, there is no information about such relatively large distances in olfactory input: nothing comparable to the echoic effects that allow us to place sounds at varying distances from us. Bearing in mind W. C. Clement's point noted towards the end of the previous chapter, note that I am not suggesting that olfactory distance perception is *impossible*. The relevant point is that such a possibility is unrealized for us at least some of the time: there are actual instances where smell is at most merely voluminous. Whereas you see and hear things *at* a distance, and feel spatially located objects *with* your hands, you typically experience smells *in* (or just behind) your nose. And yet smell is a *perceptual* sense. Taste is even less inherently spatial: its "voluminousness" is restricted to the mouth. Von Békésy has discovered, once again, that precise localization of taste is possible, with time delays again having their localizing effects;[9] but such tastes are localized on the tongue. (The primary purpose of von Békésy's discussion, indeed, is to point out the similarities between the mechanisms of taste localization and those of cutaneous *sensations* generally.) Taste is, as such, a bodily sensation, one entirely lacking the kind of spatiality we are concerned with here. Tastes are in the mouth as headaches are in the head. Similar remarks apply to felt temperature. If you put an inert new-born baby under a sun lamp, it will not feel itself bathed in heat; it will, surely, only feel its body heating up.[10] And yet we speak of ourselves perceiving smells and temperatures.

In fact, taste can, I believe, be quickly set to one side on the grounds that it is merely derivatively perceptual. When you pop a mint into your mouth, we certainly say that you are tasting the mint. This is taken to be a perception, not a mere sensation. It is intentional, having an object—the physical mint, or at least one of its qualities—distinct from itself. Taste is perceptual, however, only because it relies upon another sense modality: you take yourself to be tasting the mint only because you *feel* the mint with your tongue. Compare this with the situation in which, as we say, you have a taste "in your mouth." This taste is not attributed, non-inferentially, to any object whatever. It is certainly not attributed to your mouth. It is not your mouth that tastes minty, in the sense in which we say that a mint does: there is, rather, simply a taste *in* your mouth. This is a pure gustatory event. Indeed, it is a mere gustatory sensation, having no "object distinct from itself." It is phenomenally located, of course; but then so is a headache. Nor is the taste attributed to your tongue. When you are said to taste "physical objects," you taste them *with* your tongue, and this is only because you *feel* such things with your tongue, caressing them and "extracting" the flavour from them. Similar remarks hold for the perception of surface temperatures with the skin. This cannot, however, be said of smells; nor of radiant heat. Perhaps the attribution of a smell, or of heat, *to a physical object*—such as a piece of cheese, or a fire—is dependent on the operation of some other sense; but considered in themselves, as "physical phenomena," we have non-derivative perception of them. They therefore constitute counter-examples to the proposed necessity of spatiality for perceptual consciousness.[11]

Indeed, sight constitutes such a counter-example. For although, for almost all of us, sight presents objects at a distance, it does not do so universally, even when that sense is functioning perceptually. We find the exceptions in those people who, as it is commonly put, have had their sight restored later in life having been born "blind": subjects of the well-known Molyneux Question. For such subjects are not, in fact, totally blind before their operations. Were they so, no operation would be of any avail, since, in the absence of all visual stimulation, the optic system atrophies. Their vision is, rather, extremely impaired; so impaired that they wholly fail to see objects as being at any distance from them. Indeed, they can hardly be said to see "objects" at all. Nevertheless, they can (just about) see. Nor is such seeing merely the enjoyment of visual sensations. What they see is light and shadow—public, objective, physical light and shadow.[12] Vestigial though such visual perception may be, it also constitutes a counter-example—doubtless the most significant one—to the suggested necessity of spatiality for perceptual consciousness. It looks, therefore, as though we must search for a second phenomenon that will account for those cases of perceptual consciousness where appeal to spatiality fails.

Fortunately, a candidate is on hand. For there is another suggestion that at least meets the constraint that we be able to account for perceptual consciousness at the simple level of sensing animal life. It is that we pay attention to the way in which perception is integrated with *movement*—specifically, movement on the part of the perceiving subject. Moreover, our discussion of spatiality has already provided a clue as to the kind of movement that is relevant here. For what we have so far seen to be of perceptual significance is the apparent three-dimensional locatedness of objects of perception in relation to a sense-organ. Hence, the kind of movement that is of perceptual significance is the *movement of sense-organs in relation to perceived objects.* Not all such movements are relevant, however. For given that we are at present interested in how perceptual experience is to be distinguished from mere sensation qua experience, the movements in question must be ones of which the subject is aware. So the fact that visual perception involves constant small movements on the part of the eyes is not relevant, since they are not something of which we have any experiential appreciation whatsoever: it at least seems to us that we can keep our eyes perfectly still while seeing something, at least for very short periods. What such unconscious eye movements facilitate is the occurrence of visual sensation itself, whereas what we are interested in are conditions over and above the aetiology of sensation that sustain the enjoyment of fully perceptual consciousness. Similarly, the opening and closing of our eyelids are not movements of the right kind, even though we are aware of them. For they, too, have a merely facilitating function in relation to the genesis of visual sensation. The reason why the opening of our eyes is at all relevant to visual perception is that it allows a *mobile sense-organ* to function. It is the movement of this sensitive organ itself in relation to perceived objects that is of phenomenological significance for perception. More specifically, the bodily movements with which we should be concerned are those *by which we come to enjoy different perspectives on perceptible objects.* Hence, not the tremor of the eyeballs, nor the movement of eyelids, but the turning of our eyeballs in their sockets as we gaze across a scene or follow the outline of an object is the sort of movement we are concerned with here. Such independent movement of a discrete sense-organ within the body as a whole is, of course, the exception rather than the rule for us. Some animals can cock their ears, but we cannot; the chief activity associated with the nose is sniffing, which does not, in the relevant sense, involve movement in relation to perceived objects at all. The nearest we come to an analogy to the movement of our eyes in the other senses is the manipulation of an object by our hands as we feel its shape—though there is no discrete organ of touch. Whether an autonomous, identifiable organ of sense can be independently moved is not, however, the issue. The issue is simply whether a part of the body serving as an organ of perception can be moved in relation to possible objects of perception in such a way as to give rise to changing sensation, whether or not this involves movement of all, or large parts of, the body. Even though our ears, for example, are themselves effectively immobile, they can be moved in relation to sounds and sounding objects in virtue of our head or our whole body moving.

I should stress that our enquiry is at present phenomenological in nature, and will remain so for the rest of this chapter. So claims concerning necessary or sufficient conditions for perceptual experience are claims about conditions that may only *seem* to the subject to hold. The previous claim about the movement of sense-organs is thus, strictly, to the effect that it should seem to the subject that such an organ is in movement—whether it objectively is or not. We are not, here, concerned with psychophysics. To put the point dramatically: the distinction between perceptual and merely sensory experience is one that needs to be made even for a "brain in a vat."

The claim that there is an important role in perception for its seeming to a subject that its sense-organs are in movement is no doubt too crude a way of stating the truth. For is a baby ever aware that it has eyes, or ears, or a nose that it can move in relation to any currently perceived object? In one sense, clearly not. We need have no anatomical appreciation of the nature, or even existence, of our organs in order to perceive. There is, however, a sense in which a perceptual appreciation of sense-organs, and moving sense-organs in particular, is an integral part of most perception. For in perceiving, the subject is, in a manner to be explored, typically aware, as a dimension of the perceptual experience itself, of the functioning of what are in fact, in normal cases, sense-organs—even though they are not themselves objects of awareness.[13] I shall express this by saying that an appreciation of a mobile sense-organ is (at least) "implicit" in perceptual consciousness.[14]

Such movement of a sense-organ in relation to an object of awareness is wholly absent from the level of mere sensation, for such movement again introduces *perspectives*. You cannot enjoy different perspectives on the inner light-show, or on any element in it; you cannot turn away from a headache. This phenomenological criterion allows us to grant perceptual status to the kinds of case that were problematic for the spatiality criterion. Persons with cataracts can be credited with seeing objective photic phenomena because certain changes in the disposition of visual sensation will be consequent upon movements of their eyes. Even though a dark patch in such a subject's visual field will not be seen as at any distance from him, he will immediately take such a patch not to be a mere sensation, but something "external" to him, because of the way in which movement of the operative sense-organ kinetically structures the sensory field. As the subject turns his head, the patch will occupy different parts of his field of vision, or will disappear from view, depending upon the direction of his gaze. This minimal ability to have different "perspectives" on the object indicates that we have a case of perception, and not mere visual sensation. For none of this is true of the inner light-show, or of any other mere field of sensation. A sense of such self-movement opens up an objective realm by instituting a distinction between how sensorily things *are with us* and how, although they are themselves directly registered in sensation and veridically perceived, things *are with the objects of perception.* (More on what will turn out to be this *crucial* point will come in Chapter 6.)

Smells and radiant heat are similarly objects of perception because we can move in relation to them, and be aware of so doing.[15] Our awareness of how we stand kinetically with respect to these two kinds of phenomenon is, however, extrinsic to the sheer sensory experience of them, even though instinctive. For it is based upon a primitive appreciation of causality, and this on two levels. Note, first, that these two problem cases involve "physical phenomena" rather than "physical objects" in the philosopher's usual sense: they are not "bodies." Still, we do attribute them *to* bodies: we can smell a flower, or feel the fire in the hearth. Such attributions of heat and smell to a "physical object" require, however, the perception of such an object *by a different sense* (as does taste, as we have seen). A blind person will not attribute the warmth he feels to the fire before him unless he is otherwise apprised of its functioning presence. Even we who can see the fire do not see its producing the heat, nor do we feel this: we just feel the heat, and surmise, or know, that this seen or felt physical object is responsible for it. Radiant heat is not a "quality" of a "physical object," but a physical phenomenon in its own right, one that is related to a physical object only extrinsically, if at all: to its producer or emitter. So is a smell. If a particularly malodorous cheese is carried through the room, the smell remains. If we now attribute the smell to any physical object, it will be to the room: the room smells, we say. But really, of course, it is the air in the room that smells—hardly a paradigm case of a "physical object." Hence, we speak of foul air, and the fragrance of the air. If I put a rose to my nose, I am coming into proximity with the *source* of the smell;

and even then, I appreciate the smell only by drawing the odour into my nostrils—that is, the air that has been sweetened by the immediate presence of the rose. Reference to bodies is thus derivative whenever we are dealing with physical "phenomena"—even with sound, where spatiality is present. For although locating a sound is typically locating the object that emits the sound, such a physical object bears but an extrinsic, causal relation to the sound itself. In Chapter 1 I cited Merleau-Ponty as claiming that we hear the solidity of the cobbles in the sound of a carriage that is passing over them. This is true if by it he means merely that we can *hear that* a carriage is passing over cobbles; for this simply means that we know that this is happening on the basis of what we hear. The sound itself, however, carries no reference to solidity, or cobbles, or wheels. A wholly naive subject could hear the same sound *sounding the same way* and have no thought of cobbles at all. The sound contains no information about cobbles except to someone who already knows what kinds of sound various physical processes give rise to—a knowledge that necessarily relies on the functioning of some sense other than hearing. An auditory perception of a carriage is, as Reid would have said, an "acquired" perception. Indeed, it is not a priori that a sound has any physical object as its cause at all. Moses heard a voice coming from the burning bush, but he didn't suppose that the bush was *speaking;* nor did he think that there was a larynx hidden among the flames. Again, "Where should this music be? I' the air, or in the earth?" wonders Ferdinand in the *Tempest.* "Sitting on a bank, / Weeping again the king my father's wreck, / This music crept by me upon the waters." Smells and radiant heat, unlike sounds, posed a particular problem for the earlier appeal to spatiality when they were considered as physical phenomena in their own right, because, experientially, they are not spatially located. We are now in a position to see that they can nevertheless be regarded as objects of perception because a second type of causal attribution is involved. Since, unlike hearing, these two senses effectively fail to present their phenomena as at any distance from us, we can only sense their presence to our sensing bodies; *but our bodies can sensibly move in relation to them.* If I move out of the cheesy room, awareness of the smell gradually ceases. Such a coincidence of movement and change of experience would be of the kind that is intolerable in our cognitive lives were the smell not located back in the room. We do not smell (or see, or feel) the odour's departure: we simply detect its lesser intensity, and instinctively put it down to our relocation. And if I silently remove the bar fire that is warming you, you will not feel the warmth's relocation, but only its diminishing—an experience that will be identical to what you will have if I simply turn the fire off. There is nothing analogous, for these two senses, to our hearing footsteps departing. Nevertheless, it is only thanks to the integration of self-movement with sensory fields that we are dealing with perception here at all. Once again, it is only thanks to self-movement that we have a distinction between how sensorily things are with us and how, although they are themselves directly registered in sensation and veridically perceived, things are with the objects of perception.

We are now in a position to understand more precisely what I earlier referred to as the at least "implicit" awareness that we have of ourselves as sensing subjects when we perceive. Since whenever there is a kinetic change in my perceptual experience it is always immediately taken to be either the movement of an object in my environment or merely the consequence of my relocating myself in relation to such an object, I must always have an at least implicit sense of my position vis-à-vis perceived objects. Only because of this can I have any appreciation of the possibility of my body being in motion in relation to a stationary object, so that the experiential changes consequent upon my movement are immediately taken to be merely "perspectival." Whenever one perceives movement, it is perceived relative to oneself. All perception of movement is egocentric. Even when we perceive an object moving while at the same time we ourselves move, the former movement is perceived as being such that it would still be perceived if we were to become stationary. This is not to say that movement is perceived as mere relative displacement; it is not. Basic experiences of movement are either of something moving past us, or of ourselves moving past objects (though many experiences comprise both, of course). This basic distinction is possible because the perceived movement of objects is relative to an irrelative origin: ourselves. The experience of ourselves moving or being at rest is an absolute phenomenological datum. If this were not so, no immediate, uncalculated action would be possible; and if no uncalculated action is possible, no action at all is possible.[16]

Such implicit "apperception" is also essentially present in the first basic perceptual phenomenon discussed earlier—phenomenal three-dimensionality—even though we may suppose that movement is excluded. For whenever I perceive an object at a distance, it is always perceived as at a distance *from me*—and, moreover, in some direction: over there, up to the left, not too far away, towards the edge of my visual field.[17] Hence, my standing in the converse relation to it is phenomenologically embodied in my experience without the need for any explicit self-awareness. If the object is seen "up there," that very experience situates me "down here." The closest that we come to "self"-consciousness as an essential aspect of perception is (usually implicit) consciousness of one's own sensitive body in relation to the environment.

So we have two phenomena that suffice for perceptual consciousness. Are they, however, wholly independent of each other? Although we have seen that an adequate account of perception cannot leave out the role of self-movement and make do with the simple fact of perceived spatiality, perhaps we can make the kinetic criterion do all the work. At the very least, if phenomenal spatiality can be shown to be itself possible only thanks to the offices of self-movement, we shall have achieved a pleasingly more unified account of perception. A related issue also calls for our attention. For several philosophers have claimed that specifically *active* self-movement is a necessary endowment for any genuine perceiver: to perceive is to be an agent. Husserl, for example, believed that what he termed "the kinaestheses"—that is, modes of active self-movement, phenomenologically construed—are absolutely necessary for the "constitution" of physical objects; and Merleau-Ponty followed him in this.[18] In the "analytical" tradition, we find Stuart Hampshire writing that "the line that we draw between 'inner sensations' and features of the external world depends upon this distinction between the *active subject*, who is a body among bodies, and who from time to time changes his own point of view, and the common object observed from many points of view."[19] A related claim is that active movement is necessary for phenomenally three-dimensional experience. Are any of these claims true, however?

One line of psychological research may be thought to show that active movement is at least necessary for phenomenally three-dimensional perceptual experience.[20] The research in question concerns the way in which our tactile sense, the classic "contact sense," can become a distance sense. Paul Bach-y-rita and his associates have devised the *TVSS*—a television substitution system that receives information from the environment through a television camera and transforms it into patterns of impulses that cause an array of solenoid vibrators in contact with the subject's skin (usually the back) to vibrate. Subjects, whether blind or merely blindfolded, quickly adapt to the device, being able accurately to detect and discriminate objects at a distance.[21] That these subjects have been given a novel distance sense is indicated not only by the fact that blindfolded sighted subjects attested to experiencing the "kinetic depth effect,"[22] but also, and most dramatically, by the reaction of one congenitally blind subject when the input from the *TVSS* was suddenly magnified so as to produce the same kind of output to the vibrators as would be produced by an object hurtling towards the camera lens: "The startled subject raised his arms and threw his head backward to avoid the 'approaching' object. It is noteworthy that, although the stimulus array was, at the time, on the subject's back, he moved *backward* and raised his arms in front to avoid the object, which was subjectively located in the three-dimensional space before him."[23] What is of relevance to us in this research is the crucial role that is attributed to active self-movement in the transformation of mere bodily sensation into perceptual, indeed phenomenally spatial, experience. One of the reports contains the following significant passage: "The results thus far point to the great importance of self-generated motions on the part of the observer . . . With fixed camera, [subjects] report experiences in terms of feelings on their backs, but when they move the camera over the displays, they give reports in terms of externally localized objects in front of them . . . [T]his finding raises the interesting possibility that external localization of percepts may depend critically upon such movements."[24] Bach-y-rita himself goes so far as to say that "a translation of the input that is precisely correlated with *self-generated* movement is the *necessary* and sufficient condition for the experienced phenomenon to be attributed to a stable outside world. Conversely, in the absence of such a correspondence, the origin is perceived as being within the observer."[25] I can, however, find nothing in Bach-y-rita's experimental findings that warrants such a claim—as opposed to the claim merely that some self-movement is required. The earlier quotation, after all, only contrasts active self-movement with being static; but these are not the only alternatives, of course. I see no grounds in the research for supposing that the switch from sensation to perception could not be facilitated by the subjects being passively moved while hooked up to the *TVSS*, so long as such movement registered with them. In fact, even if this were shown not to happen, it would be a huge leap to claim that it is wholly impossible that passive movement should have such a facilitating effect on any possible subject.

Such a response to Bach-y-rita's claim will make sense, however, only if passive movement can be registered by the subject. But indeed it can. In fact, there are two ways in which information concerning our passive movement through the environment is made available to us. First, there are the deliverances of the *vestibular* and *somatosensory systems*. May not the operation of these allow even a wholly paralyzed subject an awareness of his or her own movement? To be sure, the vestibular system detects only accelerations, and our musculature and joints give us information only about the movement and position of our limbs; neither, therefore, provides any information about a constant translation of our whole inert body through an environment. Nevertheless, all we require is that a kinetic structuring of a sense-field be apparent to the subject *at all* in a given sense. If someone picks up your hand and moves it passively over a surface, you feel the kind of passage across a sense-field that is wholly absent from the domain of mere sensation.

Secondly, J. J. Gibson has argued at length that there is sufficient information in the "optical flow" present to the eye when we move through a scene to specify both the three-dimensional layout of our environment and our movement through it. Now, although Gibson himself has tended to stress the active involvement of the perceiver in extracting from this flow the "higher-order invariants" that specify the layout of the environment and the subject's relation to it, there are features of the optic flow itself that provide information about whether the subject is in motion, irrespective of whether or not such movement is actively brought about by the subject.[26] The availability of such information in the optical flow leads Gibson, indeed, to speak of "visual proprioception" and "visual kinesthesis."[27] For example, only when the observer moves or is moved is there a change in texture gradients across the whole visual field, whereas when an object moves towards or away from us, there is but a local textural change. Of course, the mere fact that certain aspects of the optic array contain unambiguous information about the observer's movement through the environment is not of itself of perceptual significance; we need evidence that we can and do *extract* such information.[28] That such is the case is, however, beyond

question. One indication of how powerful such purely visual information can be is the phenomenon of "visually induced self-motion" (or
"vection" as it is also sometimes called). A vivid sense of both trans-
lational and rotatory movement by oneself can be induced in this
way—the optical flow at the periphery of the visual field being a particularly powerful stimulus to this effect. An everyday example of this is
being under the impression that one's own train is moving off from the
platform when what we actually see is the adjoining train moving off.
Here visually detected movement wholly overrides the vestibular information that we are stationary.[29] So perhaps a wholly paralyzed
subject's visual experience could suffice to give him a sense of self-
movement. Despite the obvious evolutionary importance of a creature's being active in its environment, I therefore believe that it would
be unwarranted to insist that specifically active movement is an absolute prerequisite for either of our two basic perceptual phenomena. I
should stress that I am here exploring a mere metaphysical possibility.
It is, to be sure, difficult to credit the existence of a naturally occurring,
purely visual paralytic. Brian O'Shaughnessy speaks of the possibility I
am envisaging as "a *colossal* departure from the animal condition as we
know it."[30] I should not dissent from that.

If, therefore, our two basic perceptual phenomena are to be unified
in the way imagined, we must ask if a sense of self-movement as such,
whether active or not, is necessary for any phenomenally spatial awareness. Now, I believe that a good case can be made for this with respect
to the sense of touch, at least as this sense is usually construed.[31] I shall
shortly be suggesting that the experiences of a constitutionally inactive
subject that were the result of objects touching or striking his body
would not be phenomenologically perceptual in character. I shall suggest that it is solely the integration of touch with movement—giving
rise to active touch, or "haptic" perception—that furnishes us, within
the "tactile" domain, with perceptual consciousness at all, and, therefore, with any phenomenally spatial experience possessed by this sense.
What, however, of sight and hearing? Can it really be stated with confidence that the idea of a wholly inert subject, but one who has visual or
auditory perceptual experiences as of objects at various distances from
him in three-dimensional space, is a metaphysical impossibility? I cannot, myself, see how this could be demonstrated.[32] It is certainly possible for us to be completely paralyzed as far as active, consciously reg-

istered movement is concerned, and continue to perceive the world visually. One such temporarily paralyzed subject reports as follows: "I tried to move my eyes as hard as I possibly could and nothing happened, *the world was just there*."[33] Moreover, in the Gibsonian phenomenon of "vection," where self-movement is experienced, it is not as if the visual world is perceived three-dimensionally *because* of such self-movement. Here, it is the three-dimensional, and hence perceptual, visual field that is primary—as the alternative phrase for this phenomenon, "*visually induced* self-motion," indicates. So it looks as if self-movement, whether active or not, must indeed be relegated, when considered as a wholly independent, autonomous source of perceptual consciousness, to the task of accounting for those few kinds perceptual experience that are not phenomenally three-dimensional in character—at least as far as any *essential* contribution to an analysis of perceptual consciousness is concerned. (I take it that it hardly needs saying that both fundamental phenomena work in concert in most perceptual experiences.)

SO WE HAVE two distinct phenomena that suffice for perceptual consciousness. Could there be more? I claimed in the previous chapter that the intrinsic sensory character of different sense-modalities cannot by itself introduce a distinction between sensation and perception: *any* type of sensation can occur either perceptually or non-perceptually. One could, however, have doubts about this. That the case against the supposed necessary intentionality of visual, auditory, olfactory, and gustatory sensation is secure, I believe there can be little doubt. But what about tactile sensations? It has, after all, been common for philosophers and psychologists to hold that it is the sense of touch that originally establishes perceptual contact with the world. Perhaps the most striking instance of this is Condillac's fable about the statue, upon which one sense after another is bestowed. It is, according to Condillac, only with the gift of touch that an "external world" is opened up for the statue.[34] So is not intentionality *essentially* embodied in the intrinsic character of tactile sensations? By appeal to such phenomena as the "inner light-show" it is easy to discount such a suggestion for vision, but is there anything analogous for touch? In particular, is it not touch that essentially gives us an appreciation of *solidity*? And does not such an appreciation suffice for perceptual consciousness?

The answer to this last question must surely be affirmative; but do touch sensations necessarily embody an awareness of solidity? In addressing this question, we need to make sure that we are considering touch sensations *independently of the two phenomena already recognized.* So what we need to ask is whether such sensations could furnish an awareness of solidity in an experience that was not phenomenally three-dimensional, and in the complete absence of possible movement by the subject. In an attempt to find an analogy to the inner light-show for touch we should not, therefore, think of our experiences of handling objects and ask if a subject could have such tactile experience and yet be unaware of a solid object, since the dimension of movement (and three-dimensionality) is clearly present in such cases. Nor should we think of the experience of holding a stick in our hand and feeling its mass extending away from us, since three-dimensionality would then be present. We need, in short, to focus on the simple experience of either the contact or impact of things on our bodies. What I suggest is that when we do this, we shall indeed find something analogous to the inner light-show, and hence see that no mere tactile sensations are any more intrinsically intentional than visual sensations.

Try and conceive of a wholly immobile subject, one who possesses no sense of movement, not even of passive movement, but who yet enjoys tactile sensations. Such a subject would not, I suggest, simply in virtue of having tactile sensations resulting from something touching its skin, have any appreciation of solidity at all. For such a subject would not be, as we say, "feeling" an object: he would not be palpating or holding or even actively pressing against anything. Tactile sensations for such a subject would be merely that: tactile *sensations*, giving no awareness of coherent, solid, physical objects.[35] I believe that the only remotely plausible way to develop the present suggestion is to claim that what would give our subject an appreciation of solid, and hence "external," objects would be an *impact* by an object on the subject's body. Not even this would suffice, however. For we cannot suppose that the experience of impact by a paralyzed though sensitive subject would be just as it is with us in such a situation. For we can move, our muscles are in working order, and we *react* to such impacts, since they are adventitious impacts or checks on the habitual control we have over our bodies. Our bodies move under such pressures, and we feel them doing so. I cannot see, in the absence of such a mobile setting, that any tactile sensation would constitute an awareness of a solid object impacting from outside—any more than does, say, the onset of a heart attack or any other sudden commotion in the body. That *we* know that in the imagined case the impact is on the subject's body from outside is neither here nor there. *For the subject*, without any sense of possible motor control, there is as yet no sense of inner or outer. Such a subject would only be the locus of sensations, some starting up suddenly: a veritable *rudis indigestaque moles*.

Another suggestion for a sufficient condition for perceptual consciousness arises, by contrast, precisely from reflection on the importance of movement for perception. For it may be suggested that the reason this is of such importance is simply because it involves an interplay between passivity and activity. Perhaps all we require for perceptual consciousness is an appreciation that some changes are brought about by the subject, whereas others are due to the environment; and perhaps the former activity does not have to take the form of moving one's body. There is, after all, such a thing as mental activity—doing mental arithmetic, for instance. Why do we need specifically to bring in a body in order to make out a distinction between sensory change that is and sensory change that is not brought about by us? We need, obviously, to consider a non-corporeal form of agency that is quite different from doing mental arithmetic; but is not such conceivable? Can we not, in particular, coherently entertain the possibility of a being who can directly bring about changes in the layout of a sensory manifold, and appreciate just when it is doing this?

Such active power, even over a sensory field, would, however, be inadequate for perceptual experience. This is because, if we can genuinely conceive of a such a being, we can conceive of ourselves as analogously having control over our bodily sensations: I have a sensation of pins and needles in my right index finger, which I move across my palm and up into my little finger. Or, to give an example in relation to non-bodily but yet non-perceptual sensation: I change the shape and location of a phosphene in my closed-eye visual field. It is clear, I take it, that we should not have perceptual experience in these situations; we should simply have an uncanny control over our sensations. They would remain sensations, despite the fact that sometimes changes in them were a result of our activity, and were known to be, and sometimes not. The interaction of agency and passivity as such is not of perceptual significance. What is missing is exactly what is present in our second basic perceptual phenomenon: that agency, when it is exercised, is exercised in moving a sense organ in relation to a perceived object. Bodily sensations, even if they could be moved about, would be moved about within the phenomenal body; they would not be displayed before us in the "external world." Since the previous kinds of sensation are not experienced as being independent of us, there are no varying perspectives to be had on them, no varying approaches that we can make to them by actively moving our sense-organs in relation to them. Being perspectival, as far as we have seen so far, is the fundamental factor that serves to differentiate perception from sensation.

Although neither touch sensations nor the active / passive distinction suffices for perceptual consciousness, when the two are taken together we *do* find something that suffices—something, moreover, that is sufficiently distinctive to count as a third fundamental perceptual phenomenon in its own right. Although no mere impact on a sensitive surface as such will give rise to perceptual consciousness, *we* certainly feel objects impacting on us from without. This fact needs to be recognized in any adequate perceptual theory. I shall name the phenomenon that is central here by the term that is at the heart of Fichte's treatment of the "external world," or the "not-self": the *Anstoss*. This phenomenon is that of a *check* or *impediment* to our active movement: an experienced obstacle to our animal striving, as when we push or pull against things.[36] I am, I should say, appropriating Fichte's term for my own purposes, since in Fichte's own philosophy the *Anstoss* is a check to the infinite self-positing that is our fundamental *intellectual* act; whereas I am concerned with a check to bodily movement. I nevertheless employ his term since much of what he says rings true even of the humble animal phenomenon with which we are concerned,[37] and because hardly anyone before Fichte had said anything that comes even close to recognizing the phenomenological irreducibility of agency at all.[38] It was not until shortly after Fichte's work, in the early nineteenth century, that the distinctively active dimension to bodily movement started properly to be appreciated—by such figures as J. J. Engel and, more famously, Maine de Biran (though de Biran, too, restricts the phenomenon to the exercise of distinctively human freedom).[39] The subsequent swift incorporation of the *Anstoss*, or at least of the deliverances of the "muscular sense," into perceptual theory is one of the most notable developments in the Philosophy of Perception during this period. It was soon widely claimed that this phenomenon is what *originally* gives us any perceptual appreciation at all of physical bodies "without the mind," with the most penetrating discussion of this topic I know coming from Dilthey, at the end of the nineteenth century.[40]

The *Anstoss* must be distinguished from two related phenomena. The first is the experience of active movement of a part of the body *ceasing* at a certain point—perhaps inexplicably. This, by itself, is of no perceptual significance. But neither is this second phenomenon: the experience of an *inner limit* to one's bodily agency. You experience such a limit when, for example, you separate the index and middle fingers of one hand as far as possible. Here, you engage in a certain active movement, and at a certain point *can proceed no further.* Neither of these constitutes what the *Anstoss* affords: your sensibly encountering an alien force. They will not achieve this even if they are supplemented with the coincidental occurrence of a so-called pressure sensation at a suitable point on the arrested bodily part. What is required for the *Anstoss* is that the subject *push* against the foreign body, however minimally. Or, rather, bearing in mind that we are at present engaged in a phenomenological enquiry, that the subject have a sense of so doing.

Although the *Anstoss* involves self-movement, the type of self-movement that is here in question is significantly different from that which went to constitute our second fundamental phenomenon. For one thing, it is immaterial for the latter whether the self-movement that is involved is passive or active; whereas here activity on the part of the subject is vital. Moreover, what is of moment in the *Anstoss* is not the movement of a sense-organ across or "into" a sensory manifold giving rise to changing perspectives. In order clearly to bring out the way in which the present phenomenon is genuinely distinct from the earlier form of self-movement, it will be useful to imagine a creature whose limbs are movable only in one direction; for if a variety of movement is allowed, we shall have introduced haptic perception because of the possibility of moving a limb *across* the surface of an object, and the case will be subsumable under the earlier account. So, rather than a "limb," we should perhaps think of a "spine" that can be extended outwards in only one direction from the creature's body. The *only* sensory function of such a spine is to register a collision with an alien body. In order to consider this third phenomenon in its purity, this will have to be the sole possibility of active bodily movement for the creature. Moreover, the creature should also be thought of as being bereft of any sense of passive movement, for otherwise the creature might be able to feel the end of its spine being dragged across the surface of an object, giving it different perspectives on the object, and the case would again not be genuinely independent of our second basic phenomenon. All this being stipulated, however, it looks as though we have found an irreducible and fundamental third perceptual phenomenon.

Could it not be, however, that the *Anstoss* is subsumable not under the second, but under the first, of our two basic phenomena? For when we consciously collide with an object, we do so in three-dimensional space, and take ourselves so to do. So are we not simply dealing here with phenomenally three-dimensional awareness? Though this is in a sense true, we can see the problem with this suggestion when we recall the earlier attempt to reduce the first to the second of our fundamental phenomena. I there suggested that such a reduction is plausible for the sense of touch. Touch, I suggested, is spatial only when it is active, or "haptic." What we call "pressure sensations" do not, of themselves, vouchsafe spatial, and hence perceptual, awareness. *No* sensations, qualitatively specified, of themselves constitute perception. In fact, it is precisely the *Anstoss* itself that introduces three-dimensional spatiality *at all* into haptic perception. It is only the experience of a collision, or at least a resistance, as the result of active bodily striving that opens up genuine spatiality for touch. Sheer movement of limbs, as in the flailing movements of babies, in the total absence of any contact made with external objects—even if it be only other parts of the subject's body—would embody no perceptual awareness. Although they no doubt in some sense embody "three-dimensionality," such movements would not be in a space that is *perceptual*—any more than were the four non-planar bodily sensations considered at the beginning of this chapter. Moreover, perceptual three-dimensionality does not emerge simply in virtue of bodily movement being attended by "pressure" sensations. Imagine that our subject, in flailing its limbs in empty space—in a sensory vacuum, we might say—experiences a pressure-sensation at what is in fact the surface of a limb *while the movement is yet uninterrupted*. This would give the subject no sense of encountering a foreign body. It is *resistance* that is crucial. "We first discern a pressure-sensation in the impression of resistance," writes Dilthey.[41] Only here, where "pressure-sensations" accompany a felt resistance, do we have *true* pressure-sensations. Take such felt resistance away from haptic experience, and it would not be spatial at all in our sense: it would not operate in a phenomenal space in which things can be encountered. Dynamically encountering a resistant body *at one and the same time* establishes a space in which *both* any foreign body *and* our own active body are first located (though the "foreign" body may be another part of our own physical body).

Over recent years both Brian O'Shaughnessy and Michael Martin have made related and valuable contributions to the subject of tactile perception, bringing out the way in which this sense differs significantly from all the other senses. One aspect of their approach is an emphasis on the obvious, but insufficiently appreciated, fact that we perceive things tactually through the medium of our bodies. "In touch a body investigates bodies as one body amongst others, for in touch we directly appeal to the tactile properties of our own bodies in investigating the self-same tactile properties of other bodies. Whereas we do not smell or hear or see through smelling or hearing or seeing ourselves, the space and solidity of our bodies provides the access to the space and solidity of other bodies," writes O'Shaughnessy.[42] "The model of touch here is that of the body as template . . . One measures the properties of objects in the world around one against one's body. So in having an awareness of one's body, one has a sense of touch," writes Martin.[43] The picture that their writings tend to suggest, however, is that we *first* have an appreciation of our bodies as spatially located and articulated things, in relation to which we can then feel foreign bodies. Now, everything they say is true of mature tactile perception, but they skate over the issue of, to use Husserlian terminology, the original "constitution" of one's own body itself. What we call "bodily" sensations are, claims O'Shaughnessy, "from the start necessarily putatively of body parts";[44] and Martin writes that "one's sensations . . . feel to be within one's body. This is not some special quality each one has which it might lack, for then we could imagine the case of a bodily sensation which felt to be completely external to the body. Contrary to that, every sensation which feels to be located feels to be located within the body."[45] Well, *my* sensations certainly feel to be in my body. But a new-born baby's? Or those of a sightless creature that has never touched anything, even itself? Would such a being have any sense at all of its body—of its body as "an object in a space extending beyond it," as Martin says? For it is not as if the only alternative to feeling a sensation in one's body is feeling it to be outside the body. Another alternative, as Condillac brought out vividly in his tale about the statue, is that such a distinction between inner and outer gets no purchase: a wholly pre-objective state of sentience in which, we are tempted to say, you just *are* your sensations. Or, as T. H. Huxley, who has a remarkably good discussion of this whole issue, says of such a subject, "His feelings would be his universe, and his tactile sensations his *'moenia mundi.'"*[46]

In O'Shaughnessy's account of these matters, what we are in effect offered is a *dual component* account of our relation to our own bodies: "The truth is, that certain sensations, say, in muscles and joints, play a *causal role* in determining an immediate awareness of the limb that *is not* an awareness of those sensations. The so-called 'postural' and 'kinaesthetic' sensations are *the causes and not the objects* of an *immediate* though fallible awareness of the limb."[47] Now, such a theory certainly has considerably more plausibility as an account of our relation to our bodies than it had as a theory of perception; but I do not believe it will do even here. The problem arises from the role that is given to mere sensations. Their role is as unintelligible here as it was in the dual component account of perception: more natural magic, in effect. Since such sensations can occur without giving the subject any awareness of its body, their ability to provide such awareness remains wholly unilluminated. Simply bringing in a causal relation explains nothing. The general point remains firm: sensations, however causally configured, of themselves give us notice only of themselves. It is not sensation that originally provides awareness of our bodies, but our *activity*, and specifically the *Anstoss*. O'Shaughnessy does, indeed, say that "bodily" sensations are necessarily projected on to the body-image, and that the existence of such a body-image has preconditions. In particular, the body-image is constituted out of practical knowledge: it is only when we move our bodies that there arises any phenomenal articulation of the kind that is necessary for anything that deserves to be called a *body*-image.[48] What I am suggesting is that mere movement, even active movement, is not enough. Not that O'Shaughnessy himself thinks that it is enough: he rejects the idea that "body-sense" is neatly prior to "tactile-sense"—as the "picture" I have been discussing would have it. Tactile-sense, he says, is "conditionally presupposed" by body-sense. What I am suggesting is that the presupposition is more than conditional, and that the crucial presupposition is the *Anstoss*. If, with eyes closed, you move your arm to and fro in empty space, you will no doubt feel the whole extent of your arm, with a hand at its end, describing a path in space. This, however, is an *acquired* perception (if "perception" is the right word). A sightless being, whose *first* action this was, would surely have no such knowledge. Here experience would be, if I may so put it, of sheer "kinesis" in a void, not movement in a space that is appreciated as a realm potentially holding alien entities. There would be no sense, here, of any bodily *limits* beyond which things might be located. Such a limit, and hence a phenomenal body itself, and hence a tactile distinction between inner and outer, and hence a genuine felt space in which we are located along with possible other things, emerges only when *contact is made* with something. Such contact, involving the *Anstoss*, is our sole mode of access in this modality to spatially located objects. The *Anstoss* simultaneously reveals both an outer object and our own body by establishing a space in which both are located, and, thereby, confers spatial meaning on what would otherwise be meaningless kinesis. The story told by Martin and O'Shaughnessy is true to everyday tactile perception, but the *Anstoss* is its precondition.

So, to return to the central point at issue, the *Anstoss* cannot be reduced to our first perceptual phenomenon of three-dimensionality, since, in the haptic domain, which is alone relevant, it is itself the precondition of such three-dimensionality. Take away the *Anstoss* from the tactile domain, and we shall be left, as far as any genuinely perceptual consciousness is concerned, with a tactile analogue of the visual perceptions of cataract patients: we should be left with only a sense of something foreign moving over our skin. All we should have left, therefore, would be our second basic phenomenon. Since we have already seen that the *Anstoss* cannot be reduced to this latter phenomenon, and since I can think of no other remotely plausible candidate phenomenon that would suffice for perceptual consciousness, I conclude that a perceptual theory should recognize precisely three equiprimordial sources of perceptual consciousness.

WE ARE NOW in a position to address in a concrete way the issue that was raised at the beginning of this chapter: the non-sensuous and yet non-conceptual dimension to perceptual consciousness. If our three phenomena are indeed the only fundamental forms that perceptual consciousness can take, we should be able to discern such a dimension in each case. And indeed we can.

Consider, first, the difference between the three-dimensionality of the typical visual field and the merely two-dimensional array of visual sensation as it is found in the inner light-show. This difference is not a matter of more, or of new kinds of, visual sensations being present in the former. No such alteration in mere sensation could give rise to a change in the phenomenal *dimensionality* of experience. The distinction here is "sensory" in the sense that it is a simple function of the senses, and is experientially manifest to us; and yet it is not "sensuous," not a matter of the "quality" of visual sensation. Something similar is found in the kinetic structuring of sensation that we find in our second basic perceptual phenomenon. The distinction between the drifting of lights across the visual field in the inner light-show and the phenomenally distinct occurrence that features the movement that we introduce into the open-eye visual field when our eye or head moves is not a matter of sensation. A non-sensuous dimension to sensory experience is even more obvious, however, with the *Anstoss*, for here an object is presented to consciousness *otherwise than by sensation*. Here an object is manifest to us in the sheer check to our active movement—a check that is not embodied in sensation. For not only can such a check not be reduced to sensation—something that is equally true of the other two basic perceptual phenomena—sensation is, or may be, *entirely absent* in its customary role of being a subjective registration of the presence of an object to our senses. When we press against a solid object, we do, indeed, usually feel "pressure sensations" in our body at the point of contact; and here sensation is playing its usual role in perception. Such sensations are not, however, necessary for the experience of the *Anstoss*. We can feel such a check to our agency even if the relevant body-part is anaesthetized, or if we use some implement to feel the object's renitent bulk. In both of these cases, certain sensations will indeed be present: in the first, there will, at least usually, be muscular sensations,[49] and in the second, there will (normally) be pressure sensations where we are holding the implement. Such sensations, however, do not occur *where* we feel the obstacle to our action. In the first case, the obstacle is certainly not felt as being in our muscles, but as resisting our anaesthetized bodily extremity; and in the second, the resistance is felt at the other end of the implement we are using.[50] Here, sensations are not playing their usual role of themselves presenting the object that is perceived, but have a more ancillary function. It is not these sensations that, according to Hume and Prichard, we *mistake* for physical objects. No sensation, in these cases, is a candidate for any such role. This is hardly surprising, since we are here dealing with a quite unique mode of perception: one where the passive givenness that is characteristic of all perception is manifest exclusively in the dynamics of agency, which is itself phenomenologically basic. Maine de Biran, citing Hans Berhardt Mérian, one of the very few writers before his time to appreciate this latter fact, wrote that "the will cannot be *encompassed* in any *passive* succession," for such a thing would have "nothing *active*" about it, whereas we know that "the will is an essentially actional [*agissante*] force."[51] It has taken philosophers and psychologists a long time to recognize this fact. Even when, after the beginning of the nineteenth century, the need to give a distinctive account of the role of animal agency in "touch" was fully recognized, the sense of agency was repeatedly confounded with experiencing sensations. The commonest phrase throughout the nineteenth century for the sense of agency was "muscle (or muscular) sense"—as if the appreciation of our activity could be reduced to an awareness of sensations in our muscles.[52] Even the later talk of "innervation-feelings," though it recognized the need to represent agency as that which is itself *responsible* for the contraction of muscles, and hence for muscular sensations, still failed to do justice to agency by representing our appreciation of activity as a matter of "feeling." But there is no way of constructing a sense of agency out of *any* set of sensations, since any such hypothesized sensations could be passively experienced. In and of itself, sensation is passive in its very essence.[53] So the *Anstoss*, which is specifiable only in relation to such agency, similarly transcends the level of sensation.[54] Indeed, so different is the *Anstoss* from all other forms of perception, that we may well hesitate to term it "sense-perception" at all. Here it is our activity, rather than our senses, that reveals something foreign to us. And because of the unique way in which an object is manifested to us, *what* is manifested has a unique character too. It is manifest to us simply *as a force:* a force that resists the counter-force of our animal striving.[55] No "qualities" of the object are perceived by this unique form of perception, except incidentally. What we register is the bare presence of an alien something checking our movement.[56]

Although we have found a non-sensuous and yet pre-conceptual dimension to each of our three fundamental perceptual phenomena, we need to consider carefully the significance of this fact. For although it should by now be clear that it is necessary, in order for a sensory modality to be perceptual, that it feature such a non-sensuous dimension, it would be rash to infer that it is sufficient. Indeed, not only would it be rash, it would undermine the three foundations for a perceptual theory that I have attempted to lay in this chapter. This is because, once we are alert to their existence, *many* cases of sensory awareness with such non-sensuous aspects can be discovered, and some of them seem not to derive from *any* of our three basic perceptual phenomena. Let us briefly consider a small selection from the variety of such cases that can be discovered.

There is, to begin with, the phenomenon of perceptual organization of which the Gestalt school rightly made so much, and of which the well-known "Gestalt pictures" are but a special case. Such "organizational" changes are hardly a matter of a change in perceptual *sensation*. What psychologists call the *psi-phenomenon* is another clear demonstration of a non-sensory dimension to perceptual awareness. If a bar is flashed on a screen, and shortly afterwards an identical bar is also flashed on the screen a short distance away from the first, there are a number of perceptual possibilities, depending on the time interval between the flashes. With a relatively long interval, you simply see what is on the screen: one bar appears, disappears, and then another bar appears. With a very short interval, you seem to see only one bar *moving* from one position to the other. At a range of intervals between these two extremes, however, something quite different is experienced: one gets a sense of a single bar shifting position but without describing a continuous spatial path. The bar "goes" from one position to another *without visibly moving*. This is the psi-phenomenon. (One sometimes perceives this effect in the switching lights of neon advertisements. You can also get an idea of the effect by holding up a finger and looking at it while alternately opening and closing each eye as rapidly as possible.) It is easy to come up with a description of a course of visual sensation that would be adequate to our experience in the first two cases, but not in this third one. Again, consider the way in which certain two-dimensional line drawings can, as it is often put, look three-dimensional—or, as I shall put it, *quasi-three-dimensional*.[57] Particularly instructive in this connection are figures that imperfectly sustain such quasi-three-dimensionality. Such figures often at first appear merely as flat line-drawings, but then an impression of quasi-depth suddenly emerges.[58] Such phenomena of quasi-three-dimensionality are no more a matter of facts concerning mere visual sensation than are those of the genuine three-dimensionality of typical visual perception. Finally, it is also possible to find cases where, as in the *Anstoss*, something is presented to sensory consciousness that is not registered in sensation *at all*: cases of "amodal perception" as it is now commonly termed.[59] Particularly striking are the diagrams due to Gaetano Kanisza that feature amodal, or "subjective," contours.[60] When you look at these diagrams, you immediately perceive a shape, such as a white triangle standing out against a white background, even though there is no real difference on the page between the figure and the background—no objective contour—as far as most of the figure is concerned. Moreover, there is not even any difference in *sensation* corresponding to the perceived difference between figure and ground.

All of these varied examples are, of course, instances of perceptual consciousness because the objects in question are perceived by sight, which is phenomenally three-dimensional in character. The question is whether the non-sensuous features that they all exhibit would, by themselves, suffice for perceptual consciousness; and if so, whether they can all be traced back to one or other of our three basic sources of perceptual consciousness. Now, given that none of the examples concerns the tactile sense, they cannot be derived from the *Anstoss*. Also, since none of them necessarily involves self-movement, they cannot be educed from our second basic phenomenon. It would not be implausible, however, to claim that at least some of them can be educed from phenomenal three-dimensionality. Quasi-three-dimensionality would be a prime candidate for such treatment. What we need to do, in order to test this suggestion, is to ask if any of these non-sensuous phenomena are possible in the absence of visual three-dimensionality—possible, for example, in an experience that would be analogous to the closed-eye visual field. As I have just suggested, this is perhaps not possible for quasi-three-dimensional objects. It seems likely that such things are possible objects of experience only for subjects capable of genuine three-dimensional perception. Other examples, however, are not so plausibly explained away. To take the most extreme case, consider the "subjective contours" that were the final examples in our list.

Is it at all clear that it would be impossible for Kanisza's figures to appear in a merely two-dimensional, static visual field? But if this is not impossible, we may seem to have a serious problem, since surely the "amodal"—that is, non-sensory—presence to consciousness of an object is not possible at the level of mere sensation. What clearer way could there be, it may be said, of distinguishing between sensation and perception than having perception *without sensation?*

One might attempt to get round this difficulty by suggesting that the "amodal" objects in Kanisza's drawings are not in fact truly amodal. Most subjects see the "subjective objects" as differing ever so slightly in *brightness* (or darkness) from their backgrounds. So although the contours would indeed be "subjective," they would not be amodal. What the relevant parts of the diagrams would achieve, on this interpretation, would be the induction of a lightness boundary in visual sensation. One ground for doubt concerning this interpretation is that the difference in perceived brightness, when there is one, is minute, whereas the presence of the subjective figures is quite manifest. Another is that there are certain figures where, according to most subjects, Kanisza-type contours are seen without any apparent difference in lightness.[61] On the other hand, it has been suggested that quasi-three-dimensional cues are operative in perceiving such figures, one indication of this being that certain geometrical illusions, of the sort commonly explained by reference to such cues, are sustained by such "illusory contours."[62] It is far from clear, however, that this warrants the claim that experiences of such illusory contours are wholly impossible in the closed-eye visual field. And it is even less clear that certain "organizational" factors, such as grouping, must be absent from such a field. Another of our examples is equally difficult to dismiss: the psi-phenomenon. I am not clear how it could be demonstrated that this would be wholly impossible in something analogous to the closed-eye visual field.

If these doubts are unsupportable, and all of my examples (and others that could have been mentioned) are possible only in a field of vision that is phenomenally three-dimensional, then there is, of course, no problem for the tripartite account that has been developed in this chapter. But there is equally no problem if this is not the case. For surely what we are imagining when we imagine any of these phenomena occurring in something like the closed-eye visual field is imagining them featuring at *a non-perceptual level of mere sensation.* If you close your eyes, it is not that difficult to imagine a couple of phosphenes giving rise to the psi-phenomenon. But would that render the visual experience perceptual in phenomenological character? Surely not. What this means is that we should reject the initially plausible assumption that possession by a sensory state of a non-sensuous dimension suffices for perceptual consciousness. There is, moreover, a solid reason for such a rejection. For what all these cases signally fail to embody is any sense of independency or "over-againstness," which is essential to perceptual consciousness as such. All three of our basic perceptual phenomena possess this feature. The first presents us with objects that are straightforwardly separated from us in space, and hence ostensibly independent. The second presents us with objects that are independent of, but that stand in relation to, our movements. And the third presents us with an object that stands over against us as a check to our activity. So it is not merely the fact that each of these three possesses a non-sensuous dimension; it is that they possess it in such a way that we have a sense of encountering something independent of us: of encountering the "Not-I" as they used to say in the nineteenth century, echoing Fichte. I cannot see that this is possible in any way other than by virtue of one or other of our three basic phenomena.

Although I believe we can now return to our three basic phenomena with renewed confidence, it will, as yet, be far from clear how a recognition of their fundamental role in relation to perception is supposed to help us with our problem of answering the Argument from Illusion. It is to that task that we turn in the following and final chapter of Part I.

The Solution

6

HOW MAY our three fundamental perceptual phenomena, and the non-qualitative aspects to perceptual consciousness that can be discerned in them, enable us to respond to the Argument from Illusion? I believe that our discussion of one of these phenomena, the *Anstoss*, has put us in a position to give an immediate answer: the Argument simply does not apply to it. It is not that illusions cannot occur in the realm of the *Anstoss*. As we saw in Chapter 1, there is no form of perception that is immune to illusion. It is, rather, that the unique non-sensory nature of the *Anstoss* allows it to slip through the Argument's net. For the Argument's central claim was that when we perceive, we are immediately aware not of normal physical objects, but of sensations. In the case of the *Anstoss*, however, it is just such focal sensations that are absent. There is simply no such sensuous item to interpose itself between us and the external physical force that we experience. We experience it, therefore, directly.

More needs to said, however, since we are obliged to give a positive account of what is going on when illusions occur in this area. Now, because of the extremely limited character of what manifests itself in the *Anstoss*—sheer force, or renitency—the scope for illusion is limited. Indeed, since force itself is exhaustively specifiable by its intensity and direction, illusion here must be limited to precisely the following possibilities: the force appears to us as either greater or less than it is, or it appears at a point in space other than where it really is, or it appears to be acting in a direction other than its real direction. When any of these obtains, we are faced with the obligation of answering the two challenges that make our Argument a problem. Let us consider them, first, in relation to degree of force. If, because of illusion, I mistakenly judge a resistance to my active movement to be greater than it actually is, *why* do I so judge—unless it is because I am immediately aware of something that actually has that greater degree of resistant force? Secondly, and in case this former question is thought to involve reliance on some form of the "Myth of the Given," we need a positive account of the phenomenology of the illusory situation. A force's perceptually appearing strong differs experientially from that force's appearing weaker; how is this to be accounted for, given that one and the same physical force may be involved in the two situations, unless we introduce some immediate object of awareness that really does vary in the two situations? Perhaps what so varies in this case is not sensation; but *something* must vary, something of which we are aware—for otherwise our account of the phenomenal situation will be inadequate.

The answer to these questions is that, in illusory cases of the *Anstoss*, what varies, and so what underlies our mistaken judgements, is our appreciation of the force *with which we ourselves act* on the alien force. When our muscles are tired, or when they are injected with a debilitating substance such as curare, a given resistance feels greater than it actually is. It is now generally agreed that such appearances are not a function of the state of tension in our muscles, skin, or joints, since these will typically be as they should.[1] As two leading researchers in the field put it, in relation to weight, "There is a perceived command to the muscles, or 'sense of effort,' which is used in estimating the weight of a lifted object."[2] We are not aware of the differing degrees of effectiveness of our motor commands to our muscles as such. When the effectiveness of "innervation" is weakened, subjects do not report a sense of diminished strength, but of a "heaviness" in the object they are lifting.[3] It is the appearance of the external force itself that is an immediate function of a varying sense of effort. So we have a way of satisfactorily answering our two questions without introducing any intermediary item of awareness, whether sensuous or not. We can, therefore, say that it is some external force itself of which we are directly aware in the *Anstoss*, even when it appears other than it is. For the alien force appears only as a check to our activity, and it appears *how* it does as a result of the dynamical interplay of force against force. No object other than the external force itself needs to be brought into the picture in order to do justice to its variable appearances. All that needs to be brought into the story is the variable play of force against force, which is the context of the very emergence into consciousness of the alien object through the *Anstoss*.

The other two possibilities of illusion in this area concern the spatial location and the direction of the force. Suppose that you extend your arm straight out in front of you, but that, blindfolded, it feels as though you are extending it out to the side. You meet a resistance half-way. Because you seem to meet a resistance where there is in fact none, must we introduce an object at that point (or at a "corresponding" point in some subjective space) to account for your experience?[4] Again, no. For, once again, the experience is adequately accounted for by your mistaking the true trajectory of your active movement. Once again, departure from the true appearance does not need to be accounted for by bringing in some non-normal *object* of awareness, since this is adequately done by reference to the character of one's activity. The same goes for mistaking how far out from the body the resistance is encountered, and which direction the force is acting in.

This reply to the Argument hinges entirely on an irreducibly active component to the phenomenon of the *Anstoss*. We can appreciate the full significance of this if we consider again the account of tactile perception offered by Michael Martin—but this time with an eye firmly on the issue of Direct Realism. In the previous chapter I suggested that Martin pays insufficient attention to the absolutely fundamental role of the *Anstoss* in haptic perception. In so doing, he deprives himself of the ability to give a cogent response to the Argument from Illusion. Imagining someone pressing his finger against the rim of a glass, Martin writes that "the place where one feels the sensation to be shares certain spatial properties with the object which impedes one's movement; it is in the same place in space. So the spatial location that the sensation feels to have can provide an awareness of the spatial location of the point on the rim which keeps the fingertip there."[5] What is wrong here is the excessive concern with sensation. The incidental reference to the rim's *keeping* the finger immobile at a point in space affords a glimpse of the truth. It is not, of course, the objective facts concerning a balance of physical forces between a glass and a digit that are relevant, but the phenomenology of such a dynamical situation—as I am sure Martin would be the first to acknowledge. It is precisely this phenomenology, however, that cannot be captured by reference to sensations at the end of one's finger. No sensation, of itself, can give us an awareness of the glass's rim, but only in concert with the *Anstoss*. Elsewhere, Martin writes that "to feel an object pressing against one's skin is to feel one's skin to be a certain way such that one can feel the object which presses against it."[6] In general, of course, this is true, but it involves two accomplishments that are left unexplicated: how a mere sensation can give one an awareness of the surface of one's body (a problem I raised in the previous chapter), and how feeling one's skin to be a certain way can constitute feeling the physical object that is pressing against it. Martin takes Reid to task for distinguishing between sensation and perception; Martin's own account is, however, as unilluminating as Reid's appeal to a natural kind of magic in its claim that sensations themselves just do give us an awareness of physical objects. Stressing the fact that "bodily" sensations are phenomenally located is not adequate for two reasons. First, a throbbing at the end of my finger does not reveal the rim of the glass to me, even if it is in contact with the glass. Secondly, we need an account of how the body itself, with a boundary, located in space, is itself constituted in experience. What is missing, in relation to both points, is the *Anstoss*. Most importantly, for our purposes, a failure to pinpoint the essentially *dynamic* way in which objects are revealed to us in haptic perception would deprive us of an ability to answer the Argument in the present manner.

The *Anstoss* is a unique perceptual phenomenon. I presume that it was ignored for so long, and is still insufficiently appreciated, because we tend to divide animal functions into the active and the passive, and treat perception as a mode of passivity. What we have in the *Anstoss*, however, is a mode of perception that emerges only at the point of an exercise of activity. Objects are revealed to and through our animal striving. Passivity in some sense is involved, of course; but it is a passivity that only makes sense in relation to activity, since it is but a shock or check to our activity—a check that reveals the independency of something from ourselves that is the hallmark of perceptual consciousness. Because any object is so perceived only as the reciprocal to our activity, there is no need to introduce a passively received sensation to account for illusions in this area, since how an alien force is perceived will be conditioned by the character of the striving that reveals it. The Argument from Illusion would seem to have been answered with respect to one of our fundamental perceptual phenomena.

Although I initially presented our Argument as one that claimed to show that Direct Realism is incoherent, so that no possible object could possibly be directly perceived in any possible sense-modality, and although we have just seen that, by failing to encompass the *Anstoss*, the Argument fails to deliver this strong conclusion, no Direct Realist is likely to be happy with such a limited victory. For nothing has yet been said by way of resolving our Problem in relation to any form of perception that is independent of the *Anstoss*—those that are independently grounded on one or the other of the two additional basic sources of perceptual consciousness. But the situation is worse than this. For the previous line of argument does not demonstrate that Direct Realism may be true even for perceptions grounded on the *Anstoss*. This is because, at the mere cessation of effort, the *Anstoss* passes over into mere tactile perception. Can it seriously be supposed that as soon as we stop pushing against an object, and merely feel its contact upon our body, we cease being immediately aware of it? When we begin to push against an object, surely we are, albeit in a different mode, perceiving *the same* object that we may feel merely touching our skin. Unless we can defend Direct Realism in the domain of tactile perception where the *Anstoss* is not operative, we shall not be able to say these things, and Direct Realism even in relation to the *Anstoss* will have been compromised. We need, therefore, to turn our attention to the other two basic forms of perceptual consciousness, those that are focally sensory in character, to see if Direct Realism can be defended there.

WHEN WE TURN to address our Problem in relation to these other two basic phenomena, we yet have a guiding thread: the non-sensuous dimension that we have already discerned in these two cases. This must be where our solution lies, if one there be, since focusing on the specifically sensuous character of any perception will get us nowhere—it being precisely this that perceptions have in common with mere sensations. If, however, the non-sensuous aspect of each of the remaining perceptual phenomena will allow us to see our way round the Argument, it will not be in anything like the previous straightforward way—one that was possible precisely because of the essentially non-sensory nature of the presentation of the *Anstoss*'s object. For we are now turning to forms of perceptual consciousness where an object is not presented to us as simply a counter to our agency, but where physical objects are passively *registered in sensation*. Here our Argument is on its home ground, and, hence, most challenging and problematic. Although we have two independent sources of perceptual consciousness to consider, with their two non-sensuous aspects—phenomenal three-dimensionality and kinetic structure—they can, I believe, be encompassed by a single theory that will lead us to our goal. For our two basic non-sensuous features, distinct though they may be, function in their respective forms of perceptual consciousness to achieve an identical phenomenon—one that alone can confer perceptuality upon sensuous modes of awareness.

The key to the Problem of Perception, as it relates to distinctively sensuous experience, is the following insight, the importance of which was first recognized, as far as I know, by Kant. It is that, where we have perception we can, but where we have mere sensation we cannot, draw a distinction between what is merely *a change of experience* and what is *an experience of change in the object of experience.*[7] With mere sensation, any change in experience is simply a change in the quality, distribution, intensity, or duration of the sensation itself. That our experience changes entails that the sensory object of our attention changes, because, as Reid says, there is no object distinct from the sensation itself. When we turn to perceptual consciousness, the situation is wholly different. For what the Kantian distinction highlights is what are known by psychologists as the "perceptual constancies." I believe that it is a proper appreciation of precisely these constancies, phenomenologically interpreted, that will allow us finally to answer the Argument from Illusion.[8] Moreover, since it is, I shall be arguing, precisely perceptual constancy that is at work in the non-sensuous dimension of our remaining two basic perceptual phenomena, such constancy allows these two to be comprehended by a single account.

The term "perceptual constancy" is used by psychologists to refer to any veridical perceptual situation in which an unchanging physical feature of an object gives rise, because of its changing relation to the perceiver, to changing proximal stimulation at our sense-organs, while the perceived feature of the object appears unchanged. Now, when such changing proximal stimulation gives rise to *changing sensations*, we shall have a "constant" perception despite inconstant sensation. It is this latter discrepancy alone that will be of concern to us, not that between perception and proximal stimulation. The distinction between the two arises when changing proximal stimulation fails to give rise to changing sensations. It is, for example, generally thought that retinal and immediately post-retinal *adaptation* accounts for at least certain instances of "colour constancy"—the notable constancy of the apparent colours of objects despite differing lighting conditions, and hence despite differing forms of light entering the eyes.[9] Similarly, it used to be thought that so-called lightness constancy—our ability to perceive objects as equally white (or grey, or black) despite their reflecting significantly different amounts of light into the eyes—involves "lateral inhibition" at the retinal and immediately post-retinal level.[10] Neither account involves perceptual constancy in the sense that is of interest to us. For although such accounts acknowledge a constancy of perception despite highly varied proximal stimulation, there is no constancy despite variation *in sensation:* adaptation and lateral inhibition introduce constancy at the post-retinal level before any sensation ensues, so that there is a *constancy* in the relation between sensation and perception. Such accounts are of no *phenomenological* relevance. We, however, are interested in a constancy that is manifest to reflexion on perceptual consciousness itself. We are also only interested in a constancy in an object *as it appears to the subject* despite variation in perceptual sensation: we are not concerned with the objective state of such physical objects. In order to avoid ambiguity, I shall sometimes refer to the kind of perceptual constancy that alone is our concern here as "phenomenological constancy."

In contrast to the above two merely "psycho-physical" constancies, here are some examples of phenomenological constancy. When I move my eyes while viewing my surroundings, although the character of my visual experience changes, what I am observing does not appear to move: I detect no movement in (what I take to be) the *objects* of my visual awareness. This is termed "position constancy." Again, when I walk up to an object, it projects an increasingly large image on my retinas, and comes to occupy a larger portion of my visual field; the object does not, however, typically look any larger as a result of these changes. This is called "size constancy." A third example is one that is of some historical significance. The informed reader will have noticed that although in my original presentation of the Argument I went out of my way to stress the potential ubiquity of illusion, there was one commonly cited instance of this that I did not mention. This is the claim that when you look at a round, flat object otherwise than straight- or side-on, it looks elliptical. Many of the classic expositions of the Argument use this claim to get it under way.[11] I did not myself use this example because the suggestion that pennies, for example, look elliptical when seen from most angles is simply not true—they look round—and in no sense, not even in the extended sense given to the term in these pages, is the look of such a tilted penny an illusion. Such a penny (usually) looks just the way it is: round and *tilted away from you.* This is called "shape constancy." All such constancies involve a change in visual experience, a change in visual sensation, despite the fact that the object of awareness does not itself appear to change at all. This is because the changes in sensation *themselves have objective significance:* there is a change in how the physical world perceptually appears to us. For such sensations are not merely overlooked, as Reid supposed. What happens because of the changing visual sensations involved in size constancy, for example, is that the object *looks nearer.* The same goes for all the phenomenological constancies: the changing sensations always manifest to us a changing *relation* in which an intrinsically unchanging object comes to stand to us. Only so is such constancy intelligible at all.

My proposal is that, with one qualification soon to be noted, *the operation of some phenomenological constancy in a sense-modality is* sufficient *for that sense to be perceptual; and that if the modality in question is, unlike the* Anstoss, *sensuously presentational in character, it is* necessary—*such constancy alone enabling sensation to function here perceptually.* That any such constancy suffices to render any sensory modality perceptual is, I take it, evident. Indeed, this simply *is* the Kantian insight as I have been construing it: any perceptual constancy opens up a distinction between the appearance of an object and the sensations that are thereby experienced—a distinction that is essentially absent from mere sensation. The more controversial thesis is the claim to necessity. Now, if it is agreed that our two fundamental phenomena are indeed alone sufficient for sensuously presentational modes of consciousness to be perceptual, this issue can be addressed by asking whether perceptual constancy is necessary for each. This can be swiftly demonstrated.

As concerns three-dimensional spatiality, it surely makes no sense to suppose that it is inconceivable that an object should appear to be at a distance from you, that this object should appear to come closer to you, and yet that it should not appear to change size; or that a non-spherical object should appear to turn around its axis and yet not appear to change shape. It also makes as little sense to suppose it inconceivable that a sound should be heard as getting closer, and yet not as getting any louder—"loudness constancy." It is of the very essence of the perception of things as located in three-dimensional space that they can appear to move without necessarily appearing to undergo any other— that is, intrinsic—change. Since in any such appearance both the relational change and the intrinsic lack of change must be registered in consciousness, we have a case of constancy. The sheer *possibility* of such experiences shows that perceptual constancies are in play in that sense-modality—for where mere sensation is concerned, such constancy phenomena are excluded *in principle*.[12]

The demonstration that perceptual constancy is entailed by the kinetic structuring of a sense-field through self-movement is even simpler, for the kind of integration of such movement with sense-fields that is here in question *itself constitutes* a species of perceptual constancy. If there is movement "into" a three-dimensional field, we shall have size constancy (or, if the field is auditory, loudness constancy); and if there is movement "across" a sense-field, as when we shift our gaze, we shall have position constancy. I can have a sense of myself, or of a part of myself, moving in relation to a sense-field only if movement on my part does not entail subjectively registered movement on the part of the object of awareness. Where there is self-movement, but no possibility of such independence—as in the experience of the inner light-show, where the "lights" move with each movement of the eyeballs or head—there can be no sense of movement in relation to an object of awareness. In the total absence of such a kinetic structuring of sense-fields, we have mere sensation. Conversely, the most minimal presence of such kinetic independence—and it is difficult to think of a more minimal presence than we find in the visuo-motor experience of cataract patients—suffices for perception.[13] Constancy in relation to self-movement is perhaps most in evidence, however, in haptic perception. As you run your hand over an object, the rapidly changing series of touch sensations at your fingers' ends is wholly compatible with the appearance of a solidly motionless object.[14]

It is true that there is not exactly perceptual constancy in our perception of smells and radiant heat.[15] We may *judge* that a smell or a thermal
phenomenon is objectively unchanged and that a less intense perception is due to our having distanced ourselves from it; but we do not
smell or feel this. And there is no sort of constancy whatever for taste
and surface temperature. All these perceptions are, however, as I argued earlier, derivative or acquired. They all presuppose perception
of the world through some other sense—one that *does* feature some
genuine phenomenological constancy. This is the reason for the qualification mentioned above. The precise claim to be defended here,
therefore, is that the operation of perceptual constancy in a sensuously
presentational sense-modality is necessary and sufficient for *original
perception* in that sense.[16]

Although we began this section with two irreducible sources of perceptual consciousness, the phenomenon of perceptual constancy allows
a unitary account. Indeed, it seems that we may be able to go even further in the direction of unity. For all the perceptual constancies we
have so far examined crucially involve movement. Not specifically self-
movement, and even less active self-movement, but movement as such,
occurring between a sense-organ and an object of sensory awareness, is
what sustains an independence between the course of our experience
and the experienced nature of the objects that is required by all the
perceptual constancies that have been mentioned (as well as others
that have not).[17] Even phenomenal three-dimensionality, in abstraction from self-movement, not only entails the possibility of perceiving objects move in the space in which they are visibly situated; it
is such movement in relation to the observer that alone introduces
those changes in sensation that are involved in the constancies that are
entailed by such spatiality. So the question naturally presents itself
whether it is always and necessarily movement on which perceptual
constancy immediately depends. In fact, it is not.

Consider colour and lightness constancy. If these are phenomenological constancies, then, according to the present suggestion, they suffice for perceptual consciousness. And yet it is not clear how movement
is it all relevant to them. Now, many instances of both colour and lightness constancy are not, in fact, phenomenological, but merely psycho-
physical. Adaptation is thought to play a role in colour constancy, for
example. This seems to be the reason why the colours of most objects

look more or less the same in daylight and electric light, even though, as photographs with the same colour film testify, different ranges of wavelengths enter your eye in these two situations. (In photographs of indoor scenes taken with outdoor film under ordinary electric light, yellow is surprisingly prominent, and blues look washed out.) Still, not all colour constancy can be accounted for in this way, for some is genuinely phenomenological—as can be demonstrated, ironically, by reference to that favourite example of philosophers: rose-tinted spectacles. If you put on such spectacles, white objects do *not* typically look pink; they look white. The same is generally true if you view a white object in a room illuminated by a coloured light-bulb. Here one's colour sensations are certainly different from what they would be if one were viewing these white objects in daylight and without coloured spectacles. Many cases of lightness constancy are like this too. So such cases do pose a problem for the suggestion that movement is fundamental for perception.

In fact, however, both of these constancies do, albeit indirectly, presuppose movement, for they are possible only within sensory modalities *that are already phenomenally three-dimensional,* and that, therefore, already feature some constancy that involves movement. For recall that the variations in sensation involved in phenomenological constancy are neither wholly overlooked, nor are they without objective significance. An object appears intrinsically unchanged despite such variations in sensation only because they manifest to us a change in the object's relation to us. Generally, this relation is straightforwardly some perspectival relation in which we stand to the object, where there can be change only as the result of movement. This is not what we find in the present cases. But what kind of indicated relationship to us do we find here? The answer is that in these two cases of perceptual constancy the varying sensations indicate to us a changing relation of the perceived object to something else in space. This other thing is *light.* For we do not merely see physical objects; we see such objects in a relation to surrounding light as more or less illuminated. It is because (and only because) of this that, although a weakly and a strongly illuminated sheet of white paper give rise to qualitatively different sensations in the visual field, they can both look white, indeed equally white. The former does not look grey, because the latter looks, not whiter, but *brighter* than the other. This is so even though the very same local sensations could, in a different context, give us appearances of a grey and a white object—as the following phenomena nicely illustrate. If you see a white piece of paper reflected in a shiny black tile, it will look white; however, by an act of attention you can bring yourself to see it as a mere patch *on* the tile, and then it will appear distinctly grey. Again, obscuring with a solid border the penumbra of an attached shadow will make the shadow look like a darker patch. And coming to see a border as merely the effect of illumination can also lead to a switch in appearance. Once again, as with all genuine constancies, this is not a matter merely of "judging" that things are objectively of the same or different colour; it is a matter of simple perceptual appearances. A dramatic illustration of this can be had using the "Mach strip" mentioned in Chapter 1. If you place the "roof," as suggested, so that one side is turned towards, the other away from, the light, the two sides look equally white, though one looks shaded. When, after viewing the object monocularly for while, the "roof" flips up to look like two pages of an upright book, lightness constancy is suddenly disrupted: the side that is objectively in the shade now definitely *does* look grey. It simply did not have that appearance before. As with all the perceptual constancies, the changing sensations involved in brightness constancy have the "objective significance" of indicating a changing relationship in which the intrinsically unchanging object stands to something else. Although, in contrast to all the other constancies I have mentioned, this "something else" is not ourselves, but the illuminating light, the relationship involved is a *spatial* relationship. No such thing is possible with the inner light-show, or any such two-dimensional array of "colour patches." Since such spatiality must already characterize the operative sense, the movement-involving constancies that are entailed by such spatiality are equally entailed by these lightness constancies. The same can be said of the colour constancies that are phenomenological in nature. When you don the rose-tinted spectacles, it is the ambient light that looks pink, and white objects look white, though bathed in pink light. Since I can think of no other perceptual constancy where movement fails to be immediately implicated, I believe we may conclude that a perceptual theory is able to be unified at least to the extent that it can be asserted that it is both necessary and sufficient, in order for a sensuously presentational sense-modality to be perceptual, that it feature *some* perceptual constancy that is of such a character that it is specifically *movement* that introduces the variable sensory elements into such constancy.

Movement is also, of course, essentially involved in the *Anstoss*. Indeed, it also functions there in such a way as to give rise to perceptual constancy in virtue of the dynamic interplay between ourselves and the appearing object. For we distinguish between our pressing more strongly against some alien body and the latter's pressing more forcibly on us, even though this gives rise to the same pressure on our bodies, and hence, typically, to the same pressure sensations. Here again we have a case where the variable element in experience reveals a change in the relation in which we stand to an unchanging object. We have what we might term "force constancy." So the pleasing thought presents itself that we may now have a totally unified perceptual theory—one embracing all three of our basic sources of perceptual consciousness. For have we not discovered that it is always movement that allows us to home in on a perceptual object that transcends the sheer flux of subjective sensation? Always movement that sustains the emergence of that *unum e pluribus* which is of the essence of perceptual consciousness? The bipartite, or tripartite, nature of the present account is perhaps simply a reflection of the different ways in which movement can function in perceptual experience.

Although this last point is, I believe, true, perceptual theory cannot be as unified as is here suggested. For there is, first, the sobering fact that the *Anstoss* involves movement in a wholly different way from the other two basic phenomena. With the *Anstoss* it is *agency* that is crucial. This underlies the fact that, secondly, and more importantly, although perceptual constancy is possible within the narrow limits of the *Anstoss*, it is not *necessarily* to be found there. For it is surely not a necessary truth, concerning any possible agent, that if it can push against something, it can push harder, or more gently, against it. Surely a creature could have but a single level of physical energy available to it with which to accomplish any of its activities. Take away such variability, however, and we have lost the only relevant variable that could feature in perceptual constancy in this area. The failure of this attempt at a "general unified theory" of perception is perhaps not to be wondered at, given not only the wholly unique character of the *Anstoss*, but also the fact that we have been able to reply to the Argument from Illusion in relation to the *Anstoss* without mentioning perceptual constancy.[18] Appealing to perceptual constancy is necessary only in order to rebut the Argument on its home territory of specifically sensuous perception. It is time to try to bring the investigations of Part I to a close by seeing precisely how the perceptual constancies are supposed to help us defeat the Argument in this remaining problematic area.

THE KEY TO AN ANSWER to our Problem in relation to sensuously presentational forms of perceptual consciousness is the recognition that we are not, even in this domain, aware of perceptual sensations as objects because, *if we were, perceptual constancy would be wholly absent:* the object of awareness would appear to change whenever there was a change of sensations, because such sensations would *be* our objects. For what must a sense-datum theorist say of the typical situation in which an object is seen to approach me? He must say that the sense-datum, that which is "given to sense," that of which I am most fundamentally and immediately aware, *gets bigger.* But that of which I am most fundamentally and immediately aware, what is *given* to me, does not appear to change at all in such a situation. This is a plain phenomenological fact. Or consider position constancy. If you move your head from side to side while looking at this page, the page will not seem to move. Compare this with viewing the "Mach strip" whilst similarly moving your head, where the visual object *does* appear to move. Most people are quite astounded when they experience this latter phenomenon for the first time—for it is not an experience that they have whenever they move their heads. With the Mach strip, position constancy startlingly fails. Such constancy is not the function of any "judgement" that supplements the deliverances of the senses; it characterizes what we are *aware of* in the most "basic" and "immediate" sense. Such constancies are present in the simple movement of an eye, a limb, or a head for all animals for almost all of their waking lives. The eye or the paw moves; the object seen or felt appears not to. In this and kindred phenomena we find the wholly pre-conceptual birth of distinctively *perceptual objects* that are beyond the capacity of mere sensation to deliver. Since the only alternatives presented by the Argument are that in perception we are aware either of normal physical objects on the one hand, or of sense-data or sensations on the other, and since we have seen that we can deny, on purely phenomenological grounds, that we are aware of either of the latter (since that would be incompatible with perceptual constancy), we may conclude, for all that the Argument has to offer to the contrary, that we are directly aware of normal physical objects, just as Direct Realism contends.

We are really pretty good at telling, simply by looking, when nearby objects change in size, shape, or location. If you move your eyes closer to this page, you can see perfectly well that it does not get larger. The same may be said of the position constancy that holds sway throughout haptic perception. If you run your finger over this page, it will not at all seem, even with your eyes closed, that the surface is moving under your finger: that is a wholly different kind of experience. Similarly with the sense of hearing: in most circumstances you can immediately tell if someone is speaking appreciably more loudly, or whether he is approaching you while speaking at a constant volume. The reliability of our senses is not, however, what is of importance here. The perceptual constancies are, indeed, far from perfect; but even if they were worse than they actually are, that would be of no significance. What is important is that they characterize, and fundamentally characterize, perception *at all*. Relatedly, it should not be supposed that the present defence of Direct Realism applies only when some perceptual constancy is actually operative. For since the operation of a constancy involves a variation in sensation, and such variation always involves movement, this would mean that we could never have perceptual awareness of an unmoving normal object while we ourselves were stationary and wholly inert—which is certainly false. The justification of applying the constancy-based defence of Direct Realism outside the occasions when some constancy is actually operative resides in the fact that we have perceptual consciousness of an object that *would* emerge as a single object of awareness, in virtue of the operation of some constancy, *if* a relevant movement were to occur. Consider, for example, a cataract sufferer staring fixedly at the light streaming from a brilliantly lit window in the dark. Although this subject is aware of but a two-dimensional array of light and shade, this ought, I have suggested, to be recognized as a case where the subject perceives, albeit extremely poorly, the light of the window. The reason for this is that, if the subject were to turn his head, the light would not, or might not, appear to him to move. The sheer possibility of the operation of such a perceptual constancy serves to confer perceptual status on the original static experience; for in the realm of mere sensation, such constancy is *impossible*. During the actual operation of the constancy, the object of awareness has an unchanging identity amidst the flux of sensation. When the subject begins to turn his head, thus bringing position constancy into operation, the object retains an unchanging character. Since this object of awareness cannot be equated with sensation while the constancy is in operation, neither can it be so equated before movement introduces the constancy. This is even clearer when we consider perceptual experience that is phenomenally three-dimensional. To perceive an object at a distance is to perceive it as being in a space through which it could move without undergoing any apparent intrinsic change. Should it move towards you, the sensations that register this movement will be changing, but the object will appear not to: only its relation to you appears to change. The phenomenal three-dimensionality of perceptual objects that gives them "external reality" is a phenomenal manifestation that such spatial perceptual constancies are potentially in play.

This, I believe, is how Direct Realism may be defended against our Argument in all the areas in which it is desired: all those cases where we are, intuitively, perceptually conscious of a normal physical object (or "phenomenon"). In supplementing the *Anstoss* by the perceptual constancies, all this intuitively delimited terrain has been covered; and, equally importantly, we have defended the *Anstoss* itself from being undermined. The task we have set ourselves in the first part of this work is effectively at its end. There is but one further point to consider.

ADVOCATES of the Argument from Illusion have failed to see that the perceptual constancies can play an essential role in blocking that Argument for one simple reason. For what has been vital to this attempt to block the Argument is the claim that when a perceptual constancy is in operation, although perceptual sensation is changing, what I am aware of, in the most basic and immediate sense, does not appear to change. Advocates of the Argument have consistently asserted that this is simply not true. When, for example, I walk up to an object while looking at it, what I am immediately aware of visually *does*, they say, increase in size. What I have been referring to as "perceptual" constancy is in fact no more than the content of a judgement that I make, perhaps on the basis of past experience, in response to what I am immediately aware of.

In giving examples of illusion in Chapter 1, I focused on cases where the manifest character of perceptual appearance differed from the true nature of the perceived physical object—cases where the object would naturally be taken to possess a sensible character that was simply in ac-

cord with the character of perceptual sensation. As a result of considering the constancies, however, we have come increasingly to see the way
in which the character of such sensation can *diverge* from the character
we take the object to have. And in fact it is not uncommon for support-
ers of the Argument to point precisely to aspects of perceptual experience of which we are usually ignorant in order to introduce a notion of
immediate awareness that is intended to undermine Direct Realism.
C. W. K. Mundle, for example, writes that "if one suspends one's normal perceptual preoccupation—with identifying physical things of familiar kinds, etc.—there is what we may call another 'dimension of perceptual experience.' If one starts paying heed to the contents of one's
'visual field,' it is possible to go on noticing things that had never been
noticed before."[19] He goes on to claim that it is "phenomenology" that
pays attention to this other dimension; that phenomenology deals with
phenomena; that a phenomenon is "an immediate object of awareness"; and that therefore these usually overlooked aspects of perceptual
experience are "*immediate* objects of perception," or are "sense-given."
Mundle also speaks of such "sense-given" facts in terms of how an object "looks$_{(ph)}$"—that is, looks phenomenologically. So, according to
Mundle, a penny seen at an angle looks$_{(ph)}$ elliptical. He recognizes,
of course, that we commonly speak of how a thing looks in a non-
"phenomenological" sense. This common, everyday sense of a thing
looking a certain way is, however, supposed by him to be a matter of *estimating* the real characteristics of an object. I have suggested, contra
such writers as Broad, Russell, and Price, that the appearance of a circular object seen from the side is not a case of illusion in *any* sense.
This, however, is perhaps of little theoretical importance. Perhaps it is
indeed, as Mundle suggests, on this "other dimension" of perceptual
experience that we should all along have been focusing in order to introduce the notion of direct awareness that is to cause trouble for Direct Realism. And, to be sure, the trouble for Direct Realism would be
overwhelming if we followed this approach, since it would block a reply
to the Argument based on the perceptual constancies—the only satisfactory reply, I suggest, that is available. If Direct Realism is to be se-
cured, therefore, we need to insist that it is the character of the most
basic sensible appearances of things that are determined by the operation of the constancies.

It is certainly the case that the character of one's visual experience is different when looking at a penny from an angle when looking at it full-face. This difference is, however, seriously mis-described as a case of an object *looking differently shaped*. After all, if something really does perceptually look elliptical to me, I shall, if I notice the thing, and if I have no countervailing information to hand, take the thing to *be* elliptical—for I have nothing else to go by.[20] In the case of the tilted penny, however, no such thing occurs. I am not even inclined, the tiniest bit, to take the object to be elliptical, or to react to it as to an elliptical—one can even say elliptical *looking*—object. If set to perform discrimination tests, I should naturally and unthinkingly class together, on the basis of their visual appearances, what I see when I look at the titled penny with *round* objects seen full-on. Animals react in the same way. Indeed, the relatively difficult identification test in this area is trying to identify objects that have the same look$_{(ph)}$ in Mundle's sense. That kind of painterly, or so-called innocent, attitude to what we are presented with visually is an unnatural and sophisticated one that is difficult to attain.[21] This is equally the case with haptic perception, or active touch. For the analogy in this domain to what constitutes looking$_{(ph)}$ would be the series of sensations of contact and texture at our fingers' ends as we handle an object. We noted earlier that one of Reid's more intuitively compelling claims was that we are hardly perceptually intent upon *these* when we explore an object tactually. By lumping together all uses of "looks" other than "looks$_{(ph)}$" as being a matter of estimation, Mundle is, to use the terminology of Chapter 1, assimilating the evidential and the genuinely perceptual uses of this term.

The reason why, in the past, so many philosophers and psychologists have thought otherwise, in relation to sight, is that they held that what we are immediately aware of visually is a two-dimensional array of colour patches—"a party-coloured plane," as Samuel Bailey put it.[22] Hume stated the then standard view as follows: "'Tis commonly allowed by philosophers that all bodies which discover themselves to the eye, appear as if painted on a plain surface, and that their different degrees of remoteness from ourselves are discover'd more by reason than by the senses."[23] These patches were conceived as being, in effect, two-dimensional projections of three-dimensional objects. If the sizes and shapes that physical objects look to have are either identical to, or a function of, such patches, then the claim that round objects look elliptical and that approaching objects look bigger will indeed be a natural consequence. In fact, I can think of *no other reason* why anyone should deny that a tilted round penny looks round other than such a presumption that properly visual experience is phenomenally two-dimensional. Since I have elsewhere discussed at some length this idea that sight, touch, and hearing are "originally" at best two-dimensional in phenomenal character—that such senses basically lack an awareness of what Berkeley termed "outness"—I shall here simply state that there is nothing whatever to be said in its favour.[24] And if there is no reason to deny the fundamental nature of the perceptual constancies in relation to phenomenally three-dimensional perceptual experience, there is equally little reason to deny it in relation to our second basic perceptual phenomenon—where the critical suggestion would be that all that is originally given in this domain is the movement of objects of awareness, and that we then come to attribute some of these movements to ourselves. "Position constancy" is, however, as irreducible in this domain as are the three-dimensional constancies. This being so, and if such misguided claims are the only way in which it could be argued that perceptual constancies are not absolutely basic perceptual phenomena, we can return to our defence of Direct Realism with confidence.

It is important, however, that we should not go to the extreme to which some have been led in their accounts of perceptual constancy. When I walk up to an unchanging object while looking at it, there is *some* sense in which something grows in extensity. The extreme to be avoided is the denial of this (and of analogous facts in connection with the other constancies). "Consider again the circle seen at a slant," writes Irwin Rock, one of the most theoretically sophisticated of recent perceptual psychologists. "Many students in introductory classes in psychology are likely to shake their heads when the instructor points out that the circle looks circular and not elliptical. They often say 'it looks elliptical but I know it is circular'. In saying this, they are advocating the classical thesis the Gestaltists opposed so vigorously and successfully . . . In this I believe they are mistaken. We do *perceive* the circle at a slant as circular, but we *also* are aware that its projected extensity relations are 'elliptical'. The point is that we would be seriously distorting the phenomenal facts if we chose to speak *only* of the constancy aspects of perception. In this respect the students have been right and we have been wrong."[25] We should not dissent from this. Rock is right to stress that such "projective" facts concerning sensation have phenomenological significance. That a certain object gives rise to greater "extensity" in the visual field than another identically sized object is, after all, necessary if the one is both to look nearer than the other and to look the same size as it. To recognize only the aspect of constancy in perception is, in effect, to treat perception as if it were thought, and to forget that it is a sensory phenomenon we are dealing with. Rock, however, claims that to recognize such "projective" (or, as he puts it, "proximal mode") facts is to recognize a level of merely two-dimensional phenomenal description of visual experience. For otherwise, he suggests, "the existence of the proximal mode would seem to be a curious, redundant, unexplained phenomenon."[26] A feature such as "extensity" is, however, neither curious, redundant, nor unexplained, since it is a *phenomenological necessity*. Given two objects that look the same size, one of them *must* have greater extensity if it looks closer to you than the other one. This is not a real feature of a two-dimensional visual array, but an abstraction from the three-dimensional field with which one is phenomenally presented. But, one may object, must one not at least recognize that an object looks to be the size that it is *because* of its extensity in the field of vision? And does not such an admission take us back to the dual component theory—with visual sensations *causing* us to judge the sizes of perceived objects? We have seen that such a "judgement" ought not to be seen as a conceptual representation of the environment; but that granted, have we not still to recognize the core truth of the dual component theory? We have not, since the "because" here should not be misinterpreted as having causal force. It expresses, rather, the phenomenological necessity in question. For it is equally true to say that an object has the "extensity" that it does because it is seen as having such and such a size at such and such a distance. These are but two inter-dependent aspects of the phenomenally three-dimensional visual experience that is created at one stroke by the operation of the visual system. (And analogous remarks hold for the other senses that embody any perceptual constancy.)

Indeed, we are finally in a position to see that the language of "perceptual sensation," though it has the virtue of recognizing the reality of sensory qualia while yet avoiding the invocation of sense-data, has a limited value and is a potential source of misunderstanding. For it is tempting to think that, if sensation is ingredient in perceptual experience, it must be *the very same thing* that is present there that might occur non-perceptually. If one thinks in this way, however, the Argument from Illusion will be unanswerable. At best we shall end up with the dual component theory. What mere sensation and perceptual experience have in common is not sensation—a type of sensory state in its own right—but sensory qualities, or qualia. There is no common sensory state to perception and sensation that such qualities characterize. In the one case they characterize, or "inhere in," perceptual experience, in the other, sensation. We should not try to understand perceptual experience by trying to construct it out of independently intelligible psychological states such as sensations. Perceptual consciousness is a distinctive and irreducible type of psychological state, which shares with sensation only the fact that it is possessed of a qualitative character. We should not ask how mere sensation can *become* perceptual—for it cannot. All we can do is seek to understand how perceptual consciousness itself can emerge and possess the same qualitative character as sensation. I have suggested that we should understand this emergence in relation to three fundamental sources of perceptual consciousness. It is the non-sensory functions that are at work in these three basic phenomena that render them perceptual—that, indeed, constitute any perceptual act as perceptual. These functions do not supplement independently constituted sensations, but rather, together with sensory qualia, characterize that type of state which is perceptual consciousness.

THE ARGUMENT FROM ILLUSION has, I believe, been answered. It has been answered, moreover, on phenomenological grounds. The present account should not, however, be confused with what one may call the "cheap phenomenological response" to the Argument. "I've never seen a sense-datum in my life!" a former colleague once said to me. It is astonishing how many philosophers are of the opinion that simply pointing out that mature perceptual experience is not a matter of registering, as Charles Taylor puts it, "raw uninterpreted data," that such experience is "suffused with concepts," or at least that certain principles of perceptual "organization" are at work, suffices to defuse the force of the Argument.[27] Such a tack gets us nowhere—even if the almost inevitable reference to "concepts" is ignored. The sense-datum theorist can happily accept all of this.[28] "Interpret," "conceptualize," and "organize" all you like, the question still remains: What are the immediate objects of awareness that are involved in any such activity? Even bodily sensations are not "raw uninterpreted data" in the relevant sense, and yet they are mere sensations. What is of vital importance, rather, is that a feature of perceptual experience be isolated that is both sufficiently basic to be involved in all conscious animal perception, and that will allow us to distinguish between an object of perceptual awareness and either sensations or sense-data. In relation to sensuously presentational perception, this is to be found in perceptual constancy, elsewhere in the *Anstoss*, and nowhere else. Here and here alone do we find within sense-experience itself the phenomenological independence of object from subject that is the hallmark of perceptual consciousness. Here we find the distinctive intentionality of perception: one that is distinct from, and indeed more basic than, that to be found in thinking.

Nevertheless, some readers may be surprised that merely phenomenological observations should be thought capable of delivering Direct Realism. After all, what is of central concern in this area is the issue of perceptual "transcendence": how we can pierce the "veil of perception," break out of the circuit of our own experience, and come into immediate cognitive contact with an "external world." How, it may be objected, could mere phenomenology, which is just a matter of how things stand *within* experience, be thought to be of decisive importance here? Such an objection would, however, betray misunderstanding on one or other of two points. First, the Argument that we have been wrestling with concerns illusion, not hallucination. It does not presuppose that we fail to be directly aware of normal physical objects when we experience an illusion: that is part of what it is supposed to prove. Until this is achieved, we are allowed to assume that we *are* so aware of such physical objects. It is not we who have to prove that we are; it is the proponent of the Argument who has to prove that we are not. The *only* proof that is offered, however, proceeds by pointing out that the sensory qualities that feature in illusory perceptual experience are inherent in sense-experience itself. It forces us to recognize sensory qualia. This, however, does not constitute the proof; it is but one stage of it. What has to be shown in addition is that we are *directly aware* of these sensory qualities—or, rather, of whatever it is that possesses them—as objects. Only then will the normal object be edged out of its presumed position as object of immediate awareness. Only then will "transcendence" have been lost. So all we have to show, in order to block the Argument, is that we are not directly aware of whatever it is that possesses such qualities, so that awareness of the latter does not cognitively mediate our awareness of normal physical objects. Showing that such bearers are sense-data would carry the Argument through; but that, I have suggested, is what has not been, and cannot be, demonstrated.[29] An alternative is that what bear such qualities are sensations. As soon as this is said, however, phenomenological considerations do become relevant. It can be shown, and I have shown, the way in which sensations, though "in" consciousness, are not objects for consciousness. They are not objects for consciousness either in relation to the *Anstoss*, nor in relation to the perceptual constancies. Phenomenology by itself cannot, to be sure, prove transcendence; but that has never been the question here. What phenomenology can do is block an argument that would seek to deprive of us such transcendence. This achieved, we can interpret the constant appearance of a single unchanging object amid varying sensations in perceptual constancy and the *Anstoss* as what, in the absence of an argument to the contrary, and in accord with the very meaning of the term "illusion," we should naturally take it to be: the varying appearance of the normal object of perception.

Secondly, I do not suggest that what has been achieved so far suffices to vindicate Direct Realism even within what I have delimited as the Philosophy of Perception. What I suggest is that it is capable of sustaining Direct Realism *in the face of the Argument from Illusion*. This work is in two parts because we have a second argument to consider: the Argument from Hallucination, where the issue of transcendence will take centre stage. It is, indeed, far from obvious how the present account of perceptual consciousness can put us in a position to answer this second, and much more serious, challenge to Direct Realism.

The **Argument** from **Hallucination**

II

The Argument

7

IN THE INTRODUCTION to this work I suggested that all arguments against Direct Realism can be seen as employing the principle of the Indiscernibility of Identicals. They all attempt to find some discrepancy between the perceived normal object and the immediate object of awareness. In Part I we looked at an argument based upon qualitative discrepancy. In this part we turn our attention to a discrepancy concerning existence. The most obvious such case, falling with the domain of the Philosophy of Perception, is that of hallucination, where a subject seems to perceive a normal physical object, but where none such exists at all. Or rather—since there could be a situation in which a subject hallucinates an object just where there really is such a one—where the subject seems to perceive a physical object, but where there is in reality no physical object which is the one he seems to perceive. (If I hallucinate a stain on a wall exactly where there really is just such a stain, it is not *that* stain that I seem to see. Although in some sense "accurate," this experience is not "veridical" in the sense in which I shall employ the term.) This is definitive of hallucination, as philosophers have come to use the term, and pinpoints the essential way in which hallucination differs from illusion. In illusion, although a physical object appears other than it actually is, that very object is really perceived; in hallucination, "that" physical object does not exist. No doubt most actual hallucinations are partial, in the sense that an object is hallucinated against a genuinely perceived background: you hallucinate a pink rat, say, in the middle of the carpet, just to the right of that chair, both of which you genuinely perceive. As far as the specifically hallucinatory aspect of such a situation goes, however, it remains the case that there is an element of your perceptual field that constitutes, or goes towards constituting, a perception of no physical object whatsoever. If you are misperceiving a part of the carpet as a pink rat, we have a case of illusion, not hallucination.[1]

Another situation that has been used for motivating an argument against Direct Realism based upon a discrepancy in existence is double vision. Hume believed that such a phenomenon allowed him to refute Direct Realism in a couple of sentences: "When we press one eye with a finger, we immediately perceive all the objects to become double, and one half of them to be remov'd from their common and natural position. But as we do not attribute a continu'd existence to both these perceptions, and as they are both of the same nature, we clearly perceive, that all our perceptions are dependent on our organs, and the disposition of our nerves and animal spirits."[2] In such cases a normal object is, we naturally believe, indeed perceived; the problem is that there are *two* objects of awareness, at least one of which, it would therefore seem, must be non-identical to the normal object. It is sometimes objected that in such cases of induced double vision one of the apparent objects always appears more intangible and ghostly than the other, and also that the former eventually dissolves into the latter, more substantial one. True though this is, it could be replied in turn that, ghostly or not, a second object of some sort is there, so that we must recognize at least one non-normal object of awareness in such cases. Doubtless, however, the ghostly nature of the supplementary objects will render implausible the eventual claim that all objects of perception have the same ontological status as such spectres. As a matter of fact, however, in a different type of case of double vision the situation is quite different. If one focuses on a distant object, any interposed physical object will appear double, as Reid emphasized. Here, although it is still the case that one of the apparent objects always looks insubstantial—we can, for example, see "through" it—we can, by shifts of attention, make *either* object the substantial one and the one into which the other "dissolves," and so, it would seem, paradoxically determine which object is the "real" one. The problem with all such double vision cases, however, is that the Direct Realist can deny that two objects are seen: rather, he will say, one object is perceived twice or perceived double or as double. Although this manoeuvre may eventually prove unsatisfactory, the case of hallucination is not beset with such an additional difficulty. Any problem that double vision may genuinely present for Direct Realism will surely emerge in an analogous, and simpler, form in a consideration of hallucination.

Another perceptual situation that is commonly discussed as involving a discrepancy in existence is the having of an after-image.[3] As a result of an after-image I can take myself to be seeing a dark patch on a facing surface when there is no such patch there that I am seeing. Here, too, we seem to have a non-normal object of awareness. The weakness with such a reliance on after-images, however, is that they become apparently normal objects of awareness for us only when "projected" on to other objects; and it is open to a Direct Realist to claim that it is these latter normal objects of which we are aware, the after-image merely serving to mislead us as to the characteristics of these objects. We are dealing, in short, with cases of illusion. I shall, therefore, in this part focus specifically on hallucination, and we may term the argument against Direct Realism with which we are to be concerned for the remainder of this work the "Argument from Hallucination"—henceforth "the Argument."

The preceding remarks about after-images may, however, suggest a worry about the ability of even hallucination to ground an objection to Direct Realism. For perhaps it is the case that all hallucinations are only partial. If the pink rat is always hallucinated against a genuinely perceived background, is this not also a case of "projection" on to a real object in the physical environment? Perhaps to hallucinate a pink rat in the middle of the carpet is always to misperceive a patch of carpet. If so, we should again have reverted to nothing better than the Argument from Illusion. Such a manoeuvre has very little plausibility, however. If the rat seems to jump through the air, across an open window, what can we say it is that you are misperceiving? The air (though air is not visible)? Part of the distant sky (though the object seems to be but a few feet away from me)? In any case, although I shall myself, for ease of exposition, sometimes use examples of partial hallucination, the Argument can be based on the possible occurrence of *total* hallucinations: cases where an entire perceptual field is hallucinatorily induced. Perhaps there are no actual cases of such total hallucination, but as we shall

see, as with the Argument from Illusion the mere *possibility* of hallucinations is enough to inaugurate an argument against Direct Realism.
That said, let us turn to the Argument itself.

The Argument from Hallucination has a structure closely parallel to
that of the Argument from Illusion, so we can be relatively brief in its
presentation. The first stage is the simple claim that hallucinations are
possible; or, more precisely, that for any veridical perception, it is possible that there should be a hallucination with exactly the same subjective character. So a subject could hallucinate in such a way that he
seems to see a book in front of him, and seems to be reading it, in a
manner that exactly matches your own present experience of reading
this book.[4] Guido Küng, for one, has objected to this: "It is often
claimed that as far as the experience of the subject is concerned a naive
hallucination [that is, one where the subject is taken in] is not distin-
guishable from a genuine perception. I do not think that this is true.
But it may happen that the experiencing subject does not pay attention
to distinguishing features which are present in the experience."[5] What
might these telltale features be? I can only think that Küng has in mind
the possibility that the object should follow one's gaze, as an after-image does; or that the "image" does not properly occlude objects in front
of which it is apparently situated; or at least that the experience in some
way fails to embody a full sense of reality. If the suggestion is—as it
must be if it is to carry any weight at this point—that a hallucinatory
state of perceptual consciousness that lacked any such telltale signs is
an *absolute impossibility*, I find it to be wholly without plausibility.

Having claimed that lifelike hallucinations are possible, the Argument proceeds to claim, as its second stage, that a hallucinating subject
is aware of something. When you hallucinate, though you are indeed not
really seeing or smelling or otherwise perceiving any real object or
phenomenon in your environment, you are surely aware of *something*.
Since, however, you are, ex hypothesi, not aware of a normal object, we
have to recognize a non-normal object of awareness—an image, or
sense-datum, or what have you—for any case of hallucination. Having
established this, the Argument proceeds to its generalizing stage: what
holds true of possible hallucination goes for all perceptual experience.
Even in so-called veridical perceptual situations you are never aware, at
least directly, of a normal physical object.

When we compare our two arguments, from illusion and from hallucination, I believe a natural initial reaction is the following. With respect to the Argument from Illusion, the dubious step was the very introduction of non-normal objects of awareness. Once this is granted, the generalizing step seems plain sailing. With the Argument from Hallucination the opposite seems to be the case. For the claim that a hallucinating person is aware of *nothing whatever* seems initially preposterous. Consider your present perceptual state: you are certainly aware of something. Now consider the possible hallucinatory course of experience that is qualitatively identical to your present one. It would, for such a subject, be subjectively *exactly* as it is for you now. This subject, if asked to report on what he was aware of, would reply just as you would now. This subject too can shift his attention from one to another part of his visual field, or from what he sees to what he is hearing; he can scrutinize objects more closely and can describe what he is aware of. Such reports would not be mere make-believe. Does the subject not say what he does because he is aware of things possessing a manifest phenomenal character? Here Broad's question comes back with full force: if such a hallucinating subject is not aware of anything, why does he say that he sees a page of print, as opposed to a motor-car or nothing at all? In relation to the Argument from Illusion, Broad's challenge was seen to have less than complete authority. In Part I, I attempted to show how we can defend our conviction that it is a normal object of which we are aware when we are subject to illusory appearances. In the hallucinatory case, however, there would seem to be no such candidate normal object; and so it is not clear how we can avoid the introduction of a non-normal object of awareness. As we shall see in the following chapter, the denial that a hallucinating subject is aware of anything has been made—and by not inconsiderable philosophers. I think it must be granted, however, that such a denial has very little initial plausibility. Indeed, I think it fair to say that such a denial is made only as a last desperate effort to defend Direct Realism at all cost.

On the other hand, although the introduction of non-normal objects to account for hallucination may seem quite reasonable, the generalizing step may initially appear to have no plausibility whatsoever. Why on earth should the same kind of object be involved in such radically dissimilar cognitive situations as hallucination and genuine perception? Indeed, the very plausibility of recognizing non-normal hallucinatory objects may seem to work against the plausibility of the generalizing move. For the Argument from Hallucination, unlike the Argument from Illusion, initially introduces a non-normal object of awareness only in the case of the radical loss of perceptual contact with the environing world that is involved in hallucination. The following restricted form of Direct Realism may therefore seem to be a plausible response to the Argument: That we are, in perceptual consciousness, always immediately aware of normal objects, except when we hallucinate. This, indeed, bids fair to be called the view of enlightened common sense. (Incidentally, I shall be using the term "genuine perception" to cover veridical and illusory perceptions, but not hallucinatory states. I shall, however, often speak of hallucinatory states as being phenomenologically "perceptual" in character—since the claim that there could possibly be states that are phenomenologically identical to genuine perceptions is simply the first premise of our Argument.)

As with the Argument from Illusion, it is at this point that the possible qualitative identity, or indiscernibility, of veridical and hallucinatory experiences is generally emphasized. Although some weight was accorded to the issue of qualitative identity in motivating acceptance of the generalizing move in the context of the Argument from Illusion, it will be recalled that the conclusive reason for making the move in that context arose from the very concept of illusion itself, according to which we are aware of the same object in illusion as we could perceive veridically. To deny the generalizing move there would effectively have been to deny the existence of illusions, and to treat them all as hallucinations. Such a reason is, of course, inapplicable when we are, as now, explicitly concerned with hallucination. What, therefore, a proponent of the Argument needs to do is to find some undeniable ground for holding that hallucinations, qua experiences, share a common nature with genuine perceptions, in virtue of which hallucinations, equally with genuine perceptions, must be allocated a non-normal object as the immediate object of awareness. The possible subjective indiscernibility of genuine perceptions and hallucinations may well appear to be such a ground. And perhaps the most intuitively compelling way of marshalling such possible indiscernibility is to suppose that a hallucination occurs that precisely matches what the subject would see (or otherwise perceive) around him if he were not hallucinating, and then that genuine perception is so deftly restored that *no subjective change at all* is experienced by the subject. If it is granted, by the second step of the Argument, that the subject is at first aware of a non-normal object in this situation, how can the subject be aware, at least directly, of anything other than this self-same non-normal object when nothing whatever experientially changes for the subject? Surely, the subject is, here, continuously aware of the *same* persisting object.

Nevertheless, a denial that hallucination and genuine perception have a common nature is central to an increasingly influential account of perception, deriving from the work of J. M. Hinton—one that is commonly known as the "disjunctive" account of perception. This view denies that subjective indiscernibility—which only means sameness as far as the subject can tell—is a true guide to the actual nature of experiences, to the "what-it-is" of such experiences, as Hinton puts it.[6] On the disjunctive account of these matters, although the subject may definitely know something about the character of his conscious state while yet being unsure whether he is hallucinating or genuinely perceiving, it is denied that such knowledge indicates that there is an identifiable component in such experiences that is a "common core"— one that, if it were to occur in isolation, would be a hallucination, but is, or is a constituent of, a genuine perception when it is supplemented by various extraneous, primarily causal, factors relating that experience to the physical environment. That is to say, it is regarded as a temptation to jump to the conclusion that it is just such a sensory state that our subject definitely knows to obtain. The target of the disjunctive theory is, as Hinton puts it, "the doctrine of the 'experience' as the common element in a given perception and its perfect illusion," "a sort of as-it-were-picture-seeing [that] occurs as a common constituent of illusion and true perception."[7] (Given our present concerns, for "illusion" read "hallucination.") To use John McDowell's often echoed phrase, what is rejected is a "highest common factor" account of experience.[8] Perhaps it is true that a certain subject cannot tell whether he is genuinely perceiving something or merely hallucinating, and yet know that he is at least having an experience of a certain character; nevertheless, such epistemological facts should not lead us to infer that the subject is aware of enjoying a kind of experience of a determinate nature that is independent of whether he is genuinely perceiving or hallucinating. To underline the falsity of such an inference, the disjunctive theory proposes that we best express what our subject definitely does know in such a situation as his knowing *either* that he is perceiving something of such and such a sort *or* that he is hallucinating such a thing.[9] This is, to be sure, something that our subject definitely does know; and yet there is no suggestion that what he knows is that he is enjoying an experience with a determinate nature. Indeed, the nature of the state is precisely what is left open by such a construal of the situation. Such an either / or statement is, it is claimed, the bottom line in specifying *what is occurring*—something that is not further decomposable into an inner state (common to perception and hallucination) and extra conditions, the holding or not of which determines whether the case is that of perception or hallucination. In short, we should not follow Taine's famous characterization of perception as a "true hallucination"—an intrinsically world-independent sensory state plus various other conditions (though no doubt ones involving causality as well as "truth").[10] So even the most initially compelling employment of subjective indiscernibility —the switch from a hallucination to a genuine perception without any noticeable change at all—is simply rejected by the disjunctivists: despite the lack of any subjectively registered change, the subject in such a situation would indeed be aware of two different objects—one hallucinatory, and one real—that he cannot tell apart from one another. If the disjunctive account of experience is accepted, the generalizing move of our Argument will, of course, have no plausibility, since there will be no common nature to hallucinations and genuine perceptions to warrant the generalization of the introduction of non-normal objects of awareness from hallucinations to all perceptual situations.

A number of writers have argued that the generalizing step can be forced through, and hence the "disjunctivist" proposal refuted, by appeal to the principle that the same kind of total, proximate cause gives rise to the same kind of effect.[11] The idea is perhaps best explained by reference to a well-known passage in Russell: "Science holds that, when we 'see the sun,' there is a process, starting from the sun, traversing the space between the sun and the eye, changing its character when it reaches the eye, changing its character again in the optic nerve and the brain, and finally producing the event which we call 'seeing the sun.'"[12] If we replicate just the last events in the optic nerve and brain, shall we not generate exactly the same kind of visual experience as we have when we really see the sun—one that because of its unusual aetiology cannot be regarded as a genuine seeing of the sun, but must count as a hallucination? The suggestion is that since any hallucination involves awareness of a non-normal object, and since, moreover, such a hallucination may be generated in a subject by precisely replicating the proximate afferent inputs to the brain that occur during any veridical perception—so that any such veridical perception has the very same kind of total immediate cause as some possible hallucination—such veridical perceptions, too, must, by the causal principle, also involve awareness of a non-normal object.[13]

In fact, however, a blanket application of such a causal principle to the psychological domain is not something that can be uncontroversially relied upon these days. Hinton, for example, writes that "there is the feeling that if not everything, then at any rate every effect, must be what you might call 'narrowly identifiable'; meaning that one can state the what-it-is of it, to a degree of exactitude which satisfies normal human interest in the matter, without having to know what its proximate, let alone more remote, cause is."[14] He clearly means this to be a diagnosis of an error. And Paul Snowdon explicitly claims that perceptual experience is "essentially tied to a certain sort of cause."[15] Indeed, a position commonly known as "externalism" is widely accepted by philosophers today. The central tenet of externalism is that what cognitive state you are in is not a matter that can be specified independently of your relationship to an environment: that, as far as the cognitive domain is concerned, "methodological solipsism"—the claim that one can fully determine the nature of one's mental states by reflexion or apperception—is false. Externalists admit that there will indeed be *something* inner that is common to those in subjectively identical states, but insist that what can be thus identified as common is not identifiable as something *cognitive*. As McDowell says of such supposed inner contents, "These 'contents' could not yield answers to the question what it is that someone thinks; there is really no reason to recognize them as contents at all."[16] They are at best content "bearers" or "vehicles."[17] Applied to the topic of perception, the externalist claim is that the notion of *being aware of an object* is, though no doubt distinct in various ways from thinking, at least cognitive in the relevant sense, and so escapes the application of the causal principle.

It should not be thought that the following argument, due to C. D. Broad, suffices to rule out the viability of externalism, at least with respect to perception: "Suppose it could be shown that the occurrence of a certain disturbance in a certain part of a person's brain at a certain time is the immediate *sufficient* condition of his then having an experience which he would naturally describe as seeing or hearing or feeling a foreign object of a certain kind in a certain place. Then it would follow at once that the actual presence of such an object at that place at that time *cannot* be a *necessary* condition of the occurrence of the experience. From this it would follow at once that the experience *cannot* be, as it appears to be to the person, a prehension [a direct awareness] of the object in question."[18] This is not adequate to rule out the possibility in question because, for one thing, the logical principle on which Broad seems to rely here—that if X is sufficient for Y, then nothing else is necessary for Y—is unsound. The correct principle is that if X is sufficient for Y, then nothing else is necessary for Y except what is necessary for X itself. In the case in question, Broad's argument leaves it open that the "foreign object" may itself be necessary for the cerebral disturbance in question. Doubtless Broad assumed that no such necessary dependence would be present, but whether such an assumption is warranted depends upon precisely how we are to understand what it is for which such a brain disturbance would suffice. Broad characterizes it as "an experience which [the subject] would naturally describe as. . . ." One way of reading this is as saying that a certain type of brain event is sufficient to give rise to some experience or other with a certain phenomenal character. So read, the claim is doubtless true; and given that no *type* of brain event is necessarily the result of the presence of any "foreign object" at all, Broad's assumption would also be justified, and we should be warranted in concluding that no subjectively specified type of experience requires the presence of any such object. This, however, falls short of the conclusion Broad intends to secure: that no such object can be necessary to any *individual* experience with a given subjective character. In order to reach *this* conclusion, Broad will have to defend both of the following two possibilities: first, that a particular brain disturbance that was caused by a certain object could have been caused by another object (or none)—that is to say, a certain thesis about individual essences; and second, that neurological facts suffice to determine not only the phenomenal, but also the cognitive, character of an experience—to determine, for example, whether it is a case of direct awareness of a normal object or not. Failing to address these issues is simply to beg the question against "externalism," which claims, in relation to perception, that two subjectively identical experiences may differ in that one is, and one is not, the direct awareness of a normal object—

with the implication that the latter, *that very experience*, could not exist
without its normal object. No possible development of neurology or
psychophysics could have any bearing on these issues. Although the
causal principle in question may perhaps be acceptable at a purely scientific or naturalistic level of description, the currently widespread acceptance of externalism in the philosophy of mind and cognition shows
that it would be at least strategically weak to rely on the principle in
cognitive contexts. Because of this, I propose not to rely on any such
blanket appeal to the causal principle, but to attempt to push through
the generalizing step, *given that the earlier stages of the Argument have
been accepted*, on a different, though related, basis. The qualification
here is important. What I hope to demonstrate in the rest of this chapter is strictly conditional in nature: that *if* non-normal objects are accepted as objects of immediate awareness for cases of hallucination, the
generalizing step goes through, and Direct Realism is shown to be
false.[19]

What both genuine perceptions and possible hallucinations have in
common, experientially, is that they are both *sensory* in character. In
other words, the very same sensory qualities, or qualia, that are actually
present to consciousness when we genuinely perceive may be present
in a merely hallucinatory state. The first step to take in order to push
through the generalizing move is simply to claim that such a hallucinatory realization of sensory qualities is metaphysically possible, and to
interpret the initial premise of the Argument—that hallucinations are
possible—in this sense.

A number of writers have, however, denied even this weak claim.
R. J. Hirst, for example, writes that "Naive Realism can escape . . . by
denying that having an hallucination is perceiving or perceptual consciousness . . . [D]espite subjective similarity the mode and objects of
consciousness in hallucination differ in kind from those in genuine perception . . . The Argument from Hallucination is thus answered by the
suggestion that hallucinations are vivid, and especially eidetic, mental imagery; and where the subject is deceived by this imagery it is being confused with genuine perception owing to various disposing factors."[20] More recently, Brian O'Shaughnessy has written, in relation to
vision, that "neither [hallucinatory nor dream] experience is a visual experience, being instead episodes in the visual imagination that are of
such a kind that necessarily and delusorily they seem at the time to
their owner indistinguishable from visual experience"; later he claims

that "all hallucinations necessarily are caused by a diminution in the sense of reality."[21] And even more recently John Hyman has contended that, far from being qualitatively indistinguishable, genuine perception and hallucination sustain only "a non-symmetric doxastic relation"— that is, hallucinating subjects at best merely believe that they are experiencing the way a genuine perceiver does—so that hallucination is but "a *pseudo* experience."[22] The drawing of some such distinction has, indeed, an ancient pedigree: the Stoics, for example, distinguished between *phantasia* and *phantasma*, the latter being a "fancy of the mind [*dokēsis dianoias*] such as occurs while asleep," whereas the former is an "impression [*typōsis*] in the soul."[23] If hallucinations are intrinsically of a different character from genuinely perceptual experiences, and if it is only confusion in the subject that leads him to mistake a non-sensory state for a sensory one, then there is little prospect of convincing anyone of the plausibility of the Argument's generalizing step.

Now, I believe it would be unwise to dispute the claim that most, and perhaps all, actual cases of hallucination are instances of the kind of vivid imagery suggested. Nevertheless, the Argument can proceed even if this is true. Indeed, it is possible for the Argument to proceed even if we were to accept, for reasons deriving from the work of Hilary Putnam and Saul Kripke on reference and essence, that if this is true, hallucinations are *necessarily* such vivid imaginings, and essentially not sensory states. (The occurrence of the term "necessarily" in the previous quotation from O'Shaughnessy seems to indicate that he holds such a position.) For it would be a mistake to infer from this concession that the kind of state required by the Argument is not possible, and that it can therefore be blocked at its very first stage. This would be a mistake because, as with the Argument from Illusion, all that the present Argument requires is that there *could possibly be* genuine sensory experiences of the same intrinsic, qualitative character as veridical perceptions, but which are not veridical, nor even merely illusory: subjectively perceptual states that are not the perception of any normal object—a claim that O'Shaughnessy, for one, accepts.[24] Whether such states are properly to be called "hallucinations" is a question of little moment. This being so, I shall continue, in the absence of any handy term, to refer to the possibility in question as one concerning hallucination. Perhaps perceptual experiences of the same subjective character as genuine perceptions never actually occur in the absence of a normal object. Perhaps it would be fiendishly difficult, or practically impossible, for a neurophysiologist to replicate precisely the conditions for perceptual experience. Is it, though, *absolutely impossible* that such a thing should occur? If not, the Argument is up and running.

Although the assertion of the mere possibility in principle of truly sensory states of consciousness that are not genuine perceptions is so extraordinarily weak that I believe it would be absurd to deny it, in case any reader should have doubts on this score, the assertion is supported by both of the following considerations. First, I believe that in Part I we have seen beyond a shadow of a doubt that no sensation, of whatever kind, is necessarily intentional in character. Now, hallucinatory states are certainly not a matter of merely enjoying "meaningless" sensations. They are genuinely perceptual in phenomenological character, being at least ostensibly directed intentionally to objects in the physical environment. But in virtue of such an extra phenomenological richness they can hardly be thought necessarily to *lose* the sensuous character that even sheer sensation possesses! Secondly, although it is debatable whether the previously discussed causal principle applies unrestrictedly to the psychological domain, it is surely not open to serious question that it does apply with respect to the merely sensory character of conscious states. If the activity of your optic nerve when you are genuinely perceiving something green is precisely replicated artificially, you will, other things about you being normal, seem to see something green *in a genuinely sensory manner.* Doubt has recently been cast by several writers on whether intentional states are truly attributable to a "brain in a vat"—a subject who would indeed fall within the class of hallucinators here in question. (Indeed, a suitably stimulated brain in a vat is perhaps the simplest case to have in mind when thinking about the Argument: a case of total hallucination in all sense modalities.) But a denial that such an envatted subject could possibly enjoy sensory experiences at all would be, as they say, heroic. A brain in a vat may perhaps wholly lack cognition of its environment; but it cannot, if it is otherwise functioning normally, seriously be supposed to be wholly non-conscious, like a stone. If such a brain were before you, would you happily excite it in a way that is known to give rise to excruciating pain in a normal embodied subject? McDowell sometimes characterizes a subject isolated from interaction with a physical environment in terms of inner darkness.[25] Now, perhaps McDowell does not wish to deny all sentience to such a subject;[26] perhaps he means merely to express in a dramatic way the fact that such a subject radically lacks any cognition of the outside world, and that opposition to the disjunctive account of experience works with a picture of inner subjectivity which entails that the "world has to be conceived as letting in no light from outside."[27] But the metaphor is wholly misleading. It is possible for the subject of a disembodied, but suitably stimulated, brain to be conscious; it is possible that it be with this subject experientially as though he were ordinarily perceiving a world. Indeed, by direct stimulation of the brain we can already induce flashes of light in the visual experience of embodied subjects. Such phosphenes are incompatible with everything being "dark within" in any straightforward sense of these words. To deny all of this is to deny that there is such a thing as psychophysics at all.

So, the initial premise of our Argument is that it is a metaphysical possibility that a conscious state with the same sensory character as any veridical perception should obtain even though that state is not the perception of any physical object or phenomenon: a state that is neither a mere belief, nor a dream, nor a vivid mental image, nor a state analogous to post-hypnotic suggestion, hunch, or premonition, but one that is truly sensory. Even the sheer metaphysical possibility of such states occurring is supposed to motivate acceptance of the generalizing step of the Argument, because we now have a common nature shared by genuine perceptions and possible hallucinations. In virtue of this common nature, it may be thought, what *would* be true of such a hallucination—namely, that the subject would be aware of a non-normal object—*is* true of any genuine perception.

In fact, however, our newly formulated premise, even though it now explicitly contains the claim that genuine perceptions and hallucinations can have at least a common sensory nature, does not by itself clearly warrant the generalizing step. That is because accepting such a premise is compatible with accepting the disjunctive account of perceptual experience. For although at least some disjunctive theorists, such as McDowell, do seem to deny the premise, the essential target of the disjunctivists is independent of any issue concerning the possibly sensory character of hallucination. For their primary claim is that the content of a veridical perceptual state cannot be adequately specified without mentioning the particular real-world objects of which the subject is (directly) aware in virtue of so perceiving.[28] What is being opposed here is the conception of perceptual experiences as "amongst the events, the intrinsic natures of which are independent of anything outside the subject," a "tract of reality whose layout would be exactly as it is however things stood outside it," so that "worldly circumstances are only externally related to experiences."[29] On the contrary, when a subject perceives a normal physical object, that very object, as John McDowell puts it, "figures in" perceptual consciousness.[30] As another recent disjunctivist has put it, "To think of conscious experience as a highest common factor of vision and hallucination is to think of experiences as states of a type whose intrinsic features are world-independent; an intrinsic, or basic, characterization of a state of awareness will make no reference to anything external to the subject."[31] The central disjunctivist claim is, therefore, that phenomenology cannot deliver the final answer concerning the intrinsic nature of our experiences, even qua experiences. Phenomenology does not tell us the "what-it-is" of at least some states of consciousness.

Now, this central contention of the disjunctive theory is surely nothing but Direct Realism itself. For, as McDowell puts it, what is being opposed is the view that, even in cases of genuine perception, "one's experiential intake must . . . fall short of the fact itself"—that is, of the worldly fact that is perceived to obtain.[32] There can, for the Direct Realist, be no adequate characterization of a genuine state of perception as an experience, as a form of awareness, that leaves out the worldly object of which one is aware. For if one attempted such a characterization, either one would have to postulate an object of awareness more immediate than the worldly object, which simply denies Direct Realism, or one would have to suppose that the perception in itself is wholly objectless, which is absurd. Hence, McDowell can characterize the non-disjunctivist conception of even genuine perceptions as being "blank or blind."[33] By itself, however, such a claim is not inconsistent with the simple recognition that hallucinations are genuinely sensory in nature—or, more precisely, with the claim that non-veridical and not merely illusory sensory states of perceptual consciousness are possible—and if it were, that would only show that the disjunctive account, and, hence, Direct Realism itself, is false. For it is still open to a disjunctivist to claim that two states that are sensorily identical in nature can yet differ in cognitive status, in that one is, and the other is not, an immediate awareness of some normal physical object.

So we need one more consideration if we are to motivate the generalizing step of the Argument. The relevant consideration involves highlighting the importance of the *second* step in the Argument: the claim that the subject of a hallucination, in the sense now explained, is aware of a non-normal object. This second step is not supposed to be a second premise in the Argument: it is supposed to be *entailed* by the initial premise—entailed, that is to say, by the very nature of hallucination as it is being understood here. And for the moment we are accepting this entailment. Now, although the problem posed for Direct Realism by the possibility of hallucination is usually seen as that of how merely changing the causal antecedents of a type of sensory state, by plugging it into an environment, can make it the case that the immediate object of awareness is changed—so that we become immediately aware of a physical object in public space, rather than merely hallucinating—a much more challenging question is not how another object, a normal physical object, can intrude itself upon consciousness in virtue of our installing certain causal links, but *how the original non-normal object can thereby cease to be an object of awareness.* The impossibility of answering this question satisfactorily arises from the precise reason why a non-normal object is allocated to hallucination in the first place. Hallucinatory consciousness is sensory in nature. It is not like merely thinking or imagining an object. Rather, an object seems, as Husserl put it, to be *bodily present.* We do not speak of being "aware" of an object when we merely imagine one before us, however concretely we do it. It is precisely the sensory character of hallucination that leads us to speak of an *awareness* of objects here. In short, if we believe that a hallucinating subject is aware of a non-normal object, it is *only* because hallucination is, or involves, a sensory state. It is specifically the sensory character of such experiences that means that we are being genuinely *confronted by* a qualitatively characterized, non-normal object. Since genuine perception differs from such hallucination only in that more is present, any perception includes awareness of such a non-normal object.

Once again, we can bring in causal considerations to make the foregoing line of thought yet more compelling. When we suitably stimulate a subject's brain or afferent nerves, we *generate* a sensory experience in the subject. Now, to be sure, not any sensory experience is phenomenologically perceptual, as we saw in Part I. If, however, the subject is otherwise suitably constituted, such a stimulus will, other things being equal, generate an experience that *is* perceptual in character: sensory and at least apparently intentionally directed to a normal object. After all, given that I am the way I now am, *all* that is required for me to seem to see as I now do is that my retinas be stimulated as they now are being. So, although we cannot uncontroversially assume that the same proximal physical cause necessarily gives rise to the same effect cognitively construed, it would be heroic to deny that it may give rise, even in the absence of a normal distal cause, to the same effect phenomenally, or sensorily, construed. In short, it is possible to generate a hallucination in the sense operative here. Let us consider such a possible hallucination and the veridical perception that it perfectly matches from the subjective viewpoint. Although the latter is a case of genuine perception, the ultimate stages of the causal chain leading from the environment to the subject's perception may be identical in character to that of the matching hallucination. This final stage alone suffices to generate a state characterized with respect to its phenomenal character. Therefore, given stage two of the Argument, a non-normal object is generated, as in hallucination. There is no getting round this fact. By virtue of having, in genuine perception, a more extended causal chain that goes right out into the environment, in a way that reliably carries information to the subject about the layout of that environment, we may, perhaps, find something *more* in the resulting perceptual state than is to be found in any proximately excited hallucination; but we cannot find any *less*. In particular, we cannot suppose the non-normal object to be absent. If any further cognitive function in relation to the environment is achieved in virtue of the hooking-up of a subject with an environment, it is one that must go through the non-normal object of which we are directly aware. If we are aware of a physical world, realistically conceived, in such perception at all, our awareness of it is indirect. Once you introduce immediate, non-normal objects as real constituents of any state of perceptual consciousness, they will be ineliminable from the analysis of any such state, genuine or not. Once you accept stage two of the Argument, you must accept the Argument as a whole and deny Direct Realism.

At this point, however, it may be suggested that the idea of being sensory should itself be subjected to a disjunctive analysis, since there are two radically different ways in which a state can be correctly so described. In a hallucination the sensory aspect of the experience is entirely a characteristic of a conscious state generated in the subject: sensation is generated by the operation of the sensory centres of the brain.

In genuine perception, on the other hand, the sensuousness that is present in consciousness is a qualitative feature of a normal object in the physical world, a feature of which we are transparently aware. This particular disjunctive manoeuvre is, however, opposed by two facts. First, the suggestion conflicts with an earlier finding of ours. For it relies upon the truth of Naive Realism with respect to sensible qualities; and the falsity of this view was, I believe, demonstrated in Chapter 1. For I argued there that in order to escape the Argument from Illusion, sensory qualia had to be regarded as going toward constituting sensory experience itself, in such a way that the realization of such qualia entails that a sensory experience is occurring. No such quale can therefore characterize an insentient, merely physical object. In short, the suggestion conflicts with the primary / secondary quality distinction, which, I have argued, a Direct Realist must accept if he is to withstand the Argument from Illusion. Secondly, although the suggestion does not conflict with the pure form of the Argument from Hallucination as I have presented it in the present chapter, as one that relies for its first premise on the sheer possibility of genuinely sensory hallucinatory states of consciousness, it does conflict with the causal considerations that I have introduced to lend extra plausibility to that premise, should it be needed. For if it is accepted, as I think it must be, that the proximate causes of a hallucination suffice for the generation of a sensory state, a state whose sensuous character is *internal* to that state, then such a state is also generated when that causal chain is part of the more extended chain that we find in the case of genuine perceptions. At least the purely sensory nature of that state cannot, therefore, depend on the character of the more distant states of the causal chain involved in genuine perception, as the present proposal suggests.

As with the Argument from Illusion, therefore, once non-normal objects are introduced to account for certain perceptual phenomena, the generalizing step is unavoidable, and we are led to acknowledge the falsity of Direct Realism. Once again, if our Argument is to be blocked at all, it must be at the second stage, where non-normal objects are first introduced. Once these objects get into your philosophy, Direct Realism is sunk.

An Extreme Proposal

8

THE ARGUMENT FROM HALLUCINATION presents a substantial challenge to Direct Realism—one that, moreover, may seem not to be touched by anything that was said in the extended defence of Direct Realism in Part I of this work. This is because the present argument, like the Argument from Illusion, will go through once we allow the introduction of non-normal objects of awareness at the argument's second stage. But whereas the defence of Direct Realism in Part I essentially consisted in an attempt to make comprehensible a resistance to any such introduction of non-normal objects in relation to the phenomena of illusion, it may well seem that any such resistance will be wholly implausible in relation to hallucination, since it looks as though it could only take the form of a denial that a hallucinating subject is, qua hallucinator, aware of *anything*. Such a denial, as I have said, seems initially preposterous. Nevertheless, in recent years just such a denial has notably been made by Gareth Evans and John McDowell—who have, moreover, succeeded in convincing a significant number of other philosophers on this point.[1] We need to see, therefore, what may be said in favour of such a suggestion. Evans states the view pointedly: when someone hallucinates, "there is literally nothing before his mind."[2] I shall term the view in question, not unfairly I believe, the "extreme" position. Because the claim in itself is so utterly implausible, we could be led to embrace it only by being shown that it is an implication of certain other theses that we have overwhelming reason to accept. If this can be

209

shown, the intrinsic implausibility of the extreme position will have to be weighed against the implausibility of denying the facts on which these other theses are based. Perhaps it will turn out that our intuitive rejection of the extreme position conflicts with certain other equally "obvious" things we believe.

There is, in fact, only one line of argument that goes any way at all towards sustaining the extreme position. This is the demonstration that the position is entailed by an account of *thought* that is itself unavoidable. This account of thought is, to be sure, itself deemed extreme by many. It is, however, considerably less so than the allied position with respect to hallucination, and perhaps a convincing case can be made for it. We need, therefore, to examine this extreme account of thought to see whether it stands up; and, if so, whether it entails something as surprising as the denial that a hallucinating subject is, as such, aware of anything.

The extreme position on thought is the claim that people can mistakenly be under the impression that they are thinking something—even people who are not psychologically confused in any sense. As Evans and McDowell like to put matters, such a subject, although "essaying" a thought, can fail in the enterprise, and come up with but a "mock thought."[3] Evans again states the case bluntly: "A subject may essay a thought and literally think nothing at all."[4] We here witness a further development of the anti-"Cartesian" perspective that we encountered in Chapter 7 in connection with the disjunctive account of experience. "In a fully Cartesian picture," writes McDowell, "the inner life takes place in an autonomous realm, transparent to the introspective awareness of its subject."[5] Disjunctivism, as we have seen, denies this in so far as it claims that we do not necessarily know whether our current experience is a hallucination or a perception of a normal object, even though the difference between the two is seen as an *intrinsic* difference in the nature of two kinds of experience. Since there is no cognitive "core" common to the two cases of which we are immediately aware in Cartesian fashion, a core of "facts infallibly knowable by the subject involved in them,"[6] we just do not necessarily know what kind of mental state we are in. What we now find is the suggestion that we may even mistake whether we are having a thought at all or not.

You may perhaps be wondering, especially if you have accepted the claim made in Part I that thought and conceptualization are essentially irrelevant to the issue of our perceptual contact with the physical world, what bearing any claim about the nature of thought could have on the problem posed by hallucination. In fact, the extreme view of thought does have such a bearing, because of what I shall term the "Bridge Principle"—one bridging the spheres of thought and perception. The principle, which I take to be incontrovertible, is that if we are aware of an object, if it appears to us a certain way and we notice this, then we are, if we are thinking beings, in a position to entertain a *de re* thought or judgement about that object—at least the judgement *that is F*, or *that seems F*, where $\ulcorner F \urcorner$ is the way the thing appears to us. If the advocates of the extreme account of thought can convince us that no such thought is possible in cases of hallucination, we must indeed conclude that a hallucinator is not, as such, aware of any object.

The ground for this extreme extension of the anti-Cartesian account of thought is the idea that certain kinds of thought are *object-dependent*. Certain thoughts—*de re* thoughts—are so directly about their object that they are simply not thinkable if that object does not exist. Since we are not infallible as to whether there really is an object in the world about which we are purportedly thinking, we are not infallible about whether we are entertaining such a thought or not. On the contrary, there is, as Evans puts it, a "grave liability of thinking";[7] for we are able to mistake for true thinking what is but a "mock thought"—something that is not genuinely a thought at all, since, as Evans says of the relevant cases, "There is no such thought to be had."[8] The extreme position is, indeed, commonly viewed as just a matter of thinking through disjunctivism to its natural conclusion. After all, if, as the disjunctive theorists claim, objects themselves can *figure in* thoughts, it may seem that in the absence of a suitable object, no such thought is available to be thought. Opposition even to this extreme position is perhaps but yet another expression of adherence to an outmoded "Cartesian" view of the mind.

This extreme view on thought has itself been almost universally arrived at as a result of certain recent developments in semantics. On the basis of considerations too well-known to need rehearsing here, certain classes of word are taken to be "directly referential"—that is, to secure reference otherwise than by expressing a descriptive condition that some object happens to fit. It is also commonly held that a "canonical" understanding of such a term must mirror its direct referentiality by functioning as the referential component in a *de re* thought. Yet although it is such developments in semantics that have persuaded almost everyone today that there really is a distinctive class of judgements that are both world-directed and genuinely *de re*, this is, in fact, something that anyone who pretends to defend Direct Realism must accept anyway, since perceptual judgements, as we saw in Chapter 2, are paradigmatically *de re*, since they involve *acquaintance* with objects. For the Direct Realist, perception does not *stop short* of its (normal) object. So, in relation to perceptual judgement, it must be denied that such judgement can be possessed of some referential content that is not object-involving. Hence, any perceptual judgement essayed in the absence of its purported object would seem to be bereft of any distinctively perceptual content by virtue of being, as Evans puts it, radically *ill-grounded*.

Once the *de re* character of perceptual judgement has been recognized, the road to the extreme position may seem clear. For one thing that is distinctive of a genuinely *de re* thought is that its object is essential to it. From this it is an immediate inference that the non-existence of the object of a *de re* thought takes away the very possibility of entertaining that thought. There cannot be a *de re* thought without a *res*. What the extreme view on thought holds is that, if you start with a subject entertaining a *de re* thought about a certain object, and then consider the situation—the "deficient" situation, as I shall call it—which differs from the first only in that that object does not exist and never has (together, of course, with anything entailed by such a switch), then the subject will be left with but a mock thought. For there may appear to be but two alternatives to this conclusion, and both may seem unacceptable.

The first is the suggestion that in the deficient situation, the subject could indeed be having a thought, and one different from the original *de re* thought, but one that has no object. An immediate problem with following through such a suggestion is that there is no way of making sense of the idea of a thought that lacks an object except in terms of *descriptive* thoughts, where the thinker secures reference "attributively." There is, for example, relatively little problem in explaining how I can think that the tallest giraffe in Tunisia is over ten foot tall, even if there are no giraffes in Tunisia. Doubtless something along the lines of Russell's Theory of Descriptions, according to which such thoughts are to be accounted for in terms of the exercise of general concepts and logical notions, applies here. There is little problem in accounting for such thoughts in the absence of any relevant object because, as Keith Donnellan remarks about attributive statements, they embody "reference in a very weak sense."[9] In the cognitive sphere, McDowell states, wholly justifiably in my view, that "the difference [between *de re* and descriptive thoughts] is sufficiently striking to deserve to be marked by the stipulation that only the former should count as being in the strictest sense about objects."[10] Merely descriptive thoughts do indeed "stop short" of any individual real-world objects. If, by contrast, you take the *res* out of a *de re* thought, it is far from clear how you could be left with any coherent thought at all. For it cannot be sensibly proposed that we should be left with some merely descriptive thought here, precisely because a "deficient" situation is *minimally* different from its original. In particular, in the present context we are concerned with two situations that are phenomenologically identical: a veridical perception and its possible subjectively perfect hallucinatory replica. Now, whether a subject is having a descriptive thought or not is something that will be open to reflexion by the subject himself. That certain terms are directly referential and not descriptive, for example, is something that has been realized as a result of a priori reflection. As Evans says, in connection with the understanding of proper names, "Knowing 'NN' to be an ordinary proper name, no one would dream of responding to a challenge to the statement 'NN is the ϕ' by saying 'Oh! I was under the impression that "NN" is just our name for whoever is the ϕ'."[11] A deficient subject—one in the situation where "NN" is empty—would respond in exactly the same way, of course. Whatever happens when we move from a case of *de re* thought to its deficient counterpart, what does *not* happen is that we get a case of descriptive thinking—for that would not be a minimally different counterpart situation. Deficient *de re* thoughts are still purportedly *de re*. Indeed, we may say that they *are* de re *in character.* Bringing in descriptivism at this point would not allow our deficient subjects even to seem to make immediately object-directed judgements. It, equally with the extreme view, denies to such subjects the kind of thought they take themselves to be having. This applies even more obviously to perceptual judgements than it does to the understanding of names.

The second alternative is to hold that when there is no real-world object about which a subject is thinking, such a person could still be having a thought, indeed an object-dependent thought, albeit one about a different object. In many cases, however, this suggestion has little plausibility. We now have it on the highest authority that there was no such person as St. George. If this is so, then, according to the extreme view, we have all been mistaken in believing that we have ever thought about St. George. We have "essayed" such thoughts, but since there are no such thoughts to be had, we have on such occasions repeatedly failed really to think anything. The present suggestion rejects this initially implausible view—but only by suggesting that we were really thinking of something else! And what would that be? Given that merely descriptive thinking has been ruled out, no remotely plausible candidate suggests itself. Since, therefore, the extreme view on thought seems to have powerful considerations in its favour, let us now see what effect accepting it has on the issue of hallucination.[12]

The extreme position on the nature of thought may be felt to entail the extreme position with respect to hallucination in virtue of the Bridge Principle: that if we are perceptually aware of an object, we are in a position, in principle, to think *de re* about that very object. So let us suppose that a perceiver of some normal object makes a perceptual judgement about it. Now, a hallucinator may differ from this perceiver only minimally. As far as the hallucinator can tell, he is in the same situation as the genuine perceiver. The hallucinator could, therefore, "essay" the same kind of world-directed *de re* thought as the genuine perceiver succeeded in thinking, although of course he would come up with but a mock thought. If, however, no *de re* judgement is possible in the hallucinatory situation, we must conclude, by the Bridge Principle, that a hallucinating subject is not, qua hallucinator, aware of anything at all. It is perhaps as a result of a line of reasoning such as this that Evans can assert that the extreme view on hallucination "is really no more than a corollary" of Direct Realism, since the latter is nothing but the claim that "if in perception anything is before the mind, it is the public objects themselves, not some internal representative of them."[13]

Once again, there may appear to be but two alternatives to the extreme construal of the deficient, hallucinatory variation of a genuine perception; and once again the descriptive alternative has no plausibility whatever, for essentially the same reasons as before. But although the second suggestion mentioned earlier in connection with St.

George—that when we "subtract" the object from a *de re* thought, we end up with a *de re* thought with a *different* object—had little plausibility in that non-perceptual case, in the present context it is a much more reasonable suggestion. For in the present case, talk of subtraction means that we are dealing with a case of hallucination; and prior to the last couple of decades almost every thinker who turned his attention to this issue was of the opinion not only that it is plausible, but also that it is overwhelmingly obvious, that a hallucinating subject is aware of something different from a normal object: a sense-datum, or sensation, or sense-impression, or whatever. *This* is the view that at least initially presents itself as the obvious alternative to the extreme position; indeed, as an obviously more plausible alternative. We need, therefore, to look for additional support for the extreme view if it is to make good its case. We shall find no such argument in the writings of John McDowell. He prefers, rather, to engage in the following strategy: to argue that the extreme view is entailed by Direct Realism, then to be rude about those who would abandon such Realism, and finally to offer diagnoses for their mistake. As will shortly emerge, I believe that the case against the extreme view in relation to hallucination is so overwhelming that if the state of play is indeed as McDowell suggests, it is Direct Realism that should be abandoned.[14] When we turn to the writings of Gareth Evans, however, it is possible to find the suggestion of an argument for the extreme position, which at least deserves serious consideration.

THE ARGUMENT we are to consider for the extreme view of hallucination centres on the conditions that are necessary for understanding. The crucial claim is that understanding perceptual reports is impossible in the absence of an actual, real-world object. So the argument concerns a certain type of linguistic understanding. Because of this, the overall argument requires there to be a necessary relationship of some sort between thought and language. The argument that I am about to reconstruct from Evans's writings relies specifically on two principles here, the first of which Evans never explicitly propounds, but which I believe he would endorse (and which is anyway extremely plausible). I shall call it the "Expressibility Thesis." It is the claim that any thought we have is expressible in a significant linguistic utterance. One could, indeed, reasonably have doubts about such a claim in an unrestricted form. Why should it be that all of the enormous variety of states of consciousness, even the variety that would be deemed to be of "cognitive" or "epistemic" significance, are necessarily capturable in language? Some reasons for being doubtful about this were, indeed, presented in Part I, when we investigated the suggestion that concepts are necessarily implicated in perception. There is, however, a restricted version of the Expressibility Thesis that is all that the present argument requires. For although it may be that not everything in consciousness can receive adequate expression in language, would it not be deeply puzzling if a linguistically competent subject could not, even in principle, and in the most favourable of circumstances, give expression to the fact that he is aware of something—indeed, of something of a certain sort? The Bridge Principle already has it that if a hallucinating subject is aware of an object, he is in a position to make a *de re* judgement about it. It is difficult to understand why such a judgement should be incapable of receiving expression—if only in the form "That is F," where "F" stands for some property sensibly possessed by the supposedly hallucinated object.

The second principle, which Evans does explicitly propound, I shall call the "Comprehensibility Thesis": any meaningful linguistic utterance is capable, in principle, of being understood. A necessarily incomprehensible utterance is hardly an "expression" of anything at all, but just meaningless mouthing. As Evans says, "If nothing counts as understanding what is said, then it must be the case that nothing is said."[15] It is Evans's central contention that in the absence of a public object of reference, no understanding of an expression of a perceptual judgement is possible. If this last claim can be substantiated, it would seem that we have all the materials necessary for a cogent argument for the extreme view in relation to hallucination. The argument would go as follows. Suppose that a hallucinating subject is, qua hallucinator, aware of something. By the Bridge Principle, such a subject is in the position to be able in principle to make a *de re* judgement about the object of awareness. If the subject is indeed in such a position, then, by the Expressibility Thesis, that judgement must be capable of receiving expression in a semantically significant utterance. By the Comprehensibility Thesis, such an utterance must be capable of being understood. Evans's final and crucial claim is that in the absence of a normal object of awareness, no understanding of any expression of the perceptual judgement is even in principle possible. Since, however, there is no normal object of awareness in the original hallucination, we may, by a series of steps of *modus tollens*, conclude that the subject was not aware of any object (in so far as he was hallucinating). Since the Bridge Principle and at least a qualified version of the Expressibility Thesis are surely beyond question, the cogency of the Evansian argument effectively concerns the question whether a hallucinating subject can possibly give voice to a comprehensible expression of his supposed awareness of an object.

The prospects for such a possibility do not, to be sure, initially look promising. For suppose that I hallucinate an object and make an explicit judgement about it—to the effect that it is red, let us say. How am I supposed to formulate my judgement in words so that you may understand what I am saying, and so apprehend what I am thinking? Well, I could "baptize" the object: bestow a name upon it and refer to the object by using that name. But not only would such a procedure be quite bizarre, the question would then arise how you are supposed to understand this attempt of mine to refer by using the name. Trying to get you to interpret any such remark of mine would in the long run have to resort to what in any case is the natural way for me to express my judgement: by making a demonstrative statement. You will, however, fail to understand any such utterance of mine. Obviously, any utterance I might reasonably make in such a situation will not be wholly unconstruable by you. If I say "That is red," this sentence has a perfectly familiar lexical meaning. An ability to parse such a sentence semantically and syntactically does not by itself, however, constitute an ability to understand what is said in my uttering it.[16] For although a phrase like "that one" has a uniform lexical meaning whereby it is a term serving to refer to an object that is either salient in the context of utterance, or is indicated by the speaker to the hearer in some natural or conventional fashion, in uttering my sentence I am not saying *that the object I am indicating to you* is red. If that were what I was saying, I should have said exactly the same thing even if I had pointed out an entirely different object to you. If my utterance was referentially successful, what I should actually have said, of some object, is that *that* thing is red. When you hear me say "That is red," your first and natural reaction, if you do not simply ignore me, will be to look and see which object I am referring to. Uses of "this" and "that" call upon the hearer to go beyond the sentence uttered, and to interpret it by determining the reference of the demonstrative expression. Without this I could, for anything you know, be referring to practically anything in our environment, and each such possible point of reference would constitute a difference in what would be said: whether it is of *this* or of *that* object that I am saying it is red. Without such an advance beyond the mere sentence uttered, you are not even in a position to *mis*understand me: you have simply not bothered to try to determine what I am saying. And if you do look up, and yet take me to be referring to an object other than the one I had in mind, or the one that I "demonstrated," you will have misunderstood me. Truly to understand me you must both advance beyond the sentence and advance to the *right* object. It may well seem, therefore, that in order to understand what I am saying in such circumstances, it is necessary that you know which object I am making a judgement about, or at least be acquainted with that object.[17] The problem now is that if I am hallucinating, there seems to be no chance that you could be acquainted with the object I intend to speak of when I give expression to my perceptual state. Hallucinatory objects, of the kind we are ultimately trying to avoid, are "private," so that you cannot become aware of the same one as I, nor know which one it is that I am aware of.

Evans is surely correct when he says that "perceiving something makes a thought of a certain kind possible."[18] Suppose there is an object that I have never perceived and of which I have never heard. I can have no thought, at least no *de re* thought, of that object at all. If, however, I come to perceive it, I shall be in a position to make a judgement about it. If you also have neither perceived nor heard of the object before, then if I am to be able to express my judgement about the object in a way that is intelligible to you, I shall, it may seem, have to bring you to perceive it. For how else could I bring the right object into your mind? If, however, I am hallucinating, you will neither have heard of nor perceived the object before. Nor can I get you to perceive it now. It seems that any attempt on my part to express my judgement in a way that is intelligible to you must end in failure.[19] It should not be thought that furnishing you with a fuller description of what I am hallucinating will answer to the present difficulty. This is because no such additional descriptive specification will of itself secure communication, even in the case of genuine perception. "That's red," I say, and you look up blankly.

"The vase, in the middle of the table," I continue. This descriptive supplement is not meant to substitute for, or to constitute, my getting you to entertain a *de re* thought about the object of my judgement. It is meant, rather, to help you to move beyond your present cognitive situation and entertain a *de re* thought in virtue of coming to perceive the right object. If you do not follow my directions and yourself actually perceive the vase, you will not have the kind of *de re* thought that is alone sufficient to comprehend the expression of my *de re* thought. Without the move to perception, all you know is that I am saying that there is some vase in the middle of the table and that it is red, or that I am saying *of* some vase or other on the table (or which I believe to be on the table) that it is red. In thinking either of these thoughts, however, you would yourself be entertaining a thought the identity of which is independent of which individual vase happens to be on the table—independent, indeed, of whether there is any vase there at all. You have not, therefore, succeeded in having a *de re* thought. In any case, the suggestion that such descriptive filling-out could suffice for communication in this kind of situation is a non-starter, since all such descriptions will be false of the object of which the hallucinator is supposedly aware. Whatever the opponents of Direct Realism say a hallucinated object precisely is, it is not going to be anything like a vase on a table.

Is there any possible response to this line of argument? Since the argument has it that it is *impossible* for the hallucinator to express his supposed state of awareness, we must give him every opportunity to attempt to do so. One thing that we have seen he would naturally resort to would be providing the hearer with a descriptive supplement to his bare demonstrative utterance—"the vase in the middle of the table," and so forth. Although, in the preceding stretch of argument, I discounted this as being sufficient to allow the hearer to entertain a relevant *de re* thought on the grounds that such material would function merely descriptively, perhaps that dismissal was too quick. For perhaps such descriptive filling-out can be exploited in a *de re* fashion by the hearer. After all, Evans himself recognizes what he calls "testimony demonstratives," which allude to the possibility of my entertaining *de re* thoughts in virtue of information that you impart to me in conversation.[20] I need not perceive the object you are talking about in order to pick up such information, nor need you employ either demonstrative expressions or proper names. The notion of the *de re* is, as I suggested in Chapter 2, something of a catch-all for whatever escapes treatment by Russell's Theory of Descriptions or some descendent of it; but perhaps we are still letting that theory have too wide a field of application. Perhaps even definite and indefinite descriptions can serve to establish an informational, and hence a not merely descriptive, link with an object. Perhaps the hallucinator's descriptive supplement furnishes us with an informational link to that of which he speaks in such a way as to meet the requirements of the Expressibility Thesis.

One way of making this plausible is to consider cases where the hallucinator has knowledge of the situation he is in, and the ability to explain the situation to his listener. "Look, I'm hallucinating," he may say. "I know there's really nothing there, but I seem to see a vase in the middle of the table. There is this vase-shaped thing clearly in the middle of my visual field, and *it is red.*" Could not such "testimony" put the listener in a position to think about that hallucinated object? If Evans would not have accepted this way of allowing hallucinatory situations to conform to the Comprehensibility Thesis, his overall position is in deep trouble indeed, since it would then follow that no one ever feels pain or any other bodily sensation. After all, I cannot show you my pain so as to allow you to entertain a perception- (or feeling-) based *de re* thought about that pain. It is, of course, a very common view that such "inner states" are in need of "outward criteria" if the former are to be possible objects of thought. In order to answer to the present problem, however, such a view would have to take the form of saying that, necessarily, every sensation we are capable of having can be manifested in overt behaviour in such a way that another person, in witnessing such behaviour, would perceive (or experience?) the first person's sensation. This has no plausibility whatsoever.

The argument that I am culling from Evans's writings in fact fails to address the most obvious alternative to the extreme position in relation to hallucination. That alternative, as we have seen, is that a hallucinator is aware of a private object. But Evans's primary target is the suggestion that thought and communication are possible in the absence of *any* object. A consequence of this is that, when he deals with cases of hallucination, he focuses on cases where the subject is naive with respect to his hallucinating. Suppose, to take one of Evans's own examples, I hallucinate in such a way that there appears to be a little green man sitting on a wall before me. In such a situation, what I should try to get you to think about, in my attempt to express myself, is *that* little green man. But there is simply no such object. Here it may seem that we have putative awareness and thought and expression without an object; and if so, perhaps Evans's line of argument stands up. The problem is that from the fact that there is, in the situation described, no such object as the little green man, it does not follow that I am aware of no object at all. A much more plausible suggestion is that I am aware of some private visual entity—a sense-datum, or sensation, or whatever. This is certainly a natural suggestion when the subject is *not* naive with respect to his hallucinatory situation—and can it really be thought that the mere difference between naiveté and knowledge of circumstances suffices to sustain a difference between being aware of nothing at all and being aware of something? When I suddenly realize that I am hallucinating, I do not suddenly become aware of an object. I come, rather, to have a different opinion about the selfsame object of which I am continuously aware. If one denies that even the non-naive subject is aware of anything, we are faced with the unacceptable conclusion we have recently reached: that none of us ever experiences bodily sensations of any sort.

Although I have been attempting to undercut the argument for the extreme position by indicating how hallucination can be seen as conforming to the Comprehensibility Thesis, there is, in fact, a shorter way with this whole line of argument—one that emerges when we ask what Evans exactly means by this thesis. We know the claim to be that any genuine thought is capable of receiving expression in an utterance that can be understood. But understood by whom? Now, it is perfectly clear—both from Evans's explicit statements and from the fact that the argument requires this interpretation—that the proposal is that the utterance in question be understandable *by someone other than the speaker*.[21] Let us therefore term the Comprehensibility Thesis, thus understood, the "Communicability Thesis." In non-perceptual contexts, this requirement is eminently reasonable. The suggestion that the name "St. George," though empty, has a meaning even though no one can possibly understand any utterance by anybody else of any sentence containing this name, has nothing to recommend it whatever. Where reference is not backed by perceptual acquaintance, the only possibility is that it be mediated by public language—something that immediately brings in the requirement of mutual comprehensibility. Is it, however, equally clear that the Communicability Thesis applies to the perceptual cases in which we are principally interested? Is it, that is to say, at all obvious that a subject can be aware of something only if he can convey what it is that he is aware of, the individual thing of which he is aware, to another person? The original Expressibility and Comprehensibility Theses are, perhaps, eminently reasonable; but why should it not suffice to meet their requirements that the hallucinating subject *himself* understand what he is saying? Now, there are of course several lines of argument, all deriving more or less directly from Wittgenstein's Private Language Argument, that would cast doubt upon any such possibility—though I must say that I find little plausibility in any of them. Be that as it may, let us be quite clear about the crux that now presents itself. On the one side we have a fairly contentious, highly theoretical position that requires the communicability in principle of any genuine thought. On the other we have the claim that a hallucinating subject is aware of something. If there were no other grounds for dissatisfaction with Evans's line of argument, and if Evans could convince us that the content of a hallucinator's supposed awareness is in principle incommunicable—so that we should have to choose between these two claims—I think it pretty obvious which way we should jump. I wrote at the beginning of this chapter that the claim that a hallucinating subject is aware of nothing is so immediately implausible that we need to find an equally powerful thesis that is incompatible with it if we are to abandon it. The Communicability Thesis is not it.

In order to underline this last point, let us be perfectly clear about just how outrageous the extreme view of hallucination really is. It is, precisely, phenomenologically outrageous. This emerges clearly when we ask the extreme view for its characterization of the subjects who, according to that view, have failed to be aware of anything despite hallucinating. As proponents of the view themselves fully acknowledge, a hallucinating subject's mind—and, in general, the mind of anyone who entertains merely a mock thought—is hardly a complete blank. So, although McDowell can say of such cases that "there is a gap—an absence—at so to speak, the relevant place in the mind," he also firmly denies that the mind of a hallucinating subject is "simply void," and questions whether anyone has ever really suggested such a thing.[22] Although someone who essays a singular thought and fails "may think there is a singular thought at, so to speak, a certain position in his internal organization although there is really nothing precisely there," perhaps a nice explication of "precisely" will settle all serious phenomenological worries.[23]

That someone may utter words, even syntactically well-formed sentences, and fail to say anything is not a claim that it would be sensible to dispute—least of all on phenomenological grounds. When we turn to cases where such sentences are uttered with apparent understanding—apparent, that is, to the subject himself—we enter territory where phenomenology is relevant; but perhaps the extreme position can stand up here. It will be instructive to consider a case of "ungroundedness"—that condition of our informational relationship to the world that supposedly renders genuine *de re* cognition impossible—other than hallucination. For although, for obvious reasons, we have been focusing on hallucination, this is not for Evans the only source of ungroundedness. Suppose, to take one of Evans's other examples, that you have met a certain girl on a number of occasions, and on a number of other occasions her identical twin, but that it has never occurred to you that two different girls were involved. There is, as far as you are concerned, a single she. Suppose that you now essay the thought that she is intelligent. According to Evans, there is no genuine thought of this kind that you can entertain. For what thought can I possibly ascribe to you? I cannot say "You are thinking that she is intelligent," and understand what *I* am saying, without determining what the "she" here refers to; but there is no single "she" to whom reference can be made. Crediting you with a thought about one rather than the other of the two girls is not only arbitrary, but wholly falsifies the situation, as does the suggestion that you are thinking about *both* girls (as you would if, aware of the true situation, you had thought that *they* were intelligent). The problem is that we can specify such thoughts only by specifying which object is thought of; and here there is no suitable object that we can refer to. So, perhaps, the claim that you are merely essaying a *de re* thought, but wholly failing in the enterprise, is not really phenomenologically objectionable. Perhaps even the extreme position can credit you with enough genuine psychological and cognitive reality to achieve descriptive adequacy. After all, you may be genuinely exercising concepts. In attempting to think that "she" is intelligent, you were at least exercising your grasp of the concept of being intelligent. Moreover, you are not abstractly entertaining the concept of intelligence, but ascribing it, or at least attempting to. Any amount of mental imagery can also be supposed to be going on, including verbal imagery—"She is intelligent," for example, may run through your head. Although McDowell speaks of a "gap" at a certain place in the mind, he also says that "what there is at that place . . . is a putative *bearer* or *vehicle* of content."[24] We can make such vehicles as phenomenologically rich and salient as we wish. Furthermore, many allied thoughts may genuinely be entertained—such as the thought that there is a girl whom I have met who is intelligent. As Evans says, "It is not part of this proposal that [the subject's] mind is wholly vacant; images and words may clearly pass through it, and various ancillary thoughts may even occur to him."[25] Perhaps, once all this is admitted, the situation of the mere essayer of singular thoughts is not under-described. If the extreme position is indeed false of such cases, it is surely not for phenomenological reasons.

When, however, we turn to hallucination, the situation changes completely. Here, not only is the subject apparently entertaining a demonstrative thought, but the object of this thought is, phenomenologically, *present bodily*, as Husserl would put it. To say simply that our subject is not aware of *anything* is surely to under-describe this situation dramatically. Perhaps we can make sense of there being "mock thoughts," but can there really be such a thing as mock sensory awareness? Perhaps there can be "an illusion of understanding," but can there be an illusion of awareness?[26] Well, doubtless there can. After all, we should perhaps allow that in cases such as dreaming, post-hypnotic suggestion, merely fancying that you have perceived something momentarily, serious mental confusion, and so on, subjects may take themselves to be sensorily presented with an object when a relevant sensory state simply does not occur. Such cases, however, are not our present concern, since our Argument is concerned solely with genuinely sensory states of consciousness—possible "hallucinations" that are sensorily identical to cases of veridical perception. In particular, we need to be able to account for the *perceptual attention* that may well be present in hallucination. A hallucinating subject may, for example, be mentally focusing on one element in a hallucinated scene, and then another, describing in minute detail what he is aware of. In what sense is all this merely "mock"? Here it is not enough to say that the subject is exercising concepts, having visual imagery, and engaging in descriptive thoughts. The sensory features of the situation need to be accounted for. How can this be done if such subjects are denied an object of awareness? Indeed, one could suddenly induce in a subject a hallucination of an *extremely* loud scream, which might make the subject jump out of his skin—even though he is, supposedly, aware of . . . *nothing*. It is not enough, in order to patch up the extreme theory's deficient phenomenology of hallucination, simply to add a sensory state to the list of mental items that can occur in the absence of awareness, for such a state could obtain unnoticed; and it if *is* noticed, it will itself be an object of awareness. If we take as our example subjects who are fully attentive and focused, we need to do justice to the fact that such subjects in some sense take cognizance of, indeed fully attend to, sensory presentations. But if so, what else can we say other than that the subject is, as the Argument requires, aware of a non-normal object?

Evans attempts to diffuse any such opposition to the extreme position in the following passage: "To hallucinate is precisely to be in a condition in which it seems to one as though one is confronting something. So of course it will seem right to the hallucinator to say that he is actually confronting something; the situation is very like one in which he *is* confronting something . . . If after it has been acknowledged on all sides that it seems to the hallucinator that he is confronting something . . . one says that it seems reasonable to the generality of mankind to suppose that the hallucinator is actually confronting something, . . . then one is attempting to double-count the fact that has already been acknowledged."[27] What, however, is it for someone to *seem to confront* something? Unless more is said, we are left without any means of distinguishing the hallucinatory cases we are interested in from such quite different states as post-hypnotic suggestion, gross mental confusion, inattentiveness, jumping the gun, and so on. Alternatively, to equate hallucination with such cases would, in effect, be simply to deny the premise of our Argument: that hallucination is possible. Hallucination, as the term has been employed in these pages, involves a conscious state that is sensory in character, thereby differing intrinsically from any hunch or premonition.

THE CRITICISM that I have levelled against the extreme view of hallucinations is also telling against a somewhat less extreme version of the view, originally due to Harold Noonan, that has been gaining currency in recent years.[28] Whereas I have criticized the extreme position on phenomenological grounds, Noonan and others have criticized it on the grounds that it would render impossible any rational explanation of actions in circumstances in which they are clearly called for. If I hallucinate a little green man sitting on the wall before me, I may walk up to the wall and speak to "him." This would be an intentional action of mine, calling for an explanation in terms of reasons, not merely causes. A full specification of such reasons will have to mention my beliefs, and specifically my beliefs concerning the target of my actions. Since, for familiar reasons, bringing in merely descriptive thoughts will not serve here, and since the extreme view denies me any relevant *de re* beliefs, such a view leaves us with no resources by which to represent my actions as intentional, as they clearly are.[29] Although what we may call Noonan's "less extreme" position rejects the object-dependency—that is, the *normal object*-dependency—of perceptual judgements, it still views such judgements as essentially dependent on something objective, and so distinguishes itself from adherence to "methodological solipsism." What such judgements are dependent upon are *places* in physical space. So my action in relation to the little green man can be rendered intelligible by reference to truly *de re* beliefs, for the target of my action and my beliefs is the place where I seem to see the man.

This less extreme position, however, both succumbs to a phenomenological objection and is intrinsically inadequate. As to its intrinsic merit, note that the account has the following bizarre aspect. In order to distinguish between mentally or perceptually focusing on a location, and focusing on an object that is present at that location—a distinction that must be made even for a subject who is hallucinating, even though the only object available to him is a location—Noonan suggests that a hallucinating subject *mistakes locations for physical objects*. In connection with a hallucination of a pill, for example, Noonan writes that "one's demonstrative thought 'that pill . . . ,' though not a thought about any pill, is nevertheless *a thought about the place* at which it seems to one that there is a pill."[30] This seems barely intelligible. Moreover, we should note that the targeting of a spatial location—which is critical, on this view, for a hallucinator being capable of suitable demonstrative judgement—is spelled out in terms of the subject's dispositions. "The capacity to employ a particular demonstrative mode of identification of an object," writes Noonan, "can rest upon a disposition which can be possessed whether or not that object exists . . . [M]y thought has the *content* it has because of what I am disposed to do—which would be the same if I were hallucinating or not."[31] These dispositions are, of course, dispositions to act with respect to a certain location, for "a demonstrative thought is always a thought about a place."[32] It is precisely because one can have such a behavioural disposition targeted on to a given place, whether or not it is occupied by an object, that an identity of content is possible between a perception and a hallucination: "It is a consequence of this account of the dispositions underlying a demonstrative thought that such a thought, when it has an object, will be as much a thought about a place (or a connected series of places) as about an object, and can be a thought about a place even when it is not a thought about an object."[33] In the absence of such a determinately targeted behavioural disposition, there can be no demonstrative thought, on this account. Speaking of the subject hallucinating a pill, Noonan writes that "unless one's demonstrative thought 'that pill . . . ,' though not a thought about any pill, is nevertheless a thought about the place at which it seems to one that there is a pill then one *will* have no thought about the place one in fact reaches out to, and one's action *will* be psychologically inexplicable."[34] In fact, however, it is false that a demonstrative judgement, even a wholly successful one grounded on genuine perception, necessarily involves a cognitive fix on the location of the object perceived, or, indeed, on any determinate location. Consider, for example, the effects of lenses that displace the apparent locations of seen objects. If a pair of such lenses is surreptitiously placed on my nose while my eyes are closed, on opening my eyes and seeing that pill of Noonan's, I shall be "disposed" to move to a location quite other than that occupied by the pill. This is a problem for the account because in cases of genuine perception, the object about which a demonstrative judgement is made is supposed to be the object "on which, in fact, my dispositions are uniquely targeted," and because this is supposed to sustain the same content as I should judge even if I were hallucinating.[35] If, however, we consider my visual experience while wearing the displacing lenses, and its hallucinatory counterpart, what I am disposed to do if I want to pick up the pill is, we may suppose, to walk into a wall. To be sure, as soon as I start moving whilst wearing these lenses, my initial behavioural dispositions will change in a way that is guided by the actual location of the object in relation to me. But if I simply open my eyes and close them again while the lenses are in place, and the lenses are then promptly removed, no such story is available. Moreover, there is a certain type of brain-damaged subject who is constitutionally incapable of directing action on to objects that are clearly perceived. One report speaks of a subject's "inability to seize or touch directly any object presented to him, and even to extend his hand in the proper direction towards it, though he could perceive and recognize it . . . When a pencil was held up in front of him he would often project his arm in a totally wrong direction, as though by chance rather than by deliberate decision, or more frequently he would bring his hand to one or other side of it, above or below it, or he would attempt to seize the pencil before he had reached it, or after his hand had passed it."[36] These subjects could certainly *see* the objects in question. As one of the subjects himself reports, "When I wished to pick up something from my plate I even put my hand in to the cup or under the bed-table instead of on to the plate. I could see the things quite well, but when I tried to take hold of them my hand would miss them."[37] Locomotion was similarly awry: "In moving about he ran into and collided with such objects as beds and other patients standing in the wards, as though they were not there. This occurred even when there could be no doubt that their images fell in the seeing portions of his retinae; in fact in moving about he showed none of that hesitation or tendency to groping his way with the hands which occurs in a blind person."[38] This is hardly a matter of behavioural dispositions being uniquely targeted on the objects that are seen. Not even eye movements can be brought in to salvage the theory: "When requested to look at my finger he generally stared with open eyes in a wrong direction and then rolled his eyes about in search of it."[39]

The other weakness of the less extreme proposal is that it, equally with the extreme view, is phenomenologically inadequate, albeit for a narrower range of cases than with the extreme view. The cases in question are total hallucinations. For all the examples that Noonan discusses are partial, in the sense that an object is hallucinated within a scene that is itself genuinely perceived. In such situations one will, indeed, in virtue of hallucinating, at least usually have a disposition with respect to a location within that scene: to the place where the object seems to be. One is in cognitive contact with that place in virtue of one's perception of the surrounding space. If, however, your entire visual field is a hallucination, there is no hope of crediting the experiencing subject with a thought about a location in physical space.[40] But if so, then according to the current proposal the total hallucinator can make no *de re* perceptual judgement at all. From this it follows, by the Bridge Principle, that the hallucinator is aware of nothing. For cases such as this, the less extreme position is as unacceptable as the extreme view.

The Solution

9

THE GAME may now really seem to be up for Direct Realism. We cannot sensibly deny that a hallucinating subject is aware of an object; and yet such a subject is clearly not, in so far as he is hallucinating, aware of any real physical object. It would seem to follow immediately that such a subject is therefore aware of some non-normal object: a sense-datum, or sensation, or image, or what have you. If this is accepted, however, the generalizing step of the Argument will be irresistible: such non-normal objects will be the immediate objects of awareness for all states of perceptual consciousness. Such a refutation of Direct Realism is compelling, however, only if it is the case that for a hallucinating subject to be aware of something is for him to be aware of a non-normal object. What now remains to us as the *only* way of blocking the Argument, and of defending Direct Realism, is to challenge this assumption. I believe that the force of the Argument can indeed be turned at this very point, and that this assumption can be undermined on phenomenological grounds.

It is doubtless not immediately clear how this assumption about awareness in a hallucinating subject could possibly be doubted. A hallucinating subject is aware of something; but since he is hallucinating, the object of awareness is not a normal physical one; therefore it must surely be a sense-datum, or sensation, or some such thing. The findings of Part I of this work should, however, give us pause here. For there we not only found it necessary to distinguish carefully between sensations and sense-data, but also saw our way to denying, on phenomenological grounds, that we are aware of *either* of these as an object when we perceive. The whole of Part I was devoted to avoiding sense-data altogether, so only perceptual sensations need to be countenanced. And it was finally argued that perceptual consciousness as such differs subjectively from merely having sensations. Only the non-perceptual having of sensations, I argued, would involve such sensations as objects of awareness. Hallucination, however, is a form of *perceptual* consciousness. It is, in the cases we are focusing on, phenomenologically identical to perception, being not only sensuous in character, but also intentionally directed to ostensible objects in a physical environment. So how can something like sensation, as a supposed object of perceptual consciousness, re-enter the picture so easily? Perhaps, by bearing fully in mind the findings of Part I, we shall see a way of avoiding the introduction of non-normal objects even in relation to hallucination.

One writer who also believes that the Argument can be blocked for phenomenological reasons is Reinhardt Grossmann. What is primarily needed, according to him, is that we make a clear distinction between acts of sensing and perceptual acts. "No doubt, there are sense-impressions and acts of sensing," he writes. "But plain experience also shows that there are perceptual mental acts. The mental act of, say, seeing a penny is quite different from sensing a round patch. Plain experience shows, moreover, that perceptual acts occur not only in veridical perceptual situations; they even form the essential ingredient of every hallucinatory perceptual situation. The man who sees a pink rat in his hallucination does not just experience sense-impressions. Nor does he inspect sense-impressions. He truly *sees* something."[1] He goes on to say that "one of the crucial (factual) mistakes of the phenomenalist"—by which we can take him to mean all who accept the Argument from Hallucination—"consists in his asserting that hallucinatory perceptual situations cannot contain perceptual acts, but (at most) mental acts of sensing." Now, mere acts of sensing do not, according to Grossmann, present us with sense-impressions as objects. For this to occur we must *inspect* our sense-impressions.[2] And there is a manifest, phenomenological difference between straightforward perceptual consciousness (which may be hallucinatory) and the introspective inspection of sense-impressions. We can always engage in such introspection, but it is a different activity from perceiving—one involving a switch in attention, a switch to a reflexive mode of awareness.[3] Since one is not, usually, inspecting sense-impressions when one is aware of, say, a hallucinatory penny, it is simply false to say that the conscious state of seeing such a penny has a sense-impression as its object.[4] This, however, is precisely the assumption that we have just seen the Argument make. For does not the reference to non-normal objects at step two of the Argument simply assume that states of perceptual consciousness are mere acts of sensing?

Most of Grossman's observations are, I believe, true; but we must be careful how we proceed from this point. Grossmann himself, for example, after expressing these phenomenological insights, immediately goes astray from any possible route to Direct Realism.[5] This wrong turn emerges when we ask what it is of which the hallucinating subject is perceptually aware, if it is not a sense-impression. Grossmann terms the objects of all perceptual acts "perceptual particulars"; and when the acts are hallucinatory, the perceptual particulars are "wild." On Grossmann's view, any real perceptual object is a family of perceptual particulars; and a wild, hallucinatory perceptual particular is wild in virtue of not being contained in a suitable family: "A perceptual object . . . has spatio-temporal parts; these parts contain perceptual particulars. We may therefore say that a family of such particulars 'constitutes' a perceptual object. In veridical perception, certain perceptual particulars are presented, and these particulars belong to a certain family . . . A hallucinatory perceptual situation (also) contains perceptual particulars. But these particulars are not part of a family—they are 'wild'."[6] Though in detail Grossmann's position differs from Phenomenalist and Neutral Monist constructivist accounts of the physical world, it is surely reminiscent of them. And despite the differences in detail, his position is no more tenable than these as a form of Direct Realism. For, according to Grossmann, the object of which I am aware when I hallucinate an orange is, in itself, *as fully real and existent* as the object of which I am aware when I see a real orange. This is simply not compatible with Direct Realism. For according to such Realism, when I see an orange, it is that very orange, or at least its surface, of which I am directly aware. That object is different in either kind or status from any entity that I may be aware of when I hallucinate. The difference is not merely that certain other entities form a family with it. The real world is not, for the Realist, merely a coherent hallucination. So, despite

Grossmann's careful distinction between sensing and perceiving, his perceptual particulars are hardly any better than sense-data in their role as constituting the very existence of physical objects. Let us, therefore, return to the phenomenological insight, and see if we can stake out another path.

Grossmann's suggestion that the crucial distinction is between perceptual consciousness and the "inspection" of sense-impressions is already somewhat phenomenologically off-key, since it is not only when we engage in the reflexive, apperceptive act of introspection that we are aware of "sense-impressions" or sensations. I am not necessarily introspecting when I have spots before my eyes, or when I "see stars," or when I enjoy the "inner light-show," any more than I am when experiencing a pain in my toe. If we are not aware of sense-impressions when we hallucinate, that is not because we are not introspecting (though that, of course, is generally true). Nor is it that we are doing more than sensing—for that lands us with the dual component view, and possibly intellectualism. It is, rather, that when we perceive, we sense *in a certain manner*. Sensory experience that is phenomenologically perceptual embodies, as we saw in Part I, a non-sensuous dimension in such a way as to present us with objects of awareness that transcend the mere flow of sensation. We cannot identify a perceptual object with a sensation, or series of sensations, because of the nature of the two ultimate sources of perceptual consciousness: perceptual constancy and the *Anstoss*. As for the first of these, the principles of identity and change that govern the merely sensory and the perceptual domains are distinct: there is a coherence and identity of perceptual objects that transcend the flux of perceptual sensations. If I hallucinate an orange, and if the hallucination is lifelike, then it will be a single, intrinsically unchanging orange of which I am apparently aware when I walk up to it and view it from different sides, even though my visual sensations are changing constantly. The crucial phenomenological issue here is this very *unum e pluribus*. And with the *Anstoss* there is simply no plausible candidate sensations with which the ostensible object of awareness may be identified.

This phenomenological truth is suggestive of, and indispensable for, a way forward, because it is the *same* non-sensory functions that we have seen to be present in veridical and illusory perception—where they give us, for all we have seen so far, direct access to the physical en-

vironment—that constitute the phenomenologically perceptual nature
of hallucination. In both cases, such functions give us, not mere sensations, but an *intentional object* that transcends the flux of sensation. This,
of course, is simply to dwell on the fact that perceptions and possible
hallucinations are phenomenologically identical; but let us dwell on it
yet further, for here alone shall we find the answer to our Problem.
Since they are thus identical, they have *the same kind of objects* for consciousness. Hallucination, equally with veridical perception, presents
us not with sensations, or sense-impressions, or sense-data, but with
normal objects: normal *physical* objects, to boot, in the sense that they are
presented in three-dimensional physical space. The only way to answer
the Argument is to say that the only difference between a veridically
perceived object and a hallucinated object is that the latter *does not exist*,
or is *unreal.* When Macbeth hallucinated a dagger, he was not aware of
visual sensations. What he was aware of was, I shall initially suggest, a
dagger, located at some point in physical space before him, though one
that was non-existent, or unreal. Since his state was hallucinatory, his
object of awareness was *merely* an intentional object. *This* is the path
suggested by the phenomenological insight—and no other whatsoever
remains to us to follow if we are to save Direct Realism from our Argument. Heidegger expresses the view in question straightforwardly:
"Let us suppose that someone suffers a hallucination. Hallucinating, he
sees here and now in this room that elephants are moving about. He
perceives these objects even though they do not exist. He perceives
them, he is perceptually directed to them. We have here a being-di-
rected to objects without these existing."[7] I shall again employ the term
"intentionalism" to name the theory to be developed along these lines.[8]
All accounts of awareness other than intentionalism require objects of
awareness to be actually existent or, as I shall usually put it, *real.* Central to intentionalism is the denial that the expression "is aware of"
must express a relation between two entities. On this view, to speak of
an object of awareness is not necessarily to speak of an *entity* that is an
object of awareness; for some objects do not exist. They are, as I shall
call them, "nonentities," or "non-existents."[9]

   It is clear, I hope, how intentionalism allows us to block the Argument. The crucial generalizing step of the Argument does indeed go
through if a *real, non-normal entity* is assumed to be an object of hallucination—the very existence of which, at least given attentiveness on the

part of the subject, gives rise to awareness of itself. For since genuine perception differs from hallucination only in that *more* is involved in the situation, such an entity, and such an awareness, will be present in the more inclusive situation. This is best brought out by considering the possibility of *inducing* a hallucination in a subject by stimulating the subject's sensory systems in a way that perfectly matches the stimulation involved in a genuine perception of the environment. For if such stimulation is regarded as causing a real entity or process to exist, it can hardly be supposed that giving this same type of stimulus one rather than another type of causal antecedent can annihilate or prevent the occurrence of this sensory entity, and the consequent awareness of it. But the generalizing step goes through *only if* such a view is taken of hallucinatory objects. According to the present proposal, however, there is no such hallucinatory entity to obtrude itself upon our awareness in veridical perception. When we generate a hallucination in a subject, certain real sensory items are indeed produced; and they may be identical in nature to what they would have been if that same type of stimulation had had the right aetiology to count as a stage in a genuine perception of the world. These real sensory items are, however, perceptual *sensations* or *qualia*, which, as we saw in Part I, are not the *objects* of awareness when we perceive: they are not "sense-data." Neither, therefore, are they our objects in the phenomenologically identical states that I have been calling "hallucinations." What we are aware of when hallucinating are, phenomenologically, of exactly the same kind as the objects of genuine perception. That, after all, is why they can be subjectively identical. There are thus *two* levels of qualitative identity when perceptions and minimally different hallucinations are compared: that of sensations (or qualia), which are not objects of awareness, and that of intentional objects. In a hallucination and its minimally different veridical counterpart, we do, indeed, have qualitatively identical kinds of object of awareness; but in a hallucination this object is not real, whereas in the veridical case it is.

If the disjunctive theorists are right—as they must be if Direct Realism is true—in saying that the same-total-cause-same-total-effect principle does not apply to the cognitive or epistemic status of conscious states, this can only be because facts concerning the object of perceptual awareness are not exclusively to be analyzed in terms of the *realities* involved in the causal process. Since, however, hallucinatory objects are not realities, the causal principle does not apply to them. Although qualitatively identical to real physical objects, they differ in status. It is precisely this sort of "cognitive" or "epistemic" fact that escapes the causal principle. There is no reason to infer from the fact that in hallucination we are aware of a non-existent object that we are aware of such non-existents whenever we perceive veridically or illusorily. Although genuine perception does, indeed, differ from hallucination only in that *more* is present, when viewed in the light of the present account this "more" turns out to be nothing short of reality itself. Direct Realism therefore escapes our Argument.

To quote Hume out of context, "an intelligent reader will find less difficulty to assent to this system, than to comprehend it fully and distinctly."[10] I shall, therefore, spend the remainder of this work clarifying the intentionalist position and defending it from criticism. Such clarification aside, however, our path towards a vindication of Direct Realism within the confines of the Philosophy of Perception is at an end.

THE TERMS "object" and "entity" are, to many, more or less synonymous. My own use of the term "object" earlier in this work can be read in this manner. But it is now time to draw a distinction. For according to a fairly widespread alternative usage—to be found, for example, in both the Germanic and the Scholastic traditions—the term "object" specifically connotes being an object *for a subject*. The relevant German and Latin terms themselves suggest this: a *Gegenstand* is that which *stands opposite*, over against a cognizing subject; and an *objectum* is that which is *thrown towards*—towards a cognizing subject. In this sense, any entity that is not in any way cognized is not to be termed an "object"— or an "ob-ject" as I shall sometimes write it, so as to emphasize the point. Even those who would strenuously oppose any talk of non-existent intentional objects can accept this usage—as did Bertrand Russell, for example.[11] The proposal now to be considered goes beyond this, however, and suggests that nonentities too must be discussed as being in some sense "over and against" consciousness; or, to put the matter somewhat less paradoxically, that there is a phenomenological "over-againstness" to cognition even in cases where no real object is cognized. As Alexius Meinong, doubtless the most famous, not to say notorious, exponent of intentionalism put it, "Nothing is commoner than to represent [*vorstellen*] something or to make a judgement about something that does not exist."[12] Now, such a view may be false; it at least needs spelling out and defending. It cannot, however, simply be ruled out of court on the grounds of some merely parochial presumption that "object" just means "entity," so that the notion of a non-existent object would be simply a gross *contradictio in adjecto*.

One immediate objection that many will have to the invocation of non-existents is that it cannot possibly do justice to the *real* sensory states that are involved in perception. Suppose you hallucinate a vivid green patch on a wall. You attend to it carefully, perhaps describing its particular colour and brightness. Although intentionalism does not follow Evans and McDowell in claiming, absurdly, that in this situation you are aware of nothing, is it really any better to be told that you are not aware of anything that actually exists? Surely there is, in the situation just described, a concrete exemplification of green (or green'). Surely *something* really exists, something that you are attending to. Although perhaps initially tempting, this reaction in effect simply ignores the analysis of perceptual consciousness developed in Part I of this work. "Something," indeed, really does exist in the situation in question: you exist, and your visual experience with its sensory character exists. In particular, there is, actually in your sensory experience, something corresponding to the greenness that you see on the wall: namely, an instance of a chromatic quale. Neither this quale, nor the sensory experience of which it is a characteristic, is, however, the *object* of awareness—as we saw in Part I. Your object is a patch on a wall. It is only *that* that doesn't exist.

Nevertheless, intentional objects are, for many people, creatures of darkness. At least to philosophers trained in the analytical tradition they summon up the spectre of Meinong—the "unspeakable Meinong," as William James would have it—whose supposed proliferation of entities Russell supposedly demonstrated both to be unnecessary, and also to run counter to that "feeling for reality which ought to be preserved even in the most abstract studies."[13] Can one seriously be supposed, today, to follow Meinong into his "jungle" in order to solve the problem of perception?[14] In so far as the position to be defended here is that in hallucination a subject is sensorily aware of an object that does not exist, the answer to this is perhaps Yes. I have, however, not termed the position to be defended here "Meinongian," but more broadly "intentionalist," for good reason. Since the introduction of non-existent objects is, in the present work, restricted to the case of hallucination, we have not entered the domain of full-blown *Gegenstandstheorie*, which is the proper home of Meinongianism, and which deals with "the object as such in its generality."[15] In particular, we are concerned only with objects that are "ob-jects" for a cognizing subject; whereas Meinong explicitly distanced himself from such an approach, from "the relativistic interpretation of the concept of an object which, appealing not without etymological support to the *'Gegenstehen,'* will hear only of an 'object for the subject'."[16] We shall, according to Meinong himself, be operating merely in the domain of "psychology," which "can take interest only in those objects on to which some psychological event is really directed."[17] In true Meinongian *Gegenstandstheorie*, not only are such "pseudo-existing" objects, as Meinong called them, recognized as objects, but "all objects, even those which are objects of our knowledge only in possibility."[18] (Meinong's pupil Mally even went so far as to include within the domain of *Gegenstandstheorie* objects that are not even thinkable.)[19] Roderick Chisholm gives us perhaps the clearest expression of such unrestricted Meinongianism when he writes that "the round square need not be thought of in order not to exist. We draw these objects, so to speak, from the infinite depths of the *Außerseiend,* beyond being and non-being."[20] Since only adherence to such total *Gegenstandstheorie* deserves to be described as Meinongian, the merely "psychological" thesis to be advanced here, a thesis restricted, indeed, not just to cognition, but specifically to perception, would not properly be so called.[21] Certainly the standard approach of present-day Meinongians, or neo-Meinongians, goes far beyond the confines adopted in this work.[22] More importantly, certain neo-Meinongians, as we shall see, explicitly exclude perception from their theories. Indeed, the only philosopher in this camp who to my knowledge has defended the kind of blunt intentionalist answer to the Argument from Hallucination to be defended here is Richard Routley (*rené* Sylvan): "One simply sees what does not exist."[23]

The restricted domain with which we are concerned relates closely to the question whether something *really exists*. As a number of writers have pointed out, questions of existence and of real existence are subtly different. Gareth Evans gives a couple of nice illustrations of this. "When we say that, if *x*'s parents had never met, he would not have existed, we are not saying that if his parents had never met, he would not have been real"; "when we say 'John does not know that this beach exists', we do not intend to assert that what John does not know is that this beach really exists, or is real."[24] Similarly, Richard Cartwright has pointed out that "it is not of *anything* non-existent that unreality may be correctly predicated: given only that a person has no brothers, we can hardly say that his brothers are unreal."[25] The reason for this is that the notion of something being real is, as J. L. Austin clearly showed, essentially contrastive—with notions of what is fake, illusory, pretend, merely apparent, and so forth.[26] Although many of Austin's observations apply only to the notion of something's being *a real F*, not of something's *really existing*—a decoy duck is not a real one, but it really exists—and although the latter alone is our sole concern here, Austin's discussion does show that for the question of unreality to arise, we must be dealing with something that is *in question*, and hence something that is "psychologically" an ob-ject. So, we should say that John did not know that the beach was real, or that it really existed, only if it were in some way an ob-ject for John—if, that is, he were somehow apprised of it, through perception or word of mouth—but he had discounted or questioned the information.[27] For certain purposes—logical purposes, for example—an untrammelled realm of non-existents may perhaps serve a function. Such, however, is not ours. Here we are concerned solely with objects that do not *really* exist, or are *unreal*.

In fact, it is *only* of objects that we can say, quite simply, that they are unreal, or that they do not really exist. A decoy duck, we say, is not really a duck; it is a fake or pretend thing. Yet a decoy duck really is, for instance, a piece of wood fashioned in such and such a manner; and it really exists. Whenever such a thing is said not to be real, what is meant is that it is not really a certain *kind* of thing. Whenever such a thing is not really of that kind, however, there is some other kind of which it really is an instance—a piece of wood, for example. It is only of ob-jects, like Macbeth's dagger, that we can say that it is not really a dagger *without implying that it really is something else*. And this is because it is only of objects that we can say that they are not real, or do not exist, *at all*. Nevertheless, although the position to be developed here is not Meinongian, because it is genuinely related to certain aspects of Meinong's philosophy it is perhaps advisable to begin a clarification of the intentionalist answer to the Argument by addressing certain initial misunderstandings of the position that tend to arise through association with Meinong—through the very mention of his name, indeed.

Gilbert Ryle once referred to Meinong as "the supreme entity-

multiplier in the history of philosophy," and Keith Donnellan alludes
to "the Meinongian population explosion," both thereby expressing a
common view that lies behind the *bon mot* that we should cut back
Meinong's jungle with Occam's razor.[28] Such remarks, however, betray
misunderstanding—one that must be traced back to Russell. For although, as we shall see, early in his career Russell made certain informed criticisms of Meinong's theory, later in life he fell into speaking
of the "desire to avoid Meinong's unduly populous realm of being."[29]
When one thinks about it, however, the suggestion that a position that
recognizes *non-existent* objects infringes a rule not to multiply *entities*
beyond necessity is bizarrely off target. No one is suggesting that there
are entities—that is, existents—that do not exist. What fail to exist are
certain *objects*. The objects in question are precisely those that are not
entities, or "things," in any sense whatever.

This is not the only serious misunderstanding that still plagues intentionalism. Another idea that is still around is that although "Meinongian" objects perhaps do not exist, at least they *subsist*. They do not.
Subsistence is the mode of being of things like numbers, relations,
states of affairs, universals, and propositions: things that are "ideal," or
"irreal." Meinong was an unabashed "Platonist" about such things—as,
of course, was Russell. The question whether such Platonism is tenable, however, is irrelevant to our present enquiry.[30] Meinong's infamous
golden mountain was not supposed by him to subsist; and nor am I suggesting that hallucinated objects subsist. Since the subsistence / existence contrast is precisely correlative to that between what is abstract,
or "irreal," on the one hand, and what is "concrete" on the other, it is a
categorial contrast: between things that are timeless and things that are
temporal (or, perhaps, spatio-temporal).[31] If a golden mountain or a
hallucinated dagger were to be real, they would be at some location in
space and endure through time, and so would *exist*. Subsistence is just
the wrong kind of being to ascribe to them. For it is not as if by failing
to exist they at least manage to subsist. That would be a "category mistake." Meinong used the term "being" *(Sein)* to cover both existence
and subsistence, which are thus two ways of being.[32] The important
point is that when a categorially concrete object, such as a hallucinated
dagger, fails to exist, it thereby fails to have *any kind of being whatever,*
even of a very "thin" kind that Roderick Chisholm, on a related issue,
once spoke of as "short of actuality but more than nothingness."[33] Mei-

nong explicitly characterized his own work as embodying an attempt to get by "without recourse to a new, third kind of being beside existence and subsistence." Ironically, given subsequent history, Meinong went on to present as one reason for such an attempt the "law of parsi-mony."[34] The figure of Meinong is relevant to us not because he popu-lated the realm of being with Platonic irrealia, but because of his claim that "there 'are' [es 'gibt'], as we know, many objects that do not exist, and also many which do not even subsist," and that there is "a grasping of an object that is unconfined by the bounds of being."[35]

Although there are, in fact, some grounds for thinking that Meinong himself wavered somewhat over this issue of crediting non-existents with some form of being, other major intentionalists were consistently forthright in the rejection of any such idea—as I shall be.[36] Husserl, for example, whose views I shall be following more closely than anyone's, was quite explicit in rejecting the suggestion that non-existent inten-tional objects have any weak form of existence: "That the object is a 'merely intentional' one does not, of course, mean: it *exists*, albeit only in the *intentio* (and so as a real [*reelles*] constituent of it), or that some kind of shadow of it exists in it. Rather, it means: the intention, the in-tending [*Meinen*] of such an object exists, but the object *doesn't*. If, on the other hand, the intentional object does exist, then the intention, the intending, doesn't exist alone, but what is intended does also."[37] Cer-tain recent philosophers in the analytical tradition who are not Mei-nongians, or otherwise soft-headed, such as J. L. Mackie, Gilbert Har-man, and Sidney Shoemaker, have endorsed the necessity of reference to non-existent objects.[38] They are quick, however, to point out the lack of ontological implications of such a position. Mackie, for exam-ple, writes that "we must insist that the only entity involved is, for ex-ample, [the subject's] having an experience of a certain sort. Talk about its intentional object can be no more than a way of characterizing it, of saying what sort of experience it is by indicating its content."[39] Though we may well want to question the conflation here of intentional object and "content," as far as the ontological issues are concerned what I am suggesting is that we should not see this as a recent, disinfected, "analytical" version of intentionalism, but as wholly in keeping with the mainstream of the tradition. Compare, for example, the passage from Mackie with the following, from Husserl: "Intentional experi-ences have the peculiarity of relating to represented objects in various ways . . . There is nothing else to this than that certain experiences are present, which have the character of intention . . . [O]nly one thing is present, the intentional experience, whose essential descriptive character is just the relating intention . . . When this experience is present, *eo ipso* . . . the intentional 'relation to an object' is accomplished, *eo ipso* an object is 'intentionally present.'" Husserl goes on to speak of such intentional "relatedness" as a matter of *being minded (Zumutesein)* in a certain descriptive fashion.[40] Brentano and his followers make similar remarks. Throughout its history intentionalism has been at least predominantly free of excess existential commitments. I intend to cleave fully to this majority view.

What ontologically neutral sense, however, can possibly be attached to the claim that *there are* non-existents? Meinong said that "whoever likes a paradoxical manner of expression can therefore indeed say: there are objects of which it holds that there are no such objects."[41] But could any presentation of intentionalism escape such paradox? The first step towards seeing our way here is to make a distinction. For to say that the object of a certain psychological state does not exist is not to say that that state does not have an object. That would, as Twardowski, another major intentionalist, put it, be to confuse "the non-existence of a represented object" with its "not being represented." He goes on to say that "although one would be correct to assert that the objects of certain representations do not exist, one would, however, say too much if one asserted that no object fell under such representations, that such representations had no object, that they were objectless representations."[42] Still, as Meinong himself asks, "Even if it is primarily representations which 'have' objects, what really is this kind of 'having', if that which the representation in question 'has' can completely fail to exist?"[43]

The principal thing to recognize, in considering this question, is that, right from its inception, modern intentionalism has rejected the suggestion that the "having" of an intentional object is to be construed as a *relation*. Here is Brentano on this crucial point: "The term of the so-called relation does not at all need to be given in reality. One could therefore doubt whether one really is dealing with something relational [*Relatives*] here, and not, much rather, with something that in a certain respect is similar to something relational, something which one might, therefore, call something 'relation-like' [*'Relativliches'*]."[44] What this means is that when we say of a subject that he is, say, hallucinating a dagger, we are simply characterizing the subject psychologically. No other entity is involved. As Brentano's pupil Oscar Kraus put it: "'Object' *is not here an independently meaningful word*, but merely a dependently meaningful (synsemantic) expression."[45] Talk of intentional objects is simply a way of talking about intentional experiences.

Perhaps, however, an argument due to Kit Fine can be used to force just such an "ontology" on to the "psychological" form of intentionalism that I am proposing. His argument is presented in relation to an intentionalist account of fictional objects, but it can be modified so as to be relevant to our own concerns. He objects to an "abstract or platonic conception of fictitious objects"—something that would be analogous to Meinong's "a-psychological" approach—by saying that it "runs counter to our ordinary judgements that fictional characters are created by their authors."[46] Similarly, it may be urged, we should not think of the dagger that I might just now have hallucinated as having forever been waiting non-existently to be apprehended by me. Surely it *comes into existence* when I hallucinate. If so, we seem forced to adopt a position analogous to what Fine terms a "creationist" account of fictional objects; and the conclusion that Fine draws would apply: "On a creationist view . . . there is a clear and compelling reason for ascribing being to fictional objects; for an object could not be created unless it could pass, in some appropriate sense of the term, from non-being to being."[47] The answer to this charge is already implicit, however, in the previous remarks by Brentano and Husserl. What genuinely comes into being, in the perceptual cases that are our concern, is a hallucinatory experience. To speak of that experience's intentional object is simply to talk about the "descriptive nature" of that experience, to advert to its specific intentional character. The intentional object is not any sort of being "over and above" the experience itself.

It might, finally, be thought that the very claim that reference to intentional objects is essential for psychological adequacy itself carries ontological implications. Suppose, for example, that Macbeth is frightened by the dagger he hallucinates. This may cause him to gasp. Do we not here have a case where a non-existent has actual causal effects? And is not such an idea senseless? Indeed it is; but what we should say is that the cause of the fright and the gasp is the visual experience of seeing a dagger—for that is real enough.[48] I conclude, therefore, that appeal to intentional objects should not be seen as offending anyone's ontological scruples.

In fact, the proper initial worry with intentionalism should perhaps be the reverse of the suspicion that it multiplies entities (or modes of being). For it may seem that the invocation of intentional objects is the attempt to make literally nothing do some essential work in an analysis of perception. Recall that we were led to investigate the notion of intentional objects by finding that the extreme position considered in the previous chapter lacked the resources to say what needs to be said so as to distinguish different perceptual situations: How does hallucinating an apple differ from hallucinating an orange, for example? Can we, however, really rest content with the suggestion that the difference consists in the fact that the two situations involve two different kinds of object, *neither of which exists?* How can a double invocation of nothing serve to distinguish anything? Alternatively put: in so far as intentionalism really is not multiplying modes of being, and in so far, therefore, as intentional objects really do not exist at all, how is this position to be distinguished from that of Evans and McDowell? The problem can best be put in the form of a dilemma. Either intentional objects really are nothing, in which case nothing of value can be said by appeal to "them"; or, if it turns out that they are indeed necessary for our task of giving a descriptively adequate characterization of mental phenomena, then surely, my earlier protestations to the contrary notwithstanding, they must really exist in some sense.

Talk of merely intentional objects is, however, an invocation of "nothing" only in an ontological sense. We do, indeed, need an *ontologically reductive* account of intentionality. Non-existent intentional objects supervene on intentional experiences. We should, however, sharply distinguish this from any attempt at *psychological reduction*. Talk of awareness of an object is inescapable if we are adequately to characterize certain psychological states as they are lived. Reference to intentional objects is not just "a way" of talking about perceptual experience, but the phenomenologically necessary, only adequate, way. It is necessary in order to do *descriptive justice* to the phenomenological fact of someone's being "minded" in a determinate fashion—a fashion that is phenomenologically perceptual in character, not being a matter merely of enjoying sensations. What is being thus described is an experience. It is crucial to the present position that one be able to combine ontological conservatism with the claim to the phenomenological indispensability of reference to such objects. Remember that "object" does not mean "entity": the former term is here given an *exclusively phenome-*

nological interpretation. The intentional directedness of even hallucinatory states of perceptual consciousness is simply a phenomenological fact—one that needs to be recognized in any adequate account of the mind. This fact alone sustains the intentionalist position. The theory is not an ontological, but a phenomenological, one. J. L. Mackie characterizes what he takes to be the "real puzzle about intentionality" as follows: "Is it not strange that there should be one state of affairs . . . that requires for its adequate description the . . . description of a quite different and so far merely possible state of affairs?"[49] Even if it were strange, this would hardly constitute a knock-down argument against intentionalism. Indeed, is it even that? The phenomenon of intentionality is, after all, unique. Moreover, I have attempted to sketch its perceptual genesis in the last two chapters of Part I.

AT THIS POINT we ought, perhaps, to consider Russell's explicit arguments against non-existent objects. For although, as I have mentioned, Russell succumbed later in his life to the misreading of Meinong as a multiplier of entities without a feeling for reality,[50] at an earlier period Meinong's works were an object of serious study for him, and an object of *informed* criticism. Moreover, he is supposed to have refuted modern intentionalism, in the figure of Meinong, almost at its inception. There are just two Russellian arguments to consider, and they can be dealt with briefly, since they have received thorough treatment in the neo-Meinongian literature.

The first is that intentionalists are, despite their intentions, committed to the actual existence of certain non-existents: "For if the round square is round and square, the existent round square is existent and round and square. Thus something round and square exists, although everything round and square is impossible."[51] This need not detain us. For although there may be a problem here for full-blown *Gegenstandstheorie*, or if it is supposed that an intentional object corresponds to every syntactically well-formed, or at least senseful, predicative expression that may be dreamt up, there is no such problem in relation to the realm of perceptual consciousness with which we are alone concerned here. For the concept of *being existent* is hardly part of the content of a hallucination. There is no distinction between hallucinating an apple and hallucinating an existent apple. There is, certainly, the issue of whether or not we are taken in by our experience, whether we believe that there really is an existent object of the kind we seem to perceive; but that is a different issue.[52]

Russell's other objection to intentional objects was that "such objects . . . are apt to infringe the law of contradiction. It is contended, for example, that . . . the round square is round, and also not round, *etc.* But this is intolerable."[53] Given that our concern is with hallucination, we can doubtless forgo consideration of round squares; but an analogous problem perhaps attaches to hallucinatory objects, since we can seem to perceive objects with an impossible, self-contradictory nature. Think, for example, of Escher drawings; or the well-known paradoxical figures devised by L. S. Penrose and R. Penrose. Perhaps we could hallucinate one of those. Or, since each drawing is, qua drawing, perfectly self-consistent, we might hallucinate an object the best pictorial representation of which would be such a drawing. There are also examples of genuinely three-dimensional illusions that present us with impossible objects: "paradoxical percepts" as psychologists call them, such as the "waterfall illusion," and various sounds that audio engineers have succeeded in producing.[54] Yet another example is the "Pulfrich double pendulum," a contraption that consists of two rigid bars suspended from a hinge that are made to swing one behind the other. When this is viewed monocularly in reduced illumination it looks as if the rigid bars are passing *through* one another.[55] All such normally illusory phenomena could be hallucinated.[56]

Meinong's reply to the original objection, which I regard as entirely adequate, was that although some non-existent objects are merely possible, others are downright impossible (in the sense that they could not possibly exist, or be real), and that it is hardly surprising if the latter embody contradictions. "The Principle of Contradiction is, for sure," he wrote, "applied by no one to anything other than what is real and what is possible."[57] Applied to the realm of hallucination, we simply admit that some perceptual objects could not possibly exist as real things. (If this is denied, it is in effect being allowed that there is no problem to answer on this score in relation to perception.) We need, however, to beware of a possible error. The error is to accept the following kind of inference, which I again illustrate by reference to Russell's example: Although the round square is square, it is also round; therefore the round square is not square (because it is round); therefore it is not the case that the round square is square; therefore it both is and is not the case that the round square is square. Such an inference must be resisted, of course, as must the converse inference from not being square to being non-square, for otherwise we shall have contradictions not only in the nature, or *Sosein*, of certain objects, but in our own philosophical theory. We can, however, avoid this by distinguishing between the ascription to an object of a negative property and the non-ascription, or denial, of the corresponding positive property. As Meinong put it, we must distinguish between *Nichtsosein* (being not-so) and the *Nichtsein eines Soseines* (the non-being of a being-so).[58] So we block the preceding inference by denying that if an object is non-square (for example, round), it cannot also be square: the round square, to continue for the moment with this (for us, no doubt, unhelpful) example, is both square and non-square.[59] Applied, for example, to the paradoxical perceptual phenomenon of a single tone that sounds to be both rising and falling in tone, we do not infer from its rising that it is not falling.

A related worry concerns intentional objects' lack of complete determinacy. If a card with even a very simple line drawing on it—a square or a circle, say—is held at the periphery of your field of vision, you will be able to see a shape on the card, but not what shape it is. We here have an object that is indeterminately perceived. Such a perception has its possible hallucinatory replica; in which case we should have an intrinsically indeterminate perceptual object (a point fully recognized by Meinong himself).[60] If so, do not the familiar arguments from indeterminacy directed against sense-data count equally against intentional objects? Otherwise put, do not intentional objects infringe, if not the Law of Non-contradiction, at least the Law of Excluded Middle? The reply to this simply parallels the previous one. Indeterminacy may be a problem for sense-datum theorists precisely because sense-data are real entities. Since non-existent objects do not exist, there is no cause for worry over their indeterminacy. Moreover, it is confusing to express this fact of indeterminacy as its being a matter of such objects infringing the Law of Excluded Middle, since this principle properly relates to the truth-values of propositions. Infringement of this law is avoided by denying the validity of the inference from its not being the case that a certain hallucinated shape is rectilinear to its being the case that the shape is non-rectilinear (that is, curved). The indeterminately hallucinated shape itself is neither rectilinear nor curved; but the proposition that the shape is rectilinear has a determinate truth-value: it is false, since this is simply not part of the nature of the object of awareness. So, once again, a distinction between internal and external negation, or between propositional and predicate negation, shows that intentional objects fail to infringe any law of logic—or, more precisely, that our account of such objects is not itself incoherent.[61] In general, when we remember that talk of intentional objects is, as far as we are concerned here, but a necessary way of doing phenomenological justice to the nature of perceptual consciousness, then if it is the case that we can be perceptually presented with paradoxical and indeterminate objects, such features must carry over to our characterization of such states in terms of the intrinsic features of their intentional objects; otherwise our phenomenological criterion of adequacy would be flouted. If there cannot be such paradoxical or indeterminate perceptual objects, the problem does not arise in the first place.

IN FACT, the full force of Russell's opposition to intentionalism is not to be found in his explicit criticisms of Meinong, but rather in his positive proposal of how to avoid recourse to non-existents: his Theory of (definite) Descriptions. This situation can, however, be turned to the advantage of intentionalism, because, as I shall now argue, whatever the possible merits of Russell's theory of descriptions in other areas, where hallucination is concerned it is hopelessly inadequate. Indeed, the complete failure of Russell's approach constitutes a strong factor *favouring* intentionalism, since it is but one particular way of spelling out a more general and more widely held conviction that is simply the denial of intentionalism—a denial that, following the Routleys, I shall term the "Ontological Assumption."[62] This is the claim that it is not possible to make genuine reference to what does not exist, so that no statement, at the very least no true statement, can have a non-existent as its genuine subject. Terence Parsons refers to what is, in effect, the same position as "the Russellian rut."[63] That this "rut" extends far beyond Russell's theory of descriptions is amply demonstrated by the fact that Strawson, in his famous attack on Russell's theory in "On Referring," fully subscribes to it. Indeed, the presumption in question must be traced back at least to Parmenides, whose use of it wrought so much trouble for Greek thought.[64] Since it is this Assumption that is ultimately inadequate in the face of hallucination, and since it is effectively but the denial of intentionalism, we have, as I say, a strong argument in favour of intentionalism.[65]

The Ontological Assumption, despite its almost universal acceptance by philosophers, cannot be said to have a strong intuitive basis.
Indeed, most people will already feel a certain unease about this Assumption when confronted with Quine's (wholly authentic) expression
of it: everything exists.[66] On the contrary, most people have a strong
pre-theoretical conviction that we *can* make judgements, indeed true
judgements, about what does not exist. The swiftest demonstration of
its inadequacy concerns what are known as "negative existentials."
Sometimes, it seems at first blush, we wish to deny that a certain thing
exists. As Macbeth finally says of his hallucinated dagger, "There's no
such thing." Such an assertion is surely true; and yet it also seems to be
about something in particular. The Ontological Assumption, of course,
requires viewing these initial appearances as misleading. Since no
judgement can be literally about what does not exist, any apparent
judgement that a certain object does not exist must be reconstrued
somehow. Indeed, in the interests of uniformity, Russell was led to hold
that neither judgements of non-existence nor even judgements of existence are really about their apparent subjects, whether or not they exist: "The actual things that there are in the world do not exist, or, at
least, that is putting it too strongly, because that is utter nonsense. To
say that they do not exist is strictly nonsense, but to say that they do exist is also strictly nonsense."[67] G. E. Moore similarly avers that "the
terms 'real' and 'unreal' cannot, when used in this way, be properly said
to stand for any conception whatever."[68] Now, if the Ontological Assumption can be shown to be unavoidable, we shall have to accept such
assertions; but they can hardly be regarded as grounds for making the
Assumption, since they are, initially at least, wholly counter-intuitive.
What we need to do is to see if any reconstrual of negative existential
judgements is acceptable.

Russell reconstrued such judgements as being about "propositional
functions"; Ryle has them being about attributes; and Reinhardt
Grossmann about descriptions.[69] For our purposes we do not need to
distinguish between these claims: from the intentionalist perspective
they are all of a kind, and they are all demonstrably false of perceptually
based judgements. As I have said, it need not be denied that such a
broadly Russellian approach has application in some areas. It is, perhaps, not wholly implausible to construe the claim that ghosts do not
exist as saying that there are no such things as ghosts, and to construe
the latter statement as denying that anything is-a-ghost.[70] Even when

the subject of my judgement is more specific, perhaps a Russellian approach will do. Suppose that I think that there is a can of beer in my fridge: not any particular can I seem to remember putting there—I just assume that there will be one (and only one) there. But there is not. In order to do justice to my state of belief, perhaps it is sufficient to say that I simply entertain an existentially quantified proposition. I do not relate in thought to any individual object, intentional or otherwise (except the fridge). My thought of a can of beer is a thought about the instantiation of a *kind* of thing. Such a Russellian manoeuvre is far less appealing, however, in relation to perceptually based judgements. For what if I open the fridge door and *hallucinate* a can of beer? Here the inclination to introduce some *particular* object of awareness is much stronger. In the earlier case, perhaps we are happy to credit my cognitive state with a "content," but no individual *object* at all. Now, however, we are dealing with a case of sensory confrontation: a hallucinated can of beer is "bodily present." If I am aware that I am hallucinating, what are we to make of my possible judgement to the effect that, as we are initially inclined to put it, *that can* does not really exist, or is not really there? Is such a judgement really to the effect that a certain attribute (or description, or propositional function, or whatever) fails to be instantiated? For I am certainly not of the opinion that there are no such things as cans of beer, nor even that there are no cans of beer in this fridge (since there may be one lurking somewhere in the fridge, and I may realize this). My judgement is, rather, to the effect that a certain *particular* can of beer—*this* can—does not really exist. Such a demonstrative reference, which is essential to the nature of the perceptually based judgement, is precisely what the Russellian tradition has to discount.

What gives perceptual judgements their demonstrative character is the appearance of an object as being at a certain location in our environment. So a Russellian may suggest that the attribute whose instantiation is really being denied is that of being a can of beer *located there*. There are three insurmountable problems with such a suggestion, however. The first is that perceptual location is not sufficiently precise for this generally to work (something that is especially true of auditory perception). Secondly, even when we do make perceptually based judgements about precise locations in our environment, we do so on the basis of a particular object appearing to us as at that location. As

Gareth Evans put it, "In the absence of an object to anchor our dispositions, we can make only rather gross discriminations of areas or regions
in egocentric space. Try to concentrate upon a pill-sized region on a
white wall in front of you: even if you keep looking, do you have any
confidence, at the end of fifteen seconds, that you are still looking at
the same region you began with?"[71] In other words, our grasp of the
specific spatial location that is supposedly part of the complex attribute
whose instantiation we are denying in the judgements in question, is
dependent upon our awareness of an individual object, and so cannot
be used to avoid reference to such individuals. Thirdly, even if we supposed that our perceptual ability to locate regions of space were precise
and ungrounded, there is the insuperable difficulty that I can hallucinate an object in a place where, just by chance, such an object exists,
and I can know this. Even if I do not know this, nor even believe it, if I
am sufficiently reflective I should realize that there at least *could* be such
an object there. Looking into my fridge, I need not believe that there is
no can of beer exactly there where my hallucinated can appears, since I
may realize that my hallucination may be blocking out an otherwise
possible view of a can that is really in that place. A more plausible everyday example would be an after-image projected on to a wall, giving
the appearance of there being a dark patch there. My recognition that I
am seeing no real patch is perfectly compatible with memory-based
knowledge that there really is a dark patch on just that part of the
wall—one that is of just the kind I seem to see. So it cannot be the existence of a mere *type* of physical object, even at a precisely designated
place, that I am denying when I deny the existence of a hallucinated object. Once again, we return to the fact that it is *this object*, and only this
one, whose existence I am denying in the sort of judgement in question. It is precisely the "bodily presence" that is phenomenologically
inherent in perceptual awareness as such that wrecks the Russellian
project. (A related problem stems from the fact, for which I shall argue
later, that all non-existents are necessary non-existents: no hallucinated
object could possibly have existed. The Russellian approach is incapable of recognizing this fact, since the attributes with which it deals typically could be instantiated.)

What these last reflections have done is spell out one particular aspect of the general truth that *any "Russellian" approach is incapable of doing justice to* de re *psychological states.* Advocacy of such an approach in

this area is but an expression of the "bad old philosophy of mind" encountered in Part I, since the only recourse, on such an approach, when presented with apparent reference to what does not exist, is to the machinery of denotation, or depiction. Such a line demonstrably fails whenever we are dealing with cognitions that have, as I put it in the preceding chapter, a *de re character.* Since hallucinations, being phenomenologically perceptual experiences, clearly have such a character, the entire Russellian approach wholly misfires in this connection. Russell himself, of course, would have had no time for such an attempt to construe perceptually based judgements along such "Russellian" lines. Hallucinations, for him, were clear instances of acquaintance with individuals—a cognitive situation that rendered senseless the question of the possible non-existence of the object. This, however, leads inexorably to the conclusion of the Argument from Hallucination, as Russell himself clearly saw.

Although the "Russellian" approach is hopeless, perhaps there could be some other way of handling hallucination that abides by the Ontological Assumption. I know of only one. It stems from the work of Kendall Walton on fiction, and it has been applied to hallucination by Gareth Evans. The fundamental idea in this approach is that of *make-believe* or *pretence.* I can move various everyday objects around on a table so as to represent the movements of troops in a famous battle—or, indeed, in a battle that never took place. In the latter case we can imagine how things might have gone, and enact such a scenario in our own dining room. In such a situation I make believe that, say, this salt cellar is the British First Infantry Division and that the movement of the salt cellar across the table towards the dinner plate is the advance of that division towards the French artillery. What are we to make of a statement, made in this situation, such as "The British have just advanced towards the French"? We want to say that this is in some sense appropriate; but do we really want to invoke intentional battlefields to account for this? We neither want to nor need do this, because the truths in question are merely *make-believe* or *pretend truths.* Evans and Walton signal such make-believe statements by the use of asterisks; so although it is not true that the British have advanced, it is true (really true) that *the British have advanced*.[72] We thereby avoid appeal to a realm of unreal entities because, as Walton puts it, "The pretense construal has the appreciator pretending to describe the real world rather than ac-

tually describing a fictional one."[73] Furthermore, I can myself be incor-
porated into the make-believe: I can pretend, for example, that I am the
French field commander, in such a way that when I say "Get ready to
fire," I *give a command*. Indeed the pretence might be such that I
give a command in French, even though I am actually speaking English. Even when I do not incorporate myself in the pretence in this way,
any remarks I may make that in any way rely on the pretence are themselves pretend remarks. So when I say that the French are advancing, I
am not really making a statement, but pretending to make one: I am
making a statement about the French.[74] A small manoeuvre now allows us to regard such "statements" as being both genuine and true. As
Evans says: "Now any of the games of make-believe we have been discussing can be exploited in the making of serious statements about the
game, and about what is make-believedly the case within it. One makes
such a statement by *making a statement* (*i.e.* making a move within
the game), but in such a way as to manifest the intention that what one
does should be up for assessment as correct or incorrect (*i.e.* really correct or really incorrect) according to whether or not *the statement one
makes is correct or incorrect*."[75]

We come closer to our own area of concern when we recognize that
pretence can also be, as Evans puts it, "existentially creative." In the
earlier example, the French artillery was, if I may so put it, a real plate.
If, however, we are subject to a hallucination, and know that we are, we
can yet pretend that things are actually as they seem to be. Hallucinating an apple, I say, "That apple is green." In such contexts, according to Evans, "empty singular terms are knowingly used, not in the first
instance to state how things stand in the world, but to convey the content of some *representation* of the world."[76] Such a context is existentially creative "in virtue of an initial pretence that things are as they
seem—that things are as the information . . . presents them as being . . .
[O]ne can let the automatic and habitual responses of one's cognitive
system take over and produce the make-believe thoughts, emotions,
and reactions which playing [a] game normally requires. One can
throw oneself into the pretence by suppressing the impact of disbelief."[77] Here, it may seem, we have an account of *Sosein* without appeal
to intentional objects. Since when I say "That apple is green" I am not
really making an assertion, but only pretending to, we need no intentional object to occupy the place of subject in the proposition I have as-

serted. Nevertheless, we can still do justice to the intuitions that lie behind the notion of *Sosein*, because it is really true that *the apple is
green*. Indeed, it is really true that *there is a proposition to the effect
that that apple is green*.

Such a make-believe approach has one signal advantage over the
"Russellian" one considered earlier: it need not reconstrue those cognitive situations that tempt us to invoke non-existents as all involving
thought "by description," or thought about attributes or propositional
functions. In short, the approach has no trouble in recognizing *de re
thoughts*. When I go along with my hallucination, I am not restricted
to thinking things like *there is an apple before me*; I can genuinely
think *that apple is green*. On the other hand, the pretence approach
fares no better than the "Russellian" one on another score: it too is
false. The simple reason for this is that denying the reality of a hallucination need involve no pretence whatsoever. It is, perhaps, tempting to
think that if I deny that something exists, the object of such a denial can
only be something that I in some way merely suppose or pretend to be
there. Let us, however, recall Macbeth. "Is this a dagger which I see before me, / The handle toward my hand?" he wondered. The point is
that one can be *in doubt* whether one is hallucinating or not. According
to the Walton-Evans account, however, if I am hallucinating, I can succeed in make-believedly referring to something *only if I am aware of a
pretence*. In the case of hallucination, I must be aware, or at least believe, that I am hallucinating. Recall that the proffered answer to the
problem of negative existentials hinged on the introduction of the notion of a *proposition*. This makes sense only within the scope of a
pretence. As Evans says, "If 'This does not (really) exist' is to be intelligible when 'this' is empty, it must somehow involve the exploitation of
pretence."[78] What, then, of the question "Does this exist or not?" or
the statement "I am in doubt whether this exists or not"? Are these supposed to involve doubt as to whether I am pretending or not? Not according to Evans: "The Idea involved in the thought 'Does this *G* really exist?' cannot be a demonstrative Idea. But we do not need to
suppose that it must be this Idea (whatever it is) that is employed when
there is no question of doubt—when one throws oneself into one's
thoughts and one's words."[79] The present proposal therefore makes
questions of existence *ambiguous*: "The standard situation (when there
is an object) provides the opportunity for a subject to make *two* positive

existential statements: one is a basic existential statement, and the other is the statement which the negative existential statement negates."[80] Evans is forced into this position because, as we have seen, a true negative existential must somehow involve the exploitation of a pretence. It is also, however, a negative proposition. So there must be a positive existential, of which the former is the negation, which also depends on pretence. So someone who resolves the question whether he is hallucinating in the negative, and judges that the object of his awareness definitely does exist, is in a position to make *two* judgements: one that is based on a pretence (which, it may be, was his alone, and which he does not endorse, but which he is supposed still to be able to "exploit"), and one that is not based on such a pretence. Is this really credible? Suppose that some minutes ago it was an issue for you whether you were hallucinating or not. You have now decided the issue in the negative: this book really does exist. Can you actually make the two judgements Evans postulates? Such a suggestion has no psychological basis at all. It strikes me, in its multiplication of propositions, to go beyond anything in Meinong in its disregard for a "feeling for reality." Evans attempts to assuage our disbelief here by drawing on the distinction, which we have already seen reason to endorse, between the notions of *existing* and *really existing*. Indeed, does not the mere recognition of such a distinction give Evans all he requires: a distinction between two positive existential judgements, which would naturally be expressed by "This exists" and "This really exists"? These are, indeed, subtly different, but for Evans the difference has to be *vast:* they do not even have the same subject-matter, they do not employ the same "Idea." This is specifically what is incredible in Evans's account: that the two positive existential judgements that you can supposedly make *have nothing in common at all save for the employment of the notion of existence.* Surely what we wish to say is that "This really exists" makes exactly the same claim as "This exists," except only that the former implicitly makes reference, as the term "real" contrastively always does, to some mode of unreality. Since the specific notion of reality in question is that of *really existing*, the implicit reference, as we have seen before, is specifically to at least one person for whom the object that is stated to exists is an ob-ject, but for whom the actual existence of that object is, in one way or another, in question. Such contrastive differences are a matter of context, not of subject-matter. Since I can think of no other way of attempting to handle the problem posed by negative existential judgements in connection with hallucination that abides by the Ontological Assumption, I think we should conclude that the Assumption itself is mistaken. This is a very powerful indication indeed of the unavoidability of intentionalism as a theory of perception.

It is, moreover, not only such negative judgements that cause a problem for the Assumption, claiming as it does that *no* true statement or judgement can be made about an unreal object. For it forbids us also from ever truly describing our hallucinations. If I hallucinate an apple, we surely need to distinguish, in response to the question "What are you visually aware of?" between the natural answer, "An apple" or "A roundish object," and a possible, wilfully perverse, mendacious answer, "A box of chocolates" or "Something square." The first two answers are, quite clearly, in some sense *appropriate* in the way the latter two are not. But can some notion of appropriateness be made out that falls short of truth? There is no problem here for the intentionalist, of course.[81] Although not every object exists, whether it exists or not, it is always true to say of an object that it has a certain nature: that it is one sort of object rather than another. No one working under the Ontological Assumption, of course, can say any such thing. On such a view only truly existing things can be characterized by attributes. According to Ryle, for example, "non-existent dachshunds are not dachshunds at all—for *ipso facto* they are not anything at all . . . [A] thing's being real or being an entity or being an object just consists in the fact that it has attributes."[82] But how, from within this "rut," are we at all to do justice to the undeniably applicable notion of appropriateness just mentioned? More particularly, if we do not attribute certain characteristics to certain non-existent objects, how shall we be capable of doing phenomenological justice to hallucinations? Evans and Walton will be ready with their non-"Russellian" approach; but it should be even clearer here than it was in relation to negative existential judgements that no pretence whatever need be involved in describing a hallucination.

WE NOW COME to what I regard as the most important set of problems that face the invocation of intentional objects in relation to hallucination—problems that will involve a modification, or at least a perhaps unexpected development, of the intentionalist account. These problems arise from the requirement that in veridical and illusory perception the *intentional object be a real physical object.* This, after all, is the whole point of our examining the intentionalist position as a way of sustaining Direct Realism. Indeed, such a claim, once the concept of intentionality is in place, simply is an expression of Direct Realism. For perceptual consciousness *as such* is intentional, which means it has an intentional object. A perceptual state does not forfeit its intentional object in virtue of being veridical. Rather, because of its veridicality, its intentional object is a *real* denizen of our actual environment. Its intentional object *exists.* If we deny this by suggesting that in non-hallucinatory perception the subject is aware of an intentional object *in addition* to a real object, we shall simply forsake Direct Realism. If this is how things end up, our whole exploration of intentionalism will have been in vain. We might as well have settled in the first place for the introduction of sense-data at stage two of the Argument.

This obvious requirement may yet seem to involve a genuine problem, because of the way in which intentionalism seems to allocate intentional objects, and intentional objects of a specific character, to mental states *solely on the basis of the subjective character of the states.* This is, after all, how intentional objects get into the picture in relation to the Argument at all. At step two, not a non-normal object, but an intentional object is introduced as the object of awareness in hallucination—solely on the basis of the phenomenologically perceptual character of hallucinatory states. The nature of the intentional object seems here at least, in the absence of any relevant real-world object, to be wholly determined by the subjective character of experience, by how things seem to the subject. Why, after all, do we say that the intentional object of Macbeth's vision is specifically a dagger, if not simply because that is how things visually seemed to him? The situation is surely markedly different, however, when veridical perception is in question. Here an object is allocated to a perceptual state at least partly on the basis of non-phenomenological factors: real-world factors involving the real relations between a perceiving subject and elements in his physical environment. The problem can be put as follows. So far, it seems, the only way to develop a plausible intentionalist account of perception is to make facts about intentional objects *supervene* on phenomenological facts. Clearly, however, facts about real-world, physical objects do not, for a Realist, so supervene. When a perceptual experience is non-hallucinatory, such a real object *is* the intentional object. But how can what does not supervene on phenomenology be possibly identical to what does so supervene? Clearly it cannot; so some development, or at least articulation, of the theory is required.

The problem that now faces us can perhaps best be appreciated by considering cases of illusion. When a red ball looks black to me, the normal object I am seeing simply is not black. If, however, the subjective character of experience alone suffices to determine intentional facts, the intentional object of this experience would seem to be a *black* object. But how can the intentional object *black ball* be identical to a real ball that is red? The thesis that the subjective character of a perceptual experience suffices to fix the nature of its intentional object seems to face an equally serious problem with the indeterminacy with which objects may present themselves in perception. The character, or *Sosein*, of the line drawing on the card that I hallucinate at the edge of my visual field is neither rectilinear nor curved. If we consider the possible veridical perception that is subjectively identical to such a hallucination, it seems that the intentional object here, too, must be indeterminate—something that no actual drawing can possibly be.[83]

Indeed, Gilbert Ryle has suggested that the idea that the subjective character of experience suffices to fix intentional facts leads immediately to epistemological disaster. Contrasting intentionalism with the earlier "New Way of Ideas," he wrote, "Formerly we could not be right in our thinkings; now, what is nearly as bad, we cannot be wrong in our thinkings. Object-having had been an unrealizable ambition; now it is an unevadable obligation. We are choked where we had been starved. Object-having was [on the later view] . . . petrified into an inbuilt relation to a Term. Thought's targets were made un-missable, and were therefore made un-hittable, by being cemented to thought's very arrow-heads."[84] The application of this to the domain of perception is straightforward. Whenever we are in perceptual touch with the real world, we are so, even when illusion is present, thanks to our natural involvement with a physical domain. If intentional facts are determined solely on phenomenological grounds, and so in a way that ignores such real-world factors, intentionality seems incapable of sustaining a concept of "transcendence." If intentional objects are superior to sense-data and sensations as far as the phenomenology of perceptual consciousness is concerned, epistemologically they may seem to be no better. We may still seem to be confined within a "veil of perception."

Not, indeed, a veil of sense-data or sensations, but an equally impenetrable veil of intentional objects.[85]

So it looks as if the only way to save intentionalism as a form of Direct Realism is to deny that phenomenology suffices to determine the nature of intentional objects: to deny what I shall call the "Phenomenological Criterion." But how, it may well be wondered, could such a thing be denied? Is not Reinhardt Grossmann entirely justified when he writes, as if it were a matter beyond dispute, that an intentional object "has all the features with which it appears before a mind"?[86] Have we not seen, indeed, that the only way to avoid excessive ontological baggage is for us to follow Husserl in insisting that talk of an intentional object is just a way of saying how a subject is "minded," a necessary way of being descriptively adequate to experience? Is not the notion of an intentional object fully at home only in a phenomenological setting? And is it not of fundamental importance to the project of Phenomenology that an intentional object be describable independently of whether anything really exists corresponding to it—a commitment enshrined in the phenomenological *epoché?* Surely we must be able to fix upon a pre-given object with its *Sosein* independently of the issue of whether it exists or not. Let us see.

A minimal denial of the Phenomenological Criterion would have it that it holds for hallucinatory states—where we are, as such, wholly out of touch perceptually with the environment—but that it does not hold for veridical or illusory states—where real-world relations are also essentially implicated in the determination of the intentional object. Something along these lines must, indeed, be defended. Unless, however, some fuller story can be told, such a move merely introduces, in an ad hoc manner, a wholly unmotivated asymmetry into the theory of intentional objects. The intentional objects of genuine perceptions cannot be entirely divorced from specifications of the content of perceptual consciousness in the way envisaged by this manoeuvre. In the situation where a red ball looks black to me, we cannot simply say that the intentional object is red, for characterizations of perceptual situations in terms of intentional objects will then lack phenomenological adequacy. Somehow a reference to blackness also has to be available to such an account. One suggestion might be that we should say that the intentional object *is red* but *appears black*. This simply recapitulates the everyday, ordinary-language, account of the matter, albeit with reference to an intentional object. This may initially appear a surprising suggestion, since it may well seem to imply that the introduction of intentional objects effectively achieves nothing. It should be remembered, however, that we have been forced to bring intentional objects into the present account of perception only because of the phenomenon of hallucination. It formed no part, at least explicitly, of the discussion in Part I of this work. Illusion has re-emerged as a worry only in connection with a rearguard action to defend an intentionalist account that is otherwise motivated. It would not be particularly surprising, therefore, if reference to intentional objects were to freewheel in relation to illusion. The real test for this first suggestion will come in connection with hallucinations. "Is this a dagger I see before me?" asks Macbeth. If we apply the preceding suggestion to this case, the answer is No. What we ought to say is that Macbeth was aware of an object that *looked like* a dagger (just as it looked real). We ought to say this because the preceding suggestion involves shunting all characteristics that the intentional object does not really possess into the realm of mere appearance. But Macbeth was not aware of anything that really was a dagger. The problem is, however, that Macbeth was aware of an intentional object that was *not really anything at all*. This first suggestion therefore entails that there is no *truth* at all as to the nature of the intentional object of which Macbeth was aware. Such a proposal certainly retains a close parallel to everyday modes of expression—for we should not unnaturally describe Macbeth's situation as being one in which it merely seemed to him that a dagger was before him. On the other hand, the "freewheeling" nature of this intentionalist proposal renders it nugatory; reference to an intentional object of awareness is now doing no real work at all. Macbeth was aware of an intentional object, the proposal suggests, but one about which nothing can truly be said! The only alternative to this way of filling out the suggestion is to claim that, since the appearance-reality distinction gains no purchase when hallucination is in question, appearance should be allowed to constitute truth for hallucinatory objects. If it looks to Macbeth as though a dagger is before him, then what he hallucinates *is* a dagger. When, however, we return to cases of illusion, the situation becomes extremely puzzling. For we are trying to work out the suggestion that if a red object looks black to you, your intentional object is (really) red. What is mystifying is how the subjective character of an experience can entail a true characterization of an intentional object in the case of hallucination, but not in the case of illusion. This proposed asymmetry is mystifying because wholly unmotivated. Alternatively, saying simply that in the case of our illusion the intentional object is *black* returns us to our predicament.

The way forward here requires us to develop the special sense of "object" that is involved in intentionalism. At the beginning of this discussion of intentionalism, I said that "object" must not be equated with "entity." This is required if intentionalism is to be a significant alternative to the sense-datum theory in response to the Argument. What we now see is that "object" must be distinguished from "entity" *even in relation to illusion*, where there *is* an entity of which we are aware. When we are aware of a red physical object that looks black, we should say that the entity, the "thing," of which we are aware is red, but that *qua object* it is black. The term "object" should be given an *exclusively* intentional, phenomenological interpretation. Strictly speaking, an intentionalist should not characterize our illusory situation as being one in which a physical *object* is red. The object—that is, the ob-ject—is black. What is red is a certain physical entity. But, it may be objected, does this distinction not wreck the proposed defence of Direct Realism by denying the identity of intentional object and real "object" (in the now forbidden sense) for all cases of illusion? It does not, because the distinction in question is not, in the medieval sense, a "real distinction." (Nor, indeed, is it even a "modal distinction": it is a "distinction of reason.") To recognize a distinction between an entity (that is red) and an object (that is black) is not to postulate two different entities. That, indeed, from a Direct Realist perspective, would be to attempt to divide a thing from itself. The distinction is merely between a thing as it is in itself (or objectively) and *the same thing* as it is represented by a perceiving subject.[87] We may be reminded here of the medieval (and Cartesian) practice of expressing the distinction in question adverbially: although the thing is "formally" red, it is, in a now obsolete sense, "objectively" black: that is, black qua ob-ject. This has the signal advantage of excluding any suggestion that it is anything other than the real, red, physical entity that appears black, or that is, in the medieval sense, "objectively" black. Unfortunately, this terminology will not allow us a parallel treatment of hallucination, since here there is nothing to which the formal / objective contrast can apply. So finally, and retaining the substantive "object," we may characterize our illusory situation as being one where *a black object is really red*. Once again, the characterization of the object, qua object, is determined by the subjective character of the perceptual state, but the "really" ushers in the facts that hold *in reality*. Despite the fact that "object" is a "substantive," propositions in which it occurs are to be interpreted no differently from the corresponding medieval, adverbial construals where these are available. Finally, in the case where I *hallucinate* something black, we should say that I am aware of a black object that is *not really anything at all*.

If we do so interpret "really," we need to be careful, however. In particular, we need to distinguish between these two questions: "Is the subject (really) aware of a black object?" and "Is the subject aware of an object that is really black?"[88] In the illusory case as envisaged, the answers to these questions are, respectively, Yes and No. (The answer to the former question would be No only in cases where, through confusion, post-hypnotic suggestion, or whatever, the subject mistakes the sensory state he is in.) This proposal, too, may appear initially surprising. After all, we are not generally accustomed to distinguishing between "X is black" and "X is really black." If X is not black, we tend to think, then it just is not black at all. It ought not, however, to be surprising if a form of inference that is valid for the most part fails in the domain of intentionality. Intentionality is, after all, unique in character. In this domain we are not concerned simply with characterizing the world, but this together with our representation of that world. We are concerned not just with things, but with *objects*. It is surely not untoward that subtleties should enter into the description of the interplay between reality and its representation—subtleties that are absent when we are simply concerned with the description of things in themselves.

How then, finally, are we to answer Macbeth's question? Was it a dagger he saw before him? It now looks as if our answer should be Yes. And yet this is not entirely plausible. Kit Fine terms such a response "literalism," and puts his finger on the source of our unease with it as follows: "Macbeth asked: 'Is this a dagger that I see before me?' Now, assuming this is a situation from real life, it seems reasonable to suppose that Macbeth could have been wrong in his answer to this question . . . But on a literalist view, it is hard to see how Macbeth could have made a mistake . . . [T]he object would have been a dagger and so his belief that it was a dagger would have been correct."[89] The point here, I take it, is that when one is genuinely perceiving a dagger, even veridically, one's claim to see a dagger is not incorrigible, since there are things that look exactly like daggers but are not (and similarly for objects of the other senses). To say that something is a dagger is to go beyond a specification of the mere look of a thing. If we are interested in truly specifying hallucinated objects phenomenologically, we must not employ any descriptions that go beyond the simple deliverances of the senses.

Macbeth did not see a dagger. Not only did he not see a real dagger, he did not even see a non-existent or unreal dagger. What he saw was something that *looked like* (perhaps exactly like) a dagger. It is a trivial, but important, truth that daggers look exactly like things that look exactly like daggers; and some of these latter may not be daggers. A certain misshapen carrot, for example, could look exactly like a dagger, at least given limited viewing opportunities. Since, given that we are not to sever intentionalism from phenomenology, the characterization of Macbeth's intentional object is determined by the subjective character of his visual state, and since this state is subjectively identical to *both* a possible perception of a real dagger *and* a possible perception of a real carrot, what are the grounds for saying that he is aware, phenomenologically, of a dagger rather than a certain sort of carrot? What are the grounds for saying anything other than that he is aware merely of something that *has the visual characteristics* of a dagger? The only ground, of course, is that Macbeth would, if he believed his senses, naturally take it that there was, specifically, a dagger before him. Would he believe this, however, because this is precisely what his *senses* inform him? Or would he believe this only because he possesses certain general background beliefs, so that he would believe that a dagger is present *on the strength of* what his senses inform him—where this latter is something that falls short of the content *dagger*? In fact, the only reason that Macbeth would believe that there was specifically a dagger before him is that, as things are, almost everything that looks like a dagger *is* a dagger, and Macbeth knows this. If the world had been different, if it had contained innumerable dagger look-alikes, and if Macbeth knew this, he would not automatically have formed his belief about the presence of a dagger. Again, someone wholly unfamiliar with daggers would form no such belief, even if he saw the world exactly as Macbeth did. Such a person would only acquire the belief that something possessing such and such perceptible characteristics was present at such and such a location in space relative to himself. Being a dagger is not a *visual characteristic*, since things that look exactly like daggers, but are not, share all of a dagger's visual characteristics. All that vision properly affords are the *looks* of things; and analogous remarks apply to the other senses. This is, indeed, but an application of the anti-conceptualist position that was developed in Part I of this work. This does not mean, of course, that we cannot immediately perceive daggers;[90] for if the thing that looks to us a certain way is really a dagger, then we are immediately perceiving a dagger—even if it does not look like a dagger. Perceptual attributions are in this sense "extensional." It is, however, only in cases of veridical and illusory perception, where what is seen is a *real F*, that there is any ontological grounding for a claim to see an *F*, where *F*-ness is not a "sensible quality" (in the sense of the term explained in Chapter 1). Whenever the object is unreal, there is no such ground. The most that we can say in such a case is that the subject is aware of something that looks *F*. Indeed, the claim that such a subject is aware of something that *is F* is simply false, for there is nothing that makes this claim—rather than the contrary claim that it is not *F*, but merely looks it—true. True characterizations of hallucinations cannot exceed what is *sensorily given* to the subject. This is not to revert to the "Myth of the Given." What is given is not "raw sensation," something about which we have Cartesian certainty, but which awaits an "interpretation." What is given is a physical object, or at least a physical "phenomenon," in space.

Although Macbeth did not see a dagger, by contrast it is true to say that what he saw was shaped thus and so, had such and such a colour or lustre, and so on for all sensible qualities perceptible by sight. If, therefore, we re-phrase Macbeth's question as "Is this a dagger-shaped thing I see before me?" intentionalism can give an affirmative answer. Such an affirmative answer is considerably less implausible than it is in response to Macbeth's original question. For by making reference to a dagger, Macbeth made appeal to certain non-visual features that are necessary for any thing to be a dagger, and this undermines any phenomenologically grounded reason for a positive answer to the question. Talk merely of a "dagger-shaped" thing makes no such appeal.

When characterizing hallucinated objects we also, however, need to restrict our descriptions to what a minimally different, genuinely perceiving subject would perceive "of" the normal physical object he is aware of. If by "dagger-shaped" we mean that the object is shaped *exactly* like a real dagger—that is, like a certain three-dimensional body—then our description still goes beyond what is visually given to a hallucinating subject, at least in a single view. This is because any such view of a physical body is partial. What we see of the thing is less than there is to it—less, even, than there is to the visible surface characteristics of it. Just as half an egg-shell, seen from the right angle, looks exactly like an egg, so half a dagger can look just like a dagger. Since all that we see (or feel) of a physical thing is *part* of its *surface*, all such claims go beyond what is strictly given to the senses. This somewhat traditional, even dated, claim is now given a theoretically motivated ground in the context of intentionalism as the only viable way of sustaining Direct Realism. For in the present context such a claim amounts to the observation that when the intentional object of a perception is non-existent, there is nothing to constitute the truth of any claim about the nature of the object that goes beyond such narrow traditional limits on description. If we allow our subject a more extended, coherent hallucination, in which he attains more "views" of the object, we can allow our characterizations of the hallucinated object to expand. The principle that governs all such descriptions, however, is the following: Allow all, but only, those descriptions of the object that a subjectively identical, veridically perceiving, ideally attentive and honest subject would give, and that, given veridical perception, *entail* that the perceived object really is as described. This is, in effect, simply to spell out what was meant by a "sensible quality" in Part I.

This line of argument also suffices to rule out two related possibilities that surfaced briefly in the previous chapter: that I should hallucinate the same object as you, and that I should hallucinate an object I have previously perceived veridically or illusorily. Once again, in the absence of a real object, such identity claims are ontologically ungrounded: there is nothing to make them true. In the nature of the case, there can be nothing to constitute a distinction between the two purported possibilities and situations in which I hallucinate, respectively, an object that is *just like yours* and that is *just like one I have perceived before*. This may seem far from obvious; and it has certainly been denied. Brian McLaughlin, for example, writes as follows: "When one undergoes an hallucination there can be something such that one is hallucinating it. There are, so to speak, *de re* hallucinations. Just as one can dream about an actual individual, so one can hallucinate an actual individual. One might, say, hallucinate one's father. Indeed, I am told that it is not uncommon for hallucinators to hallucinate an actual individual."[91] The fact that one can dream about an actually existent individual, however, lends no weight to the suggestion that one can hallucinate one—at least not as the term "hallucination" has been employed in the present work. For it will be recalled that, at the outset of our discussion of hallucination, the suggestion that hallucinations are but cases of vividly imagining things was set aside. Perhaps all actual hallucinations are of this nature; perhaps, indeed, this is what "hallucination" standardly *means*. I, however, have been employing the term to denote a different type of experience: one that is not a matter of imagination, but a matter of being in a sensory state that is identical to one involved in some possible genuine sensory perception of the world. Now, one can dream about, just as one can imagine, real individuals only because such cognitive states are dependent upon the offices of thought, or at least memory. The intentionality of such states, when *de re*, is *inherited* from thought or memory. Only if hallucinations are understood as falling within the same genus as such states can they be of real individuals—something that McLaughlin himself recognizes when he writes that "an hallucinatory experience can function only as a singular element that refers in a secondary way. In *de re* hallucination, the hallucinator must already have possessed a mental singular element that refers to the individual in question. Hallucinatory experiences can refer, but they cannot initiate referential chains."[92] Such derivativeness is, however, entirely lacking in the kind of genuinely sensory states of intentional awareness that we have been concerned with in these pages. Hallucinations, in this proprietary sense, are as underivative as are the genuine perceptions to which they are phenomenologically identical.

A further implication is that hallucinated objects not only do not exist, they could not possibly exist: they are *necessary non-existents*. Macbeth's visual object is unreal; but he might, on that occasion, have been perceiving veridically while his visual experience was subjectively the same. In this possible situation, must we not say that the intentional object would have been real, and yet, qua intentional object, would be the same as the object of the hallucination? We must not. In this possible situation Macbeth would have been perceiving a real dagger that was at most *exactly like* the original hallucinated object. It is not a meta-physical possibility for a nonentity to be real. In case this is not obvious, note that it is a straightforward (albeit "trans-world") implication of the preceding observations.[93] For if Macbeth's dagger could have been real, there is some possible world in which either he or someone else perceives it veridically. We are then faced with exactly the same unanswerable challenge to state in virtue of what it is that his actual hallucination is of the same object as the object of this veridical perception rather than of some qualitatively identical dagger. In all three cases it is the lack of a real entity as what is perceived in hallucination that undermines the attempt to ground an identity claim.

To return to our original question, since intentionalist characterizations of any hallucinated object must be restricted to sensible qualities, the only sorts of questions to which the intentionalist is required to give affirmative answers are questions such as the following: "Is this a curved surface I am seeing (or feeling)?"; "Is this a sweet odour I am smelling?"; "Is this a shrill noise I am hearing?"; "Is this a cold surface I am touching?"; and, if the object is small enough to be felt at one moment in its entirety, "Is this a spherical object I am feeling?" In contradistinction to Macbeth's original question, all of these seem strained and artificial. The reason for this, of course, is that it is somewhat difficult to imagine circumstances in which a subject would seriously ask any such questions, even of himself. Difficult, but not impossible. If we imagine that the subject is extremely psychologically confused, or drunk, such questions will no doubt be intelligible. But this is only because we imagine the subject having doubts as to whether he really has a grip on the character of the sensory experiences he is having: he is unable, for example, to keep track of the course of his experience from one moment to the next. If, however, we set aside such cases of subjective confusion, the questions certainly are puzzling. The intentionalist has an explanation for this. The questions are puzzling because the answer to them all—Yes—would be *perfectly obvious* to the subjects in question. So, far from the intentionalist's limited commitment to "literalism" being counter-intuitive, it actually explains why such questions, within the sphere in question, are peculiarly strained to the ear. Can we not, however, envisage questions, even within our restricted domain, that intuitively demand a negative reply? "Is this a red thing I see before me?" asks a hallucinating subject. Are there not circumstances in which "No" would be a perfectly reasonable answer? Doubtless there are. The circumstances in question, however, would be ones in which the question amounts to asking, "Is this *really* a red thing I see before me?" If the question is construed in *this* way, however, the intentionalist reply is, of course, not at all counter-intuitive, since it is a straightforward negative. That it would, indeed, be most reasonable to construe such questions in this way is again explained by the fact that they would, without the intended reference to reality, be strained and puzzling.

One final problem that may be thought to attach to the requirement that the intentional object of a non-hallucinatory experience be a real physical object concerns space. Are hallucinated objects in real physical space? The question is not whether they are really in this space, since, being unreal, they are not really anything or anywhere. The question is whether, qua objects, they are so located. When a real red tomato looks black to you, I have suggested that you are aware of a black object that is really red. The present question is whether, when you *hallucinate* a black object, you are aware of a physically located object that really has no such location. In the case of partial hallucinations, we shall need some ingenious answer to convince us otherwise. If you hallucinate an object on the table in front of you, both phenomenology and naive consciousness will testify to its presence *on the table*. Indeed, a suitably lifelike, moderately extended, and coherent hallucination could put you in a position to think about, and in general have cognitive "attitudes" (or a "comportment") towards, a particular location in space that was otherwise unavailable to you. If you look up and try and focus your attention on a small region of unoccupied space about ten feet away from you, you will, as we have already noted, quite rightly have little confidence in the enterprise. One could, however, hallucinate an object *precisely there*. But what of a complete hallucination—of which the experience of a brain in a vat is an extreme example? Could such a subject hallucinate an object ten feet in front of himself? Most of us would want to insist that in some sense he could; but the question is whether such a perceptual experience will give a fix on a place in physical space—one that is, perhaps, about ten feet from the place where the brain is located. Such a suggestion is surely extremely dubious—even when fully embodied, active subjects are in question—if the hallucination is total.[94] The natural thing to say about such cases is that not only the objects, but also the entire space in which they are located, are un-real—for the objects of a total hallucination are not located at any distance from any really existing object. It is possible, however, for doubts to arise over this. Suppose, for example, that a brain in a vat has, totally unknown to it, just been fitted with eyes in such a way that the subject will eventually be allowed to see his environment. Everything is now ready, and all that is required for the subject to see is that a switch be flipped that will cut off the artificial visual inputs to the brain that the subject up to now has been receiving, and will allow the eyes and visual system to function normally. So as not to shock the subject out of his wits, the recently induced course of visual experience has been of a scene that is qualitatively identical to what the subject is about to see of the real world. The switch is flicked, and there is, let us suppose, no subjective change at all. Is it not plausible to describe the subject's course of experience here as its being a matter of real physical entities coming to be perceived in the *same space* as he was aware of before the flicking of the switch?

In fact, the issue here is essentially the same as was involved in what, in the initial presentation of the Argument from Hallucination in Chapter 7, I suggested was the most initially compelling way of trying to motivate the generalizing step of the Argument by reference to the possible subjective indiscernibility of hallucination and genuine perception: pointing out that a subject may move from merely hallucinating to genuinely perceiving something without any subjectively registered change at all. And the response to the present objection is essentially the same as before. Here, too, the Direct Realist must reject the assumption that lack of subjective change entails a continuing identity of object perceived—for any such assumption is pretty clearly incompatible with the "externalism" that is, I have suggested, essential to Direct Realism. It is just that, in the present case, the "object" involved is space. So we should say that in the scenario now in question, the subject, upon the flipping of the switch, comes to be aware of a new, because real, space.

Such a scenario can, however, be made even more intuitively difficult for the intentionalist. For imagine that the scene the subject sees just before and after the switch is flicked is of a darkened room in which only a few obscure shapes to the left and right are visible. Shortly after the switch is flicked, the subject sees a light (really) come on in the centre of the room. Throughout this time the subject's eyes are, or seem to him to be, fixed on the centre of the room. Suppose also, however, that the flicking of the switch, which allows the subject's normal optical system to function, this time does not cause the previous artificial visual input to cease entirely; rather, it now induces a *partial* hallucination in the subject. Although the subject truly sees the central portion of the room where the light is seen to come on, the rest of the "room" is hallucinated, and, moreover, is qualitatively identical to that aspect of the visual scene before the switch was flicked. In short, what the flick of the switch brings about is that the subject begins to see only the centre of the physical room he is in, with all the rest of the apparent scene continuing to be a hallucination. Can we really avoid saying that the subject sees a real light beginning to shine in the centre of a space that was and continues to be unreal, because entirely artificially induced? It will not do to suggest that only in the centre of the subject's visual field is he aware of real space, and that the apparent space surrounding this is unreal. For if this is said, we shall have to draw the unintuitive conclusion that *no* hallucinated object can ever be located in physical space—that no hallucination can be partial. So are we not forced to conclude, absurdly, that the light is seen to come on in an unreal space, even though this perception is veridical? We do not. What we should conclude, rather, is that as soon as a real light is perceived, the subject's entire visual field gives an awareness of the one, all-encompassing space of our physical environment. One of the hallucinated dark shapes would be, for example, located by the subject just to the left and a little behind *that light*—which is itself truly located in physical space, since perception of it is veridical. Any genuine perception of even a single physical object gives the subject physical space, entire and whole, at one stroke.

THIS CONCLUDES my defence of intentionalism. I have attempted to push the theory as hard as possible, trying to come up with the most apparently embarrassing questions for it; but the approach has, I believe, held up. This defence is not, however, supposed to constitute a reason for accepting intentionalism. Those reasons were given earlier. For, in the first place, intentionalism is the only way of defending Direct Realism from the Argument from Hallucination—the most serious threat to this position within the Philosophy of Perception. It achieves this, you will recall, by virtue of not construing the object of which one is aware when hallucinating as an entity: as something *real*. Once any such non-normal entity is admitted into the story as an immediate object of hallucinatory awareness at stage two of the Argument, such will ineradicably remain the immediate object of awareness whatever the perceptual situation. In the second place, intentionalism has emerged as the most natural way of accounting for hallucination in terms of the phenomenological insights that were attained in Part I of this work in connection with illusion. For there we discovered the origin and nature of the intentionality of perception: that in virtue of which perceptual consciousness is other than a mere registering of sensation. Since this is a phenomenological fact, it is also to be found in hallucination, which is subjectively perceptual in character, whatever its causal aetiology. Here too we find a directedness to objects that transcend the flux of the real sensory elements in consciousness. But whereas in the case of illusion these objects may be identified with the normal physical entities with which we stand in real-world relations—those entities that focally govern the course of our sense-experience and, crucially, that govern those aspects of consciousness that constitute *perceptual* consciousness: the constancies and the *Anstoss*—in the case of hallucination it makes sense, precisely because of such intentionality, and in the absence of suitable real-world relations, to say that these objects do not exist—that they are *merely* intentional objects. This solution to the Problem of Perception has, I believe, been so consistently overlooked because of the idea that we can make sense of intentionality only by reference to concepts and the nature of thought. Since this idea inevitably leads to construing intentionality along the lines of Russell's Theory of Descriptions, and since this is manifestly inapplicable to perceptual awareness, such an approach is destined to fail to see the solution. The account of the wholly pre-conceptual genesis of the intentionality that is peculiar to perceptual consciousness is, therefore, as integral to a satisfactory response to the Argument from Hallucination as it was to a satisfactory response to the Argument from Illusion.

Notes

All translations of foreign texts are my own, though references are given to published translations when they exist.

Introduction

1. That such a world is at all times dependent upon an infinite creative consciousness—God—was the dominant view until the "Enlightenment." This was, however, taken to be compatible with Realism.

2. For a detailed account of the issues involved here, which I endorse, see the beginning of John Foster's *The Case for Idealism* (London: Routledge & Kegan Paul, 1982).

3. This is perhaps too narrow. In Heidegger we find the suggestion that there are forms of "comportment" towards the world that are more basic than "cognition." I shall, however, regard as Idealism any position that is truly characterized by the earlier definition even when any form of "comportment" is substituted for "cognition," since this, too, would make the purely physical domain necessarily correlative to human existence: to, if not consciousness and "subjectivity," at least *"Dasein."*

4. Jean-Paul Sartre, *L'être et le néant* (Paris: Gallimard, 1943), pp. 42–65 [*Being and Nothingness*, tr. Hazel E. Barnes (London: Methuen, 1958), pp. 8–28].

5. Cited in Sextus Empiricus, *Pyrrhoneae Hypotyposes*, I.215, in *Sextus Empiricus*, tr. R. G. Bury, 4 vols. (London: Heinemann, and Cambridge, Mass.: Harvard University Press, 1967), vol. 1, p. 128.

6. This claim will be contested by many. In relation to Husserl, I think the case is overwhelming—as I argue in a forthcoming book, *Husserl and the Cartesian Meditations* (London: Routledge). As for Merleau-Ponty, the following passage is instructive. "As Berkeley says, even a desert that has never been visited has at least one spectator, and that is we ourselves when we think of it . . . The thing can never

be separated from someone who may perceive it, it can never be effectively in it-self": *Phénoménologie de la Perception* (Paris: Gallimard, 1945), p. 370 [*Phenomenology of perception*, tr. Colin Smith (London: Routledge & Kegan Paul, 1962), p. 320].

7. Sartre, *L'être et le néant*, pp. 30–84, 219–235 [*Being and Nothingness*, pp. xxxviii–45, 171–186].

8. Heidegger does state, however, that he knows of no demonstration of the falsity of Idealism and of the truth of Realism: *Die Grundprobleme der Phenome-nologie (1919/20)*, in *Gesamtausgabe*, vol. 58 (Frankfurt am Main: Vittorio Kloster-mann, 1993), pp. 237–238 [*The Basic Problems of Phenomenology*, tr. Albert Hofstadter, rev. ed. (Bloomington: Indiana University Press, 1988), p. 167].

9. The best account I know of Heidegger's views on perception, in the con-text of his philosophy as a whole, is Jacques Taminiaux, *Lectures de l'ontologie fonda-mentale: Essais sur Heidegger* (Grenoble: Millon, 1989) [*Heidegger and the project of fundamental ontology*, tr. Michael Gendre (Albany: State University of New York Press, 1991)], ch. 2.

10. John Foster, "The Succinct Case for Idealism," in *Objections to Physicalism*, ed. Howard Robinson (Oxford: Clarendon Press, 1993), 293–313; and Howard Robinson, "The General Form of Argument for Berkeleian Idealism," in *Essays on Berkeley*, ed. John Foster and Howard Robinson (Oxford: Clarendon Press, 1985), pp. 163–186.

11. I do not choose this example lightly. Giovanni Battista della Porta's liken-ing the human eye to a camera obscura had enormous influence on, indeed was one ingredient in, the growth of the Problem of Perception in the early modern period of philosophy. For an excellent survey of optical theories in the period preceding Descartes, see David C. Lindberg, *Theories of Vision From Al-Kindī to Kepler* (Chi-cago: University of Chicago Press, 1976).

12. I intend the notion of *distinctness* to be stronger than that of non-identity. Most Direct Realists are happy to accept that when we (directly) see, say, an apple, we do so in virtue of seeing a part of the apple's surface. I, for one, certainly see no threat to Direct Realism in such an admission. For although an apple's surface is not identical to the apple, it is not "distinct" from that apple. Something is distinct from X if and only if it is neither a dependent nor an independent part, neither a "piece" nor a "moment," of X. (For the mereological notions I am employing here, see Edmund Husserl, *Logische Untersuchungen*, 3 vols., in *Husserliana*, vol. 18, ed. Elmar Holenstein, and 19/1–2, ed. Ursula Panzer (The Hague: Martinus Nijhoff, 1975 and 1984) [*Logical Investigations*, 2 vols., tr. J. N. Findlay (London: Routledge & Kegan Paul, 1970)], *Third Investigation*.

13. I here echo Moltke Gram's way of explicating the issue of Direct Realism in terms of the notion of a "proxy": see his *Direct Realism* (The Hague: Martinus Nijhoff, 1983), ch. 1.

14. When philosophers speak of "physical objects," they tend to have in mind what J. L. Austin referred to as "middle-sized dry goods." Leaving aside mere size, we also, of course, perceive such things as rainbows, shadows, sounds, and so on. Where a distinction between these latter and "bodies" would be helpful, I shall re-fer to them as physical "phenomena," though I shall also usually intend them when I use the term "physical object"—since, equally with sticks and stones, they are physical and objects of perception.

15. Bertrand Russell, *The Analysis of Matter* (London: George Allen & Unwin, 1927), p. 383.

16. The term "normal" is not meant to connote usual or standard, but rather to echo the sense of the word as it is used in the phrase "normal to the line of sight."

17. J. L. Austin, *Sense and Sensibilia* (Oxford: Oxford University Press, 1962), p. 19.

18. The phrase derives from Jonathan Bennett, who himself employed it, in effect, to denote any position other than Phenomenalism—a specific form of Idealism: see *Locke, Berkeley, Hume* (Oxford: Clarendon Press, 1971), §13. The phrase is, however, now widely used in a less theory-laden fashion to connote the general spectre of a loss of direct contact with the physical world.

19. Sextus Empiricus, *Adversus Mathematicos*, VII.354 and VII.366 in *Sextus Empiricus*, vol. 2, pp. 186, 192. Compare his *Pyrrhoneae Hypotyposes*, I.72–73.

20. The quotation is from Ayer's *The Problem of Knowledge* (Harmondsworth: Penguin Books, 1956), p. 3.

21. I construe this law here as the principle of the "indiscernibility of identicals": if X and Y are one and the same, there can be no difference between them—since they are one.

22. The term "genuine" is used, here and in (b), in order to exclude, for familiar reasons, merely apparent counter-examples to Leibniz's Law based on intensionally specified pseudo-attributes.

23. J. L. Mackie endorses such an argument in his *Problems from Locke* (Oxford: Clarendon Press, 1976), p. 8. P. F. Strawson endorses at least the incompatibility: see his "Perception and Its Objects," in *Perception and Identity*, ed. G. F. Macdonald (London: Macmillan, 1979), p. 49.

24. David Hume, *A Treatise of Human Nature*, ed. L. A. Selby-Bigge and P. H. Nidditch, 2d ed. (Oxford: Clarendon Press, 1978), pp. 210–211.

25. For an interpretation of Hume along these lines, see John Wright, *The Sceptical Realism of David Hume* (Manchester: Manchester University Press, 1983), p. 45.

26. For the earlier history of this argument, see John W. Yolton, *Perceptual Acquaintance from Descartes to Reid* (Oxford: Basil Blackwell, 1984), chs. 2–4. The argument was still popular in the nineteenth century: see, for example, Hippolyte Adolphe Taine, *De L'Intélligence*, 2 vols. (Paris: Hachette, 1870) and Thomas H. Huxley, *Hume: With Helps to the Study of Berkeley, Collected Essays*, vol. 6 (London: Macmillan, 1908).

27. Leibniz states the argument concisely: "And since rays of light take time (however short it may be), it is possible that the object should be destroyed in this interval and no longer exist when the ray reaches the eye, and what no longer is cannot be the present object of sight": *Nouveaux Essais sur l'Entendement Humain, Sämtliche Schriften und Briefe*, ser. 6, vol. 6 (Darmstadt: Deutsche Akademie der Wissenschaft, 1962) [*New Essays on Human Understanding*, tr. Peter Remnant and Jonathan Bennett (Cambridge: Cambridge University Press, 1981)], p. 135. For a modern discussion of this argument, see W. A. Suchting, "Perception and the Time-Gap Argument," *Philosophical Quarterly* 19 (1969): 46–56.

28. I spell the word "reflexion" when it bears this sense. I reserve the term "re-

flection" for contexts where connotations of pondering and ratiocination are relevant.

29. The notable exception to this observation is Wilfrid Sellars, a major postwar philosopher who returned again and again, throughout his career, to the issue of perception. His work will receive detailed consideration later.

30. A remark by Jacques Derrida is symptomatic, if extreme: "There is no such thing as perception." See *La Voix et Le Phénomène* (Paris: Presses Universitaires de France, 1967), p. 50n [*Speech and Phenomena*, tr. David B. Allison (Evanston, Ill.: Northwestern University Press, 1973), p. 45n].

31. Sextus Empiricus, *Pyrrhoneae Hypotyposes*, I.99.

32. The reference is, of course, to W. V. Quine, *Word and Object* (Cambridge, Mass.: MIT Press, 1960), ch. 2.

33. Diogenes Laertius, *Lives of Eminent Philosophers*, with English translation by R. D. Hicks, 2 vols. (Cambridge, Mass.: Harvard University Press, 1995), VII.49.

34. See, for example, J. L. Mackie, *Problems from Locke*, ch. 2, §7, and Frank Jackson, *Perception* (Cambridge: Cambridge University Press, 1977), ch. 6. (Mackie's version of Indirect Realism is, it should be said, non-standard, since his proxies are not entities but intentional objects. That intentional objects, properly understood, are not proxies, and that their recognition is compatible with Direct Realism, will be the burden of Part II of this work.)

35. Another option, of course, is scepticism—a position I shall simply not consider in this work.

36. Hume, *Treatise*, p. 193.

37. Jean le Rond d'Alembert, *Essai sur les Élémens de Philosophie*, *Oeuvres Philosophiques, Historiques et Littéraires d'Alembert*, 5 vols. (Paris: Bastien, 1805), vol. 2, p. 126.

1. The Argument

1. Frank Jackson, *Perception* (Cambridge: Cambridge University Press, 1977), p. 107. I am given to believe that Jackson no longer endorses Indirect Realism.

2. G. Dawes Hicks, *Critical Realism* (London: Macmillan, 1938), p. 76.

3. J. L. Austin, *Sense and Sensibilia* (Oxford: Oxford University Press, 1962), p. 29.

4. The phrase "perceptually appears" is something of a term of art. It will be properly explained in the following section of this chapter.

5. See, for example, Diana Deutsch, *Musical Illusions and Paradoxes* (Philomel DIDX 037 155).

6. Although it is always Berkeley who is referred to in this connection, he was not the first philosopher to make the general point, or even the first to employ it against the doctrine of primary and secondary qualities. Theophrastus, for example, makes precisely the same move against Democritus: see his *De Sensibus*, §70, to be found, with translation, in George Malcolm Stratton, *Theophrastus and the Greek Physiological Psychology before Aristotle* (London: George Allen and Unwin, and New York: Macmillan, 1917), pp. 128–129.

7. For an amusing example of what can happen when this is denied, see the Frank Cioffi anecdote in G. E. M. Anscombe, "The Intentionality of Sensation: A

Grammatical Feature," in *Analytical Philosophy*, 2d ser., ed. R. J. Butler (Oxford: Blackwell, 1965), pp. 158–180.

8. Deutsch's *Musical Illusions and Paradoxes* gives some striking examples of directional illusions.

9. The "phantom limb" phenomenon is well known, but perhaps more properly should be considered a case of hallucination than one of illusion.

10. James R. Lackner, "Some Proprioceptive Influences on the Perceptual Representation of Body Shape and Orientation," *Brain* 111 (1988): 281–297.

11. H. H. Price, *Perception* (London: Methuen, 1954), pp. 31–32. That sense-data are such fleeting products has, of course, not yet been shown; but the general thrust of Price's claim is clear.

12. Austin, *Sense and Sensibilia*, p. 52.

13. A. J. Ayer saw this point clearly: see, for example, *The Problem of Knowledge* (Harmondsworth: Penguin Books, 1956), pp. 87–88. And compare J. L. Mackie, *Problems from Locke* (Oxford: Clarendon Press, 1976), pp. 48–49.

14. We are now in a position to state the very weakest premise that suffices to initiate the Argument. It is to the effect that, for any possible physical object, some quality of that object is possibly subject to "illusion" in each possible sense by which we might perceive that object.

15. T. P. Nunn, "Are Secondary Qualities Independent of Perception?" *Proceedings of the Aristotelian Society* 10 (1909–1910): 208.

16. E. B. Holt et al., The New Realism (New York: Macmillan, 1912). I should perhaps say that Percy Nunn, referred to earlier, was not an American New Realist, but a British sympathizer.

17. Jean-Paul Sartre, *L'être et le néant* (Paris: Gallimard, 1943), pp. 372–375 [*Being and Nothingness*, tr. Hazel E. Barnes (London: Methuen, 1958), pp. 310–312].

18. "Perception" is sometimes "aisthēsis," sometimes "phantasia." The interpretative issues surrounding the Epicurean claim are delicate. For good recent discussions see C. C. W. Taylor, "All Perceptions Are True," in *Doubt and Dogmatism*, ed. Malcolm Schofield, Myles Burnyeat, and Jonathan Barnes (Oxford: Clarendon Press, 1980), pp. 105–124, and G. Striker, "Epicurus on the Truth of Sense-Impressions," *Archiv für Geschichte der Philosophie* 59 (1977): 125–142.

19. *Adversus Colotem*, 1100D, in Plutarch's *Moralia*, 15 vols. (London: Heinemann, and Cambridge, Mass.: Harvard University Press, 1957), vol. 14, p. 208.

20. Sartre, *L'être et le néant*, p. 375 [*Being and Nothingness*, p. 312].

21. Winston H. F. Barnes, "The Myth of Sense-Data," *Proceedings of the Aristotelian Society* 45 (1944–1945); repr. in *Perceiving, Sensing, and Knowing*, ed. Robert J. Swartz (Berkeley: University of California Press, 1965), p. 144.

22. D. M. Armstrong, *A Materialist Theory of Mind* (London: Routledge & Kegan Paul, 1968), pp. 284–285.

23. Such would certainly seem to be the import of Plutarch's remarks in *Adversus Colotem*, 1109D.

24. David Armstrong, *A Materialist Theory of Mind*, pp. 286–287.

25. A wide range of such cases is discussed in J. J. Gibson, "Adaptation with Negative After-Effect," *Psychological Review* 44 (1937): 222–244.

26. W. A. Thalman, "The After-Effect of Movement in the Sense of Touch," *American Journal of Psychology* 33 (1922): 275.

27. Barnes, "The Myth of Sense-Data," p. 153.

28. See Roderick M. Chisholm, "The Theory of Appearing," in *Philosophical Analysis*, ed. Max Black; repr. in Swartz, *Perceiving, Sensing, and Knowing*, pp. 168–186.

29. Roderick M. Chisholm, *Perceiving: A Philosophical Study* (Ithaca, N.Y.: Cornell University Press, 1957), pp. 151–152. In his influential article, "The Myth of Sense-Data," Winston Barnes presents such facts as a sole and sufficient basis for a wholesale rejection of the idea of sense-data. To be fair, Barnes does make two further points. First, he emphasizes what he takes to be ontologically puzzling features of sense-data, such as their identity conditions. But he holds these to be "perhaps not sufficiently serious to destroy the theory." Secondly, he refers the reader to works by Dawes Hicks for an analysis of perception that eschews sense-data. The reader will, in fact, search these works in vain for a theory of perception that is sufficiently detailed to deflect the Argument.

30. This point is forcefully made in Howard Robinson, "The Objects of Perceptual Experience II," *Proceedings of the Aristotelian Society, Supplementary Volume* 64 (1990): 158.

31. C. D. Broad, *Scientific Thought* (London: Kegan Paul, Trench, Trubner & Co., 1923), p. 240.

32. The distinctions about to be drawn are related to ones commonly made in the literature, sometimes by employing the contrasting terms "epistemic" and "phenomenological." The widespread use of the term "epistemic" in this context derives largely from Roderick Chisholm's influential tripartite division of the language of appearing into the epistemic, the comparative, and the non-comparative: see his *Perceiving*, ch. 4. (He credits the introduction of "epistemic" to H. H. Price, though the article by Price to which he refers does not in fact employ the term: cf. "Review of A. J. Ayer, *The Foundations of Empirical Knowledge*," *Mind* 50 [1941]: 280–293.) Anthony Quinton, in an influential article discussed later, had already suggested a similar division, and he has subsequently adopted the term "epistemic": see, respectively, "The Problem of Perception," *Mind* 64 (1955), reprinted in Swartz, *Perceiving, Sensing, and Knowing*, pp. 497–526) and *The Nature of Things* (London: Routledge & Kegan Paul, 1973), ch. 7. I have not myself adopted this term, however, since it perhaps implies that another, contrasted, form of appearing is *entirely* non-epistemic—a big issue that we should not take on at this stage. Neither shall I use the term "phenomenological" in this context, since it is ambiguous, as we shall see in Chapter 6. Also, I shall not be explicitly discussing Chisholm's "comparative" sense, according to which "looks *F*" means "looks the way *F* things look" (either normally, or in specified circumstances). One reason why this use does not demand further consideration is that such a phrase immediately invites the question, "And what way is that?"

33. Quinton, "The Problem of Perception," p. 501.

34. Ibid., p. 504.

35. Wilfrid Sellars, *Science, Perception, and Reality* (London: Routledge & Kegan Paul, 1963), ch. 5. See also Michael Williams, *Groundless Belief* (Oxford: Blackwell, 1977) for a particularly clear presentation of the issues.

36. Price, *Perception*, p. 69.

37. Recall that, strictly, the only certainty that is required here is that it is *possi-*

ble that there should, for any veridical perception, be an illusion that shares its sensory character with respect to one perceived quality.

38. Daniel Dennett, "Wondering Where the Yellow Went," *Monist* 64 (1981): 105–106. Such claims about what is achievable by hypnosis are, in fact, far from uncontroversial. For relevant details, and some first-person testimony, see Mary Haight, "Hypnosis and the Philosophy of Mind," *Proceedings of the Aristotelian Society* 90 (1989–1990): 171–189. I shall, however, not emphasize this point, since Dennett's questions can equally, and less controversially, be raised in relation to dreaming.

39. Gilbert Harman, "The Intrinsic Quality of Experience," *Philosophical Perspectives* 4 (1990): 35. I should say that Harman is primarily interested in psychological states that are not directed to any real object at all: cases of hallucination, which form the topic of Part II of the present work. We need, however, to consider the merits of such a pure intentionalist account as applied to the case of illusion.

40. A certain form of such a divide and conquer strategy, called the "disjunctive" account of perceptual experience, is currently much in vogue. For reasons about to be given, this is more plausibly employed in relation to hallucination than illusion. The account will, therefore, receive proper consideration in Part II.

41. Sextus Empiricus, *Adversus Mathematicos*, VII.350, in *Sextus Empiricus*, tr. R. G. Bury, 4 vols. (London: Heinemann, and Cambridge, Mass.: Harvard University Press, 1967), vol. 2, p. 184.

42. Robert C. Cummins, "Reid's Realism," *Journal of the History of Philosophy* 12 (1974): 320.

43. As a matter of fact, many proponents of the Argument accept just such a picture of sense-experience: they *agree* with Naive Realism's intuitive understanding of the structure of perceptual awareness, and differ only over the status of the objects of awareness. This is true, for example, of adherents of the sense-datum theory, which we shall encounter shortly.

44. Daniel Dennett, "On the Absence of Phenomenology," in *Body, Mind and Method*, ed. D. F. Gustafson and B. L. Tapscott (Dordrecht: Reidel, 1979), pp. 97 and 95, respectively.

45. Daniel Dennett, *Consciousness Explained* (Harmondsworth: Penguin, 1993), p. 388.

46. Daniel Dennett, "Quining Qualia," in *Consciousness in Contemporary Science*, ed. A. Marcel and E. Bisiach (Oxford: Clarendon Press, 1992), p. 544.

47. John McDowell, "The Content of Perceptual Experience," *Philosophical Quarterly* 44 (1994): 191, commenting on Dennett's *Brainstorms* (Montgomery, Vt.: Bradford Books, 1978), pp. 165–166.

48. As Dennett himself writes: "It may look as if the color is *out there*, but it isn't. It's *in here*—in the 'eye and brain of the beholder' . . . But now, if there is no inner *figment* that could be colored in some special, subjective, in-the-mind, phenomenal sense, colors seem to disappear altogether!" (*Consciousness Explained*, pp. 370–371). Dennett clearly does not consider this a reductio of his position. I do not see how it can fail to be.

49. For a fuller—indeed exhaustive and unanswerable—polemic against reductive accounts of sensory experience, see Morland Perkins, *Sensing the World* (Indianapolis: Hackett, 1983). The only criticism that I have of this fine work is that

Perkins takes his position to entail the falsity of Direct Realism. As I hope will subsequently emerge, this is not the case.

50. George Pitcher, *A Theory of Perception* (Princeton, N.J.: Princeton University Press, 1971), pp. 32–33.

51. The idea that such cases pose a problem for the inference to the existence of subjective sensory qualities dates back to Hellenistic times. The Cyrenaics were known for construing a subject's seeming to see something white or yellow in terms of the subject being "whitened" or "yellowed." Plutarch, though not in his own voice, expressed the objection that someone's seeing a horse or a wall should, therefore, and absurdly, be construed in terms of that person being "walled" or "horsed": *Adversus Colotem*, 1120DEF.

52. For a notable early attempt within the analytical tradition to escape from such a traditional perspective, see Roderick Firth, "Sense-Data and the Percept Theory I and II," *Mind* 58 (1949) and 59 (1950), repr. in Swartz, *Perceiving, Sensing, and Knowing*, pp. 204–270. Firth is also particularly notable for seeing that adopting a more "phenomenological" approach does not by itself dissolve the Problem of Perception.

53. Maurice Merleau-Ponty, *Phénoménologie de la Perception* (Paris: Gallimard, 1945), p. 265 [*Phenomenology of Perception*, tr. Colin Smith (London: Routledge & Kegan Paul, 1962), p. 230].

54. Sartre, *L'être et le néant*, pp. 235–236 [*Being and Nothingness*, p. 186].

55. I take this, and its generalization to the other senses, to be analytic. This does not imply, of course, that we cannot therefore see how things really are; for sometimes, indeed typically, things appear how they really are.

56. Such a critical paring down of features that are "immediately" perceptible has often issued in the view that it is only "meaningless sensations" of which we can be aware without a further sensory fundament. If such a view is indeed true, it requires for its demonstration considerable argument over and above the simple recognition of the present distinction. The present suggestion also does not imply that if a subject's cognitive capacities were limited to detecting only sensible qualities, such a subject would be in a position to perceive perceptible features of objects that are perceived in virtue of perceiving those sensible qualities. *We* can see that someone is looking sad; but perhaps someone incapable of feeling either sadness or sympathy would be unable knowledgeably to identify human faces that look sad. Nor is it implied that we ourselves could give a reductive specification of what it is for someone to look sad in terms of sensible qualities.

57. It is certainly part of the Argument as I have presented it that the yellowness of such a sense-datum is the very quality that a normal physical object can *look* to have. But when something normal looks yellow to me, it looks to be the way I take genuinely yellow physical objects actually to *be*. (This is an instance of Chisholm's "comparative" use of the language of appearing mentioned earlier.)

58. See, for example, Christopher Peacocke, *Sense and Content* (Oxford: Clarendon Press, 1983), ch. 1, though he takes such predicates to refer to properties of sensations or experiences, rather than sense-data—an important distinction that I shall discuss later in this chapter.

59. Sellars, *Science, Perception, and Reality*, p. 48. I should say that Sellars, like Peacocke, takes these "primed" qualities to be qualities of sensations (or sense-impressions), rather than of sense-data.

60. If such inversion is accepted as a possibility, the "priming" operation on sensible qualities will have to be relativized to a perceiver, or to classes of such.

61. Or, if one prefers to speak of a "thing," rather than a quality, as the object of awareness, the question is how we can avoid representing the bearers of such qualities as immediate objects of awareness.

62. G. E. Moore, *Some Main Problems of Philosophy* (London: George Allen & Unwin, 1953), p. 4.

63. G. E. Moore, *Philosophical Studies* (London: Routledge & Kegan Paul, 1922), p. 169.

64. Bertrand Russell, *Theory of Knowledge: The 1913 Manuscript*, in *The Collected Papers of Bertrand Russell*, vol. 7 (London: George Allen & Unwin, 1984), p. 5.

65. The term had, in fact, been around since the closing decades of the nineteenth century; but it became a standard piece of philosophical terminology as a result of the writings of Moore and Russell.

66. Moore, *Some Main Problems of Philosophy*, p. 3. Compare Bertrand Russell, *The Problems of Philosophy* (London: Thornton Butterworth, 1912), p. 17.

67. We see, then, how close the sense-datum theory and Naive Realism are: they can share one and the same analysis of perceptual awareness itself, differing only over the status of the objects of such awareness.

68. Moore, *Philosophical Studies*, p. 17.

69. What follows is loosely based upon C. J. Ducasse, "Moore's 'The Refutation of Idealism,'" in *The Philosophy of G. E. Moore*, ed. Paul Arthur Schilpp (Evanston, Ill.: Northwestern University Press, 1942), pp. 225–251.

70. This analogy is made in Jonathan Bennett, *Locke, Berkeley, Hume* (Oxford: Clarendon Press, 1971), §5.

71. Broad, *Scientific Thought*, p. 256.

72. Hence the incredulity with which Hume's similar claim—that it is a priori possible that pains should exist "unperceived"—is usually greeted: see David Hume, *A Treatise of Human Nature*, ed. L. A. Selby-Bigge and P. H. Nidditch, 2d ed. (Oxford: Clarendon Press, 1978), p. 207.

73. For a summary of Broad's later views, see his "A Reply to My Critics," in *The Philosophy of C. D. Broad*, ed. P. A. Schilpp (New York: Tudor, 1959), esp. pp. 797–801. This is a reply to H. H. Price's "The Nature and Status of Sense-Data in Broad's Epistemology," found on pp. 457–485 of the same work, which contains a careful discussion of this aspect of Broad's account of perception, together with an unpersuasive attempt to defend the act-object analysis across the board.

74. Ducasse, "Moore's 'The Refutation of Idealism,'" pp. 232–233.

75. Panayot Butchvarov, "Adverbial Theories of Consciousness," *Midwest Studies in Philosophy* 5 (1980): 261–280.

76. Jackson, *Perception*, ch. 3.

77. See, respectively, Michael Tye, *The Metaphysics of Mind* (Cambridge: Cambridge University Press, 1989), and Wilfrid Sellars, "The Adverbial Theory of the Objects of Perception," *Metaphilosophy* 6 (1975): 144–160.

78. Such, for instance, is a major concern of Tye's.

79. The only traditional example I am aware of is from the Cyrenaics, who although, as I have mentioned, commonly speak of a subject to whom something white or yellow appears as being "whitened [*leukainometha*]" or "yellowed [*ōchrainontai*]," sometimes seem to have employed adverbial expressions—such as

"whitely [*leukantikōs*]" and "yellowly [*ōchrantikōs*]." Such adverbs occur, for example, in Sextus Empiricus's discussion of the Cyrenaics in *Adversus Mathematicos*, VII.198 (though the English translation in the edition cited earlier does not bring out this fact). For a good recent discussion of these issues, see Voula Tsouna McKirahan, "The Cyrenaic Theory of Knowledge," *Oxford Studies in Ancient Philosophy* 10 (1992): 161–192.

80. Bertrand Russell, *Logic and Knowledge*, ed. R. C. Marsh (London: George Allen & Unwin, 1956), pp. 305–306.

81. Price, "Review of A. J. Ayer, *The Foundations of Empirical Knowledge*," p. 284.

82. See, for example, Ayer, *The Problem of Knowledge*, pp. 61–62 and *Language Truth and Logic* (Harmondsworth: Penguin Books, 1971), pp. 161–162.

83. Bertrand Russell, *Our Knowledge of the External World*, rev. ed. (London: George Allen & Unwin, 1926), p. 83.

84. Many, these days, discuss the primary / secondary quality distinction in terms other than these. It is, however, only this traditional way of conceiving the issue that I am concerned with here. I have discussed this traditional issue, in more historical terms, in "Of Primary and Secondary Qualities," *The Philosophical Review* 99 (1990): 221–254.

85. Plutarch, *Adversus Colotem*, 1110F.

2. Three Theories of Perception

1. David Hume, *A Treatise of Human Nature*, ed. L. A. Selby-Bigge and P. H. Nidditch, 2d ed. (Oxford: Clarendon Press, 1978), p. 190.

2. Some public phenomena are de facto restricted to a single sense: sounds, for example. Even here, however, it is presumably at least in principle possible that such objective items should be registered by sense-organs quite different from eardrums: organs that would give rise to sensory experiences that are not at all subjectively auditory in character. Indeed, we do not even have to hypothesize new senses to make the point: it is presumably possible that an existing sense should come to be affected by objects formerly peculiar to another sense. It is not a simple contradiction to speak of seeing sound—as, indeed, some advocates of synaesthesia actually do. Should the reader have doubts about these contentions, the following weaker claim can be substituted for the one in the text: that being an object of a mode of perceptual consciousness *as such* does not rule out the possibility of that object being perceived (and directly perceived) in a different perceptual modality.

3. Dugald Stewart, *Elements of the Philosophy of the Human Mind*, 3 vols., in *Stewart's Works*, ed. Sir William Hamilton, vols. 2–4 (Edinburgh: Constable, 1854), vol. 2, p. 14.

4. Thomas Brown, *Lectures on the Philosophy of the Human Mind* (Edinburgh: William Tait, 1828), p. 126.

5. *Works of Thomas Hill Green*, ed. R. L. Nettleship, 3 vols. (London: Longmans, Green, and Co., 1885), vol. 1, p. 57.

6. Arthur Schopenauer, *Über die vierfache Wurzel des Satzes vom zureichenden Grunden*, in *Sämtliche Werke*, vol. 1 (Wiesbaden: Brockhaus, 1966), p. 52 [*The Fourfold Root of the Principle of Sufficient Reason*, tr. E. F. J. Payne (La Salle, Ill.: Open Court, 1974), p. 76].

7. Arthur Schopenhauer, *Die Welt als Wille und Vorstellung*, 2 vols., in *Sämtliche Werke*, vols. 2 and 3 (Wiesbaden: Brockhaus, 1966), vol. 1, pp. 13–14 [*The World as Will and Representation*, tr. E. F. J. Payne, 2 vols. (New York: Dover, 1969), vol. 1, pp. 11–12].

8. Indeed, Frauenstädt, the editor of Schopenhauer's works, accused Helmholtz of plagiarism on this point. See Nicholas Pastore, "Helmholtz on the Projection or Transfer of Sensation," in *Studies in Perception*, ed. Peter K. Machamer and Robert G. Turnbull (Columbus: Ohio State University Press, 1978), p. 373, n. 27. This entire paper is an excellent discussion of Helmholtz's perceptual theory—as is the chapter on Helmholtz in Pastore's *Selective History of Theories of Visual Perception: 1650–1950* (Oxford: Oxford University Press, 1971).

9. Hermann von Helmholtz, *Handbuch der physiologischen Optik*, 3d ed., 3 vols., ed. A. Gullstrand, J. von Kries, and W. Nagel (Hamburg: Voss, 1910), vol. 3, p. 29 [*Treatise of Physiological Optics*, 3 vols., ed. J. P. S. Southall (New York: Optical Society of America, 1924), vol. 3, p. 32]. For both Helmholtz and Schopenhauer such an appreciation of causality is innate, a "law of our thinking which precedes all experience," as Helmholtz put it; one "that must be furnished from the understanding itself, since it could never have come to it from outside," as Schopenhauer says: ibid., and Schopenhauer, *Über die vierfache Wurzel*, p. 79 [*The Fourfold Root*, p. 114], respectively.

10. Schopenhauer, *Über die vierfache Wurzel*, p. 53 [*The Fourfold Root*, p. 77]; and *Die Welt als Wille und Vorstellung*, vol. 1, p. 13 [*The World as Will and Representation*, vol. 1, p. 11]. Emphasis in original.

11. Helmholtz, "Über das Sehen des Menschen," *Vorträge und Reden*, 2 vols. (Braunschweig: Viewig, 1903), vol. 1, p. 115.

12. Bertrand Russell, *The Problems of Philosophy* (London: Thornton Butterworth, 1912), pp. 23–24.

13. Any such suggestion is not only blatantly false, but also has difficulty making sense of the fact that a significant number of thinkers have utterly rejected *any* causal account of perception—not to mention the many ancient writers, from Euclid to al-Kindī, who espoused an "extromission" theory of vision, according to which the causal processes involved in perception proceed *outwards* towards the object. According to the present suggestion, all such people must simply have been ignoring a manifest aspect of their everyday experience—manifest because the very intentionality of perception supposedly depends on its appreciation. (An informative account of extromission theories can be found in David C. Lindberg, "The Intromission-Extromission Controversy in Islamic Visual Theory: Al-Kindī versus Avicenna," in *Studies in Perception*, pp. 137–159, and *Theories of Vision from Al-Kindī to Kepler* [Chicago: University of Chicago Press, 1976], ch. 1.)

14. In contrast with Naive Realism and New Realism—both of which, as we have seen, essentially embody an act-object analysis of perceptual consciousness—the present account of perception also often emerges under the title "Critical Realism."

15. It also seems to have achieved this status in the post-war period in Britain, being the chief reaction against the previously prevailing sense-datum theory. Although not worked out in any great detail, Quinton's account of perception, discussed in Chapter 1, seems to be a form of it, as does that developed in the extensive writings on perception by D. W. Hamlyn.

16. Immanuel Kant, *Prolegomena zu einer jeden künftigen Metaphysik, die als Wissenschaft wird auftreten können*, in *Kant's gesammelte Schriften*, vol. 4 (Berlin: Reimer, 1911), pp. 253–383 [*Prolegomena to Any Future Metaphysics That Will Be Able to Present Itself as a Science*, tr. Peter G. Lucas (Manchester: Manchester University Press, 1962)], §§18–19.

17. Reid is sometimes claimed as the first propounder of the dual component theory, and, indeed, as the first to make an explicit distinction between perception and sensation. This is certainly not true. A separation of sensation from cognition, and the claim that both are to be found in perception, is central, for example, to the philosophy of Malebranche (surely one of the most grossly ignored of the great philosophers in history)—though with him the analysis of perception is tied up with the striking doctrine that we see all things in God. A similar approach to perception can be found even earlier in the writings of Kenelme Digby, who in turn had a strong influence on John Sergeant. I do not know whether these two English philosophers had a direct influence on Reid, but several of Reid's most characteristic theses can be found in these earlier writers. This early development of the theory in the modern period will receive further consideration in Chapter 4.

18. Thomas Reid, *Essays on the Intellectual Powers of Man*, ed. B. Brody (Cambridge, Mass.: MIT Press, 1969), II.5, pp. 111–112.

19. Ibid., VI.2, p. 557.

20. Ibid., II.17, p. 265.

21. I speak of a "quasi-causal" operation because Reid, being a firm Cartesian on metaphysical issues, found it absurd that matter should be "the proper efficient cause" of either perception or sensation. For perception see Reid, *Essays*, II.4, p. 100, and for sensation, II.20, p. 288. He does, however, commonly speak of physical impressions on the body "occasioning" sensations (and, indeed, on rare occasions, as causing them).

22. John Immerwahr has argued that although this is true of Reid's theory as presented in his early *Inquiry*, he develops a different position in the maturer *Essays*. In the later work, he claims, physical impressions *jointly cause* a perception and a sensation: the former is not itself in any way based upon the latter. (See "The Development of Reid's Realism," *Monist* 61 [1978]: 245–256.) I am unconvinced. What I propose is to consider the more usual interpretation here, and to consider the view attributed to Reid by Immerwahr on its own merits later.

23. On the first dependence, he writes that "our perceptions and sensations correspond to . . . impressions, and vary in kind, and in degree, as they vary. Without this exact correspondence, the information we receive by our senses . . . would be fallacious"; and on the second, he says that "sensations . . . serve as signs to distinguish things that differ; and the information we have concerning things external comes by their means": Reid, *Essays*, II.2, p. 83 and II.16, p. 247, respectively.

24. Ibid., II.20, p. 289.

25. Sensation and perception are "commonly conjoined by nature," but they "ought to be carefully distinguished by philosophers": Reid, *Essays*, IV.3, p. 426.

26. George Pappas has argued vigorously that Reid did not hold that sensations accompany perception, but that they are ingredient in it: George S. Pappas, "Sensation and Perception in Reid," *Noûs* 23 (1989): 155–167. Reid can certainly talk in such a manner—e.g., *Essays*, II.16, p. 246; but then he is generally very

sloppy over such niceties. I think Reid would have regarded the issue raised by Pappas as trifling.

27. Reid, *Essays*, II.16, p. 249.

28. Ibid., II.16, p. 251.

29. Ibid., II.16, p. 243 and I.1, p. 13.

30. Ibid., II.20, p. 289; IV.1, p. 405.

31. Ibid., II.16, p. 251.

32. Sellars, "The Structure of Knowledge," in *Action, Knowledge and Reality: Critical Studies in Honour of Wilfrid Sellars*, ed. H.-N. Castañeda (Indianapolis: Bobbs-Merrill, 1975), p. 303, and *Science, Perception and Reality* (London: Routledge & Kegan Paul, 1963), p. 162.

33. Sellars, "The Structure of Knowledge," p. 339. Although Sellars is less emphatic than Reid that perceiving involves belief, and although, on occasion, he contrasts perceptual taking with belief (e.g., "Carus Lectures," *Monist* 64 [1981]: 89, n. 11), he can also talk of such takings as "occurrent beliefs," differing from ordinary beliefs only in that they lack *explicit* subject-predicate form—so that they are a matter of *believing in* rather than *believing that* (e.g., "Sensa or Sensings: Reflections on the Ontology of Perception," *Philosophical Studies* 41 [1982]: 84–87). On page 101 of this work he characterizes perceptual taking as "doxastic."

34. Sellars, "The Structure of Knowledge," p. 308.

35. Sellars, "Berkeley and Descartes: Reflection on the Theory of Ideas," in *Studies in Perception*, p. 288.

36. Sellars, "The Structure of Knowledge," p. 310. This is not the only ground for Sellars's insistence on the presence of sensation in perception. Indeed, in his earlier writings the primary, if not sole, reason for their introduction was to account for the contents of mistaken perceptual *judgements*. He came, however, increasingly to stress the phenomenological requirement of sensation, as the present quotation demonstrates. Compare, also, "Sensa or Sensings," p. 89.

37. This, at least, is *one* thing that he means by this denial. Another will emerge shortly. The distinction between the terms "sensations," "sensings," and "sense impressions" is important in the context of Sellars's overall metaphysics and philosophy of mind. See especially, "Science, Sense Impressions, and Sensa: A Reply to Cornman," *Review of Metaphysics* 24 (1970–1971): 391–447 for the significance of such distinctions for Sellars's wider philosophical concerns. I shall, however, ignore this issue here.

38. Sellars, *Science and Metaphysics* (London: Routledge & Kegan Paul, 1968), p. 10.

39. Sellars, "Sensa or Sensings," p. 109.

40. Sellars, "The Structure of Knowledge," p. 311.

41. For more recent advocates of an essential role for belief in perception who also see the need for a more nuanced account, see, for example, George Pitcher, *A Theory of Perception* (Princeton, N.J.: Princeton University Press, 1971), and D. M. Armstrong, *Perception and the Physical World* (London: Routledge & Kegan Paul, 1961) and *A Materialist Theory of Mind* (London: Routledge & Kegan Paul, 1968).

42. The first such publication was Fred Dretske, *Seeing and Knowing* (London: Routledge & Kegan Paul, 1969).

43. I have discussed this matter in detail elsewhere: see A. D. Smith, "Perception and Belief," *Philosophy and Phenomenological Research* 62 (2001): 283–309.

44. The following argument is similar to one to be found in Romane Clark, "The Sensuous Content of Perception," in Castañeda, *Action, Knowledge and Reality*, p. 112. Clark, however, does not pay sufficient attention to the fact that the dual component theory makes reference to a causal connection between object and perceptual state.

45. If we imagine a world in which mothers' presence standardly causes a certain sort of headache in their offspring, we can even stipulate that my mother has caused my headache in virtue of a "non-deviant causal chain." I still do not perceive her—at least not directly.

46. Sellars, *Science and Metaphysics*, p. 16.

47. Thomas Reid, *An Inquiry into the Human Mind, On the Principles of Common Sense*, repr. 4th ed. (Bristol: Thoemmes, 1990), p. 114.

48. Reid, *Essays*, II.20, p. 294.

49. Ibid., p. 297.

50. Michael Ayers, *Locke*, 2 vols. (London: Routledge, 1991), vol. 1, p. 184.

51. Ibid., esp. chs. 15, 20–22.

52. Sir William Hamilton's editor's notes to *The Works of Thomas Reid, D. D.*, 2 vols. (Edinburgh: Maclachlan & Stewart, 1872). For a critic of Sellars, see, e.g., Romane Clark, "Sensibility and Understanding: The Given of Wilfrid Sellars," *Monist* 66 (1983): 353.

53. Russell, *The Problems of Philosophy*, pp. 30 and 42, respectively.

54. A point forcefully made by Samuel Bailey, whose own account of perception in some ways resembles that of Reid. See Samuel Bailey, *Letters on the Philosophy of the Human Mind*, 2d ser. (London: Longman, Brown, Green, Longmans, & Roberts, 1858), p. 35.

55. For example, Pappas, "Sensation and Perception in Reid," p. 160, and Timothy J. Duggan, "Critical Study: *The Scottish Philosophy of Common Sense* by S. A. Grave," *Philosophical Quarterly* 12 (1962): 89. (As I have pointed out, "causal" is not exactly the right word in connection with Reid.)

56. "Consciousness," claimed Helmholtz, "can arrive at a cognition of [bodies] only through an inference. For, in general, only through inferences can we cognize what we are not directly perceiving": "Über das Sehen des Menschen," p. 112.

57. The claim that Hume was an Indirect Realist is hardly uncontroversial, since he has often been read as not being a Realist at all. Suffice it here to say that I am wholly convinced by John Wright's ground-breaking exposition of this topic: *The Sceptical Realism of David Hume* (Manchester: Manchester University Press, 1983). It is certainly difficult for any alternative interpretation to make sense of a passage such as the following: "Properly speaking, 'tis not our body we perceive, when we regard our limbs and members, but certain impressions, which enter by our senses": Hume, *Treatise*, p. 191.

58. H. A. Prichard, *Knowledge and Perception* (Oxford: Clarendon Press, 1950), p. 68.

59. Sellars, *Science, Perception and Reality*, pp. 90–91. This is the second sense of "epistemic" mentioned above.

60. Sellars, "Carus Lectures," p. 89, n. 11.

61. Sellars, *Philosophical Perspectives* (Springfield, Ill.: Thomas, 1967), p. 205.

62. Towards the end of his career Wilfrid Sellars came increasingly to recognize the importance of the question concerning what we perceive "of" objects.

When we see a pink ice cube, "we see not only *that* the ice cube is pink, and see it *as* pink, we see *the very pinkness* of the object": "Sensa or Sensings," pp. 88–89. Somehow, indeed, this fact has to be accounted for. Reflecting on this mark of adequacy leads Sellars to go so far as to say that "visual perception itself is not just a conceptualizing of colored objects within visual range—a 'thinking about' colored objects in a certain context—but, in a sense most difficult to analyse, a *thinking in color* about colored objects": "The Structure of Knowledge," p. 305 (emphasis mine). And again: "That the relation between the sensing and the taking is at least in part that of the former (given a certain perceptual set) being the immediate cause of the latter, is, I believe, clear. Might not the relation be even more intimate?": "Some Reflections on Perceptual Consciousness," in *Crosscurrents in Phenomenology*, ed. Ronald Bruzina and Bruce Wilshire (The Hague: Martinus Nijhoff, 1978), p. 182. It had better be; but this is just what a dual component analysis of perception cannot allow. Visual perception, on such a view, is not in any sense a thinking *in* colour, but a thinking *accompanied and caused by* colour (or colour'). Any attempt within the context of a dual component account to establish a greater degree of intimacy between perceptual judgement and sensation will end up construing such sensation as itself an object of awareness. For since the sensuousness of the "very pinkness" of the ice cube that I see enters the dual component theory as a character of sensation lying outside the perceptual judgement, how can we avoid being forced to acknowledge that in the judgements that direct us to "this very pinkness," we are mentally directed to a sensation? "Is it so easy," Sellars himself asks at one point, perhaps as implicit criticism, or at least qualification, of his own earlier account of these matters, "to downplay the awareness of objectless sensings?": "Sensa or Sensings," p. 98. ("Objectless sensings" is Sellars way of expressing his allegiance to an "adverbial" account of sensation.)

63. Reid may have been influenced in this matter by a work on optics by William Porterfield, where, for example, we find the following passage: "Tho' all our sensations are passions or perceptions produced in the mind itself, yet the mind never considers them as such, but, by an irresistible law of nature, it is always made to refer them to something external": William Porterfield, *A Treatise on the Eye*, 2 vols. (Edinburgh, 1759), vol. 1, p. 364.

64. Reid, *Essays*, II.16, p. 247.

65. Ibid., II.18, p. 268. Such a claim has been made by many writers throughout the two succeeding centuries. In the last chapter we saw Quinton making effectively the same point when he denied that the "language of appearing" is used to describe our "sense-experience." And Helmholtz made similar claims: see, for example, *Handbuch der physiologischen Optik*, vol. 3, p. 7 [*Treatise of Physiological Optics*, vol. 3, p. 6]. Note, however, that despite this, Helmholtz was an Indirect Realist!

66. Hume, *Treatise*, p. 193.

67. Many such are detailed in C. W. K. Mundle, *Perception: Facts and Theories* (Oxford: Oxford University Press, 1971).

68. Helmholtz, *Handbuch der physiologischen Optik*, vol. 3, p. 13 [*Treatise of Physiological Optics*, vol. 3, p. 13]. Brian O'Shaughnessy, as we shall see later, has developed a dual component theory of the non-perceptual relation in which we stand to our own bodies. As he himself points out, such a theory has, by contrast, no plausibility at all in relation to perception, because of the way in which sensation functions to *direct attention*: see *The Will*, 2 vols. (Cambridge: Cambridge University

Press, 1980), vol. 1, chs. 6–7. (O'Shaughnessy's own response to this is to adopt a representationalist theory of perception.)

69. Reid, *Essays*, II.21, p. 300.

70. Ibid., II.17, p. 257. Reid indeed claimed that "in seeing a coloured body, the sensation is indifferent, and draws no attention," and thus classifies colour together with the primary qualities: Ibid., II.18, pp. 268–269. I shall, however, ignore this—not only because it contradicts his standard treatment of secondary qualities, of which of course he took colour to be one, but also because the suggestion that we overlook sensuous colour is as absurd as was the parallel suggestion in relation to hearing.

71. Ibid., II.17, p. 254.

72. Ibid., p. 256.

73. Actually, not entirely across the board: such "infection" does not extend to what, in Chapter 5, I shall term the *"Anstoss."* It does, however, extend sufficiently far to wreak havoc with Reid's account.

74. Not only does Reid fail to see a problem here, but also some of his remarks suggest that he assumed that merely descriptive, quantified propositions could serve as the contents of perceptual judgements. Thus he speaks of auditory, gustatory, and olfactory sensations as giving rise to "a conviction that these sensations are occasioned by *some* external object," and of the sensations produced by an ivory ball held in the hand being "followed by the conception and belief that *there is* in my hand *a* hard smooth body of a spherical figure": *Essays*, II.21, p. 302 (emphasis mine). Reid does, it is true, make an object's *qualities*, rather than the physical object itself, the immediate object of perception (*Essays*, II.17, p. 252), and he recognizes the existence of *particular* or *individual qualities*: "The whiteness of this sheet is one thing, whiteness is another . . . : the first signifies an individual quality really existing, and is not a general conception." He also says that "an universal is not an object of any external sense": *Essays*, V.3, p. 482 and V.6, p. 517, respectively. What I am suggesting, however, is that Reid cannot ultimately make any sense of our *cognition* of such individuals.

75. Sellars, *Science and Metaphysics*, p. 7.

76. Nor, of course, is it sufficient—even if we add that the belief is true. An after-image can lead me to judge that there is a shadow on the facing wall; even if there is a perfectly matching shadow there, I do not see it, since the after-image gets in the way.

77. Sellars, "Berkeley and Descartes," p. 284, including n. 27.

78. Ibid.

79. Gareth Evans, *Collected Papers* (Oxford: Clarendon Press, 1985), pp. 4–13. The view in question was until recently widespread. George Pitcher, for example, writes that "if a person should causally-receive *nothing but* false beliefs about something, or even, I should think, *too many* false beliefs about it, then he could not be said to perceive it": *A Theory of Perception*, pp. 77–78. That this is simply false might have been indicated to Pitcher by his very words: if the false beliefs are "about *it*," the subject must be perceiving *it*.

80. Sellars's account of perceptual reference would seem to have its precise analogue in John Searle's suggestion that *at least one* of the descriptions in the dossier that backs up a name must be true of the referent of that name: "Proper Names," *Mind* 67 (1958): 166–173.

81. A term is descriptive if it expresses some descriptive condition (i.e., represents a certain *kind* of thing) and it *denotes*, or is about, any object that meets that condition (i.e., that actually is that kind of object). Since we are interested in reference to, or awareness of, individual objects, there needs to be *one and only one* object fitting the descriptive specification.

82. The importance of this kind of situation was stressed in H. P. Grice, "The Causal Theory of Perception," *Proceedings of the Aristotelian Society* 35 (1961): 121–168.

83. William G. Lycan, "Thoughts about Things," in *The Representation of Knowledge and Belief*, ed. Myles Brand and Robert M. Harnish (Tucson: University of Arizona Press, 1986), p. 161.

84. The issues, here, crystallize in his term "this-suches." What I am in effect suggesting is that this notion, precisely as it is construed by Sellars, is incoherent: the demonstrative "this" conflicts with the denotational "such."

85. Among concrete entities, we perhaps could also be so acquainted with the self. Acquaintance is, in short, restricted to items about the existence of which we have Cartesian certainty. (Russell also attributed to us acquaintance with universals.)

86. See Ernest Sosa, "Propositional Attitudes *De Dicto* and *De Re*," *Journal of Philosophy* 67 (1970): 838–896, for some of the problems involved in trying to delimit the scope of *de re* attitudes; and Gareth Evans, *The Varieties of Reference* (Oxford: Clarendon Press, 1982) for a discussion of "testimony demonstratives."

87. P. T. Geach, *Mental Acts* (London: Routledge & Kegan Paul, 1957), p. 64.

88. Tyler Burge, "Belief *De Re*," *Journal of Philosophy* 74 (1977): 346. The quotations immediately following are all from this article.

89. It would be excessively generous to construe "mental" as restricted to truly conceptual items functioning descriptively, since in the very next sentence Burge characterizes sense-data as "mental."

90. I have in mind not only Tyler Burge's well-known papers arguing against "individualism," starting with "Individualism and the Mental," *Midwest Studies in Philosophy* 4 (1979): 73–122, but also his "Russell's Problem and Intentional Identity," in *Agent, Language, and the Structure of the World*, ed. James E. Tomberlin (Indianapolis: Hackett, 1983), pp. 79–110.

91. Kent Bach, "*De re* Belief and Methodological Solipsism," in *Thought and Object*, ed. Andrew Woodfield (Oxford: Clarendon Press, 1982), p. 136. The quotations immediately following are all from this article.

92. Bach stresses that he wants to remain non-committal on the "ontological structure of perception," and he does not restrict the characterization of percepts to purely sensible qualities. The crucial point, however, is that percepts are specified purely phenomenologically and do not, of themselves, have objects. Thus he uses the schema "$A_{mf_x}s$" to represent percepts—to be read: s is appeared to f-ly, in a way that physical object x can appear, in sense-modality m—and stresses that "the content of a perceptual state, the percept, is given by providing values for 'm' and 'f' (but *not* for 'x')."

93. Hence, Bach's analysis of s's perceptual judgement, in sense-modality m, that a certain object that appears f to him is G is "$(\exists \, ! \, x)(Cx(\overline{A_m f_x s}) \, \& \, G_x)$." Here "C" stands for the kind of causal relation that holds between a perceptual experience and the physical object that it is of. So the analysis runs: there is a unique x

such that x causes s to be appeared to f-ly in sense-modality m, and x is G. As Bach makes clear, only the portions of this formula under the bars "represent the perceptual and the conceptual contents of s's perceptual belief," and those parts, as such, are clearly open, being bound from outside. Outside of consciousness, we might say.

94. As mentioned briefly in the Introduction, the situation here is closely related to what is involved in understanding demonstrative utterances. Suppose you say, "I bought this in France," where "this" is entirely non-anaphoric. As is now generally recognized, I do not fully grasp what you say unless I *perceive* what it is that you are referring to by uttering "this." Perceiving the object puts me in a position to gain an understanding, to come by a *de re* thought, that would otherwise not be available to me.

95. The idea is especially popular among "cognitive scientists." Steven Pinker, for example, writes that "in no computational theory of a mental process does subjective experience *per se* play a causal role; only representations and processes do, and the subjective experience, if it is considered at all, is assumed to be a correlate of the processing": see his "Visual Cognition: An Introduction," in *Visual Cognition*, ed. Steven Pinker (Cambridge, Mass.: MIT Press, 1985), p. 34. For strenuous dissent from within the cognitive science camp itself, however, see Anthony J. Marcel, "Phenomenal Experience and Functionalism," in *Consciousness in Contemporary Science*, ed. A. J. Marcel and E. Bisiach (Oxford: Oxford University Press, 1992), pp. 121–158.

96. Michael Ayers's insistence that our perceptual knowledge is *transparent* is again of relevance here.

97. Edward Craig, "Sensory Experience and the Foundations of Knowledge," *Synthèse* 33 (1976): 8.

98. The primary text by Everett Hall is *Our Knowledge of Fact and Value* (Chapel Hill: University of North Carolina Press, 1961).

99. Romane Clark, "Sensing, Perceiving, Thinking," *Grazer Philosophische Studien* 7/8 (1979): 287.

3. Perception and Conception

1. In the 1930s, Dunker found that a leaf-shaped object was perceived as more green than an identically coloured donkey-shaped object: Karl Dunker, "The Influence of Past Experience upon Perceptual Properties," *American Journal of Psychology* 52 (1939): 255–265. Related findings have been made since; see Jerome S. Bruner and Leo J. Postman, "On the Perception of Incongruity: A Paradigm," *Journal of Personality* 18 (1949), repr. in Jerome S. Bruner, *Beyond the Information Given*, ed. Jeremy M. Anglin (New York: Norton, 1973), pp. 68–83, and John L. Delk and Samuel Fillenbaum, "Differences in Perceived Color as a Function of Characteristic Color," *American Journal of Psychology* 78 (1965): 290–293. Again, "Gestalt pictures" do not commonly switch spontaneously between the two available "percepts"; such a change in perceptual re-organization typically requires both familiarity with the depicted objects and prompting: see, for example, Irwin Rock, *The Logic of Perception* (Cambridge, Mass.: MIT Press, 1983), pp. 77–80. As for other sense modalities, it has been found that subjects think they can detect both a stronger taste and a stronger smell in fruit juices when the only difference between

them and a comparison liquid is one of colour: see Debra A. Zellner and Mary A. Kautz, "Color Affects Perceived Odor Intensity," *Journal of Experimental Psychology: Human Perception and Performance* 16 (1990): 391–397 (which although explicitly about smell, contains references to the parallel literature on taste). And if subjects are shown a film close-up of a person repeatedly pronouncing the syllable [ga] while listening to a synchronized tape of that person pronouncing the syllable [ba], they report hearing [da]: see Harry McGurk and John MacDonald, "Hearing Lips and Seeing Voices," *Nature* 264 (1976): 747–748. Judgements of noise level are also affected by whether sentences that subjects are trying to hear through the noise are familiar to them or not: see Larry L. Jacoby, Lorraine G. Allan, Jane C. Collins, and Linda K. Larwill, "Memory Influences Subjective Experience: Noise Judgments," *Journal of Experimental Psychology: Learning, Memory, and Cognition* 14 (1988): 240–247.

2. For good discussions of this important distinction, see Ralph Norman Haber, "Nature of the Effect of Set on Perception," *Psychological Review* 73 (1966): 335–351, and Lester E. Krueger, "Familiarity Effects in Visual Information Processing," *Psychological Bulletin* 82 (1975): 949–974.

3. For a level-headed assessment of such effects, see Rock, *Logic of Perception*, ch. 11.

4. These were the years when an extreme conceptual relativism was rife. Perhaps the most egregious form of this approach was the idea that the perception of colour is determined, via our language, by the colour "concepts" we possess.

5. Norwood Russell Hanson, *Patterns of Discovery* (Cambridge: Cambridge University Press, 1958), p. 7.

6. To my ear at least, "saw *a* telescope" sometimes invites the intensional reading, whereas "saw *the* telescope" does not at all. If this is right, then insisting on the intensional reading *even for the former* would bizarrely block the inference from "*X* saw the telescope" to "*X* saw a telescope." Such an insistence would also invalidate statements such as, "*The first time the native saw a typewriter,* he was puzzled." (Moreover, the italicized phrase would never naturally be employed to denote the first occasion on which our tribesman "conceptualized" a typewriter as a typewriter, if he had seen one before.)

7. Martin Heidegger, *Zur Bestimmung der Philosophie*, in *Gesamtausgabe*, vol. 56 no. 7 (Frankfurt am Main: Vittorio Klostermann, 1987), p. 72.

8. Fred Dretske and Jerry Fodor are two leading contemporary philosophers who have vigorously opposed conceptualism, as has David Marr at the "cognitive science" end of things. Dretske puts his finger on the central issue when he speaks of "a mistaken conflation of perception with conception" and of himself "trying to preserve the distinction between sentience and sapience": see his "Simple Seeing," in *Body, Mind and Method*, ed. D. F. Gustafson and B. L. Tapscott (Dordrecht: Reidel, 1979), p. 1. See also Jerry A. Fodor, "Observation Reconsidered," *Philosophy of Science* 51 (1984): 23–43, and David Marr, *Vision* (San Francisco: Freeman, 1982).

9. *Works of Thomas Hill Green*, ed. R. L. Nettleship (London: Longmans, Green, and Co., 1885), vol. 1, p. 414.

10. Wilfrid Sellars, *Science and Metaphysics* (London: Routledge & Kegan Paul, 1968), p. 12.

11. Wilfrid Sellars, *Philosophical Perspectives* (Springfield, Ill.: Thomas, 1967), p. 199.

12. Wilfrid Sellars, "Carus Lectures," *Monist* 64 (1981): 23 (by implication).

13. This is not to say, of course, that there have not been those who have affirmed that "ideas" do interpose themselves between the world and any mind that attempts to think about that world: a "veil of ideas," as it were, to parallel the "veil of perception." Reid held that the whole of the "New Way of Ideas" was committed to some such view. This now seems exegetically insensitive. But Augustus de Morgan states the view in as forthright a manner as one could wish: "The idea of a horse is *the horse in the mind:* and we know no other horse. We admit that there is an external *object,* a horse, which may give a *horse in the mind* to twenty different persons: but no one of these twenty knows the object; each one only knows his *idea*": Augustus de Morgan, *Formal Logic* (London: Taylor and Walton, 1847), pp. 29–30.

14. Thomas Reid, *Essays on the Intellectual Powers of Man,* ed. B. Brody (Cambridge, Mass.: MIT Press, 1969), VI.3, p. 573.

15. We have, in effect, already seen this argument run by Sellars. Other clear statements of this very common line of thought are to be found in, for example, Joseph Runzo, "The Propositional Structure of Perception," *American Philosophical Quarterly* 14 (1977): 211–220; and D. W. Hamlyn, "Perception, Sensation and Non-Conceptual Content," *Philosophical Quarterly* 44 (1994): 139–153. The current popularity of the slogan that "all seeing is seeing as" derives from G. N. A. Vesey, "Seeing and Seeing As," *Proceedings of the Aristotelian Society* 55 (1955–1956); reprinted in Robert J. Swartz, ed., *Perceiving, Sensing, and Knowing* (Berkeley: University of California Press, 1965), pp. 68–83. To his credit, Vesey does *not* make the easy inference from this to the concept-mediated nature of perception.

16. Wilfrid Sellars, *Science, Perception and Reality* (London: Routledge & Kegan Paul, 1963), p. 49.

17. Immanuel Kant, *Kritik der reinen Vernunft,* ed. Raymund Schmidt (Hamburg: Meiner, 1956) [*Immanuel Kant's Critique of Pure Reason,* tr. Norman Kemp Smith (London: Macmillan, 1933)], A104–105.

18. Ibid., A103.

19. Apart from "intuitions" there is no other kind of cognition except through concepts. Concepts rest on "functions," and a function is "the unity of the operation of ordering disparate representations under a common one": ibid., A68/B93.

20. Ibid., B143.

21. Ibid., A97.

22. Sextus Empiricus, *Adversus Mathematicos,* VII.294–300, tr. R. G. Bury in *Sextus Empiricus,* 4 vols. (London: Heinemann, and Cambridge, Mass.: Harvard University Press, 1967), vol. 2, pp. 154, 158. The final two chapters of Part I will respond to this challenge.

23. Arthur Schopenhauer, *Die Welt als Wille und Vorstellung,* 2 vols., in *Sämtliche Werke,* vols. 2 and 3 (Wiesbaden: Brockhaus, 1966), vol. 1, p. 44 [*The World as Will and Representation,* 2 vols., tr. E. F. J. Payne (New York: Dover, 1969), vol. 1, p. 37].

24. There is particularly strong evidence relating to the chimpanzee and to the African Grey parrot, both of whom show evidence of an ability to exercise the *same / different* concept—something that cannot be plausibly accounted for in terms of "stimulus generalization." Of significance here is that both species are able to manipulate *symbols.* For the chimp see David Premack, "Minds with and without language," in *Thought Without Language,* ed. L. Weiskrantz (Oxford: Clarendon Press, 1988), pp. 46–65; and for the parrot, see Irene M. Pepperberg, "Acquisition of the

Same / Different Concept by an African Grey Parrot *(Psittacus erithacus):* Learning with Respect to Categories of Color, Shape, and Material," *Animal Learning and Behavior* 15 (1987): 423–432.

25. Sellars, *Science, Perception, and Reality,* p. 148. See also Sellars, "The Structure of Knowledge," in *Action, Knowledge, and Reality: Critical Studies in Honour of Wilfrid Sellars,* ed. H.-N. Castañeda (Indianapolis: Bobbs-Merrill, 1975), p. 314.

26. Sellars, "The Structure of Knowledge," p. 297.

27. Sellars, *Science, Perception, and Reality,* p. 162, and "Language as Thought and Communication," *Philosophy and Phenomenological Research* 29 (1969): 513.

28. Sellars, "Language as Thought and Communication," p. 511. I ought to say that this sentence begins with the word "Roughly" in the original.

29. Sellars, *Science, Perception, and Reality,* p. 145.

30. Sellars, "The Structure of Knowledge," pp. 303–304.

31. Sellars, "Mental Events," *Philosophical Studies* 39 (1981): 326.

32. "I restrict this [namely, the claim that judgement is involved in perception] to persons come to the years of understanding, because it may be a question, whether infants, in the first periods of life, have any judgement or belief at all. The same question may be put with regard to brutes and some idiots": Reid, *Essays,* VI.6, p. 536; compare II.5, p. 117. For a discussion of this often overlooked aspect of Reid's theory, see J. H. Faurot, "Thomas Reid, On Intelligible Objects," *Monist* 61 (1978): 229–244.

33. There is a passage in Plutarch where he criticizes those who claim that animals perceive only "as it were." It might have been tailored for Sellars. See Plutarch's *Moralia,* 15 vols. (London: Heinemann, and Cambridge, Mass.: Harvard University Press, 1957), vol. 12, p. 334 (961E-F).

34. John McDowell, *Mind and World* (Cambridge, Mass.: Harvard University Press, 1994), p. 47, including n. 1.

35. Ibid., p. 66. McDowell actually presents an argument that is intended to show that his conceptualistic monism is unavoidable. The argument is to the effect that unless such an account is true, we cannot have a coherent epistemology, because the only alternative to it is to view experience, or "receptivity," as having no more status than a meaningless causal prodding of our epistemic lives from outside. This argument overlooks the possibility that perceptual experience may be *intentional* and yet not *conceptual.* That this is indeed the case is the burden of the rest of Part I.

36. Ibid., p. 63.

37. Ibid., pp. 119 and 122 (the latter by implication).

38. Ibid., p. 54.

39. To avoid confusion, it is perhaps worth pointing out that "environment" is McDowell's word for *"Umwelt,"* whereas the standard English translation of Gadamer's work for some reason uses both "world" and "environment" to translate *"Welt,"* and both "living world" and "habitat" to translate *"Umwelt":* see H.-G. Gadamer, *Wahrheit und Methode,* in *Gesammelte Werke,* vol. 1 (Tübingen: J. C. B. Mohr [Paul Siebeck], 1986), p. 447 [*Truth and Method,* 2d ed. (London: Sheed & Ward, 1979), p. 402].

40. The attribution to the mere animal of an *Umwelt* rather than a *Welt* in fact goes back to von Uexküll, but the particular slant given to this distinction by Heidegger is the immediate and determinative influence on Gadamer.

41. Martin Heidegger, *Prolegomena zur Geschichte des Zeitbegriffs,* in

Gesamtausgabe, vol. 20 (Frankfurt am Main: Vittorio Klostermann, 1979) [*History of the Concept of Time*, tr. Theodore Kisiel (Bloomington: Indiana University Press, 1985)], §28.

42. Heidegger prefers to use the term *"Umgebung"* or, more technically, *"Umring"*—an encircling ring (of captivation). See his *Die Grundbegriffe der Metaphysik*, in *Gesamtausgabe*, vols. 29, 30 (Frankfurt am Main: Vittorio Klostermann, 1983) [*The Fundamental Concepts of Metaphysics*, tr. William McNeill and Nicholas Walker (Bloomington: Indiana University Press, 1995)], pt. 2, esp. §61b.

43. Compare Heidegger's *Prolegomena zur Geschichte des Zeitbegriffs*, p. 352 [*History of the Concept of Time*, p. 255] with his *Die Grundbegriffe der Metaphysik*, pp. 274–275 and 374 [*The Fundamental Concepts of Metaphysics*, pp. 186 and 257].

44. Gadamer, *Wahrheit und Methode*, p. 446 [*Truth and Method*, p. 402].

45. Heidegger is candid about his failure to address any problems that may arise through the peculiar character of sensory consciousness. "To-day we no longer speak of experiences, conscious experiences and consciousness," he writes. Apparently, "our" forgoing such language goes together with a "transformation of existence": Heidegger, *Die Grundbegriffe der Metaphysik*, p. 298 [*The Fundamental Concepts of Metaphysics*, p. 203].

46. Ibid., p. 376 [p. 259].

47. Ibid., §§60–61.

48. Martin Heidegger, *Die Grundprobleme der Phenomenologie (1919/1920)*, in *Gesamtausgabe*, vol. 58 (Frankfurt am Main: Vittorio Klostermann, 1993), pp. 240–242 [*The Basic Problems of Phenomenology*, tr. Albert Hofstadter, rev. ed. (Bloomington: Indiana University Press, 1988)], pp. 168–170].

49. He says the same about "cosmos": Heidegger, *Metaphysische Anfangsgründe der Logik im Ausgang von Leibniz*, in *Gesamtausgabe*, vol. 26 (Frankfurt am Main: Vittorio Klostermann, 1978), p. 216 [*The Metaphysical Foundations of Logic*, tr. Michael Heim (Bloomington: Indiana University Press, 1984), p. 169].

50. Ibid., pp. 194–195 [p. 153] and Heidegger, *Sein und Zeit*, in *Gesamtausgabe*, vol. 2 (Frankfurt am Main: Vittorio Klostermann, 1977), p. 244 [*Being and Time*, tr. John Macquarrie and Edward Robinson (Oxford: Blackwell, 1973), p. 228].

51. Heidegger, *Zur Bestimmung der Philosophie*, p. 75.

52. On the animal, see Heidegger, *Die Grundbegriffe der Metaphysik* [*The Fundamental Concepts of Metaphysics*], §46 and esp. §69. Compare *Sein und Zeit* [*Being and Time*], §32 on *Dasein*.

53. Heidegger, *Die Grundbegriffe der Metaphysik*, pp. 364 and 291 [*The Fundamental Concepts of Metaphysics*, pp. 250 and 198].

54. Martin Heidegger, "Der Ursprung des Kunstwerkes," in *Holzwege*, *Gesamtausgabe*, vol. 5 (Frankfurt am Main: Vittorio Klostermann, 1977), pp. 10–11 ["The Origin of the Work of Art," tr. David Farrell Krell, in *Martin Heidegger: Basic Writings* (New York: Harper & Row, 1977), p. 156. I follow this translator in substituting "Volkswagen" for Heidegger's reference to the little-known *Adlerwagen*].

55. Note, however, that the qualification "probably" is required here: you need to be reasonably attentive, the lighting must be sufficient, the hammer should not be at too unusual an angle, and so on. Moreover, this "Heideggerian" point carries most conviction in relation to sight. If you are perceiving something by touch, you will typically have to *discover* that the thing is a hammer. Typically, touch *does* primarily reveal the basic material features of things.

56. "Concept" is not the right word in relation to Heidegger. His overall position is, however, in the present context, of a piece with conceptualism in its focus on more than merely animal achievements. (This is in no way to impugn the depth or seriousness of his quest for a mode of thinking that is more fundamental than the conceptual.)

57. Heidegger, *Sein und Zeit*, pp. 90 and 82 [*Being and Time*, pp. 95 and 88].

58. He suggests, indeed, that our primary response to a forest is as a source of timber, and to a mountain as a possible quarry. He then, amazingly, goes on to suggest that such a view, rather than the traditional one, will allow us to understand how we can be enthralled by a landscape. See ibid., pp. 94–95 [p. 100]. (Note that this perspective seems to be abandoned in Heidegger's later writings.)

59. Ibid., p. 108 [p. 112]. See also Heidegger, *Zur Bestimmung der Philosophie*, pp. 71–72.

60. It will not do to try and extricate Heidegger from this predicament by suggesting that the emphasis on instrumentality is but an illustration of something more general with which he is "really" concerned—such as things simply having some sort of significance in relation to a subject's active life. For this would allow Heidegger's account to apply to the animal, whereas being concerned with "gear" is the source of the "as"-structure and of understanding, which are explicitly denied the animal.

61. McDowell, *Mind and World*, p. 64.

62. Ibid.

63. Ibid., p. 122.

64. Ibid.

65. So the issue here is closely related to that of the reductivist accounts of sensory experience that were considered in Chapter 1. Although we there noted McDowell's objecting to Dennett's ludicrously impoverished account of sensory experience, it would seem that his objection only holds in relation to human beings. Where animals are concerned, the two of them would appear to be bizarrely allied. Compare, for example, McDowell's position with the following remark of Dennett's: "Nonhuman, nonverbal creatures have no print-out faculties, or at best very rudimentary and unexpressive print-out faculties, yet some philosophers—notably Nagel—insist that full-blown, phenomenological consciousness is as much their blessing as ours. I think one can be skeptical of this claim": Daniel Dennett, *Brainstorms* (Montgomery, Vt.: Bradford Books, 1978), p. 152.

66. Gareth Evans, *The Varieties of Reference* (Oxford: Clarendon Press, 1982), p. 158.

67. Kant, *Critique of Pure Reason*, A112.

68. Ibid., A108.

69. Ibid.

70. Should there be any doubt on this score, Kant explicitly denies this to animals. See, for example, *Anthropologie in pragmatischer Hinsicht*, in *Kant's gesammelte Schriften*, vol. 7 (Berlin: Reimer, 1917), pp. 117–333 [*Anthropology from a Pragmatic Point of View*, tr. Mary J. Gregor (The Hague: Martinus Nijhoff, 1974)], §1; and *Briefwechsel*, ed. Otto Schöndörfer and Rudolf Malter (Hamburg: Meiner, 1986), pp. 398–399 [*Kant's Philosophical Correspondence*, tr. Arnulf Zweig (Chicago: University of Chicago Press, 1963), pp. 153–154].

71. According to Fichte, Transcendental Idealism holds that "all consciousness rests on the consciousness of self, and is conditioned by this": *Zweite Einleitung in*

die Wissenschaftslehre, in *Fichtes Werke,* ed. I. H. Fichte, 11 vols. (Berlin: de Gruyter, 1971), vol. 1, pp. 457–458 [*The Science of Knowledge,* tr. Peter Heath and John Lachs (Cambridge: Cambridge University Press, 1982), p. 37]. Hence he can say that "in so far as you are conscious of some object or other—the wall opposite you, for example—you are . . . essentially aware of your thinking of this wall, and only in so far as you are conscious of this is a consciousness of the wall possible": *Versuch einer neuen Darstellung der Wissenschaftslehre,* in *Fichtes Werke,* vol. 1, p. 526. This idea crystallizes around Fichte's notion of *intellectual intuition,* without which, he claims, there cannot even be sensory intuition: *Zweite Einleitung,* p. 464 [*The Science of Knowledge,* p. 39].

72. *Works of Thomas Hill Green,* vol. 1, pp. 11–12.

73. William James, *The Principles of Psychology,* 2 vols. (New York: Dover, 1950), vol. 1, p. 274.

74. Incidentally, this simple fact suffices to wreck a widely accepted attempt to get round the "absent qualia" objection to functionalism. It is originally due to Sidney Shoemaker, who attempted to arrive at a functional differentiation between conscious and non-conscious perceptual states by claiming, in effect, that the former involve *self*-consciousness. See Sidney Shoemaker, "Functionalism and Qualia," in *Identity, Cause and Mind* (Cambridge: Cambridge University Press, 1984), pp. 184–205. In fact, however, it is not wholly mistaken to hold that perceptual consciousness involves some kind of "apperceptive" awareness. How this is so will be addressed later. But it requires the exercise of no concept whatever.

75. Another "low" account—associationism—was prominent in the nineteenth century. (For a clear associationistic analysis of perception, see James Sully, *Outlines of Psychology* [London: Longmans, Green & Co., 1884], pp. 152–153.) I think it should be fairly evident, however, that the idea that we can break out of the circle of our own perceptions *merely by a bundling together of such merely subjective, meaningless, non-intentional elements* is a non-starter. For trenchant criticism of associationism along these lines, see, for instance, James Ward, "Psychology," *Encyclopaedia Britannica,* 9th ed. (1886), p. 57, and G. F. Stout, *A Manual of Psychology,* 3d ed. (London: University Tutorial Press, 1921), pp. 431–432.

76. Brian Loar, "Phenomenal States," *Philosophical Perspectives* 4 (1990): 87.

77. Such "drift" is very small, of course, if the delay is sufficiently small, but that it occurs *at all* is what is theoretically significant—and it sets in even after a delay as short as a tenth of a second. See, for example, T. H. Nilsson and T. M. Nelson, "Delayed Monochromatic Hue Matches Indicate Characteristics of Visual Memory," *Journal of Experimental Psychology: Human Perception and Performance* 7 (1981): 141–150.

78. McDowell, *Mind and World,* pp. 56–57.

79. I have in mind forms of *associative agnosia,* in which conceptual, recognitional, and identificatory capacities are impaired, but basic perceptual abilities are largely intact. The other major type of agnosia—*apperceptive agnosia*—is generally thought to be largely a *perceptual* deficit. For a good recent discussion of the various sorts of agnosia and the problems in classifying them, together with an extensive bibliography, see Martha J. Farah, *Visual Agnosia* (Cambridge, Mass.: MIT Press, 1990).

80. This case is discussed in Alan B. Rubens and D. Frank Benson, "Associative Visual Agnosia," *Archives of Neurology* 24 (1971): 305–316.

81. Glyn W. Humphreys and M. Jane Riddoch, *To See But Not to See* (Hillsdale, N.J.: Lawrence Erlbaum, 1987), p. 59. This book contains an in-depth investigation of one agnosic patient, together with interesting theoretical reflections on the significance of the phenomenon for perceptual theory.

82. B. Milner and H.-L. Teuber, "Alteration of Perception and Memory in Man: Reflections on Methods," in *Analysis of Behavioral Change*, ed. Lawrence Weiskrantz (New York: Harper & Row, 1968), p. 293. It is worth mentioning that Teuber himself doubted the existence of agnosia as thus understood. Thirty or more years ago such scepticism was not uncommon. Today it is eccentric.

83. It is true that, as a result of Hilary Putnam's advocacy of the "Division of Linguistic Labour," and of Tyler Burge's related arguments, it is now commonly accepted that someone may be credited with possession, and even exercise, of a concept of *F*-type things without possessing an ability even to discriminate, let alone to recognize, things that are *F* from things that are not. Even if this is true, it is not relevant to our present concerns for two reasons. First, it is not denied by anyone, nor could it sensibly be denied, that the type of person in question for Putnam and Burge must possess *some* recognitional ability if he is to be credited with the concept of *F*-type things; it is simply that the recognitional ability is not adequately sensitive to the specific *F* / non-*F* distinction. Secondly, I take it that no one is going to suggest that when a person exercises his deficient grasp of some such concept, it is the objective content of that concept, that which outstrips the subject's recognitional ability, that allows the subject to *perceive*.

84. This *is* standardly the case, however. Abilities to classify on the basis of features of which the subject is not consciously aware have attracted interest precisely because of their strikingly unusual nature. Normally the development of a perceptually based classificatory capacity is a matter of developing an attunement to features that are, and always were, apparent, but that were either not salient or not of interest.

85. Sellars, "Mental Events," pp. 335–336.

86. Fred Dretske, "Conscious Experience," *Mind* 102 (1993): 263–283.

87. Again, this does not mean simply that the subject lacks this (or any) *word* for trapezia, but that he has never even noticed anything special about trapezia as such. It has never dawned on him that there is such a particular class of shapes.

88. Michael Ayers, *Locke*, 2 vols. (London: Routledge, 1991), vol. 1, p. 177.

89. Kant, *Critique of Pure Reason*, A102.

90. The suggestion that I am continuously *reproducing* what I have just experienced in my imagination is one such detail, as is the psychological atomism that underlies the whole story.

91. A good account of the development of this aspect of Husserl's thought can be found in Donn Welton, *The Origins of Meaning* (The Hague: Martinus Nijhoff, 1983).

92. One of the earliest appearances of this concept, if not the term, is the following: "The originary constitution of *a single object* is, of course, always brought about through *one* thetic consciousness . . . But the unity of the object does not always necessarily presuppose a *categorial* synthesis." Husserl goes on to say that what bestows unity here "is a synthesis of a wholly different sort: we shall call it the *aesthetic* synthesis. If we seek to pinpoint the peculiar differences between these two, we find that the first distinguishing mark is that the *categorial* synthesis is, *as* synthe-

sis, a spontaneous act, whereas the sensory synthesis, on the other hand, is not": *Ideen zu einer reinen Phänomenologie und phänomenologischen Philosophie, Zweites Buch,* ed. M. Biemel, in *Husserliana,* vol. 4 (The Hague: Martinus Nijhoff, 1952), pp. 18–19 [*Ideas Pertaining to a Pure Phenomenology and to a Phenomenological Philosophy, Second Book,* tr. R. Rojcewicz and A. Schuwer (Dordrecht: Kluwer, 1989), pp. 20–21].

93. The major Husserlian text on the topic of time constitution is *Zur Phänomenologie des inneren Zeitbewußtseins,* ed. Rudolph Boehm, in *Husserliana,* vol. 10 (The Hague: Martinus Nijhoff, 1966) [*On the Phenomenology of the Consciousness of Internal Time (1893–1917),* tr. John Barnett Brough (Dordrecht: Kluwer, 1991)].

94. Wilfrid Sellars, "Berkeley and Descartes: Reflection on the Theory of Ideas," in Peter K. Machamer and Robert G. Turnbull, eds., *Studies in Perception* (Columbus: Ohio State University Press, 1978), pp. 282–283.

4. Taking Stock

1. *Works of Thomas Hill Green,* ed. R. L. Nettleship (London: Longmans, Green, and Co., 1885), vol. 1, p. 183; Arthur Schopenhauer, *Über die vierfache Wurzel des Satzes vom zureichenden Grunden, Sämtliche Werke,* vol. 1 (Wiesbaden: Brockhaus, 1966), p. 53 [*The Fourfold Root of the Principle of Sufficient Reason,* tr. E. F. J. Payne (La Salle, Ill.: Open Court, 1974), p. 78].

2. John Searle, "Response: Reference and Intentionality," in *John Searle and His Critics,* ed. Ernest Lepore and Robert Van Gulick (Oxford: Blackwell, 1991), pp. 227–237; and Michael Ayers, *Locke,* 2 vols. (London: Routledge, 1991), vol. 1, ch. 21.

3. See especially, St. Thomas Aquinas, *Summa Theologiae,* Ia, qq. 75–86. The popularity of such a non-conceptual, monistic theory of perception seems to have waned after Aristotle, until it came to dominate in the high Middle Ages—though Asclepiades of Cos is reported as holding that "sensory experiences [*aisthēseis*] are truly apprehensions [*antilēpseis*]": see Sextus Empiricus, *Adversus Mathematicos,* VII.201–202 in *Sextus Empiricus,* tr. R. G. Bury, 4 vols. (London: Heinemann, and Cambridge, Mass.: Harvard University Press, 1967), vol. 2, pp. 108–111.

4. Aquinas, *Summa Theologiae,* Ia, q14, a3.

5. Ibid., q14, a12.

6. Ibid., q85, a2.

7. Perhaps equally fundamental was the contrast between essence and existence. This contrast has, however, remained recognizably in place until our own day.

8. Aquinas, *Summa Theologiae,* Ia, q115, a3 ad 2.

9. Ibid., Ia, q76, a1. The upper limit of this hierarchy is the human rational soul, which, though it is in the form of a human body, has no corporeal operation whatever. For a good discussion of these issues, see Paul Hoffman, "St. Thomas Aquinas on the Halfway State of Sensible Being," *Philosophical Review* 99 (1990): 73–92.

10. Aquinas, *Summa Theologiae,* Ia, q75, a5. Wilfrid Sellars has an enlightening discussion of this Aristotelian account of cognition in "Being and Being Known," in his *Science, Perception and Reality* (London: Routledge & Kegan Paul, 1963), pp. 41–59.

11. John Sergeant, for example, speaks of corporeal phantasms in the brain be-

ing "gay florid pictures" and "obvious and familiar . . . appearance[s]": *Solid Philosophy Asserted, Against the Fancies of the Ideists* (London, 1697), preface, sect. 19 and Preliminary Discourse I, sect. 12, respectively. (I have taken the liberty of modernizing spelling and punctuation in quotations from both Sergeant and Sir Kenelme Digby.)

12. Ibid.

13. At least in the modern era. In the ancient world, Plato's Eleatic Stranger appears to enunciate the theory when he claims that "it appears" *(phainetai)* is a mixture of sensation *(aisthēsis)* and opinion *(doxa)*, opinion being the result of thought *(dianoia)*: Plato's *Sophist*, in *Theaetetus Sophist*, tr. H. N. Fowler (Cambridge, Mass.: Harvard University Press, and London: Heinemann, 1977), 264AB. It is also perhaps possible to interpret those Hellenistic schools, such as the Epicureans and the sceptics, who stressed the irrational *(alogos)* nature of what they called *"aisthesis,"* as holding that what *we* should regard as sense-perception requires some truly cognitive supplement—such as *prolepsis*. For the "irrational" nature of *aisthesis* in Epicurus, see Diogenes Laertius, *Lives of Eminent Philosophers*, tr. R. D. Hicks, 2 vols. (Cambridge, Mass.: Harvard University Press), 10.31; and in the sceptics, see Sextus Empiricus, *Adversus Mathematicos*, 7.293. For an interpretation of Epicurus in terms of the dual component theory, see A. A. Long, "Aisthesis, Prolepsis and Linguistic Theory in Epicurus," *Bulletin of the Institute of Classical Studies* 18 (1971): 114–133.

14. Sir Kenelme Digby, *Two Treatises: In the One of Which the Nature of Bodies; in the Other, the Nature of Men's Soul Is Looked Into* (London: Williams, 1645), *First Treatise*, ch. 5, sect. 10; compare ch. 9, sect. 3.

15. Michael Ayers, *Locke*, vol. 1, p. 185. Two influential works that take a similar line on bodily sensations are D. M. Armstrong, *Bodily Sensations* (London: Routledge & Kegan Paul, 1962) and George Pitcher, "Pain Perception," *Philosophical Review* 79 (1970)P 368–393.

16. A suggestion that was endorsed, for example, by T. K. Abbott: "In the perceptions of sight the required condition occurs from the total absence of any organic sensation, which compels us to separate the subject perceived from ourselves": *Sight and Touch: An Attempt to Disprove the Received (or Berkeleian) Theory of Vision* (London: Longman, Green, Longman, Roberts, & Green, 1864), p. 80. In our own day Greg McCulloch, among others, has made a similar proposal: see *The Mind and Its World* (London: Routledge, 1995), sects. 2.5 and 6.2.

17. One recalls here one of Berkeley's initially most puzzling and challenging considerations in favour of his view that all "sensible things" are mind-dependent: *Three Dialogues between Hylas and Philonous: The Works of George Berkeley*, ed. A. A. Luce and T. E. Jessop, 9 vols. (London: Nelson, 1949), vol. 2, pp. 175–178.

18. Total paralysis is not the only sort of defective condition that can be used to make this point. Oliver Sacks tells of one of his patients who had "perfect elementary sensations in the hands," but felt that "she *had* no hands—or arms either": *The Man Who Mistook His Wife for a Hat* (London: Pan, 1986), p. 58.

19. In practice, of course, when external optical stimulation is cut off there is always a rich array of very dim patches and points of light: optical dust, as Helmholtz nicely termed it. The point is that even if there were not, the resultant uniform darkness would still be visually experienced.

20. Edmond Wright, "Yet More on Non-Epistemic Seeing," *Mind* 90 (1981):

589. I myself recall a blind person trying to convey to the sighted what it is like to be blind. In perfect consonance with Wright, he suggested that in order to understand what it is like, you should think not about darkness, but about your visual consciousness of the region *behind your head*. We are not conscious of a vast darkness behind us; we simply have no visual experience with respect to that region.

21. Ayers, *Locke*, vol. 1, p. 184.

22. Richard Aquila, "Perception and Perceptual Judgements," *Philosophical Studies* 28 (1975): 28.

23. Ibid., p. 27.

24. This is true, for example, of John Heil, *Perception and Cognition* (Berkeley: University of California Press, 1983).

25. W. C. Clement, "Seeing and Hearing," *British Journal for the Philosophy of Science* 6 (1955–1960): 61–63. The sorts of contingencies that Clement had in mind are such facts as that sound waves are large in relation to many everyday objects, that objects do not absorb and re-emit sound as efficiently as they do light, and that there is a dearth of reliable transmitters of sound to serve as an analogue of the sun or other source of illumination.

26. Stuart Aitken and T. G. R. Bower, "Intersensory Substitution in the Blind," *Journal of Experimental Child Psychology* 33 (1982): 309–323 and "The Use of the Sonicguide in Infancy," *Journal of Visual Impairment and Blindness* 76 (1982): 91–100. These authors present powerful considerations in favour of the view that these infants are acquiring truly perceptual capacities in relation to solid objects, rather than being operantly conditioned in relation to mere varieties of sound.

5. The Nature of Perceptual Consciousness

1. William James, *The Principles of Psychology*, 2 vols. (New York: Dover, 1950), vol. 2, pp. 134–135.

2. James Sully, the eminent late nineteenth-century philosophical psychologist, certainly thought so: see his *Outlines of Psychology* (London: Longman, Green & Co., 1884), p. 147. More recently Tom Baldwin has also suggested that perception is a matter of "projecting" sensations into space: "The Projective Theory of Sensory Content," in *The Contents of Experience*, ed. Tim Crane (Cambridge: Cambridge University Press, 1992), pp. 157–177.

3. See, for example, Edmund Husserl, *Ideen zu einer reinen Phänomenologie und phänomenologischen Philosophie, Zweites Buch*, ed. M. Biemel, in *Husserliana*, vol. 4 (The Hague: Martinus Nijhoff, 1952) [*Ideas Pertaining to a Pure Phenomenology and to a Phenomenological Philosophy, Second Book*, tr. R. Rojcewicz and A. Schuwer (Dordrecht: Kluwer, 1989)], §18b and *Beilage* III; Maurice Merleau-Ponty, *Phénoménologie de la Perception* (Paris: Gallimard, 1945), pp. 348–349 [*Phenomenology of Perception*, tr. Colin Smith (London: Routledge & Kegan Paul, 1962), pp. 302–303].

4. William Porterfield, who suffered from this condition, gave vivid expression to it in the eighteenth century. "These Itchings," he wrote, "have sometimes been so strong and lively, that in spite of all my Reason and Philosophy, I could scarce forbear attempting to scratch the Part, tho' I well knew there was nothing there in the Place where I felt the Itching": *A Treatise on the Eye*, 2 vols. (Edinburgh, 1759), vol. 1, p. 364.

5. Georg von Békésy, *Sensory Inhibition* (Princeton, N.J.: Princeton University Press, 1967), pp. 220–228.

6. See Brian O'Shaughnessy, *The Will*, 2 vols. (Cambridge: Cambridge University Press, 1980), vol. 1, ch. 7.

7. If, on the other hand, such occlusion really does make sense in relation to these "sensations," we should certainly be dealing with perceptual phenomena, and not mere sensations, so that they would not count against the claim to sufficiency at all. That such bodily sensations should acquire a perceptual dimension is not impossible. Indeed, we shall consider later a way in which tactile sensations can be transformed into perceptions of objects at a distance.

8. Békésy, *Sensory Inhibition*, pp. 102–106.

9. Ibid., pp. 95–102.

10. The importance of the qualification "inert" will emerge shortly.

11. It has been plausibly argued that smell is in fact a dual sense, involving both the detection of external odours through the nostrils, and also the evaluation of substances in our mouths, via a back route into the nasal cavity, that contributes to the experience of flavour. This is a significant duality because we are pretty poor at identifying identical substances detected in these different ways: one reason why things can smell awful and yet taste delicious. (See, for example, Paul Rozin, "'Taste-Smell Confusions' and the Duality of the Olfactory Sense," *Perception & Psychophysics* 31 [1982]: 397–401.) When I speak of smell, I shall intend the former, external, sense. The latter will be covered by what I say about the sense of taste.

12. One subject—H. D., who actually acquired very little visual ability after her operation—stated that before her corneal transplant she could detect passing shadows. Indeed, "if she awoke in the night from a bad dream she would switch on the room light for reassurance": Carol Ackroyd, N. K. Humphrey, and Elizabeth K. Warrington, "Lasting Effects of Early Blindness: A Case Study," *Quarterly Journal of Experimental Psychology* 26 (1974): 115.

13. As the eminent perceptual psychologist J. J. Gibson says, "An awareness of the body, however dim, does in fact seem to go along with an awareness of the world . . . [T]he very term 'environment' implies something that is surrounded": J. J. Gibson, "A Theory of Direct Visual Perception," in *The Psychology of Knowing*, ed. Joseph R. Royce and Wm. W. Rozeboom (New York: Gordon and Breach, 1972), p. 216.

14. Actually, in the case of haptic perception, such awareness is more than implicit. You can hardly feel the shape of an object without being aware that the object is being explored by a part of your body that is sensitive to contact with the object.

15. As Alexander Bain writes in his notes to James Mill's *Analysis*, "The sensations of heat and cold are, of all sensations, the most *subjective* . . . The rise and fall of the temperature of the surrounding air may induce sensations wholly independent of our own movements; and to whatever extent such independence exists, there is a corresponding absence of objectivity . . . When the degree of sensation varies definitely with definite movements, it is treated as an object sensibility, or as pointing to the object world": James Mill, *Analysis of the Phenomena of the Human Mind*, ed. John Stuart Mill (London: Longmans, Green, 1869), pp. 30n and 35n. (For reasons already given, I believe that the prize for least objective "sensation" should go to taste, and that smell is on a par with the temperature sense.)

16. Illusions are, of course, possible in this area; but they only underscore the phenomenological point in question.

17. That perceived three-dimensional space be thus oriented is not only a phenomenological necessity, but also, once again, a precondition for any possible physical action in relation to the environment.

18. See, for example, Edmund Husserl, *Ding und Raum*, ed. Ulrich Claesges, in *Husserliana*, vol. 16 (The Hague: Martinus Nijhoff, 1974), pp. 154, 160, 176; *Ideen* II [*Ideas* II], §18(a); *Analysen zur Passiven Synthesis*, ed. Margot Fleischer, in *Husserliana*, vol. 11 (The Hague: Martinus Nijhoff, 1966), pp. 13–15; Maurice Merleau-Ponty, *Phénoménologie de la Perception* [*Phenomenology of Perception*], pt. 1, ch. 3, and pt. 2, ch. 2.

19. Stuart Hampshire, *Thought and Action* (London: Chatto and Windus, 1970), pp. 46–47 (emphasis mine). Again in the analytical tradition, David Hamlyn, as we shall soon see, espoused the same position. An emphasis on the dependence of perception on action was also characteristic of much American philosophy, largely inspired by Dewey, in the earlier part of this century. See, for example, John Dewey, "The Reflex Arc Concept in Psychology," *Psychological Review* 3 (1896): 357–370; E. B. Holt, "Response and Cognition I and II," *Journal of Philosophy, Psychology, and Scientific Methods* 12 (1915): 365–373, 393–409; and R. W. Sellars, "Referential Transcendence," *Philosophy and Phenomenological Research* 22 (1961–1962): 1–15.

20. The well-known experiments by Richard Held and his associates on the effects of passive versus active locomotion on early depth perception are inconclusive in this regard. In the most famous of his experiments, two kittens were reared in the dark until they were two or three months of age. They were then put in the same lighted environment; but whereas one kitten was allowed to walk, the other was carried along passively. It was found that only the active kitten subsequently showed the "visual placing response" and reacted to the "visual cliff." See R. Held and A. Hein, "Movement-Produced Stimulation in the Development of Visually-Guided Behavior," *Journal of Comparative and Physiological Psychology* 56 (1963): 872–876. In fact, however, R. D. Walk has subsequently shown that there is little difference between active and passive dark-reared kittens at the earlier age of one month, and that close attention to moving visual stimuli may be more important for the development of depth-perception than *either* self-induced or passive locomotion. "Active locomotion," he suggests, "may simply be a method that ensures that the animal pays attention": Richard D. Walk, "Depth Perception and a Laughing Heaven," in *Perception and Its Development: A Tribute to Eleanor J. Gibson*, ed. Anne D. Pick (Hillsdale, N.J.: Lawrence Erlbaum, 1979), p. 82. In any case, Held's findings themselves show depth perception to be impaired rather than nonexistent.

21. "When several letters were placed on a wall, the blind subjects learned to locate and walk up to them, correctly identify the required letter, and place a finger accurately on it. The task took approximately 10–15 seconds from entry into the room": Paul Bach-y-Rita, *Brain Mechanisms in Sensory Substitution* (New York: Academic Press, 1972), p. 87.

22. Benjamin W. White, Frank A. Saunders, Lawrence Scadden, Paul Bach-y-rita and Carter C. Collins, "Seeing with the Skin," *Perception and Psychophysics* 7 (1970): 25.

23. Bach-y-Rita, *Brain Mechanisms*, pp. 98–99.

24. White et al., "Seeing with the Skin," p. 25.

25. Bach-y-Rita, *Brain Mechanisms*, p. 101, emphasis mine.

26. As is pointed out by Johansson in his open letter to Gibson: see Gunnar Johansson, "On Theories for Visual Space Perception," *Scandinavian Journal of Psychology* 11 (1970): 72.

27. J. J. Gibson, "Visually Guided Locomotion and Visual Orientation in Animals," *British Journal of Psychology* 49 (1958): 182–194. The best general introduction to Gibsonian theory is probably his *The Senses Considered as Perceptual Systems* (London: George Allen & Unwin, 1968).

28. George J. Andersen, "Perception of Self-Motion: Psychophysical and Computational Approaches," *Psychological Bulletin* 99 (1986): 62.

29. For a series of experiments convincingly showing the dominance of visual over proprioceptive information for an apparent awareness of self-motion (in cases of both active and passive actual self-motion), see J. R. Lishman and D. N. Lee, "The Autonomy of Visual Kinaesthesis," *Perception* 2 (1973): 287–294.

30. Brian O'Shaughnessy, "The Sense of Touch," *Australasian Journal of Philosophy* 67 (1989): 39.

31. There is one species of perception that might be regarded as falling within the realm of touch for which self-movement is at least not clearly required: what David Katz termed "vibration-sense." He argued that our bodies' sensitivity to vibration is in many ways analogous to hearing, and that it can function as a distance sense: David Katz, *Der Aufbau der Tastwelt* (repr., Darmstadt: Wissenschaftliche Buchgesellschaft, 1969) [*The World of Touch*, tr. Lester E. Krueger (Hillsdale, N.J.: Lawrence Erlbaum, 1989)], §§39–45.

32. David Hamlyn has given an argument for its impossibility in "Perception and Agency," *Monist* 61 (1978), repr. in his *Perception, Learning, and the Self* (London: Routledge & Kegan Paul, 1983), pp. 43–56. The argument, however, relies on the following two premises: that all perception presupposes an appreciation of solidity, and that this presupposes agency. If either of these claims is false, Hamlyn's argument fails. I regard them both as false.

33. John K. Stevens, Robert C. Emerson, George L. Gerstein, Tamas Kallos, Gordon R. Neufeld, Charles W. Nichols, and Alan C. Rosenquist, "Paralysis of the Awake Human: Visual Perceptions," *Vision Research* 16 (1976): 95, emphasis mine.

34. Étienne Bonnot de Condillac, *Traité des Sensations, Oeuvres Philosophiques de Condillac*, vol. 1, pp. 219–314 (Paris: Presses Universitaires de France, 1947), pt. 2.

35. As James Mill writes, "The feelings of resistance, extension, and figure, are not feelings of touch . . . [W]hen these . . . are detached, a very simple sensation seems to remain, the feeling which we have when something, without being seen, comes . . . in contact with our skin, in such a way that we cannot say whether it is hard or soft, rough or smooth, of what figure it is, or of what size. A sense of something present on the skin, and perhaps also on the interior parts of the body, taken purely by itself, seems alone the feeling of touch": *Analysis of the Phenomena of the Human Mind*, p. 31. I believe that Mill goes too far here in suggesting that a subject restricted to such sensations would even have an awareness of something *on its skin*, implying that such a subject would have some appreciation of the layout of its own body. Even that is not true.

36. In what follows I shall focus on pushing, rather than pulling, since for crea-

tures at all like us, pulling requires that we take hold of something, and this itself involves some part of our body pushing against something.

37. Fichte says, for example, that the *Anstoss* occurs "in so far as [the subject] is active." He also speaks of "outwardly striving activity" being "forced back upon itself," and of "a passive undergoing [*Leiden*] that is possible only through an activity": J. G. Fichte, *Grundlage der gesammten Wissenschaftslehre*, in *Fichtes Werke*, 11 vols., ed. I. H. Fichte (Berlin: de Gruyter, 1971), vol. 1, pp. 212 and 228 [*The Science of Knowledge*, tr. Peter Heath and John Lachs (Cambridge: Cambridge University Press, 1982), pp. 191 and 203].

38. In the erudite notes to his edition of Reid's works, Sir William Hamilton shows that Scaliger in the sixteenth century had a clear appreciation of the way in which bodily action can give us an appreciation of weight that is significantly different from anything offered by the sense of touch: Editor's notes to *The Works of Thomas Reid, D. D.*, 2 vols. (Edinburgh: Maclachlan & Stewart, 1872), vol. 2, pp. 864–867. For a brief but useful historical survey of this subject beginning in the early nineteenth century, see Eckart Scheerer, "Muscle Sense and Innervation Feelings: A Chapter in the History of Perception and Action," in *Perspectives on Perception and Action*, eds. Herbert Heuer and Andries F. Sanders (Hillsdale, N.J.: Lawrence Erlbaum, 1987), pp. 171–194.

39. See, for example, Pierre Maine de Biran, *De L'Aperception Immédiate*, ed. Ives Radizzani, in *Oeuvres*, vol. 4 (Paris: Vrin, 1995), p. 72n.

40. This claim is made, for example, in James Mill, *Analysis of the Phenomena of the Human Mind*, ch. 1, sect. 7, and Thomas Brown, *Lectures on the Philosophy of the Human Mind* (Edinburgh: William Tait 1828), vol. 2, ch. 26. Dilthey, however, regards the *Anstoss* as the *sole* ultimate source of *all* perceptual consciousness. He reaches this position by conflating the *Anstoss* with our second, kinetic, perceptual phenomenon, and by down-playing the importance of our first—suggesting, indeed, that the objects of purely visual perception lack full reality for us because they are, as he puts it, mere scenery and decoration: Wilhelm Dilthey, *Beiträge zur Lösung der Frage vom Ursprung Unseres Glaubens an die Realität der Aussenwelt und Seinem Recht*, in *Gesammelte Schriften*, vol. 5 (Stuttgart: Teubner/Göttingen: Vandenhoeck & Ruprecht, 1982). For the conflation, see pp. 108–110; for the downplaying of three-dimensionality, p. 118.

41. Dilthey, *Beiträge*, p. 101.

42. O'Shaughnessy, "The Sense of Touch," p. 38.

43. Michael Martin, "Sight and Touch," in Crane, *The Contents of Experience*, p. 203.

44. O'Shaughnessy, *The Will*, vol. 1, p. 181.

45. Martin, "Sight and Touch," p. 202.

46. Thomas H. Huxley, *Hume: With Helps to the Study of Berkeley, Collected Essays*, vol. 6 (London: Macmillan, 1908), p. 260.

47. O'Shaughnessy, *The Will*, vol. 1, p. 217.

48. See O'Shaughnessy, "The Sense of Touch," p. 55, and, in greater detail, O'Shaughnessy, *The Will*, chs. 6–7.

49. There are, in fact, a handful of cases in the literature that have been taken as suggesting that a sense of limb movement is possible without any "afferent" feed-back whatever, though the weight of scholarly opinion is against such a possibility. It is, however, perhaps worth mentioning, since it is commonly denied by philosophers, that subjects can *perform* guided movements in the absence of any

proprioceptive feedback. See, for example, D. I. McCloskey, "Kinesthetic Sensibility," *Physiological Reviews* 58 (1978): 763–820, and J. C. Rothwell, M. M. Traub, B. L. Day, J. A. Obeso, P. K. Thomas, and C. D. Marsden, "Manual Motor Performance in a Deafferented Man," *Brain* 105 (1982): 515–542.

50. I notice that the recognition of this phenomenon is sometimes first credited to Lotze; in fact it is due to Weber, who was developing an observation of Fechner's. See the opening pages of E. H. Weber, "Der Tastsinn und das Gemeingefühl," in *Handwörterbuch der Psychologie*, vol. 3, ed. R. Wagner (Brunswick, Germany: Vieweg, 1846), pp. 481–588 ["On the Sense of Touch and 'Common Sensibility,'" tr. D. J. Murray, in E. H. Weber, *The Sense of Touch* (London: Academic, 1978)].

51. Pierre Maine de Biran, *Mémoire sur la Décomposition de la Pensée*, ed. François Azouvi, in *Oeuvres*, vol. 3 (Paris: Vrin, 1988), p. 394.

52. A few saw beyond the phrase. James Mill says that such muscular sensations are *only a part* of the phenomenon in question—the other being "the Will": *Analysis*, p. 43. Even J. J. Engel uses the phrase, though he says that he will term it *"Gestrebe"*—"striving": J. J. Engel, "Über den Ursprung des Begriffs der Kraft," *Schriften*, vol. 10 (Berlin: Mylius'sche Buchhandlung, 1844), p. 102.

53. The point has recently been argued persuasively and at length by Brian O'Shaughnessy in *The Will*, ch. 15, so I shall not belabour it here.

54. "This effort, and this resistance . . . already constitute a complete modality . . . (one cannot introduce it under the general heading *sensation* without confusing everything)": de Biran, *De L'Aperception Immédiate*, p. 57.

55. "In the experience of restraint and resistance," writes Dilthey, "the presence of a force is given us . . . For restraint and resistance contain force in themselves as much as does impulse. As in the consciousness of impulse there lies the experience that I am exercising force, so in the consciousness of restraint and resistance there lies the experience that a force is working on me": *Beiträge*, pp. 131–132.

56. Not even the shapes of such objects would be perceptible—at least not for our imagined creature with a single "spine." For that to be possible, the spine would have to be able to move in different directions, and then the distinctiveness of the present case would be lost. (The only way in which a creature restricted to the *Anstoss* could detect shapes, and then only the two-dimensional shapes of facing surfaces, would be if it were equipped with rows of such spines.)

57. I introduce this term because it simply is not literally true to say, as psychologists typically do, that such figures look three-dimensional.

58. Especially notable are figures that are quasi-three-dimensionally *reversible*, for such reversal gives rise to a changed impression of the size of one of the "faces," in accordance with quasi-three-dimensional perspective.

59. The term "amodal" comes from A. Michotte and L. Burke, "Une Nouvelle Énigme de la Psychologie de la Perception: Le 'Donné Amodal' dans l'Expérience Sensorielle," in A. Michotte et al, *Causalité, Permanence et Réalité Phénoménales* (Louvain, Belgium: Publications Universitaires, 1962), pp. 372–373, who first drew attention to the phenomena about to be described. For extended discussion, and examples, also see A. Michotte, G. Thinès, and G. Crabbé, *Les Compléments Amodaux des Structures Perceptives* (Louvain, Belgium: Publications Universitaires, and Paris: Béatrice-Nauwelaerts, 1967).

60. Many such figures are to be found in Gaetano Kanisza's *Organization in Vi-*

sion (New York: Praeger, 1979). A particularly acute theoretical discussion of the fundamental issues involved is in Gaetano Kanisza and Walter Gerbino, "Amodal Completion: Seeing or Thinking?" in *Organization and Representation in Perception*, ed. Jacob Beck (Hillsdale, N.J.: Lawrence Erlbaum, 1982), pp. 167–190.

61. Such cases are discussed in Theodore E. Parks, "Subjective Figures: Some Unusual Concomitant Brightness Effects," *Perception* 9 (1980): 239–241, and Colin Ware, "Coloured Illusory Triangles Due to Assimilation," *Perception* 9 (1980): 103–107.

62. For discussion, see Stanley Coren, "Subjective Contours and Apparent Depth," *Psychological Review* 79 (1972): 359–367.

6. The Solution

1. And if a muscle is made artificially to contract during some manual operation, the subject "'gets a feeling of relief or lessening of tension,' not a feeling of heaviness or increased force": D. I. McCloskey, "Kinesthetic Sensibility," *Physiological Reviews* 58 (1978): 798, who is citing work by K.-E. Hagbarth and G. Eklund.

2. S. C. Gandevia and D. I. McCloskey, "Sensations of Heaviness," *Brain* 100 (1977): 346. See also McCloskey's "Kinesthetic Sensibility," esp. pp. 797–805, for a review of the literature.

3. Gandevia and McCloskey, "Sensations of Heaviness," pp. 350–351.

4. The issues here are more complex than in the preceding example, since contact with objects goes to confer truly spatial value on the "trajectories" that would otherwise be aspects of what, in the previous chapter, I called mere "kinesis." It makes no sense, for example, to suppose that a sightless creature's *first* contact with an object should misrepresent the object's spatial location—for prior to establishing a relation to external objects through the *Anstoss*, "kinaesthesis" has no objective significance. We are to suppose, therefore, that our present illusory phenomenon concerns a mature tactile perceiver.

5. Michael Martin, "Sight and Touch," in *The Contents of Experience*, ed. Tim Crane (Cambridge: Cambridge University Press, 1992), p. 204.

6. Ibid., p. 209.

7. What we find in Kant is, at most, suggestive hints—hints that, moreover, Kant proceeded to develop in an excessively intellectualistic fashion. What he says in the *Second Analogy*, for example, can only fully be made sense of by reference to our second, kinetic phenomenon, and yet he fails explicitly to thematize this in his account. Indeed, his language plays down its importance. The famous description of the "changing manifold" in the appearance of a house is possible only by our *moving* round the house, or at least altering our gaze; but all that Kant says is that the house "stands before me": *Kritik der reinen Vernunft*, ed. Raymund Schmidt (Hamburg: Meiner, 1956) [*Immanuel Kant's Critique of Pure Reason*, tr. Norman Kemp Smith (London: Macmillan, 1933)], A190/B235.

8. I am in full agreement here with Ernst Cassirer, who has argued for this point more explicitly than any philosopher I know: see his "The Concept of Group and the Theory of Perception," *Philosophy and Phenomenological Research* 5 (1944): 1–35. (Cassirer also cites some of the more enlightened psychologists of his day—such as Buehler, Gelb, and Katz—as also having tumbled to the fundamental importance of the constancies.)

9. This constancy is notable, but far from perfect. Hence the possibility of citing its failures as instances of illusion in Chapter 1.

10. For references to relevant literature and an account of why such an account does not work, see Alan L. Gilchrist, "The Perception of Surface Blacks and Whites," *Scientific American* 240, no. 3 (1979): 88–97.

11. It seems, indeed, to have been C. D. Broad's favourite example of an illusion. Here is a characteristic passage: "We know, *e.g.*, that when we lay a penny down on a table and view it from different positions it generally looks more or less elliptical in shape": *Scientific Thought* (London: Kegan Paul, Trench, Trubner & Co., 1923), p. 235. Similar use is made of the supposed phenomenon in, for example, H. H. Price, "Appearing and Appearances," *American Philosophical Quarterly* 1 (1964): 3–19, and Bertrand Russell, *The Problems of Philosophy* (London: Thornton Butterworth, 1912).

12. Incidentally, given that any perceptual constancy suffices for perceptual consciousness, these three-dimensional constancies give us further reason to doubt the necessity of self-movement for perception, since it is certainly not involved in every instance of such constancy. When my distance to an object decreases and yet the object looks no larger, it is immaterial whether it was I who approached the object, or the object that moved nearer to me. This holds true of all of the three-dimensional constancies.

13. Perhaps an even more minimal case is that of *muscae volitantes*, or "floaters" as they are sometimes called: the tiny impurities in our eyeballs that sometimes come to consciousness as small wisps that float before us in a spatially indeterminate fashion. The minimal sense of objectivity that attaches to these derives wholly from the way their movements lag behind the movements of our eyes.

14. It is to be noted that *active* movement is inessential even to these constancies that involve self-movement. If your hand is passively moved over a surface, the surface does not appear to be moving. Position constancy here operates in the complete absence of agency.

15. To the extent, that is, that these senses are not phenomenally three-dimensional. To the extent that they are, or could be, they *would* feature genuine phenomenological constancy.

16. If I am correct in claiming that phenomenological constancy is sufficient for perceptual consciousness, we can apply this principle to test whether our list of two fundamental perceptual phenomena in the domain of sensuously presentational perception is indeed exhaustive, as claimed in Chapter 5. The test is simply to ask: Is there any form of perceptual constancy that is independent of each of these two? As far as I can see, the answer to this is negative.

17. There are, for example, "orientation constancy" (when you tilt your head, objectively upright things still look upright), "speed constancy (the apparent velocity of an object, even when it travels across your field of vision, is not proportional to the displacement of the retinal images and the consequent changes in the sensory array), and what we might call "roughness constancy" (the perceived roughness of a rough surface is largely independent of the speed with which the finger passes over the surface irregularities).

18. Apart, that is, from the problem of relating the *Anstoss* to the same range of objects as is given to mere tactile perception.

19. C. W. K. Mundle, *Perception: Facts and Theories* (Oxford: Oxford Univer-

sity Press, 1971), p. 10. All subsequent references to Mundle are to this work, pp. 10–23.

20. I have discussed the relation between perceptual appearances and belief, or judgement, in some detail elsewhere: see A. D. Smith, "Perception and Belief," *Philosophy and Phenomenological Research* 62 (2001): 283–309.

21. This is the truth in Quinton's remark, noted in Chapter 1, that we are commonly not aware of our "sense-experience."

22. Samuel Bailey, *A Review of Berkeley's Theory of Vision, Designed to Show the Unsoundness of that Celebrated Speculation* (London: James Ridgway, 1842), p. 36. Bailey was one of the very few in the nineteenth century not to accept this view (or its even more bizarre principal rival: that visual objects are not even two-dimensionally extended). In retrospect it is difficult not to concur with his judgement when he writes that "if the theory . . . should consequently fall, its general reception by philosophers heretofore must be considered as one of the most extraordinary circumstances to be found in the annals of speculative philosophy" (p. 238). Two excellent historical surveys of this issue are Gary Hatfield, *The Natural and the Normative* (Cambridge, Mass.: MIT Press, 1990) and Nicholas Pastore, *Selective History of Theories of Visual Perception: 1650–1950* (Oxford: Oxford University Press, 1971).

23. David Hume, *A Treatise of Human Nature*, ed. L. A. Selby-Bigge and P. H. Nidditch, 2d ed. (Oxford: Clarendon Press, 1978), p. 56.

24. See A. D. Smith, "Space and Sight," *Mind* 109 (2000): 481–518.

25. Irwin Rock, *The Logic of Perception* (Cambridge, Mass.: MIT Press, 1983), p. 263. Chapter 9 as a whole contains a convincing defence of this position.

26. Ibid., p. 265.

27. Charles Taylor, "Sense Data Revisited," in *Perception and Identity*, ed. G. F. Macdonald (London: Macmillan, 1979), p. 107. For similar remarks, see also Maurice Merleau-Ponty, *Phénoménologie de la Perception* (Paris: Gallimard, 1945) [*Phenomenology of Perception*, tr. Colin Smith (London: Routledge & Kegan Paul, 1962)], introduction.

28. A. J. Ayer, for example, accepts it in his response to Taylor: "Replies," in Taylor, *Perception and Identity*, p. 291.

29. The phenomenological objection to the alternative, "adverbial" account of sense-experience has been implicitly answered.

7. The Argument

1. Winston Barnes once wrote that "hallucinations and delusions need present no insuperable difficulties. There appeared to Lady Macbeth [*sic*] to be a dagger but there was no dagger in fact. Something appeared to be a dagger, and there are certainly problems concerning exactly what it is in such circumstances appears to be possessed of qualities which it does not possess": Winston H. F. Barnes, "The Myth of Sense-Data," *Proceedings of the Aristotelian Society* 45 (1944–1945); repr. in *Perceiving, Sensing, and Knowing*, ed. Robert J. Swartz (Berkeley: University of California Press, 1965), p. 163. If *any* such normal candidate is suggested, we shall be offered a case of illusion, not hallucination.

2. David Hume, *A Treatise of Human Nature*, ed. L. A. Selby-Bigge and P. H. Nidditch, 2d ed. (Oxford: Clarendon Press, 1978), pp. 210–211. ("Perception" amounts to "immediate object of perception" for Hume.)

3. It is, for example, the favoured example of both Frank Jackson and Brian O'Shaughnessy. See Frank Jackson, *Perception* (Cambridge: Cambridge University Press, 1977), and Brian O'Shaughnessy, *Consciousness and the World* (Oxford: Clarendon Press, 2000), pt. 3.

4. Another common way of expressing this point is to say that it is an epistemic possibility that you yourself are now actually hallucinating. I shall not myself present the matter in this way, since it raises irrelevant issues.

5. Guido Küng, "The Intentional and the Real Object," *Dialectica* 38 (1984): 144, n. 1.

6. J. M. Hinton, *Experiences* (Oxford: Clarendon Press, 1973), p. 80.

7. Ibid., p. 71, and J. M. Hinton "Experiences," *Philosophical Quarterly* 17 (1967): 10.

8. John McDowell, "Criteria, Defeasibility, and Knowledge," *Proceedings of the British Academy* (1982): §3.

9. There is some dispute among disjunctive theorists over how exactly to specify the relevant disjunction. Paul Snowdon, for example, has criticized Hinton's specific proposal—which employs the notion of *being under a perfect illusion*—and employs instead the disjunction "(there is something which looks to S to be *F*) v (it is to S as if there is something which looks to him (S) to be *F*)": "Perception, Vision and Causation," *Proceedings of the Aristotelian Society* 81 (1980–1981): 185. A weakness with this suggestion, of course, is that it applies only to visual experience (as Snowdon recognizes). We need not, however, enter into the niceties of this debate, since the general idea, in which alone we are interested here, is clear enough.

10. Hippolyte Adolphe Taine, *De L'Intelligence*, 2 vols. (Paris: Hachette, 1870), vol. 1, p. 408, vol. 2, pp. 5–6.

11. For a recent example, see Howard Robinson, *Perception* (London: Routledge, 1994), ch. 6.

12. Bertrand Russell, *The Analysis of Matter* (London: George Allen & Unwin, 1927), p. 197.

13. Paul Snowdon, one of the leading disjunctive theorists, in effect accepts this argument, or at least does not reject it. Because of this, he retreats to the claim that a disjunctive analysis of experience is not a priori false. See "The Objects of Perceptual Experience I," *Proceedings of the Aristotelian Society*, supp. vol. 64 (1990): 130–131. Although this may suffice for Snowdon's limited concern with conceptual analysis, in the present context such a response would, of course, be wholly inadequate.

14. Hinton, *Experiences*, p. 80.

15. Snowdon, "The Objects of Perceptual Experience I," p. 125.

16. McDowell, "Singular Thought and Inner Space," in *Subject, Thought, and Context*, ed. Philip Pettit and John McDowell (Oxford: Clarendon Press, 1986), p. 165, n. 54.

17. John McDowell, "*De Re* Senses," in *Frege Tradition & Influence*, ed. Crispin Wright (Oxford: Blackwell, 1984), p. 103, n. 13.

18. C. D. Broad, "Some Elementary Reflexions on Sense-Perception," *Philosophy* 27 (1952); repr. in Swartz, *Perceiving, Sensing, and Knowing*, p. 39.

19. Many disjunctivists will, in fact, be happy to accept this conditional conclusion, since they deny that a hallucinator is aware of anything at all. This initially preposterous claim is the topic of Chapter 8.

20. R. J. Hirst, *The Problems of Perception* (London: George Allen & Unwin, 1959), pp. 40–44.

21. Brian O'Shaughnessy, *The Will*, 2 vols. (Cambridge: Cambridge University Press, 1980), vol. 1, pp. xvii and 174.

22. John Hyman, "The Causal Theory of Perception," *Philosophical Quarterly* 42 (1992): 286 and 290.

23. Diogenes Laertius, *Lives of Eminent Philosophers*, tr. R. D. Hicks, 2 vols. (Cambridge, Mass.: Harvard University Press, 1995), VII.50.

24. Hence, as mentioned above, his turning to after-images in order to mount a parallel to the Argument from Hallucination against Direct Realism.

25. See, for example, McDowell, "Singular Thought and Inner Space," §8.

26. This is a big "perhaps." Speaking of the brain of a normal embodied subject that is then disembodied and envatted, McDowell says that "perhaps memory can give subjectivity a tenuous foothold here": John McDowell, "The Content of Perceptual Experience," *Philosophical Quarterly* 44 (1994): 201. Greg McCulloch, a follower of McDowell's, is even less concessionary: see his *The Mind and Its World* (Routledge: London, 1995), VIII.5.

27. McDowell, "Singular Thought and Inner Space," p. 160.

28. Disjunctivism also has another target. Hinton, for example, can characterize the target of his criticism as the idea of a visual experience as "'inner' independently of the extent to which it is given meaning by the subject's experience of life"; or as the idea that there is "a gap between one's report of such an experience and any proposition as to how some external object, event, or process looks; a gap exactly as wide as the gap between such an experience-report and *any* sort of proposition about the 'external world'": Hinton, *Experiences*, pp. 60 and 61. What seems to emerge from such passages as the real target of the disjunctive theory, at least for Hinton, is a traditional view according to which we are first aware of bare sensations, which we have then to interpret in a some objective way, and according to which we can always return to such a bare reporting of experience uncontaminated by objective interpretation. Now, this may indeed be a wholly mistaken account of perceptual consciousness. Perhaps the most authentic way of expressing either a perception or a hallucination is saying *how things appear to you*. Perhaps an at least apparent presentation of an "external world" is indissociable from perceptual consciousness as such. But the Argument requires the denial of none of this. The Argument from Hallucination does not need, any more than the Argument from Illusion, to be based upon poor phenomenology.

29. Snowdon, "The Objects of Perceptual Experience I," p. 123, and McDowell, "Singular Thought and Inner Space," pp. 151 and 157.

30. McDowell, "Singular Thought and Inner Space," p. 146.

31. William Child, "Vision and Experience: The Causal Theory and the Disjunctive Conception," *Philosophical Quarterly* 42 (1992): 300–301.

32. McDowell, "Criteria, Defeasibility, and Knowledge," p. 471.

33. McDowell, "Singular Thought and Inner Space," p. 152.

8. An Extreme Proposal

1. Although almost all of those who have adopted this approach have been influenced, either directly or indirectly, by Evans and McDowell, for someone who

seems to have reached the position independently, see Barry Smith, "Acta Cum Fundamentis in Re," *Dialectica* 38 (1984): 158–178.

2. Gareth Evans, *The Varieties of Reference* (Oxford: Clarendon Press, 1982), p. 200.

3. Ibid., pp. 29–30. McDowell follows this usage: e.g., "Singular Thought and Inner Space," in *Subject, Thought, and Context*, ed. Philip Pettit and John McDowell (Oxford: Clarendon Press, 1986), p. 144. Evans derives this phrase from a passage in Frege. In fact, Evans holds that Frege is himself committed to something like the extreme position. This specific hermeneutical claim has met with vigorous dissent: see, for example, David Bell, "How 'Russellian' Was Frege?" *Mind* 99 (1990): 267–277.

4. Evans, *The Varieties of Reference*, p. 45.

5. McDowell, Singular Thought and Inner Space," p. 146.

6. Ibid., p. 148.

7. Evans, *The Varieties of Reference*, p. 148, n. 12.

8. Ibid., p. 46.

9. Keith Donnellan, "Reference and Definite Descriptions," *Philosophical Review* 75 (1966): 303.

10. John McDowell, "Truth-Value Gaps," in *Logic, Methodology, and Philosophy of Science*, vol. 6, ed. L. J. Cohen (Amsterdam: North-Holland, 1981), p. 308.

11. Evans, *The Varieties of Reference*, p. 378.

12. The account of perception to be developed in Chapter 9 will afford us a perspective from which to contest the "extreme view" of thought. I leave the development of that idea, however, for another occasion.

13. Evans, *The Varieties of Reference*, p. 199.

14. In Chapter 9 I shall, however, argue that the situation is not how McDowell takes it to be: such a view is *not* entailed by Direct Realism.

15. Evans, *The Varieties of Reference*, p. 70.

16. I shall be brief, and therefore somewhat dogmatic, on this issue, since it has been widely argued in the literature and is by now fairly uncontroversial. The general point at issue was seen years ago by Moore: "Can we say 'that thing' = 'the thing at which I am pointing' or 'the thing to which this finger points' or 'the nearest thing to which this finger points'? No, because the prop[osition] is not understood unless the thing in question is *seen*": G. E. Moore, *Commonplace Book, 1919–1953* (London: George Allen & Unwin, 1962), p. 158. (The point is clearly not meant to be restricted to the sense of sight.) Husserl also anticipated much of the recent work on demonstratives: see, for example, *Logische Untersuchungen*, 3 vols., in *Husserliana* vol. 18, ed. Elmar Holenstein, and vol. 19/1–2, ed. Ursula Panzer (The Hague: Martinus Nijhoff, 1975 and 1984) [*Logical Investigations*, 2 vols., tr. J. N. Findlay (London: Routledge & Kegan Paul, 1970)], *Sixth Investigation*.

17. It is not difficult to imagine situations in which two subjects perceive the same object, do not know they do, and yet can converse about that object. Although Evans commonly insists upon the requirement for understanding that an audience *know which* object is in question, he himself indicates that he appreciated that such knowledge was an excessively strong requirement, and that perceptual acquaintance may suffice. He writes, for example, that "if someone wrongly took himself to be deceived by the appearances, and on the basis of this false belief entered into a pretence comprising such utterances as 'This little green man is F',

then . . . he would in fact be demonstratively identifying a little green man whom he could see, and entertaining various thoughts about him": Evans, *The Varieties of Reference*, p. 370.

18. Ibid., p. 143.

19. It may be suggested that I could hallucinate something you have seen before, and so exploit this information-link to secure understanding. It might even be suggested that I could hallucinate the same object that you are hallucinating. In Chapter 9 I shall argue that neither of these is a possibility.

20. Evans, *The Varieties of Reference*, p. 306. See also p. 123.

21. E.g., ibid., p. 311.

22. John McDowell, "*De Re* Senses" in *Frege Tradition & Influence*, ed. Crispin Wright (Oxford: Blackwell, 1984), p. 103, and "Singular Thought and Inner Space," p. 145, n. 17, respectively.

23. McDowell, "Singular Thought and Inner Space," p. 145.

24. McDowell, "*De Re* Senses," p. 103, n. 13.

25. Evans, *The Varieties of Reference*, pp. 45–46.

26. McDowell, "Singular Thought and Inner Space," p. 138.

27. Evans, *The Varieties of Reference*, p. 200.

28. See Harold Noonan, "Russellian Thoughts and Methodological Solipsism," in *Language, Mind, and Logic*, ed. Jeremy Butterfield (Cambridge: Cambridge University Press, 1986), pp. 67–89; Thomas Baldwin, "Phenomenology, Solipsism, and Egocentric Thought I," *Proceedings of the Aristotelian Society*, supp. vol. 62 (1988): 27–43. Baldwin is one among several who have adopted this line of thought.

29. For the familiar reasons, though from an extreme perspective, see Christopher Peacocke, "Demonstrative Thought and Psychological Explanation," *Synthèse* 49 (1981): 187–217. Noonan's own paper itself contains some relevant observations independent of that perspective.

30. Noonan, "Russellian Thoughts," p. 88, emphasis mine.

31. Ibid., pp. 82–83.

32. Ibid., p. 89.

33. Ibid., p. 88.

34. Ibid., pp. 88–89.

35. Quotation from ibid., p. 83.

36. Gordon Holmes, "Disturbances of Visual Orientation," *British Journal of Ophthalmology* 2 (1918): 451–452.

37. Ibid., pp. 462–463.

38. Ibid., p. 459.

39. Ibid., p. 465.

40. As David Bell says of such a scenario, "When it seems to me (quite wrongly) that I am sitting in the gallery of a large theatre, watching Napoleon Bonaparte down below me on the stage, there is certainly an apparent place at which he seems to be; but no objective spatial coordinates can be given for that place. (If I undergo this hallucination while sitting in my kitchen, then the attempt to identify a place in objective space with one in apparent space will put the place I am thinking of some sixty feet below the house next door but one to mine. But I think we can safely assume that I have neither explicit thoughts about, nor behavioural dispositions towards *that* place!)": "Phenomenology, Solipsism, and Egocen-

tric Thought II," *Proceedings of the Aristotelian Society*, supp. vol. 62 (1988): 48–49. The case is even clearer with respect to the brain in a vat.

9. The Solution

1. Reinhardt Grossmann, *The Structure of Mind* (Madison: University of Wisconsin Press, 1965), p. 226. For "sense-impression" we may substitute "sensation," "sense-datum," or anything similarly non-normal.

2. "A sense-impression can only be the object of a conscious state of inspecting": ibid., p. 34.

3. "I first perceive a certain perceptual object, its shape, its color *etc.* Then there occurs a shift from perceiving to sensing. After the shift, I inspect certain sense-impressions. But to perceive a perceptual object is one thing; to scrutinize sense-impressions is something else again": ibid., p. 8.

4. Ibid., p. 34.

5. In addition to the issue about to be explored, a problem appears to lurk in the following statement of Grossmann's: "For there does occur, *in addition* to the experience of sense-impressions, an act of seeing": ibid., p. 34, emphasis mine. By making acts of sensing ingredient in perceptual consciousness along with a *distinct* "perceptual act," he seems to embrace a form of dual component theory, with all its attendant difficulties.

6. Ibid., p. 229.

7. Martin Heidegger, *Die Grundprobleme der Phenomenologie (1919/20)*, in *Gesamtausgabe*, vol. 58 (Frankfurt am Main: Vittorio Klostermann, 1993), p. 84 [*The Basic Problems of Phenomenology*, tr. Albert Hofstadter, rev. ed. (Bloomington: Indiana University Press, 1988), p. 60].

8. This is the third context in which this term has been employed in these pages. In Chapter 1 we considered certain absurdly reductive intentionalist accounts of perception. And in Chapter 4, as well as in the last section of Chapter 2, we considered non-reductive accounts of perception that falsely suppose all sensation to be essentially intentional in character. Intentionality is, indeed, the key to understanding perception, but it has to be understood aright. In a sense, the whole course of the present work has been an attempt to develop a satisfactory account of the intentionality characteristic of perception.

9. On occasion Grossmann can write as if he himself endorses such a position. "The person who in his hallucination sees a pink rat does indeed *see* something. His experience consists just as much of an act of seeing as the experience of someone who sees a white rat which actually exists. But, of course, what the hallucinating person sees, the pink rat, does not exist": Reinhardt Grossman, *Meinong* (London: Routledge & Kegan Paul, 1974), pp. 131–132. By making hallucinatory perceptual particulars real existents, however, Grossmann falls well short of a fully intentionalist position. Only going whole hog offers any hope of evading the Argument. (If it were possible for some particulars not to be real, the use to which Grossmann puts the part-whole relation between particulars and families of particulars, noted earlier, would be redundant and unintelligible.)

10. David Hume, *A Treatise of Human Nature*, ed. L. A. Selby-Bigge and P. H. Nidditch, 2d ed. (Oxford: Clarendon Press, 1978), p. 209.

11. After commenting on his eventual rejection of an analysis of consciousness

into act and object in favour of one according to which "the object remains alone," Russell remarks that this latter "ought no longer to be called by the name 'object,' since this term suggests a relation to a subject": *Manuscript Notes, Collected Papers of Bertrand Russell*, vol. 8 (London: Unwin Hyman, 1986), p. 252.

12. Alexius Meinong, "Über Gegenstände höherer Ordnung und deren Verhältnis zur inneren Wahrnehmung," in *Gesamtausgabe*, vol. 2 (Graz: Akademische Druck- und Verlagsanstalt, 1971), p. 382.

13. Bertrand Russell, *Introduction to Mathematical Philosophy* (London: Allen & Unwin, 1919), p. 169.

14. So far as I can tell, this now popular trope derives from William Kneale, *Probability and Induction* (Oxford: Clarendon Press, 1949), pp. 12 and 32.

15. Alexius Meinong, "Über Gegenstandstheorie," in *Gesamtausgabe*, vol. 2 (Graz: Akademische Druck- und Verlagsanstalt, 1971), p. 485 ["Theory of Objects," tr. Isaac Levi et al., in *Realism and the Background of Phenomenology*, ed. R. M. Chisholm (Glencoe, Ill.: Free Press of Glencoe, 1960), p. 78]. In terms of Kit Fine's useful three-tiered typology of accounts of non-existents, the account to be developed here is "empiricist": see "The Problem of Non-Existents: 1. Internalism," *Topoi* 1 (1982): 97–140.

16. Alexius Meinong, *Über Annahmen*, 2d ed., in *Gesamtausgabe*, vol. 4 (Graz: Akademische Druck- und Verlagsanstalt, 1977), p. 61 [*On Assumptions*, tr. James Heaune (Berkeley: University of California Press, 1983), p. 49].

17. Meinong, "Über Gegenstandstheorie," p. 497 ["Theory of Objects," p. 89].

18. Ibid., p. 500 [pp. 91–92].

19. Ernst Mally, "Untersuchungen zur Gegenstandstheorie des Messens," in *Untersuchungen zur Gegenstandstheorie und Psychologie*, ed. A. Meinong (Leipzig: Barth, 1904), §3.

20. Roderick M. Chisholm, "Meinong, Alexius," in *The Encyclopaedia of Philosophy*, ed. P. Edwards (London: Macmillan, 1967), vol. 5, p. 262.

21. I do not, however, deny a wider sphere of application for the intentionalist approach. There is, in particular, a strong motivation to extend it to all *de re* cognitive states. But that is a topic for another occasion.

22. Although not that many years ago Gilbert Ryle was indisputably expressing the philosophical consensus when he said (at a conference in honour of Meinong) that "*Gegenstandstheorie* itself is dead, buried and not going to be resurrected" ("Intentionality-Theory and the Nature of Thinking," *Revue Internationale de Philosophie* 27 [1973]: 255), in fact not an insignificant number of philosophers and logicians have since proclaimed themselves Meinongians. Terence Parsons is one of the best known, and in his theory there is an object corresponding to every set of properties (even the null set). See, for example, Parsons, *Nonexistent Objects* (New Haven: Yale University Press, 1980), pp. 17–22.

23. Richard Routley, *Exploring Meinong's Jungle and Beyond*, Departmental Monograph no. 3, Philosophy Department, Research School of Social Sciences, Australian National University (Canberra), 1980, pp. 667–668.

24. Gareth Evans, *The Varieties of Reference* (Oxford: Clarendon Press, 1982), p. 352.

25. Richard L. Cartwright, "Negative Existentials," *Journal of Philosophy* 62 (1960): 638.

26. J. L. Austin, *Sense and Sensibilia* (Oxford: Oxford University Press, 1962), ch. 7.

27. This also applies to Cartwright's example. Evans's first problematic statement is multiply unsatisfactory, with the previous issue concerning ob-jectness being only one strand in the tangle. Another, to which we shall return, concerns the fact that reality (and unreality) are essential properties.

28. Gilbert Ryle, "Review of J. N. Findlay, *Meinong's Theory of Objects*," *Oxford Magazine* 52 (1933–1934): 118; Keith S. Donnellan, "Speaking of Nothing," *The Philosophical Review* 83 (1974); 12.

29. Bertrand Russell, *My Philosophical Development* (London: George Allen & Unwin, 1959), p. 13.

30. In fact, despite the use to which it has been subsequently put, William Kneale's reference to the Meinongian "jungle," alluded to earlier, was specifically to Meinong's "jungle of subsistence"—which he correctly interpreted.

31. One possible source of confusion here lies in the fact that German authors commonly use the term "real" (in German usually *real*, but sometimes, and especially in Meinong, *wirklich*) to describe things that are temporal (or spatio-temporal). To say, therefore, that something is in this sense "real" is not to say anything about the "furniture of the world," but is to raise the issue of the ontological kind to which a thing belongs. Such a notion of "reality" is also, therefore, categorial, not existential, in its import. I shall *not* be using the term "real" in this sense.

32. Meinong's theory is actually more complex than this suggests, for he can speak of existence as one form of subsistence, and also state that "what can exist must, before anything, subsist, so to speak": "Selbstdarstellung," in *Gesamtausgabe*, vol. 7 (Graz: Akademische Druck- und Verlagsanstalt, 1978), p. 18, and *Über Annahmen*, p. 74 [*On Assumptions*, p. 58]. Since the point I am emphasizing is that the whole notion of subsistence is a red herring as far as our own enquiry is concerned, I shall not delve into this matter.

33. Chisholm, "Meinong, Alexius," p. 201.

34. Meinong, *Über Annahmen*, p. 79 [*On Assumptions*, p. 62].

35. Alexius Meinong, *Über emotionale Präsentation*, in *Gesamtausgabe*, vol. 3 (Graz: Akademische Druck- und Verlagsanstalt, 1968), p. 306 [*On Emotional Presentation*, tr. Marie-Louise Schubert Kalsi (Evanston, Ill.: Northwestern University Press, 1972), p. 19], and *Über Annahmen*, p. 234 [*On Assumptions*, p. 170].

36. Throughout his career, Meinong was impressed by "the peculiar positivity that seems to lie in the 'pre-givenness' of everything graspable, that is, (in principle) of every object": *Über Annahmen*, p. 80 [*On Assumptions*, p. 62]. This led him to wonder whether *Außersein* might not be a third determination of being, beside existence and subsistence. Although at one stage he in effect rejects any such suggestion, in later work it is still an open question: compare "Über Gegenstandstheorie" ["Theory of Objects"], §4 with *Über Annahmen*, pp. 79–80 and 242 [*On Assumptions*, pp. 62 and 176]. At the end of his career, Meinong could insist that at least something "being-like" must attach to any object: *Über emotionale Präsentation*, pp. 306–308 [*On Emotional Presentation*, pp. 19–21]. Richard and Valerie Routley thus go too far when they claim that "only in very early work which he later rejected . . . did Meinong allow that non-entities [have] a sort of existence": "Rehabilitating Meinong's Theory of Objects," *Revue Internationale de Philosophie* 27 (1973):

227, n. 3. (Richard Routley later abandoned this claim: *Exploring Meinong's Jungle and Beyond*, p. 857, n. 2.)

37. Edmund Husserl, *Logische Untersuchungen*, 3 vols., in *Husserliana*, vol. 18, ed. Elmar Holenstein, and vol. 19/1–2, ed. Ursula Panzer (The Hague: Martinus Nijhoff, 1975 and 1984), vol. 19/1, pp. 439–440 [*Logical Investigations*, 2 vols., tr. J. N. Findlay (London: Routledge & Kegan Paul, 1970), vol. 2, p. 596].

38. J. L. Mackie, *Problems from Locke* (Oxford: Clarendon Press, 1976), chs. 1–2, and "Problems of Intentionality," in *Phenomenology and Philosophical Understanding*, ed. Edo Pivcevic (Cambridge: Cambridge University Press, 1975), pp. 37–52; Gilbert Harman, "The Intrinsic Quality of Experience," *Philosophical Perspectives* 4 (1990): 31–52; and Sidney Shoemaker, "Self-Knowledge and 'Inner Sense,'" *Philosophy and Phenomenological Research* 54 (1994): 266.

39. Mackie, "Problems of Intentionality," p. 46.

40. Husserl, *Logische Untersuchungen*, vol. 19/1, p. 386 [*Logical Investigations*, vol. 2, p. 558].

41. Meinong, *"Über Gegenstandstheorie,"* p. 490 ["Theory of Objects," p. 83].

42. Kasimir Twardowski, *Zur Lehre von Inhalt und Gegenstand* (Vienna: Alfred Hölder, 1894), pp. 24–25 [*On the Content and Object of Presentations*, tr. R. Grossmann (The Hague: Martinus Nijhoff, 1977), p. 22].

43. Meinong, *Über Annahmen*, pp. 223–224 [*On Assumptions*, p. 163].

44. Franz Brentano, *Psychologie vom empirischen Standpunkt*, 2d ed., ed. Oskar Kraus, 2 vols. (Hamburg: Felix Meiner, 1955), vol. 2, p. 134 [*Psychology from an Empirical Standpoint*, tr. Antos C. Rancurello, D. B. Terrell, and Linda L. McAlister (London: Routledge & Kegan Paul, 1973), p. 272].

45. Brentano, *Psychologie vom empirischen Standpunkt*, vol. 2, p. 292 [*Psychology from an Empirical Standpoint*, p. 271]. Compare Twardowski, *Zur Lehre von Inhalt und Gegenstand*, pp. 24–25 [*On the Content and Object of Presentations*, p. 24].

46. Kit Fine, "Critical Review of Parsons' *Non-Existent Objects*," *Philosophical Studies* 45 (1984): 132.

47. Ibid., p. 133.

48. It does not follow from this that Macbeth was, in the usual sense, *frightened by* his visual experience—for that involves construing the experience *intentionally*.

49. Mackie, "Problems of Intentionality," p. 48.

50. The first such reference I have found occurs in the Logical Atomism lectures. See Bertrand Russell, *Logic and Knowledge*, ed. R. C. Marsh (London: George Allen & Unwin, 1956), pp. 216, 223–224.

51. Bertrand Russell, "Critical Notice: *Untersuchungen zur Gegenstandstheorie und Psychologie*," *Mind* 14 (1905): 533. Meinong himself offers the equally problematic "possible round square": *Über Möglichkeit und Wahrscheinlichkeit*, in *Gesamtaugabe*, vol. 6 (Graz: Akademische Druck- und Verlagsanstalt, 1972), p. 278. Richard Routley and William J. Rapaport, among latter-day Meinongians, discuss yet other, related problem cases: see, for example, Richard Routley, "The Durability of Impossible Objects," *Inquiry* 19 (1976): 249, and William J. Rapaport, "Intentionality and the Structure of Existence," Ph.D. diss., Indiana University, 1979, p. 91.

52. Any reader not persuaded by this swift deflection of the first argument may be directed to the extensive neo-Meinongian literature, where it is addressed head-

on. For those who are interested, here is a brief guide. Responding to the objection requires unrestricted *Gegenstandstheorie* to be, in William J. Rapaport's phrase, "two-sorted"—see Rapaport, "To Be and Not To Be," *Noûs* 19 (1985): 258—and there are two sorts of two-sorted accounts on the market. The first in effect draws on the Kantian point that existence is not a "real predicate": it is not, as Meinong himself put it, a "piece" of an object: *Über die Erfahrungsgrundlagen unseres Wissens*, in *Gesamtausgabe*, vol. 5 (Graz: Akademische Druck- und Verlagsanstalt, 1973), p. 390. Because of this, "there is no object whose existence follows from its nature, and hence a priori": Meinong, *Über emotionale Präsentation*, p. 391 [*On Emotional Presentation*, p. 95]. So we block the argument by ruling that an object's nature, or *Sosein* (its "being so"), is specifiable only by "real" predicates, in Kant's sense. Such a line of defence has been taken by Richard Routley and Terence Parsons, who, on the basis of Meinong's own distinction between *Sosein* and *Sein*, distinguish between two kinds of properties: *nuclear* and *extranuclear*. The former intuitively specify the nature of an object in itself, and exclude such ontological or "status" notions as being existent, fictional, and so forth. See Routley, *Exploring Meinong's Jungle and Beyond*, pp. 264–268; and Terence Parsons, "The Methodology of Nonexistence," *Journal of Philosophy* 76 (1979): 655, and more formally in his "Nuclear and Extranuclear Properties, Meinong, and Leibniz," *Noûs* 12 (1978): 137–151. For Meinong himself, see, for example, *Über Möglichkeit und Wahrscheinlichkeit*, pp. 278–280. (Nuclear properties also exclude what Chisholm calls "converse intentional properties," such as that of *being thought of by Smith*: see Roderick Chisolm, "Converse Intentional Properties," *Journal of Philosophy* 79 (1982): 537–545. There are other extranuclear properties as well: see Routley and Parsons for details.) Given this, the reply to Russell is straightforward. As Parsons puts it: "Russell's example of 'the existent golden mountain' unfairly treated a *Sein* predicate as a *Sosein* predicate": "The Methodology of Nonexistence," p. 655 (compare Richard Routley, "The Durability of Impossible Objects," p. 250). On this approach, what Routley calls the unrestricted Assumption or Characterization Postulate—that for any predicative expression whatsoever, there is an object specified by it—is restricted. The second two-sorted approach, endorsed by Rapaport, Hector-Neri Castañeda, and Ed Zalta, and which can accept the unrestricted Assumption Postulate, distinguishes between two modes of predication: see William J. Rapaport, "Meinongian Theories and a Russellian Paradox," *Noûs* 12 (1978): 153–180; Hector-Neri Castañeda, "Thinking and the Structure of the World," *Philosophia* 4 (1974): 3–40; and Ed Zalta, *Abstract Objects: An Introduction to Axiomatic Metaphysics* (Dordrecht: Reidel, 1983) and *Intensional Logic and the Metaphysics of Intentionality* (Cambridge, Mass.: MIT Press, 1988). On this approach, Russell's example is accepted: existence ought to be ascribed to the existent round square, but only in the sense that existence goes to constitute the object as such—by way of "constituency," as Rapaport puts it. It does not follow from this that such an object "exemplifies" existence.

53. Russell, *Logic and Knowledge*, p. 45; compare his "Critical Notice: *Untersuchungen zur Gegenstandstheorie und Psychologie*," p. 533.

54. Waterfalls are not very common. What is essentially the same phenomenon can be created by using a circular piece of paper on which a bold spiral has been drawn, spiralling into the centre of the paper. Place this on a quickly revolving turntable, stare at it for a couple of minutes, and then abruptly stop it from revolv-

ing. The bands of the spiral will seem to expand, but the overall form seems not to get any larger. In the case of sounds, there is, for example, a continuous tone that sounds as if it is uniformly falling in pitch, but never leaving its original octave: illustrated in A. J. M. Houtsma, T. D. Rossing, and W. M. Wagenaars, *Auditory Demonstrations* (Philips 1126–061), track 52. Perhaps even more astonishing is a tone that, in a manner impossible to convey fully in words, seems both to increase and decrease in pitch at the same time: illustrated in John R. Pierce, *The Science of Musical Sound* (New York: Scientific American Books, 1983), track 4.6.

55. See J. A. Wilson and J. O. Robinson, "The Impossibly Twisted Pulfrich Pendulum," *Perception* 15 (1986): 503–504.

56. Although I am relating these phenomena to the present context by suggesting that we could hallucinate any of them, their paradoxical character is present, of course, non-hallucinatorily—as simple illusions. What this indicates is that even mere illusion may have problems in store for intentionalism. This issue will be addressed later.

57. Alexius Meinong, "Über die Stellung der Gegenstandstheorie im System der Wissenschaften," in *Gesamtausgabe*, vol. 5 (Graz: Akademische Druck- und Verlagsanstalt, 1973), p. 222.

58. Meinong, *Über Möglichkeit und Wahrscheinlichkeit*, p. 173.

59. As Parsons says, "It is unfortunate . . . that Meinong and Russell agreed in referring to this state of affairs [namely, something's being round and square] as a violation of 'the law of non-contradiction'; for the *real* law of noncontradiction—that no object can satisfy $Ax \ \& \sim (Ax)$, for any A . . .—is not violated by any object at all, even the round square": Terence Parsons, "A Prolegomenon to Meinongian Semantics," *Journal of Philosophy* 71 (1974): 573. Compare Routley and Routley, "Rehabilitating Meinong's Theory of Objects," p. 231.

60. See, for example, Meinong, "Über die Stellung der Gegenstandstheorie," §21, and *Über Möglichkeit und Wahrscheinlichkeit*, §25.

61. For similar observations see, for example, Routley and Routley, "Rehabilitating Meinong's Theory of Objects," pp. 231–232. A related problem, arising from the fact that an intentional object may be determinately *F or G* but not determinately either, is answered by Richard Routley along similar lines: *Exploring Meinong's Jungle and Beyond*, pp. 450–456.

62. Routley and Routley, "Rehabilitating Meinong's Theory of Objects," p. 227.

63. Parsons, *Nonexistent Objects*, p. 1.

64. See especially fragments 3 and 6 in G. S. Kirk and J. E. Raven, *The Presocratic Philosophers* (Cambridge: Cambridge University Press, 1957).

65. Because the issues to be discussed here principally arise in the domain of "Philosophical Logic," which concerns itself with propositions and concepts, I shall in the first instance be discussing perceptual *judgements*. Because of the Bridge Principle discussed in Chapter 8, however, if, by Russellian manoeuvres, or more generally, manoeuvres based on the Assumption, we can avoid reference to non-existents as the objects of perceptual judgements, we can be assured that they are avoidable as objects of perceptual awareness.

66. W. V. Quine, "On What There Is," *From a Logical Point of View* (Cambridge, Mass.: Harvard University Press, 1953), p. 1.

67. Russell, *Logic and Knowledge*, p. 233.

68. G. E. Moore, "The Conception of Reality," in his *Philosophical Studies* (London: Routledge & Kegan Paul, 1922), p. 212.

69. Russell, *Logic and Knowledge*, p. 232: "Existence is essentially a property of a propositional function." (Russell also claimed, however, that "a propositional function is nothing": *Logic and Knowledge*, p. 230); Gilbert Ryle, "Imaginary Objects," in his *Collected Papers*, 2 vols. (London: Hutchinson, 1971), vol. 2, p. 65: "In the proposition '*x* exists' or '*x* does not exist' the term *x* which, from the grammar seems to be designating a subject of attributes, is really signifying an attribute. It is a concealed predicative expression. And the proposition is really saying 'something is *x*-ish' or 'nothing is *x*-ish'"; and Reinhardt Grossmann, "Nonexistent Objects versus Definite Descriptions," *Australasian Journal of Philosophy* 62 (1984): 370: "When you assert that Pegasus does not exist, then there is before your mind a fact which contains, not Pegasus, but some description of Pegasus."

70. I am not saying that such a view is correct: problems have, indeed, been raised for it. For not only have certain neo-Meinongians argued that the Russellian approach is mistaken across the board, in an important non-Meinongian paper to which reference has already been made, Richard Cartwright long ago argued that the issues here are at least far more complex than were envisaged by Russell.

71. Evans, *The Varieties of Reference*, p. 172. Evans, as a proponent of the "Extreme View" discussed in Chapter 8, of course himself restricts this observation to non-hallucinatory cases.

72. Walton's most recent and extended treatment of these matters does not in fact use this device, though earlier ones did. There is no change of position, however, and I shall use the device in expounding Walton's views generally. Kendall Walton, *Mimesis as Make-Believe* (Cambridge, Mass.: Harvard University Press, 1990) is the recent work; asterisks are used in "Pictures and Make-Believe," *The Philosophical Review* 82 (1973): 283–319. Evans's contribution to this debate is based on this earlier paper and on Walton's "Fearing Fictions," *Journal of Philosophy* 75 (1978): 5–27.

73. Walton, *Mimesis as Make-Believe*, p. 392.

74. See ibid., §§10.2–3.

75. Evans, *The Varieties of Reference*, p. 358.

76. Ibid., p. 343.

77. Ibid., p. 359.

78. Ibid., p. 370.

79. Ibid., p. 148, n. 12. The term "Idea" has a technical sense for Evans; see ibid., §4.4.

80. Ibid., p. 352, n. 16.

81. It is answered by Meinong by appeal to his notion of *Sosein* ("being so"), backed up by the principle of the Independence of *Sosein* from *Sein*. See Meinong, "Über Gegenstandstheorie," p. 489 ["Theory of Objects," p. 82]. Meinong seems to have adopted the independence principle from his pupil Mally, who himself formulated it as follows: "The *Sosein* of an object is, in its being, independent of the being of the object": "Untersuchungen zur Gegenstandstheorie des Messens," p. 127.

82. Ryle, "Imaginary Objects," p. 64.

83. Richard Aquila, one of the leading present-day intentionalists, believes that this problem wholly undermines any attempt, such as the present one, to con-

strue intentional objects as individuals: "If there *are* such objects whenever they are apprehended by sense, then those objects will be, in some respects at least, incomplete objects . . . It is nonsensical, however, to suppose that such an entity as this might *be* an existing physical object, even if there might be such an entity which stands in certain relations to physical objects. This sort of objection can be avoided if we suppose that the proper objects of sensory awareness are not particulars at all": Aquila, *Intentionality*, p. 51. Aquila's own proposal is that intentional objects be construed as universals. Such a suggestion is, however, as incapable as the "Russellian" account considered earlier of doing justice to the *de re* character of perceptual consciousness. (We should also, of course, reject Aquila's characterization of merely intentional objects as "entities.")

84. Ryle, "Intentionality-Theory and the Nature of Thinking," p. 261.

85. J. L. Mackie, indeed, developed an Indirect Realist account of perception with intentional objects in the place of sense-data. See Mackie, *Problems from Locke*, ch. 2.

86. Reinhardt Grossmann, "Meinong's Doctrine of the *Aussersein* of the Pure Object," Noûs 8 (1974): 78.

87. To deny that this makes sense is not only implausible in itself, and an implicit rejection of Direct Realism; it also flies in the face of the findings of Part I of this work, where I attempted to *earn* the philosophical right to speak of a physical object as "appearing" other than *it* is.

88. We also need to distinguish both of these questions from "Is the subject aware of a real black object?" The answer to this, in the present case of illusion, is Yes—for the subject is aware of a black object, and that object, though not really black, is indeed real. The answer to this question will be negative only if the subject is hallucinating, when the object itself is not real.

89. Fine, "Critical Review of Parsons' *Non-Existent Objects*," p. 139.

90. Nor does it mean that it is impossible to *see that* a dagger is before one, for all this means is that one comes to know that a dagger is before one in virtue of its so looking to one. Certain *epistemological* positions may entail that this is never a possibility; but it is not entailed simply by denying that *being a dagger* is a strictly visible characteristic.

91. Brian McLaughlin, "Why Perception Is Not Singular Reference," in *Cause, Mind, and Reality*, ed. J. Heil (Dordrecht: Kluwer, 1989), p. 116.

92. Ibid., p. 117.

93. If it is not obvious in itself, the issue is closely parallel to the situation with fictional objects, where it has been discussed at some length in the literature: Sherlock Holmes, it is generally conceded, exists in no possible world. (See, for example, Saul Kripke, "Naming and Necessity," in *Semantics of Natural Language*, ed. Donald Davidson and Gilbert Harman [Dordrecht: Reidel, 1972], p. 764.) In fact *all* non-existents are necessary non-existents. If this also is not obvious, note that the term "non-existent" (as a noun) has been used in these pages as strictly correlative to cognitive acts that are *de re* in character. Just as any real object of any *de re* act is essential to that act, so is any non-existent object.

94. Recall David Bell's remarks cited at the end of Chapter 8.

Index